WORD QUICK REFERENCE

	F1	F2	F3	F4	F5	(Next Pane)	(Spelling)	(Extend)	(Update)	(Activate menu bar)
	Help	Move	Glossary	Repeat	Go To	Next Pane	Spelling	Extend	Update	Activate menu bar
Shift-	Help pointer	Copy	Change case	Repeat find/Go to	Go back	Previous pane	Thesaurus	Shrink selection	Field codes	Activate Button bar
Ctrl-		Bigger font	Spike	Close window	Restore window	Next window	Move window	Size window	Insert field codes	Maximum window
Ctrl-Shift-		Smaller font	Unspike		Insert bookmark	Previous window	Update link	Column select	Unlink field	Ruler mode
Alt-	Next field	Save As		Quit Word	Restore window	Next window			Minimize window	Maximize window
Alt-Shift-	Previous field	Save				Previous window			Double-click field	

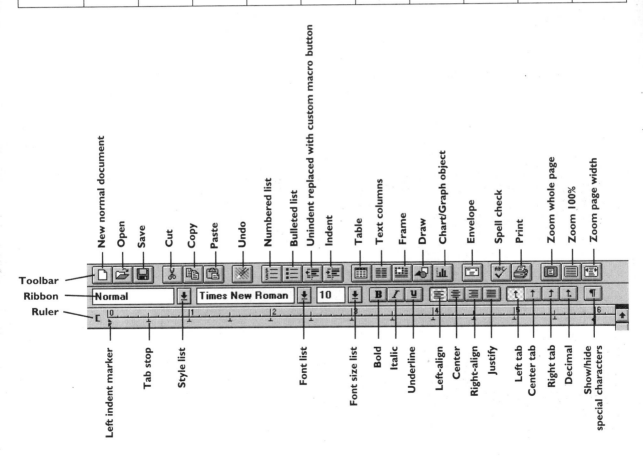

Toolbar — New normal document, Open, Save, Cut, Copy, Paste, Undo, Numbered list, Bulleted list, Unindent replaced with custom macro button, Indent, Table, Text columns, Frame, Draw, Chart/Graph object, Envelope, Spell check, Print, Zoom whole page, Zoom 100%, Zoom page width

Ribbon — Normal, Times New Roman, 10, Bold, Italic, Underline, Left-align, Center, Right-align, Justify, Left tab, Center tab, Right tab, Decimal, Show/hide special characters

Ruler — Left indent marker, Tab stop, Style list, Font list, Font size list

Computer users are not all alike.
Neither are SYBEX books.

We know our customers have a variety of needs. They've told us so. And because we've listened, we've developed several distinct types of books to meet the needs of each of our customers. What are you looking for in computer help?

If you're looking for the basics, try the **ABC's** series. You'll find short, unintimidating tutorials and helpful illustrations. For a more visual approach, select **Teach Yourself**, featuring screen-by-screen illustrations of how to use your latest software purchase.

Running Start books are really two books in one—a tutorial to get you off to a fast start and a reference to answer your questions when you're ready to tackle advanced tasks.

Mastering and **Understanding** titles offer you a step-by-step introduction, plus an in-depth examination of intermediate-level features, to use as you progress.

Our **Up & Running** series is designed for computer-literate consumers who want a no-nonsense overview of new programs. Just 20 basic lessons, and you're on your way.

We also publish two types of reference books. Our **Instant References** provide quick access to each of a program's commands and functions. SYBEX **Encyclopedias** and **Desktop References** provide a *comprehensive reference* and explanation of all of the commands, features, and functions of the subject software.

Our **Programming** books are specifically written for a technically sophisticated audience and provide a no-nonsense value-added approach to each topic covered, with plenty of tips, tricks, and time-saving hints.

Sometimes a subject requires a special treatment that our standard series don't provide. So you'll find we have titles like **Advanced Techniques**, **Handbooks**, **Tips & Tricks**, and others that are specifically tailored to satisfy a unique need.

We carefully select our authors for their in-depth understanding of the software they're writing about, as well as their ability to write clearly and communicate effectively. Each manuscript is thoroughly reviewed by our technical staff to ensure its complete accuracy. Our production department makes sure it's easy to use. All of this adds up to the highest quality books available, consistently appearing on best-seller charts worldwide.

You'll find SYBEX publishes a variety of books on every popular software package. Looking for computer help? Help Yourself to SYBEX.

For a brochure of our best-selling publications:

 SYBEX Inc., 2021 Challenger Drive, Alameda, CA 94501
Tel: (510) 523-8233/(800) 227-2346 Telex: 336311
Fax: (510) 523-2373

 SYBEX is committed to using natural resources wisely to preserve and improve our environment. As a leader in the computer book publishing industry, we are aware that over 40% of America's solid waste is paper. This is why we have been printing the text of books like this one on recycled paper since 1982.

This year our use of recycled paper will result in the saving of more than 15,300 trees. We will lower air pollution effluents by 54,000 pounds, save 6,300,000 gallons of water, and reduce landfill by 2,700 cubic yards.

In choosing a SYBEX book you are not only making a choice for the best in skills and information, you are also choosing to enhance the quality of life for all of us.

The
Compact Guide to
Windows,
Word
& Excel

The
Compact Guide to
Windows,™
Word
& Excel

Ron Mansfield

SYBEX®

San Francisco
Paris
Düsseldorf
Soest

Acquisitions Editor: Dianne King
Developmental Editor: Christian T.S. Crumlish
Project Editor: Barbara Dahl
Editor: Mark Woodworth
Technical Editor: Linda Rose
Word Processors: Scott Campbell, Ann Dunn, Chris Meredith
Book Designer: Ingrid Owen
Chapter Art: Ingrid Owen
Screen Graphics: Aldo Bermudez
Page Layout and Typesetting: Len Gilbert
Production Assistant: Arno Harris
Indexer: Ted Laux
Cover Designer: Ingalls + Associates
Cover Photographer: Michael Lamotte
Screen reproductions produced with Collage Plus.

Collage Plus is a trademark of Inner Media Inc.

SYBEX is a registered trademark of SYBEX Inc.

TRADEMARKS: SYBEX has attempted throughout this book to distinguish proprietary trademarks from descriptive terms by following the capitalization style used by the manufacturer.

SYBEX is not affiliated with any manufacturer.

Every effort has been made to supply complete and accurate information. However, SYBEX assumes no responsibility for its use, nor for any infringement of the intellectual property rights of third parties which would result from such use.

Library of Congress Card Number: 92-64216
ISBN: 0-7821-1142-4

Manufactured in the United States of America
10 9 8 7 6 5 4 3 2 1

To my fine son Scott,
who hung in there through some long, tough years.
Congratulations on your graduation.
I know you'll do well.

ACKNOWLEDGMENTS

It takes a lot of people to put a book in your hands. There's editor-in-chief R. S. Langer, acquisitions editor Dianne King, not to mention the project editor, copy editor, technical reviewer, proofreaders, typesetters, artists, and others named on the credits and copyright page. Hats off! You've made it a pleasurable experience, as always.

I want especially to thank my young son Adam, who provided several of the examples for this book, and his second grade teacher, Ms. Apffel, for getting Adam so interested in spiders, writing, and statistics at such a wonderful age.

On this book more than ever, my loving wife Nancy was there with much-needed encouragement and perspective.

Thanks again, one and all!

CONTENTS AT A GLANCE

CONTENTS

5 Printing Tricks and Tips   **70**

6 Personalizing Windows   **83**

7 Running Non-Windows Applications   **97**

PART TWO
WORD PROCESSING AND MORE

**PART THREE
EXCEL SPREADSHEETS**

PART FOUR
SHARING INFORMATION

Why did *you* pick up this book? Do you own Windows 3.1, Word for Windows 2.0, and Excel for Windows 4.0—or are you considering adding them to your arsenal? Do you hate wrestling with manuals that outweigh you? Do you wish you could quickly put your finger on answers to specific questions and shortcuts without trying to remember which of ten hefty Microsoft manuals to pick up? Do you think that learning new computer skills should be fun, and do you even like to laugh out loud once in a while? Do you travel with a notebook computer and need documentation to-go? Have you heard that information from Word and Excel file can be integrated, but wonder how to do it?

If you answered yes to *any* of these questions, *The Compact Guide to Windows, Word & Excel* was written expressly with you in mind.

There are *four* major sections—one about *Windows*, another about *Word*, a third about *Excel*, and a final section that shows you how to tie everything together with object linking and embedding (OLE). Each section starts with an overview of the tools and capabilities of the program being discussed. Experienced computer users can probably read the first chapter or two in a section, then immediately use the programs for routine projects. Beginners will find helpful examples, screen shots with important areas and tools identified, and just the right number of tutorials to smooth out those early rough spots. The examples are small enough that you won't spend all day typing if you want to recreate them.

Topic headings, the book's overall organization, and even the page layouts have been designed to help you use this compact guide as a *reference* tool, when that time comes.

Thanks to the similarity of commands and tools in today's Windows programs, many of the techniques you'll read about in Part I need not be repeated in later sections. For example, once you have learned about cutting and pasting in the *Windows* section, you'll be able to use those same techniques in Part II with *Word* and Part III with *Excel*. That's one of the reasons this book is a manageable size. It assumes that you can reuse and build upon new skills once you've learned them.

To keep this from becoming *The Not-So-Compact Guide to Windows, Word & Excel*, we've left out software installation instructions, as well as some of the more esoteric technical trivia found in bigger books. For instance, if you need to know that the "*P data type* is a pointer to an OPER structure," you can find *that* information on page 478 of Microsoft's *Excel Function Reference* manual.

But, if you want to know how to print envelopes quickly without retyping a letter's inside address, or if you'd like to add up a column of numbers with a single click of the mouse button, or if you want to amaze your friends and co-workers with an on-screen "slide show"—keep reading. You've found the right book. Pay for it if you haven't already, then let's get to work!

PART ONE

WINDOWS
Basics

Introducing Windows 3.1

Saying that Windows 3.1 is a powerful add-on to MS-DOS is like saying that the pope lives in a nice house. Few computer products have been as eagerly embraced as Microsoft Windows 3.1, which offers you unprecedented power, great simplicity, and ample opportunity to personalize your computer environment. Perhaps best of all, Windows 3.1 lets you work easily with more than one program at a time, automating the exchange of information with something called object linking and embedding, or OLE (pronounced *oh-lay*). More and more software developers are creating programs that run under Windows, making it a must-have for many business, home, and academic computer users.

HOW WINDOWS 3.1
DIFFERS FROM VERSION 3.0

While users of earlier Windows versions loved using the graphic interface and being freed from the need to type cryptic DOS prompts, many were frustrated by Windows 2.0 and 3.0's sluggishness and vulnerability to crashes from ill-behaved programs. When it was clear that version 3.1, released in early 1992, solved many of these problems, it received rave reviews and became an instant best-seller. Here are some of the reasons why.

GREATER RELIABILITY AND SPEED

Before its release, Windows 3.1 was tested by over fifteen thousand "beta" sites, making it one of the most-examined new software products in history.

Beta testers found many dramatic improvements. Gone were those cryptic messages and unrecoverable system lock-ups when a program crashes. A feature called *Application Reboot* kept Windows and other programs running while users rebooted a problem application.

With version 3.1, users found that many operations now happened noticeably faster, such as screen scrolling and disk access. In some cases they saw a tenfold speed improvement.

ADDITIONAL HARDWARE SUPPORT

Windows 3.1 supports literally hundreds of printers and virtually all popular 286, 386, and 486 computers. *Multimedia* device support is provided for many popular audio boards, CD-ROM drives, and video equipment. Windows 3.1 is even ready for the latest handwriting stylus or "pen" computers.

NEW FONT AND PRINTING FEATURES

While Windows 3.1 will still work with your old font collection, you'll want to check out its new *TrueType* scalable fonts that produce high-quality printing on most printers. An enhanced *Print Manager* noticeably speeds printing tasks and printer selection.

WINDOWS

EASIER TO SET UP AND LEARN

Windows installation is much easier now, due in part to the experiences of those fifteen thousand version 3.1 beta testers. *Express Install* totally automates installation for most users, while *Custom Install* puts advanced users in control of hundreds of Windows options.

And, once you get Windows installed, new tutorials will put you in control of your computer sooner than ever before. Context-sensitive, on-line help screens will give you the answers to a wide variety of questions on the fly.

BETTER SUPPORT FOR PORTABLE COMPUTERS

If you've ever used a mouse or other pointing device on a portable computer, you know how difficult it can be to see a moving mouse pointer on a liquid crystal display (LCD). Windows 3.1's *Mouse Trails* feature solves that problem. Moreover, Windows 3.1 offers a number of screen settings designed specifically for LCD and plasma portables. There are even Windows features designed to prolong battery life when you are on the road.

BETTER MS-DOS SUPPORT

Ironically, some of the slickest Windows 3.1 features are aimed at MS-DOS applications. There are *DOS session fonts*, for instance, and the ability to change the number of lines displayed from 25 to 50 in many DOS programs.

MUCH MORE

As you explore Windows 3.1, you'll find dozens of little things that will please and amuse you—like a choice of animated screen savers, or, if you own a sound board, the freedom to choose different "system sounds" to alert you to certain events. Overall, Windows 3.1 was worth the wait.

TERMS AND CONCEPTS YOU'LL NEED TO KNOW

"The beginning of wisdom," to paraphrase a Chinese proverb, "is knowing the names of things." While computers are getting faster and easier to use, there are still some terms and concepts you'll need to understand to become productive. Unless you are an experienced Windows user, take a few moments now to review the remainder of this chapter. If you already know about the *Windows desktop, files, subdirectories, dialog boxes, check boxes, icons,* and the like, feel free to skip ahead to Chapter 2.

THE WINDOWS DESKTOP

You'll do your work on the Windows desktop. You see it almost immediately after you run Windows itself. Like a wooden desktop, your Windows desktop can be cluttered or tidy, colorful or bland. Windows gives you control over the appearance of your on-screen desktop. Figure 1.1 shows a fairly busy desktop where someone is working with Microsoft Word, Microsoft Excel, and a number of other Windows programs.

FILES

You undoubtedly know that your computer records information on disks in things called *files*. These files make it possible for your computer to

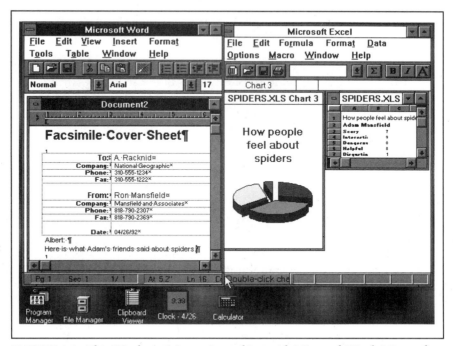

FIGURE 1.1 *This Windows 3.1 user is working with Microsoft Word, Microsoft Excel, and other Windows programs on the Windows "desktop."*

"remember" things when you turn off the power. Files are identified by unique *file names*, containing up to eight characters and an extension of up to three characters. Examples of file names include LETTER3.DOC, BUDGET93.XLS, WORD.EXE, and so on. Windows users ordinarily need only concern themselves with two general types of files: *application files* and *document files*.

Application Files

Application files (also called *programs*) are complex lists of instructions for your computer, created by programmers. Examples include Microsoft Word and Microsoft Excel. Your computer uses such programs to assist you with word processing, spreadsheet creation, and other tasks. It is the availability of affordable applications programs like these that lets you use the same computer for creating newsletters, composing music, and designing skyscrapers.

Document Files

Document files are collections of information that you and your computer create while working on projects. Examples of document files include memos, letters, mailing lists, budgets, musical scores, drawings, and the like.

Groups

Windows lets you *group* related files, making it easier for you to find them when you need them. You will learn more about groups in the next chapter.

Directories, Subdirectories, and Paths

Speaking of grouping things, MS-DOS and Windows help you organize your disks into *directories*, and even directories within directories (called *subdirectories*). These let you keep all of your correspondence together, or all of your programs in the same place, and so on. Suppose, for instance, you wanted to keep your letters and memos in the same proximity, but separated. You might create a directory called CORRESP (for correspondence), a subdirectory of it called LETTERS, and a second subdirectory called MEMOS. You would store your letters in the LETTERS subdirectory and your memos in the MEMOS subdirectory. All of your letters and memos would be contained in the CORRESP directory.

For your computer to keep track of where you put things and find them when asked, you are expected to include the exact name and order of directories and subdirectories when you save or retrieve files. This location information is called the *path*. If you saved a letter to Bob on a floppy disk in drive A, the path to it might be A:\CORRESP\LETTERS\BOB.DOC. Fortunately, the Windows 3.1 *File Manager* simplifies this cumbersome process for you. It lets you visualize disk organization using a *directory tree* together with graphic representations of subdirectories and files. You'll learn more about the File Manager in Chapter 4.

WINDOWS

When running Windows 3.1, you do most of your work in things called *windows* (note the lower case *w*). Don't be confused by the fact that the *program* "Windows 3.1" and these *tools* share the same name. The Windows 3.1 *program* lets you display different windows on your screen simultaneously.

Regardless of how many windows (workplaces) you can see on your screen at once, you work in one window at a time, and that window is called the *active window*.

Figure 1.2 shows two typical windows, one within another. Most Windows 3.1–compatible programs provide similar looking windows, so once you learn the basics of working with windows you will find it easy to learn new programs by using the same principles. You'll learn the ins and outs of window use in Chapter 2, and also when you run the Windows tutorials.

ICONS

Icons are simply on-screen pictures representing files and other Windows elements. In Figure 1.2 you can see Print Manager, File Manager, and other program icons.

MENU BARS, COMMANDS, AND KEYBOARD SHORTCUTS

Many windows (including the Program Manager window shown in Figure 1.2) contain *menu bars* with drop-down *menus*. These menus contain

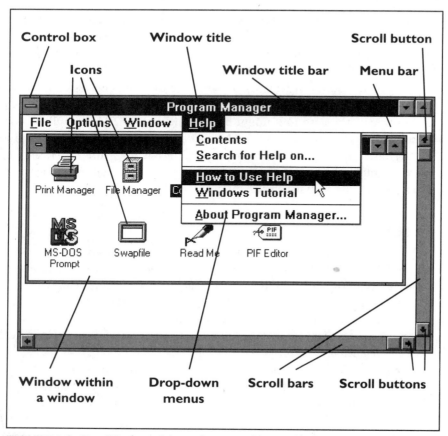

Control box **Window title** **Scroll button**

Icons **Window title bar** **Menu bar**

**Window within
a window** **Drop-down
menus** **Scroll bars** **Scroll buttons**

FIGURE 1.2 *Two Windows 3.1 windows are shown with their part names.*

choices called *commands*. You can reveal menus either by pointing with your mouse or by using the Alt key along with the arrow keys on your keyboard. (You'll practice executing menu commands with both mouse and keyboard in Chapter 2.)

Commands *without* an ellipsis (…) are executed as soon as you choose them. Windows 3.1 and compatible applications will ask you for additional information before executing commands containing an ellipsis. For example, in Figure 1.2 the command "Search for Help on…" will ask you for more information before it is executed.

WINDOWS

Sometimes choices will be dimmed on your menus. This indicates that something else needs to be done before the command can be executed. For instance, you can't save a document until you've created it.

Some menu choices have keyboard shortcuts that will save you a trip to the menu bar. For example, pressing the F1 function key in Windows and most Windows-compatible applications brings up a help window. Keyboard shortcuts are often listed to the right of commands on drop-down menus.

DIALOG BOXES

Dialog boxes are Windows' way of asking questions and collecting the necessary information to complete tasks. Dialog boxes also give you information and issue progress reports. The Page Setup dialog box illustrated in Figure 1.3 is an example.

Buttons

Dialog boxes contain *buttons* in a variety of sizes and shapes. You can see two examples in Figure 1.3. The OK and Cancel rectangles at the bottom of the dialog box are buttons. So are the small round option buttons near the top of it (Margins, Paper Source, etc.). Pointing to these with your mouse and pressing the right mouse button activates the choice. You will get to practice these skills in a moment.

Check Boxes

Notice the box next to the words "Facing Pages" in Figure 1.3. This is a *check box*. Clicking here with your mouse works like a toggle switch to alternately place and remove an X mark in the box. This is another way to indicate your preferences.

Text Boxes

The margin measurements in Figure 1.3 are contained in *text boxes*. Frequently, you are presented with empty text boxes like these in which you are

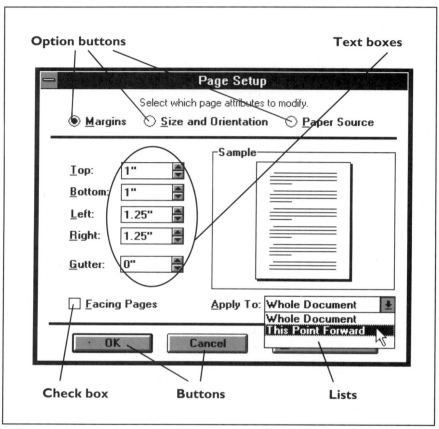

FIGURE 1.3 *Dialog boxes ask questions and supply information.*

expected to type such things as your name, values, or other text. In this example, you are presented with default entries, which you can change by typing over them.

Lists

Dialog boxes frequently contain drop-down lists like the one next to the "Apply To" label. Here you use your mouse to reveal the menu, then pick a choice.

WINDOWS

Navigating in a Dialog Box

You can move from place to place in a dialog box either by pointing with your mouse or by using the Tab key and the Shift-Tab key combination on your keyboard.

SELECTING

When working with Windows, you will often be asked to *select* things. Sometimes you will need to select text, while at other times you will be asked to select an icon or a graphic element (a picture). While the process of selecting varies, the purpose is always the same. Selecting tells the computer what item or items you want to work with next. For instance, if you wanted to italicize your name in a word processing document, you would need to select it first, indicating to the computer which words needed to be modified, then you would issue the italics command. Like most other Windows-related tasks, selecting is usually best done with a mouse or other pointing device. In this book we will use the mouse to select, sometimes also indicating how to select with the keyboard.

MOUSE AND TRACKBALL TERMINOLOGY

You now know nearly everything you need to get started, except for some mouse or trackball terminology—specifically the terms *pointing*, *dragging*, *clicking*, and *double-clicking*. The best way to gain an understanding of these concepts is to practice, something you'll do next, in Chapter 2.

Running Windows

In this chapter you'll learn how to start Windows and run applications. You'll get to practice with your mouse or other pointing device, to explore the Windows tutorials, and to learn to manage multiple windows. In no time you will be bouncing from window to window, and even finding your way back when you get lost in what might at first seem like a bewildering maze of tools, windows, and choices. This chapter also suggests directions to take if you have specific projects that you need to start in a hurry. It assumes that Windows 3.1 is already properly installed on your computer. If that's not the case, refer to your Microsoft installation documentation before continuing.

WINDOWS

STARTING WINDOWS

Windows 3.1 is actually a program itself. You start it from the DOS prompt, just as you would any other MS-DOS program. As is often the case, there are several "switches" you can include when typing the DOS command that you use to start Windows. We'll look at the easy way first.

THE EASY WAY

To start Windows in the default mode, merely type **win** at the DOS prompt, then press Enter. In a moment you should see the Windows logo followed by the Windows desktop with the Program Manager's window in view. Your screen will probably look something like Figure 2.1. Don't be alarmed if things look a little different.

A FEW START-UP POWER TRICKS

It is also possible to add to the command line the name and path of an application, and even a document name. This will start the desired program

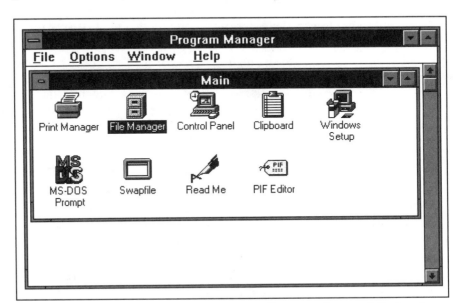

FIGURE 2.1 *Typing* **win** *at the DOS prompt will run Windows and display the Program Manager window and possibly some others.*

and open a specific document along with Windows itself. For instance, if you wanted to work on an existing Microsoft Word letter called BOB located in your WORD subdirectory, the command **win c:\word\word.exe bob.doc** would start Windows and Word and open the letter titled BOB. (DOS is insensitive to case, so you may type in either uppercase or lowercase.) Obviously you'll need to know the appropriate program and document names, as well as the drive and path information. As you'll see in a moment, the Windows StartUp group offers an easier way to run applications every time you start Windows.

If you always want to start Windows whenever you turn on your computer, add **win** as the last line of your AUTOEXEC.BAT file.

Normally, Windows will "inspect" your computer and start in the appropriate Windows mode (either *standard* or *386 Enhanced*). To force Windows to start in standard mode, type **win /s**. To force the use of 386 Enhanced mode on capable computers, type **win /3** to start Windows.

USING A MOUSE OR TRACKBALL

Running Windows without a mouse, trackball, or other pointing device is like trying to win the America's Cup without a crew. If you are going to use Windows regularly, purchase a pointing device. In instances where you can't use one, you can frequently make do with a collection of keyboard tricks. See Chapter 8 for details.

Take a moment now to read about pointing, clicking, dragging, and double-clicking in the pages that follow. After these sections, you will learn how to run the Windows tutorial, where you will get some mouse practice.

POINTING

When you move your mouse around on a flat surface you will also see the on-screen mouse pointer (frequently, but not always a large arrow). The process of moving the on-screen pointer this way is called *pointing*.

Here's a tip. Sometimes you might bump into things with your mouse (like your keyboard or soda can). Or you might run out of desk space while moving the mouse. In these instances, simply *pick up* the mouse and place it back down in a more convenient location. The pointer on your screen will not move when the mouse is moved in midair.

If you use a trackball instead of a mouse, slowly spinning the trackball with your fingers moves the on-screen pointer. Trackballs have the advantage of taking less desk space and never "bumping into" things on your desktop.

CLICKING

Mice and trackballs designed for Windows have two buttons, the *right* and *left* buttons. They each perform different functions. Pressing and quickly releasing a button is called *clicking*. Among other things, clicking is one way to *select* things.

If you are right-handed you will probably want to use the default arrangement for Window's mouse buttons. That is to say, you will use the left button as the primary button. (As you will see when you use Excel, some programs make use of the right button for special tasks, although there is no real standardization regarding the use of the second button.)

If you are left-handed, you might find it more convenient to use the mouse with your left hand. And you might wish to "swap" the functions of your mouse buttons so that you can use your left index finger for most clicking. See "Changing Your Mouse's Behavior" in Chapter 6 for details.

DOUBLE-CLICKING

You've probably guessed that since pressing and releasing a mouse button once is called clicking, doing it twice quickly is called *double-clicking*. Double-clicking often causes specific actions. For instance, double-clicking on the Microsoft Word program icon will run Word. Double-clicking does different things at different times. It is often a powerful and convenient shortcut.

Beginners sometimes wait too long between clicks when double-clicking. This makes your computer think you have issued two single clicks rather than one double-click. Practice helps, or you can change the double-click response time as described in "Changing Your Mouse's Behavior" in Chapter 6.

DRAGGING

To move icons, windows, and other things around on your screen, first point to them, then *while holding down the mouse button* move the mouse the appropriate distance and direction. The on-screen object follows obediently. Releasing the button completes the dragging. Some objects (like windows) can only be dragged if you point to a particular part of the object. In the case of windows, you move them by dragging on the *title bar*. Dragging is also a way to select areas of text or multiple cells in a spreadsheet. You drag to resize things as well.

USING THE WINDOWS TUTORIALS

When you first install Windows, the installation program asks if you'd like to run the tutorial. Any time thereafter, you can run the tutorial from a menu choice in the Program Manager window.

If necessary, start Windows from the DOS prompt (type **C:>win**, for instance). You will soon see a window titled *Program Manager* that looks something like Figure 2.2.

If you don't see the Program Manager window, hold down the Alt key and press the Tab key repeatedly until you see a box in the center of the screen

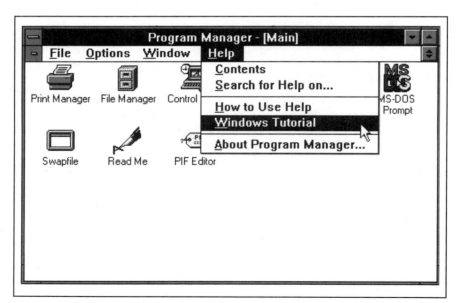

FIGURE 2.2 *To start the Windows tutorial, run Windows and make Program Manager the active window. Choose "Windows Tutorial" from the Help menu, or simply press and release the Alt, H, and W keys one at a time in that order.*

titled "Program Manager." Release the Tab key and the Program Manager window will appear.

STARTING THE TUTORIAL WITH YOUR MOUSE

To start the tutorial with your mouse, point to the Help menu in the Program Manager title bar and click once to reveal the Help menu commands. Then click once on the Windows Tutorial command. Follow the resulting on-screen instructions. The exercise will probably take you ten entertaining minutes or less. To quit the tutorial before the end, press the Esc key once or twice and follow the on-screen prompts.

STARTING THE TUTORIAL WITH YOUR KEYBOARD

To start the tutorial without using your mouse, press and release the Alt key, then press and release the H key. You will see the Help menu shown in Figure 2.2.

Now, notice the underlined letters in each command on the Help menu. Since the W is underlined in the Windows Tutorial command, pressing **w** will initiate the tutorial command. Try it. (Incidentally, this is how you make menu choices without a mouse.) Follow the resulting on-screen tutorial. Use your mouse if you have one. The exercise will probably take you ten entertaining minutes or less. To quit the tutorial before the end, press the Esc key once or twice and follow the on-screen prompts.

GETTING ON-LINE WINDOWS HELP

To get help in Windows itself and in many Windows-compatible applications, press the F1 function key. Or you can often point to the Help menu on most menu bars to reveal available Help menu commands. You will frequently see a Help window something like the one in Figure 2.3. If you click on the Contents button, you will see a list of available help topics. Clicking on a topic in the list reveals help on the subject. The Search button normally lets you type a specific topic of interest or select from a list. Back buttons take you back to the previous help topic. History buttons display a chronological list of help topics you've displayed in the current Windows session. (Clicking on an old topic in the History list takes you back to it.) The Glossary button reveals a list of Windows terms and their definitions.

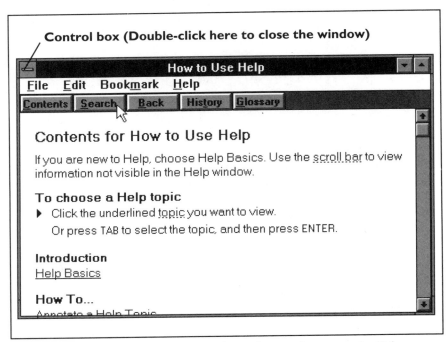

FIGURE 2.3 *To get on-line help, press the F1 function key or use the Help menu available in most windows.*

To quit help, either click outside of the Help window or choose Exit from the Help window's File menu.

QUITTING WINDOWS

It is recommended that you always quit Windows before shutting off your computer. To quit Windows, first quit any applications you are running (Word, Excel, etc.), then, from the Program Manager's File menu, choose Exit Windows... Figure 2.4 shows how.

There are two Windows "quitting" shortcuts. You can either double-click on the Program Manager's Control menu box, or you can choose Close from the Program Manager's Control menu.

In any case, you will be asked if you want to quit Windows. If you have forgotten to quit an application, you may be reminded to do so. When you

WINDOWS

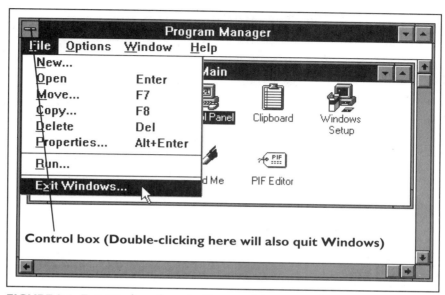

FIGURE 2.4 *Exit Windows from the Program Manager's File menu, or double-click on the Program Manager's Control menu box.*

quit Windows, it updates some disk files; wait until you see the DOS prompt before turning off your computer.

GETTING MICROSOFT PRODUCT SUPPORT

When you really get stuck, Microsoft's huge technical support staff can be a big help. They provide technical notes via downloading services, CompuServe forums, prerecorded support messages, and even real live people to answer your questions.

RYFM

The first step, as they say in tech support circles, is to "Read Your Friggin' Manuals." People who don't read documentation are referred to as RYFMs (pronounced *riff 'ems*). Only then, if you can't find the answers you need in Windows' on-line help, in your manuals, or in books like this one, is it time to call out the big guns.

DOWNLOADING TECHNICAL NOTES

If you have a modem and communications software, you can download technical notes for free from Microsoft. Call 1-206-936-6735 with your modem set for 9600 (V.32 or V.42), 2400, or 1200 BPS (baud). Your communications settings should include no parity, 1 stop bit, and 8 data bits. You will be asked for your name and city. The first time you call, you will also be asked for details about your communications software (such as whether you need line feeds and can display IBM graphics characters, and so on). If you use the same name and location each time you call, you will not need to answer the setup questions each time. Type Help for assistance.

COMPUSERVE FORUMS

Microsoft hosts a number of Microsoft forums on CompuServe, many of them Windows-related. It is even possible to rub elbows with Microsoft programmers and product managers on various CompuServe forums. Type **GO MICROSOFT** at any "!" prompt.

Free introductory CompuServe membership kits are available with most modems or communications software packages, or by dialing 1-800-848-8199.

VOICE SUPPORT SERVICE

Since many people have the same questions, Microsoft has established a 24-hour voice maze (called Fast Tips), which can be reached by dialing 1-206-635-7245 from a touchtone phone. This number will also give you information about fax-based technical support services. Have paper and pen in hand—these Microids talk faster than most people can hear. Use your phone's asterisk button (*) to skip ahead. The pound button (#) returns to the Fast Tips menu. To repeat something, press 7. To end, press zero.

HUMANS TO THE RESCUE

When all else fails, try the wonderful (and often overworked) Microsoft technical support staff. Phone them at 1-206-637-7098 between 6:00 AM and 6:00 PM weekdays, excluding holidays. (Hey, even technicians need time off; when else would they play with their *home* computers?)

WINDOWS

HELP YOURSELF

You can, of course, help yourself. When you register your copy of Windows and Windows applications, you will start receiving Microsoft newsletters, invitations for seminars, and more. Take advantage of these free and low-cost Microsoft resources.

INTERNATIONAL TELEPHONE SUPPORT

Microsoft provides worldwide support for Windows and other products. To inquire about local phone numbers for international support, contact Microsoft in the United States at 1-206-936-8661.

WINDOW MANIPULATION

The diverse window arrangements available will drive you crazy until you learn how to control them. Then you'll wonder what you ever did without them. The trick is to learn how to resize, move, and flip through windows gracefully. You do this with devices built into the windows themselves.

MOVING A WINDOW WITH YOUR MOUSE

To move a window with your mouse, point to the title bar at the top of the window, then press the left mouse button and drag. You will see a window outline that shows you where the window will be placed when you release the mouse button. When the outline is where you want it to be, release the mouse button, and the window will move to its new location.

MOVING A WINDOW WITH YOUR KEYBOARD

Skip this topic if you have a mouse. You *can* move windows using just the keyboard, but a root canal is more fun. (To quit this process midstream, press the Esc key.) Thus forewarned, to move a window with your keyboard:

1. Make sure your Num Lock feature is off.

2. If necessary, cycle through application windows with the Alt-Esc key combination to make the desired application window the active window. (It will then have a solid title bar.)

3. Next, to select a window *within* the chosen application, use the Alt-Tab key combination to cycle through your choices.

4. Once you have activated the desired window, you need to open the Control menu for *that* window. Stay awake, now. If you are working with an *application window*, press Alt and the spacebar simultaneously to view the application window's Control menu. To open a *document window* Control menu, press Alt and the hyphen key together.

5. If you haven't gone shopping for a mouse yet, choose Move from the resulting Control menu either with the arrow keys, or by typing **M**.

6. When and if the pointer changes to a four-headed arrow, say "All riiiight!" loudly, then use your arrow keys to move the window outline.

7. Press Enter when the window outline is where you want the window.

8. Put "Buy a mouse" on your To-Do list.

RESIZING AND REARRANGING WINDOWS

Increasing a window's size can give you more room to work on a project, while decreasing its size can make room for more than one window on the screen at once. The three groups of tools shown in Figure 2.5 and a mouse are all you need for most window resizing operations.

Minimizing a Window

Minimizing a window turns it into a tiny icon. This is a great way to temporarily set aside an application or other window while you do something else. The first time you minimize a window, you might think you have screwed up badly. A day's work can seemingly disappear with a single mouse click. Have faith: the work is not gone, it is just set aside. Somewhere on your screen (albeit maybe under a ton of other stuff) there is an icon with the window's name under it. Double-clicking on that icon will restore both it and your regular heartbeat.

WINDOWS

To minimize a window with your mouse, click on the Minimize button shown in Figure 2.5, or use the Minimize choice on the Windows Control menu as shown in Figure 2.6.

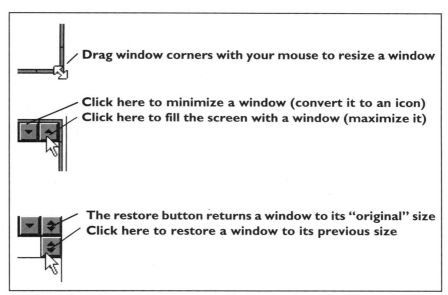

Drag window corners with your mouse to resize a window

Click here to minimize a window (convert it to an icon)
Click here to fill the screen with a window (maximize it)

The restore button returns a window to its "original" size
Click here to restore a window to its previous size

FIGURE 2.5   *Drag or click to manipulate window size.*

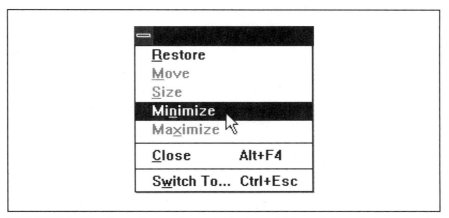

FIGURE 2.6   *The Control menu is particularly useful in resizing windows without a mouse.*

To minimize with your keyboard, follow the eight steps listed above in "Moving a Window with Your Keyboard," but pick "Minimize" from the Control menu instead of "Move." Pay particular attention to step 8.

Maximizing and Restoring a Window

Not surprisingly, the Maximize button (shown in Figure 2.5) fills your screen with a window. Don't confuse the Maximize button (a single upward-pointing triangle also illustrated in Figure 2.5) with the Restore button (a double triangle that sometimes occupies the same location). The Maximize button and its Control menu equivalent fill your screen with a single window, while the Restore features return a window to its "original" size and shape. Usually, Restore makes a window smaller than full screen.

Dragging to Change a Window's Size

When you move the mouse pointer over any corner of most windows, the pointer will turn into a large, two-headed, diagonal arrow. When this happens, press the primary mouse button (usually the left button), and drag the window to a new size and shape. Voilà!

Scrolling to See a Window's Contents

When a window is too small for an unobstructed view of its entire contents, scroll tools appear like the ones shown in Figure 2.7. They are called the *scroll arrows*, *scroll boxes*, and *scroll bars*. Some windows have horizontal scroll tools, some have vertical scroll tools, and others (like the Excel window in Figure 2.7) have both.

Clicking on scroll arrows moves things up or down or left or right incrementally within the window. Clicking in the scroll bars moves things more dramatically. It is also possible to drag the scroll box to a new position. Dragging a scroll box to the top of the scroll bar will take you to the "top" of a window. Dragging it to the "bottom" will take you to the end of a window, and so on.

Obviously, horizontal scroll tools move window contents to the right or left. With the box near the middle of a scroll bar, you will see the approximate middle of the window's contents. It takes practice, but soon you'll be able to drag to just the right spot with the boxes, even in very large documents.

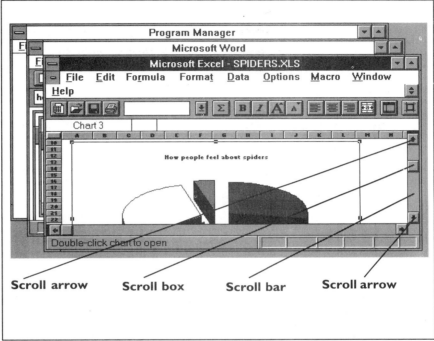

FIGURE 2.7 *Scroll tools help you view the entire contents of windows.*

Incidentally, holding down the mouse button while continuously pointing to scroll arrows or scroll bars will repeat the scrolling action.

Cascading

When you are working with multiple windows, it is possible to pile them one on top of the other, fanned out, like sheets of paper on a desk or like a series of waterfalls seen from a distance. This is called *cascading*. Figure 2.7 shows the Program Manager, Microsoft Word, and Excel windows cascaded. Use the Cascade command on the Program Manager Window menu or the Shift-F5 key combination to accomplish this.

To bring a partially-hidden window to the top of your glass desk, simply point to any part of it and click with your mouse.

Tiling

Another way to arrange multiple windows is to tile them, just as you lay out patterned tiles on a floor before gluing them down. Using the Tile command on the Program Manager's Window menu or pressing Shift-F4 will automatically arrange windows and group icons as illustrated in Figure 2.8.

CLOSING A WINDOW

There are several ways to close a window. First, you need to make the window active by clicking anywhere in it. This will change the appearance of the title bar. Then, perhaps the easiest way to close a window is to double-click on its Control Box in the upper-left corner of the window. Or, you can click once on the Control Box, which will reveal the window Control menu. Pick (click on) Close from the menu. The keyboard command for closing a window is Alt-F4.

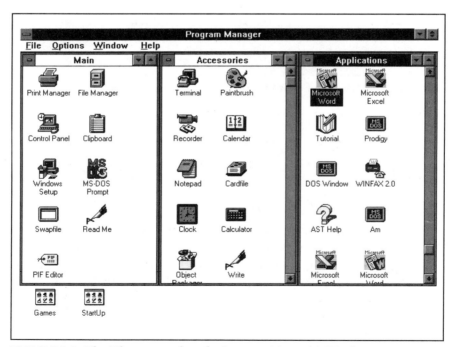

FIGURE 2.8 *The Tile command on the Program Manager's Window menu automatically arranges and sizes windows to fit your screen.*

Windows might prompt you to save your work when you are attempting to close application or document windows. Simply click the appropriate button to suit your needs.

Remember, closing the Program Manager window quits your Windows session, so you will be asked if that's what you really want to do. If you *do* want to quit, you may need to perform some housekeeping chores first (close other applications, save document changes, and so on). Windows will walk you through the necessary steps. Simply follow the on-screen prompts. Windows updates some of its files when you quit. Wait for your hard disk light to go out, or until you see the DOS prompt, before turning off your computer's power.

RUNNING APPLICATIONS
WITH THE PROGRAM MANAGER

To start an application (to load and run the program), open the appropriate window containing the program's icon, then double-click on the icon itself. Figure 2.8 shows an example of this. Notice that Microsoft Word is highlighted in the upper-left corner of the Applications window. To run Word you would simply double-click on the Word icon.

SIMULTANEOUSLY
RUNNING MULTIPLE APPLICATIONS

With Windows 3.1, it is easy to run more than one program at once. For instance, if you have enough RAM, you'll be able to run Word, Excel, and other programs, then quickly flip from one to the other and back.

SWITCHING BETWEEN APPLICATION WINDOWS

After starting one program (Word, for instance), you can return to the Program Manager and start another (Excel, perhaps). By running multiple programs this way, you can move information from one document to another. Suppose, for instance, that you had a Word document containing a list of all of your employees' names. At salary review time you decide to create a spreadsheet for budgeting pay raises. Rather than manually retyping everyone's name into the spreadsheet, you could run both Word and Excel. You would first display the Word document containing names, then *copy* those names using a Windows feature called the *Clipboard*. With the names on the Clipboard, you could then switch to Excel and *paste* the names into your new budget spreadsheet. (You'll get a chance to try this later.) As you will soon see, there are many other reasons for cutting and pasting between applications, and Windows offers other data exchange tools in addition to the Clipboard.

Now that you know *why* you'll want to run multiple programs, you'll need to know *how*. There are several ways to switch from one application to another, as well as from applications to the Program Manager and back. You can use the Task List window, or a keyboard shortcut, or sometimes a simple mouse click.

Switching Applications with the Task List

The Control box in most applications has a menu choice titled Switch To... Its keyboard shortcut is Ctrl-Esc. The Switch To... command reveals a window that looks something like Figure 2.9, except it will list the application(s) you are running.

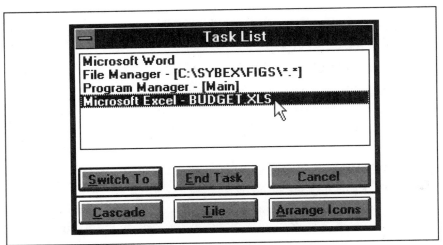

FIGURE 2.9 *The Task List is displayed when you pick Switch To... from an application's Control menu or when you press Ctrl-Esc. Use it to move from application to application.*

If you open a control box and don't see the Switch To... command, perhaps you are clicking on the wrong window Control box. You want the box for the application window (Word or whatever), not the Control box for a document window.

As you may have guessed from Figure 2.9, you can highlight the desired application and click on the Switch To... button. Double-clicking on an application name in the list will also take you directly to the application.

The Task List will also help you cascade or tile application windows. And you can use it to quit applications by selecting the program you want to quit, then clicking on the End Task button. But before you can switch from one application to another, you must have more than one running. The next section tells you how to do that.

Running Multiple Applications with the Task List

From the Task List (or using the other techniques described in a moment), switch to the Program Manager. Double-click on the program of choice. Repeat the process until you have all of the desired programs running, then use Task Manager to switch between them.

Quickly Switching Applications with a Mouse

If you can see any part of an application's window on your screen, you can switch to the application by clicking on the window. Many users adjust the sizes and shapes of their applications to facilitate this. This trick will also work in conjunction with tiled or cascaded windows.

Quickly Switching Applications with the Keyboard

Many users find it easier to employ the following shortcut instead of visiting the Task List each time they want to make a switch:

While holding down the Alt key, tap the Tab key repeatedly. Each time you press and release the Tab key, you will see an application name superimposed on the center of your screen. It will look something like Figure 2.10. When you see the name of the desired application, release the Alt key. Mission accomplished!

FIGURE 2.10 *Holding down the Alt key while repeatedly pressing the Tab key will cycle you through an on-screen list of the running applications. Release the Alt key when you see the program you want to use next (Word, in this example).*

QUITTING AN APPLICATION

It is a good idea to quit applications when you've finished using them. Remember that just hiding a window, or minimizing it, does not quit the program. Get in the habit of saving your work and quitting applications properly when you've completed a task.

Most application programs' File menus have an Exit command, the shortcut for which is usually Alt-F4. You can also quit programs from the Task List. When it is appropriate, you will be prompted to save your work or discard your most recent changes.

PROGRAM MANAGER'S MAIN WINDOW

You may have wondered about all those icons in the Program Manager's Main window. Their uses will be spelled out in more detail later in this book. For now, here is an overview of each icon.

File Manager

The File Manager helps you organize your disks and files. You use it to create subdirectories, to copy files, and to perform other tasks. See Chapter 4 for details.

Control Panel

The Control Panel lets you change the configuration of your Windows environment. For instance, you can use it to select various window color schemes. It is here that you make port assignments, install and remove fonts, alter mouse behavior, and much more. Several chapters in the book refer to the Control Panel.

Print Manager

Print Manager is used to install and configure printers. It is also the program that Windows and your applications use to manage printing tasks. For instance, when you ask Word to print a memo, the memo actually gets sent to Print Manager, not directly to the printer. Print Manager and Windows work together to send the document to your printer "in the background" while you are freed to do other work. If you are sharing a printer on a network, Print Manager will help you see and work with print queues as well. You will learn more about Print Manager in Chapter 5.

Clipboard Viewer

The Clipboard Viewer lets you see what's on your Clipboard in case you've forgotten. Some people run this program every time they start up Windows. See Chapter 39 for more details.

MS-DOS Prompt Icon

The MS-DOS Prompt icon is one of several tools used for running non-Windows programs with Windows. See Chapter 7.

Windows Setup Icon

The Windows Setup program, invoked by this icon, helps you set up Windows. It will also help you modify your setup information when things change. Chapter 6 has the details.

PIF Editor

Whenever you run non-Windows programs, Windows expects to see a program information file (PIF). This file tells Windows things about memory requirements and other compatibility issues. These days most new software is shipped with appropriate PIF files. There are other sources of PIF files, and advanced users can change the contents of PIF files. See Chapter 7 for more information.

Read Me Icon Has Last-Minute Windows News

Your version of Windows probably came with last-minute news not contained in your Windows manuals. To get the latest, double-click on the Read Me icon visible in the Program Manager's main window.

WINDOWS ACCESSORIES

Windows includes a host of powerful little applications programs that can help you keep track of appointments, make quick calculations, and much more. Chapter 3 has the details.

Grouping Applications

To help you organize your disk, Windows lets you create windows called "groups." You store related applications together in these groups. For instance, Windows comes with a Games group. Another group, called StartUp, has a unique feature: any program stored in this group automatically runs whenever you start Windows. For instance, you might place Word and Clipboard view in the StartUp group if you use them every day. Simply drag application icons (or copies) into groups.

WHEN YOU GET LOST IN WINDOWS

Finding the window you need can be frustrating at first. Making the transition from the familiar DOS prompt or even from the graphics-rich Macintosh environment to Windows is a little like moving to a new city. Things that you need may frequently seem elusive and out of place. This will pass.

Here are some tips to help you find your way around. First, remember that there are different types of windows—specifically, application windows and document windows. For example, you might see a Microsoft Word (application) window containing a memo in a *document* window. If you are looking for a Word document window, you will need to bring the Word application window into view first.

WINDOWS

Frequently, windows cover each other up. Hidden windows are still available; they are just out of sight. Use the Task List or shortcuts to bring the appropriate application into view, then use that application's window menu to get to the desired document.

The Program Manager has many windows. Use its Windows menu choice to open the window you need.

Finally, remember that if you've minimized a window you will need to bring it back to a usable size to see and manipulate its contents.

WHERE TO GO FROM HERE

As they say at Daytona Beach on spring break, "So, what d'ya wanna do next?" The next step really depends on your schedule and needs.

TO LEARN MORE ABOUT WINDOWS:

The next seven chapters cover a great many Windows features and offer techniques that you can use with a variety of programs. If you will be a regular Windows user, you might want to keep going straight ahead.

TO ORGANIZE AND UNDERSTAND YOUR HARD DISK:

Chapter 4 is essential reading for all but the most casual user. It is here that you will learn how to use File Manager, the Windows graphical replacement for the DOS prompt.

TO START A WORD PROCESSING DOCUMENT:

If you bought this book primarily to learn how to use Microsoft Word, you might want to skip ahead to Part II. You can always come back to the rest of the Windows material when you (inevitably) get to the point where you need to learn how to set up subdirectories, format disks, change the names of files, and so on.

TO START A WORKSHEET:

If you have a rush spreadsheet project waiting, skip ahead to Part III. While you will acquire tips and techniques in Part II that you can use in Part III, it is not essential that you learn Word before reading about Excel.

TO FIND HELP COMBINING WORD AND EXCEL DATA:

Once you've created some Word documents and Excel spreadsheets, be sure to check out the material in Part IV, where you will learn how to use object linking and embedding to tie your work together.

TO PRACTICE WITH YOUR MOUSE:

To get more mouse practice, run the Windows tutorial again. Or, if you've purchased and installed the Windows Productivity kit, run the tutorials that came with it.

3

Windows Accessories—Your Glass Office

Windows accessories are actually 13 small programs shipped with Windows at no extra charge. Standard accessories include a simple word processing program, a Rolodex-like card file, a calendar program, a calculator, and much more. These accessories are initially installed in the Program Manager's Accessories group. Figure 3.1 shows the icons for each.

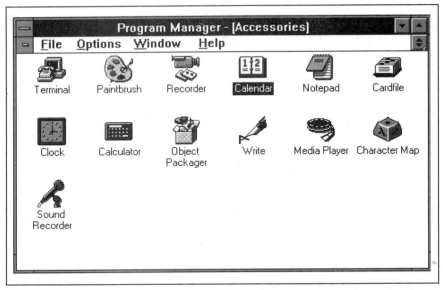

FIGURE 3.1 *Windows comes with these 13 standard accessories, located in the Program Manager's Accessories group.*

USING ACCESSORIES

Run accessories the way you do any other Windows program. *Double-click* on the desired accessory's icon, then move and manipulate accessory windows as you would any other Windows program window.

Because Windows lets you run multiple programs simultaneously, many users load one or more accessories at startup, then flip to them as needed. (To have Windows load your preferred accessories automatically at startup, use the File Manager to move or copy accessories into the StartUp group.)

WINDOWS ACCESSORY OVERVIEW

A whole book could be written about Windows accessories (Microsoft's manuals devote nearly two hundred pages to the subject), but the basics can be described in much less space. And, as you might expect, there is on-line help available for each accessory. If you don't find the answers that you need in the pages that follow, simply tap the F1 function key or visit the Help menu in any Windows accessory.

CALCULATOR

While you'll probably use Excel for your heavy-duty computations, the Windows *Calculator* desk accessory is handy for occasional calculations. You can pop it onto your screen whenever you need it and, with a few keystrokes or mouse clicks, calculate, copy, and paste the resulting answers into the projects you are working on.

For simple computations, you can use the standard calculator view. To access advance features for statistical work, trig, and number conversions, use the *View menu* to switch to scientific view with nearly seventy calculator buttons. Figure 3.2 shows both views (the smaller is the standard view).

Incidentally, you can't resize calculator windows, but you can minimize them.

You can either use your mouse to calculate (point and click on numbers and other buttons), or you can press corresponding keyboard keys. For instance, you can use the number keys along the top of your standard keyboard and the usual operator keys (that is, + for addition, – for subtraction, / for division, and * for multiplication). As you might expect, the = key executes calculations. Or, with Num Lock activated, your numeric keypad will work. The Help feature describes the keyboard equivalents for most other Calculator screen buttons, including memory buttons.

Use the Copy and Paste features located on the Calculator's Edit menu to move numbers to and from other windows. For instance, you could copy a number to the Clipboard while in a Word document, switch to the calculator, paste the contents of the Clipboard into the calculator, find the square root of the number, copy it to the Clipboard, switch back to Word, and paste it into the Word document.

(As is usually the case with Windows applications, the Calculator's keyboard shortcuts for copy and paste are Ctrl-C and Ctrl-V, respectively.)

Use the Calculator's memory feature to store intermediate results (subtotals and so on). It works like conventional pocket calculator memories. The Calculator help topic "How to Use Memory Functions" explains memory use.

CALENDAR

If you need to get better organized, check out the Windows Calendar accessory. As you can see in Figure 3.3, it is pretty impressive.

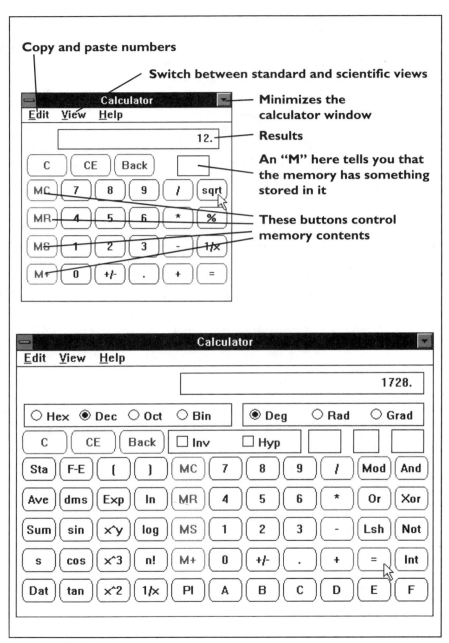

FIGURE 3.2 *The Calculator Accessory offers two views.*

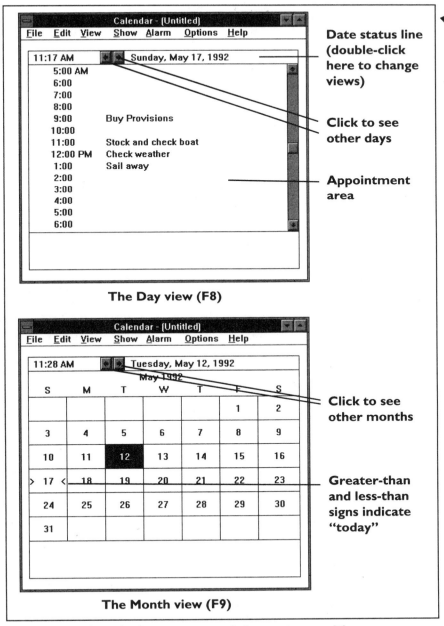

FIGURE 3.3 *The Calendar accessory can help organize your life.*

You enter your appointment dates and times using the Day view. A Month view is also available. Calendar lets you print appointment lists and will make noise to alert you if you have set alarms for the appointments. There is comprehensive on-line help available.

Both calendar views can show you today's time and date. Obviously, you will need to be sure your computer's internal time and date are properly set if you plan to use this accessory. See Chapter 6 for help setting your computer's internal clock and calendar.

Switching Views and Navigating

Switch views either with the Calendar's View menu or by pressing the F8 function key for Day view and F9 for Month view. Double-clicking in the Date Status line will also toggle (switch) views.

In Month view, the *current day* (today's date) is indicated with greater-than and less-than signs (> and <).

One way to see or make appointments for a day is to select the day in Month view by clicking on the day of interest. The day darkens. (For instance, in Figure 3.3, May 12 is the selected day and May 17 is the current day.) If necessary, you can use the scroll buttons in the Month view's Date Status line to move from month to month. With the date of interest selected, switch to Day view. Incidentally, double-clicking on a day in Month view displays the day in Day view.

Entering and Deleting Appointments and Notes

With the desired day displayed in Day view, point with your mouse to place the insertion point (the flashing stick) at the time and date where you want to enter an appointment. Enter and edit appointment reminder text using standard Windows text editing techniques.

You can remove individual appointments or all appointments within date ranges by using the Remove... choice on Calendar's Edit menu.

Printing Appointments

Calendar's File menu Print... command will print your appointment list regardless of whether you are in Month or Day view. You will be asked for beginning and ending dates.

Use the Page Setup... choice on the File menu to change margins, headers, and footers for appointment printouts. See the "Print Headers and Footers" topic in Calendar's on-line help for a list of date, page numbering, and other header and footer printing options.

Alarms

Calendar's Alarm feature lets you set as many alarm reminders as you desire. Select an appointment time in Day view, then choose Set from the Alarm menu, or press the F5 function key. To remove an alarm marker, repeat the process.

You will be reminded of appointments in one of four ways. If the Calendar is the active window, a dialog box reminds you of your appointment. If it is an inactive or a minimized window, the Calendar's border and title bar or icon will flash. Finally, the Alarm Controls... menu choice lets you turn the alarm's sound on or off.

It is possible to set alarms to give you advanced warnings of up to ten minutes. Use the Early Ring option in the Alarm Controls dialog box to set an early warning.

Personalizing Your Calendar

Calendar's Day Settings... choice on the Options menu gives you control over the Day view's display of time intervals (15, 30, or 60 minutes) and formats (12 or 24 hours).

Calendar can display five special markers in Month view to indicate different types of important dates (birthdays, holidays, and the like). Select the date you want to mark. Choose Mark... from the Options menu or press F6. Pick the desired marking from the resulting dialog box by clicking in the appropriate check box, then choose OK. To unmark a date repeat the process.

About Calendar Files

You can save and use multiple calendar files with the File Menu's Open... and Save or Save As... commands. Calendar file names must always end with .CAL. Network users can open read-only copies of Calendar files but cannot accidentally edit them. Check "Read only" in the open dialog box.

CLOCK

The Clock accessory provides three views—analog, digital, and mini-mized. They are all shown in Figure 3.4.

Clock remembers the last mode (view) you used and opens in that view when restarted. You can drag corners of clock windows to change their size and shape. Double-clicking in a clock window toggles the window's title bar. It's possible to drag a clock window, even with the title bar hidden. To change

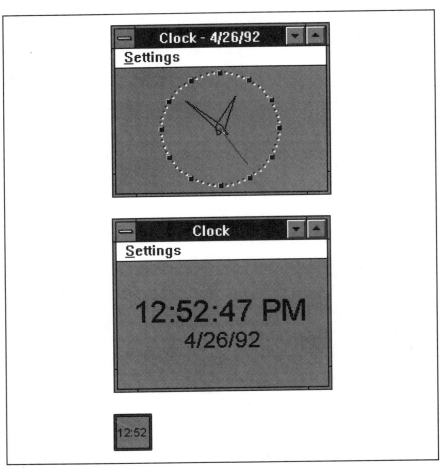

FIGURE 3.4 *The Clock accessory provides three views.*

the font used by the digital view, use the Set Font... choice on the Clock's Settings menu. TrueType fonts scale nicely when you resize the clock window. The Settings menu also lets you toggle the display of seconds in digital view and the *second hand* in analog view.

NOTEPAD AND WRITE

As you can probably tell from Figure 3.5, Notepad and Write accessories are both simple word processing (text editing) programs. They are useful for note taking or very simple correspondence.

Neither Notepad nor Write is a real substitute for sophisticated programs like Microsoft Word. For example, they can't easily produce personalized bulk mailing (as there are no mail-merge features). You won't be able to use them to create fancy multicolumn newsletters either. Nor will you find a built-in thesaurus or a spelling or grammar checker. If you need to create documents with multiple sections plus automatic tables of contents and indexes, you'll need to use Word.

Although many of Word's shortcuts and productivity tools are missing in Write and Notepad, these two accessory programs serve a purpose. If the following feature overviews intrigue you, check out the on-line help provided with both Write and Notepad for details.

Notepad

The Notepad accessory is often used to read and print the "Readme" files that come with new software. Notepad also has a handy "time log" feature that lets you quickly time- and date-stamp your notes. It's a great way to document phone calls and meetings or other events. To activate the time log:

1. Open a new note with Notepad's New command on the File menu.

2. Begin the note by typing .LOG in capital letters at the beginning of the first line of the note. (Don't forget the period in *front* of the L.)

3. Save the note using the Save (or Save As...) command.

4. Whenever you want to note something, open the saved note. The current time and date will be automatically inserted in the note for you.

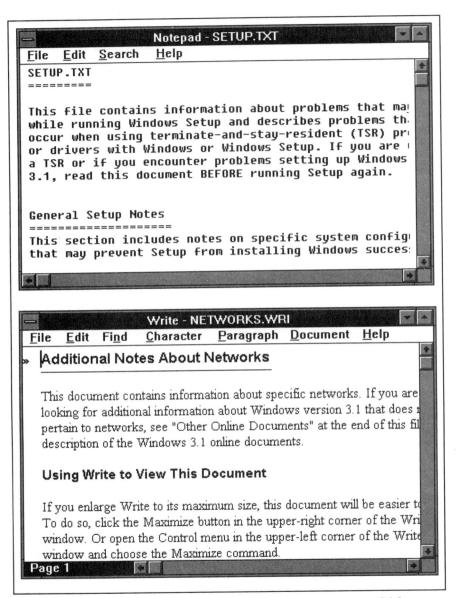

FIGURE 3.5 *Notepad and Write are simple text editing programs useful for making notes and for perusing "Readme" files.*

5. Type the text of your note, then close it (or leave it open and use the Time/Date command on Notepad's Edit menu for subsequent time-stamp entries).

Write

The Write accessory allows you to create professional-looking correspondence, including letters, memos, price lists, menus, simple signs and most of the other everyday printed items needed in your small business and personal affairs.

Write is able to import, position, and resize graphics, making it possible for you to include logos, maps, clip art, and other embellishments in your word processing documents. Write is well integrated with another Windows accessory called Paintbrush (described in a moment).

It is possible in Write to change type sizes and fonts. You can make words bold or italic, as well as create superscript or subscript characters. Text can be right- or left-justified. You can insert "optional" hyphens to even out ragged-right margins.

Write lets you add a single header and/or footer to each document and facilitates simple automatic page numbering.

You have control over things like document and paragraph margins, first line indentation, line spacing, and so on. Write will make automatic page ending decisions for you or permit you to force endings where you want them.

There are a variety of "navigational aids" built into Write, making it easy to scoot to a specific page in a long document or bounce to the beginning or end of a project. There is a useful find-and-replace feature that lets you change all or selected occurrences of words or phrases.

Each one of these features is documented with Write's on-line help. But if you own Microsoft Word, your time will be far better spent learning *it* instead.

CHARACTER MAP

Character Map provides an easy way to place unusual symbols in your Windows documents. Use it to type copyright symbols (©) as well as accented characters containing umlauts (ä) or tildes (ñ), and so on. It also tells you the keyboard shortcuts for these special characters and lets you see the various symbols available in different fonts. Figure 3.6 shows the Character Map window for the Courier font.

After loading the Character Map program, use its drop-down Font menu to pick the font of interest. You will see all the available characters for the chosen font. Clicking once on a symbol highlights the box surrounding it and lists the key combination in the lower-right corner of the window. For instance, in Figure 3.6, the copyright symbol is highlighted and the Alt+0169 key combination is displayed. If you hold down the mouse button long enough when you point, you will see an enlarged view of the chosen character.

If you double-click on characters, they will appear in the "Characters to Copy" text area of the Character Map window. You can then use the Copy button in the Character Map window to copy these characters to your Clipboard. Then, when you switch back to your Windows application (Word or Excel, for instance), you can use the Paste command to insert the special character(s) into the destination document. Realize that the font used in the destination document will need to match the font used in the Character Map if you want to see the appropriate symbol in the destination document.

PAINTBRUSH

Paintbrush is a remarkably full-featured program for creating and editing black-and-white or color drawings, logos, small signs, and other graphics.

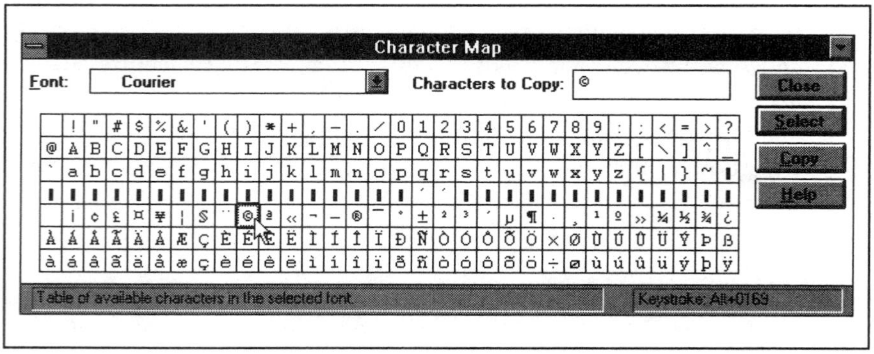

FIGURE 3.6 *Character Map simplifies symbol typing.*

You can start from scratch or use Paintbrush's Open... command on the File menu to load other people's clip art for modification.

As you can see in Figure 3.7, Paintbrush provides a host of tools and options.

For instance, you can control line width, fill patterns, the position of objects in relation to each other (above, below, and so on). Tools help you draw boxes and circles and polygons. Objects can be enlarged and reduced. Shapes can be distorted. Text tools in Paintbrush make it easy to label drawings and create things like organizational charts and signs.

Because Paintbrush supports object linking and embedding (OLE), it is possible for you to insert Paintbrush drawings into Write (or even MS Word) documents and have the drawings automatically updated in your word processing document when you make changes. For example, you could use Paintbrush to create your company letterhead. When your company phone number or address changes, you would go back to Paintbrush and change the letterhead art once. Thereafter, any documents that are "linked" to the letterhead drawing would automatically be updated when next used. The process seems a little confusing at first, but ultimately it is fascinating, powerful, and well worth exploring.

What are the drawbacks to Paintbrush? When compared to expensive drawing and CAD programs, Paintbrush is slow and lacks features like rulers and multiple drawing layers. This is probably not a program you'd want to use for mechanical drawing or for creating large-scale interior designs or scaled floor plans.

The size of the drawing area varies, based on your display adapter and available memory. The first time you use Paintbrush, a default drawing size area is established. If it is not big enough, try freeing up memory by quitting unused programs, then restart Paintbrush and visit the Image Attributes... dialog box available via the Paintbrush Options menu command. Enter new height and/or width measurements. Paintbrush comes with extensive on-line help. Paintbrush pictures can be printed from Paintbrush itself or inserted into other documents created by programs like Word and Excel.

You might want to spend some time exploring and learning Microsoft's Draw program that ships with Word before spending too much time with Paintbrush.

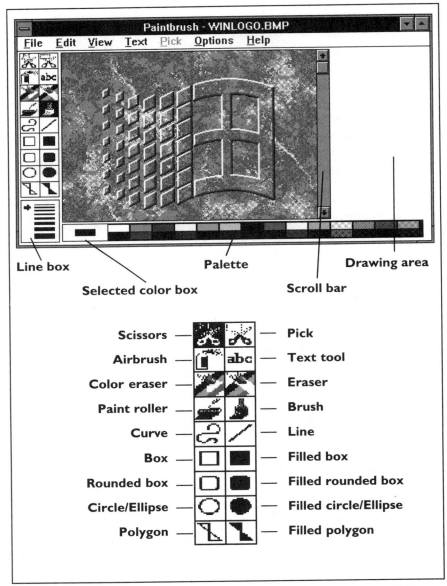

FIGURE 3.7 *Paintbrush is a robust drawing program that even creates OLE objects.*

TERMINAL

Terminal is a Windows-compatible program that will control your modem and let you access a wide variety of information on other people's or organizations' computers. For instance, you can use it to connect with CompuServe as well as local bulletin board services (BBSs). The Communications program is quite full-featured. Terminal can memorize phone numbers and affiliated log-on sequences. As you can see in Figure 3.8, it supports communications speeds (baud rates) from 110 to 19,200 bits per second (BPS) and emulates a number of popular terminal types.

You can exchange files with other computers using a variety of file exchange methods (protocols), and you can print incoming and outgoing text.

Different settings files can be created for different tasks. For instance, you can prepare a settings file for use with CompuServe and other dial-up services and a separate settings file for connecting directly to an in-house computer using a different COM port. Settings file names must all end with the extension .TRM.

The buttons along the bottom of the Terminal window in Figure 3.8 are called function keys. You can create your own communication function-key definitions for things like log-on sequences. See Terminal's on-line help for details.

CARDFILE

Cardfile is—as the name suggests—a simple way to store and retrieve the kind of information typically found on 3×5 cards. Use Cardfile to keep track of names, addresses, phone numbers, product information, and more. Data are stored in records that look like cards on your screen. The cards display in a fixed size, so there are limits to the information that you can keep on each one. As you can see in Figure 3.9, each card has an "index line" where you might type people's names or other identifiers. Cards are stored and displayed alphabetically based on the contents of the index line.

It is possible to store both text and drawings on cards. You can search for information on cards and print the information for selected cards. A "list view" feature lets you see the index lines of multiple cards and makes it easy to bring cards of interest to the top of the stack for viewing, editing, and printing.

If you have a Hayes-compatible modem installed, Cardfile can use it to dial numbers that you've stored on cards. After the modem dials the phone

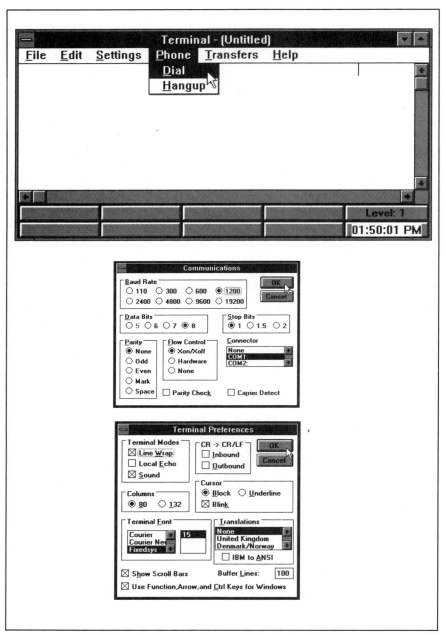

FIGURE 3.8 *Terminal offers reasonably complete communications facilities.*

WINDOWS

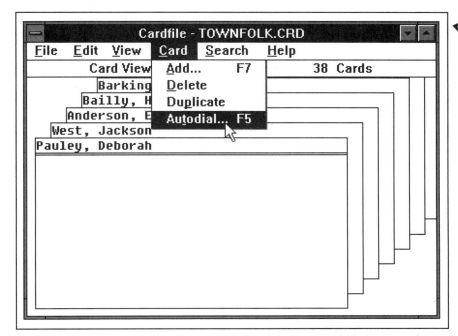

FIGURE 3.9 *Cardfile is an electronic Rolodex that can even dial phone numbers for you.*

number for you, you can pick up a telephone on the same line and talk to the person you've called. This might be a useful tool if you need to keep in touch with customers or vendors or employees over the phone.

Cardfile is not a replacement for dBASE, Q & A, or other sophisticated database management programs. But it is a useful alternative to a paper Rolodex filing system, and it offers a handy, low-cost way to get better organized.

Also consider exploring Excel's data features before spending time entering large amounts of data into a Cardfile file.

RECORDER (MACROS)

The Recorder accessory will "watch" you make a series of keystrokes and mouse moves while running most Windows-compatible programs, then record what it "sees" and repeat the steps on demand. The resulting macros are saved to disk for later use. You can even assign keyboard shortcuts to macros to speed finding and running them. Recorded Windows macro files all end with the extension .REC. Macros can be combined (merged), and one macro can "call," or use, another.

Here are some helpful Macro tips. Close (quit) unnecessary programs before recording Macros. Macros often play back more quickly and reliably if you record *keyboard shortcuts* rather than mouse actions wherever possible. The size and/or location of application windows can be a problem if they change after a macro has been recorded. Since screen resolution, mouse performance, and even keyboard settings vary from one computer to another, macros recorded on your computer may not work right on someone else's. Word and Excel both have their own macro capabilities, which you will want to explore as well.

MULTIMEDIA ACCESSORIES

Windows 3.1 provides three kinds of sound support and a variety of control features for compatible audio and video players. In fact, Windows 3.1 contains all of the multimedia functionality of Windows 3.0's optional Multimedia Extensions pack, and much more. Figure 3.10 shows two Multimedia accessories shipped with Windows 3.1—Media Player and Sound Recorder. For Media Player, you must have Media Control Interface (MCI) device drivers installed on your system. For Sound Recorder, you must have a sound driver installed on your system.

Basic Audio

Windows 3.1 supports Waveform (11 and 22 KHz), *MIDI* (General mode), and CD-quality Redbook audio standards. Thus, it is compatible with Adlib, Creative Labs Sound Blaster, and Media Vision Thunder expansion boards. Roland LAPC1 and MPU401 sound boards are also supported, as are boards compatible with the ones listed above. Your Windows subdirectory probably contains some sample files you can play.

If you have a compatible audio board and microphone or other sound source, you can record your own new Waveform audio files, then play and store them on your hard disk using Windows' Sound Recorder accessory. Waveform audio files always end with the extension .WAV. They can be embedded in sound-savvy documents like those created by Microsoft Word and Excel.

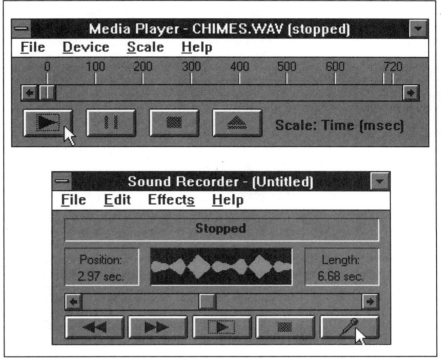

FIGURE 3.10 *Windows comes with two multimedia accessories—Media Player and Sound Recorder.*

MIDI (musical instrument digital interface) is a world standard for communicating with musical instruments and computers. Windows MIDI files end with the extensions .MID and .RMI. The Media Player accessory can play many MIDI files in conjunction with a compatible sound board or other MIDI device.

Listening to Sample Sounds

If you have a compatible sound board and speakers or headphones, run Media Player (found in the Accessories group). Then use Media Player's Open command (found on Media Player's File menu) to load the CANYON.MID file, which is probably located in your Windows directory.

You can also use Media Player to listen to files ending with .WAV. Your Windows directory probably contains CHIMES.WAV, CHORD.WAV, and other sound files. The Media Player controls will remind you of those on a cassette deck. Click on the right-pointing triangle to play, click the box button to stop, and so on.

Recording and Editing Sounds

Use the Sound Recorder and a microphone or other input device to record and edit sound files of up to one minute in length. If you've used an audio recorder, Sound Recorder will feel familiar. The wave box displays audio wave forms as you record or play them. You can record to a new file or load an existing file and add to it (append it). See Sound Recorder's help for details.

MPC (MULTIMEDIA PC) SUPPORT

If you have a true Multimedia computer and compatible accessories (such as a laserdisk player or CD-ROM drive), Windows 3.1 will support this hardware. You'll be able to use Windows as well as Windows applications software to start and stop disk players, select tracks to play, and more. When shopping for MPC devices, look for the Multimedia PC trademark (shown in Figure 3.11) to ensure compatibility.

FIGURE 3.11 *The Multimedia PC trademark, printed on Laser disk, CD-ROM, and other products, usually indicates Windows 3.1 compatibility.*

Organizing Your Files with File Manager

Today's hard disks often contain hundreds or even thousands of files. It can be frustrating and time-consuming to find what you want. File Manager is a Windows program that helps you organize and use your disks effectively. Once you've mastered the techniques in this chapter, you'll never want to go back to the DOS prompt again.

HOW DISKS ARE ORGANIZED

By now you almost certainly know that disks are often broken up into *directories* and *subdirectories* (subdirectories are directories within directories). For instance, you might have a directory called BUDGETS and two subdirectories under it called PLANNED and ACTUAL. You use directories and subdirectories to store files in an organized way. For instance, the ACTUAL subdirectory might contain budget spreadsheets called JAN93, FEB93, and so on.

The way that you and your computer access things thus organized is to use something called a *path*. In our example, if the budgets were stored on drive C of your computer, the path to the FEB93 budget would be rather long—C:\BUDGETS\ACTUAL\FEB93.

Before Windows came along, if you wanted to copy your planned budget for March into the ACTUAL subdirectory, you might type **COPY C:\BUDGETS\PLANNED\FEB93 C:\BUDGETS\ACTUAL**. With Windows you can accomplish the same thing with a few mouse movements. File Manager simplifies many other file-related tasks as well.

VIEWING DISK
CONTENTS WITH FILE MANAGER

Run File Manager the same way you run any other Windows program. Double-click on its icon in the Program Manager's Main window. (If you find yourself using File Manager regularly, as most Windows users do, drag its icon or a copy into the Windows StartUp group, and File Manager will be automatically available each time you run Windows.) When File Manager runs you will see a window something like the one in Figure 4.1.

The computer illustrated in Figure 4.1 has four available disk drives (A–D). Notice that a folder icon named SYBEX (in the left half of the window) is highlighted and that the SYBEX folder icon is "open," unlike other folder icons. This happens when you click on a folder. It becomes the *current directory*. Notice also that the SYBEX subdirectories (CHAPTERS, EXAMPLES, FIGS, and UNUSED) are shown in the right half of the window. Double-clicking on one of those folders would display its contents. For instance, double-clicking on CHAPTERS might reveal word processing files titled CH01.DOC, CH02.DOC, and so on. This is how you explore and access subdirectories easily with a mouse.

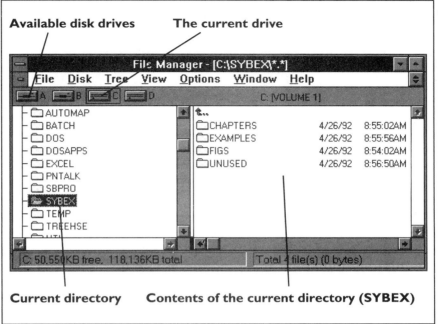

FIGURE 4.1 *File Manager shows you disk contents and organization. It provides a variety of powerful menu commands that can simplify your work.*

SELECTING A DRIVE TO VIEW

To view information about a specific drive, simply click on its icon, making it the *current drive*. (The chosen drive icon has a rectangular outline.) For instance, in Figure 4.1, drive C is the current drive.

You must properly insert a disk into a floppy drive to view its directory. If the drive you select is empty, Windows will prompt you to insert a disk and retry.

Incidentally, you may need to choose Refresh on the Window menu (or press the F5 function key) when swapping floppies. This is how File Manager knows to read and display the new disk's directory information. If you fail to refresh, you might see information from an earlier disk, since Windows has no other way of knowing that you've switched disks.

CHANGING THE
APPEARANCE OF DIRECTORY WINDOWS

Since some disk organizations are simple and sparse, while others are cluttered and complex, File Manager lets you alter its on-screen appearance to suit the task at hand.

DIRECTORY VIEWS

The File Manager's *View* menu gives you a number of viewing options. Use it to show or hide the contents of directories, as well as to increase or decrease the amount of on-screen detail. For instance, choosing *Tree Only* from File Manager's View menu hides the contents of directories. You can also use the View menu to ask Windows to sort listed items by name, type, size, or creation date.

Directory Window Sizes and Positions

Like other windows, File Manager contains scroll bars and window sizing tools to help you see the files and directories of interest.

Multiple Directory Windows Save Time

You may find it helpful to display more than one drive directory at the same time. By picking *New Window* from File Manager's Windows menu, you can display multiple directory windows, then arrange them by tiling or dragging. Figure 4.2 shows an example of this.

In Figure 4.2 the top window shows part of drive C's contents. The bottom window shows a floppy disk in drive B. Notice that two files have been selected on drive C (CH03.DOC and CH03CP.DOC). Now look for the mouse pointer in the drive B window. It is dragging an icon representing the two selected files from drive C. This is one way to copy files from a given directory to another without having to type file and directory names.

The Split Bar

Notice the mouse pointer and long black split bar in the top window of Figure 4.3. Dragging the split bar with your mouse can change the width of

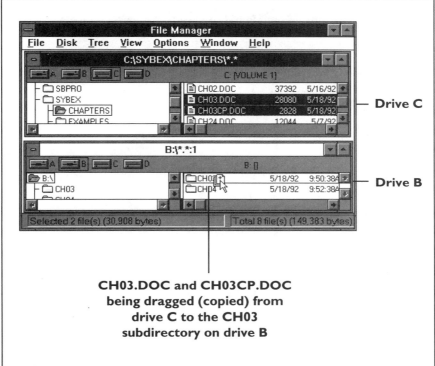

FIGURE 4.2 *Opening multiple File Manager windows can speed the copying and moving of files.*

the two window partitions. As you can see in the second part of the example, this is one way to see more of the file descriptions in the right half of the File Manager window.

Directory Window Fonts, Sizes, and Case

The Font… category in the File Manager's Option menu lets you pick a font and type size for displaying directory information. This is also where you tell Windows whether you want names to be displayed in all uppercase or all lowercase.

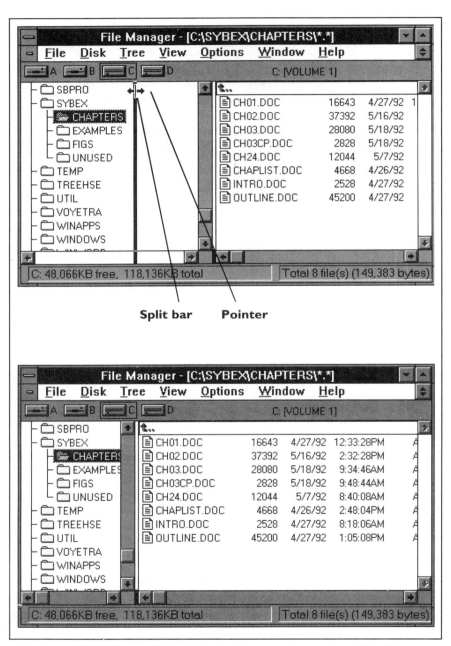

FIGURE 4.3 *Drag the split bar with your mouse to change the width of list areas.*

WINDOWS

Turning the Status Bar On and Off

The status information at the bottom of the File Manager window (bytes free, total files, etc.) can be turned on or off. The Status Bar choice on File Manager's Options menu toggles the status information.

Saving File Manager Settings

Current settings are automatically saved whenever you quit File Manager. The next time you open File Manager it will look the way it did the last time you used it.

CREATING NEW DIRECTORIES WITH FILE MANAGER

Instead of typing **MD** (for "Make Directory") at the DOS prompt, you can create new directories or subdirectories by first selecting the drive of interest in File Manager (click on the appropriate disk icon), then picking Create Directory... from File Manager's File menu. Switch to the root directory to create new directories, or switch to an existing directory to make a subdirectory. Type any valid MS-DOS directory name into the resulting dialog box (shown in Figure 4.4). Finally, click OK or press Enter to create the directory.

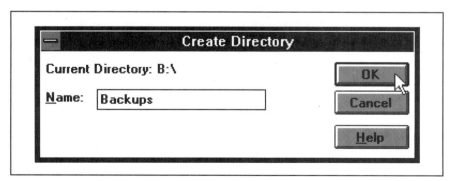

FIGURE 4.4 *Select a drive icon, then pick Create Directory... from File Manager's File menu to make a new directory.*

SELECTING MULTIPLE ITEMS IN FILE MANAGER LISTS

Several useful shortcuts will help you to deal with multiple files. To pick more than one file or directory in a File Manager list, hold down the Ctrl key while pointing. With the Ctrl key held down, each time you point to a different file or directory it will be added to the list of files previously selected. Incidentally, Ctrl-clicking on a selected item will deselect it.

To select a continuous *range* of files or directories, select the first item of interest, scroll to the last item, and hold down the Shift key while clicking on the last item. All items in between will be selected.

MOVING FILES WITH FILE MANAGER

Moving a single file from one drive to another can be as simple as pointing to the file or directory name and Shift-dragging the resulting icon to a disk icon at the top of the File Manager window. Unless you turn off this confirmation feature, File Manager will ask for confirmation before moving the file.

Moving multiple files all at once is easy too, as you saw earlier. Simply select all of the files you want (by Ctrl-clicking them), then Shift-drag them simultaneously with your mouse.

File Manager's File menu also contains a useful Move... command. (Its keyboard shortcut is F7.) When you pick Move..., you will be asked to type the appropriate name(s) and location(s) for files being moved, as well as the path to the desired new location. To avoid some typing, use your mouse *before* visiting this menu choice to select files or directories to be moved from the scrollable File Manager lists.

File Manager will attempt to move all selected files or directories without further intervention. If the destination disk does not have enough room to accept all the new files, File Manager will ask you for additional disks as necessary. Individual files will *not* be fragmented between disks when this happens.

COPYING FILES WITH FILE MANAGER

Copying works just like moving, except that you hold down the Ctrl key when dragging items. And you use File Manager's Copy... instead of

Move… for copying things. When copying from one drive to another, there is no need to hold down Ctrl.

RENAMING FILES AND DIRECTORIES

The renaming of files and directories is a snap with File Manager. Select the item of interest, then choose Rename… from File Manager's File menu. You will see a dialog box similar to the one in Figure 4.5.

If you have selected an item to rename, its old name will appear in the From box. Simply type the new name in the To box and click OK or press Enter.

Here's a great tip. If the old and new names are similar (BlkWido and BlkWido2, for instance), highlight the From text with your mouse and copy it to the Clipboard by holding down the Ctrl and C keys. Next, click in the From box with your mouse to move the insertion point. Paste a copy of the old name from the Clipboard by using the Ctrl-V key combination, then edit it.

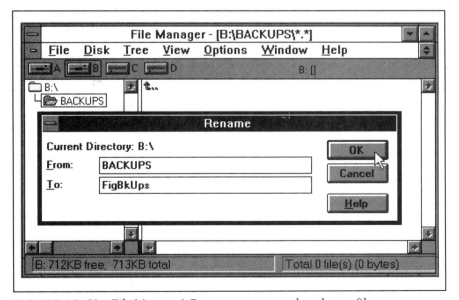

FIGURE 4.5 *Use File Manager's Rename… command to change file or directory names.*

DELETING FILES AND DIRECTORIES
WITH FILE MANAGER

To delete files or directories and their contents, simply highlight them in the appropriate File Manager list, then choose the Delete... command from the File menu or press the Del key on your keyboard. If you are using MS-DOS 5.0 or above, you may also be able to undelete files if you delete them in error and catch your mistake soon enough. This will require a trip to the DOS prompt.

CHANGING FILE ATTRIBUTES

File Manager provides a facility for seeing and changing file attributes (the hidden codes stored with a file's directory that mark its read-only or archive status and so forth). You can make a file "Read Only" or "Hidden," thereby protecting it from accidental alteration. Select the file of interest in a File Manager list, then visit the Properties... choice on File Manager's File menu. (The shortcut is Alt-Enter.) Figure 4.6 shows the resulting dialog box. Click to check and uncheck the appropriate boxes, then click OK to finish up.

Unless you know precisely what you're doing, never change the System attribute or you could cause havoc.

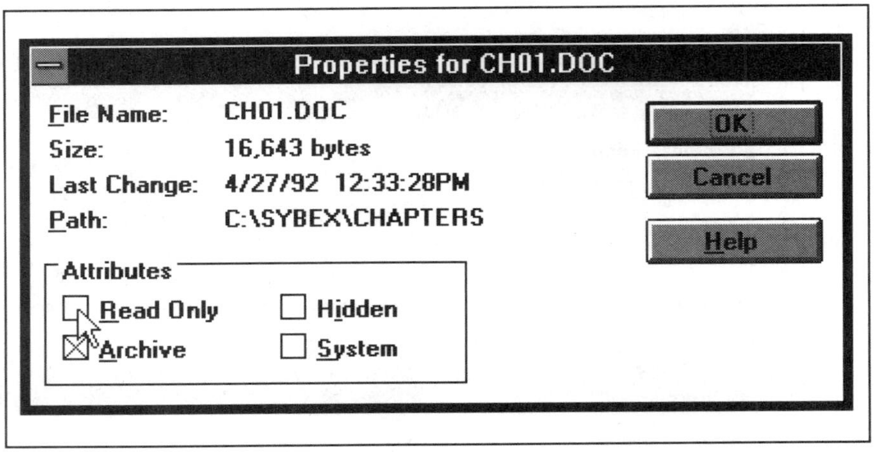

FIGURE 4.6 *Use the Properties... command found on File Manager's File menu to alter file attributes.*

SEARCHING FOR FILES WITH FILE MANAGER

"Where's that (bleeping) file?" Ever said anything like that? Check out File Manager's Search... command on the File menu. When presented with a dialog box like the one in the top of Figure 4.7, you can enter file names, parts of file names, or even just file extensions. For instance, using the asterisk wild card character in the search string "*.DOC" will ask the program to look for Word documents. The string "G*.MID" will find all MIDI files starting with the letter G, and so on. To search an entire disk, specify the root directory (C:\, for instance) as the starting location and check *Search All Subdirectories*.

When you click OK, File Manager will create and display a list of files meeting your search criteria. As you'll see next, double-clicking on the file

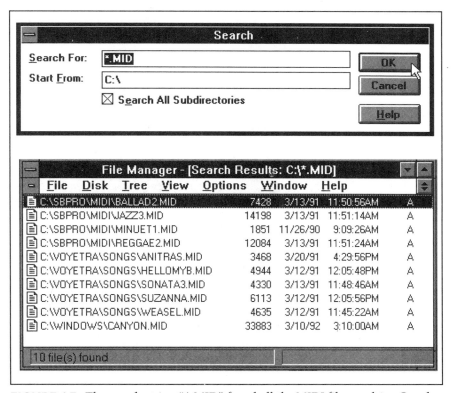

FIGURE 4.7 *The search string "*.MID" found all the MIDI files on drive C and listed them.*

you were looking for in the resulting search list will often load the file (and the application that created it, if possible).

RUNNING APPLICATIONS FROM FILE MANAGER

Memory permitting, double-clicking on the name of an executable program (WORD.EXE or CALCULATOR.EXE, for instance) in a File Manager list will often cause the program to load and run. Frequently, just double-clicking on a *document name* will *load and run* the *program* needed to use it. For instance, double-clicking on an Excel budget worksheet item in a File Manager list will first run Excel, then load the desired worksheet.

For this to work, documents need to be *associated* with applications. Many documents are automatically associated when they are created (like Word and Excel documents). Other documents can often be associated with applications, even if they don't start out life that way. Here's how:

ASSOCIATING FILES WITH APPLICATIONS

Choose the Associate… command from the File Manager File menu. You will see a dialog box like the one in Figure 4.8.

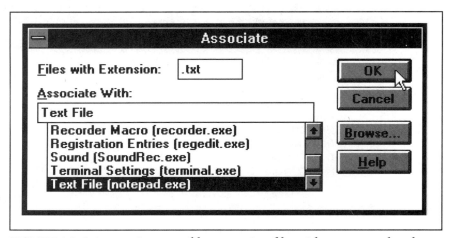

FIGURE 4.8 *It is sometimes possible to associate files with programs other than the one that created them.*

Enter a valid file extension that will be found on the files you want to associate with a program (.TXT in the example). Then, scroll through the list of available programs until you find one that is compatible with the file type with which you wish to associate it. Highlight it and click OK.

FORMATTING AND
NAMING DISKS WITH FILE MANAGER

The Format Disk... choice on File Manager's Disk menu offers a dialog box like the one in Figure 4.9.

Drop-down menus let you use your mouse to pick a disk drive and disk formats appropriate to the drive and media type. Enter an optional name for your disk in the label area, then click OK to start formatting. Since the Quick Formatting option does not check for disk flaws, its use is *not* recommended.

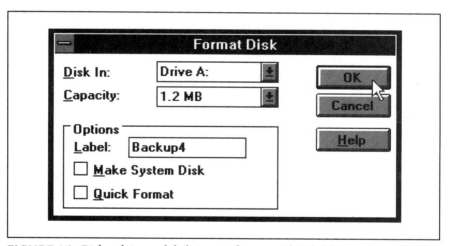

FIGURE 4.9 *Pick a drive and disk type to format with File Manager's Format Disk... command.*

CREATING SYSTEM
DISKS WITH FILE MANAGER

If you check the *Make System Disk* box in File Manager's Format Disk dialog box, Windows will attempt to create a bootable system disk. According to Microsoft, this is not always possible, and you may need to try several disks.

COPYING DISKS WITH FILE MANAGER

The Copy Disk... choice on File Manager's Disk menu offers a dialog box like the one shown in Figure 4.10.

Use the drop-down menus and your mouse to pick both a source drive and a destination drive. It is not possible to use the Copy Disk... command to copy from one disk size or format to another. For instance, if you have different drives (say, a 5 1/4" A drive and a 3 1/2" B drive), you will only be permitted to use one drive for the copying. File Manager will prompt you to enter and remove disks as needed to complete the copying. It is always a good idea to write-protect your source disks—that is, prevent accidental erasure or tampering with its contents by sliding the small tab at the top of the disk case (on a 3 1/2" disk) or putting tape over the write-protect notch (on a 5 1/4" disk).

If you have two identical disk drives, you can copy from one to the other by specifying one as the source drive and the other as the destination drive, as shown in Figure 4.10.

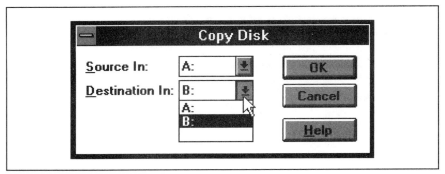

FIGURE 4.10 *File Manager's Copy Disk command will duplicate entire disks.*

HIDING AND QUITTING FILE MANAGER

Use the minimize box to put File Manager out of the way without quitting it. Double-click on the File Manager Control box to quit File Manager, or choose Exit from the File menu.

WINDOWS

5

Printing Tricks and Tips

Engineers have a saying—"The nice thing about standards," they scoff, "is that there are so *many* of them." The originator of that bit of sarcasm must have worked for a computer printer manufacturer or typeface technology company. Fortunately, Windows 3.1 does a pretty good job of isolating us from much of the world's printer and typography minutiae. You *will* need to know a few things, however, and here they are.

PRINTING PRELIMINARIES

When using Windows applications like Word and Excel, Windows 3.1 itself acts as an intermediary between the application and your printer. So, before you can print with Windows applications, Windows needs to know what printer model you have (you may have more than one) and how it is connected to your computer (via a serial, parallel, or network connection). Windows also needs to know which fonts (type styles) you plan to use.

If you are lucky enough to be running Windows on a computer that is already set up and tested, you can probably skip ahead here to the heading "About Fonts." But if you are trying to get Windows to print properly for the first time, or if you are adding a new printer, you'll need to know some details about printer drives, printer ports, and setup options.

SETTING UP PRINTERS

When you initially install Windows, it asks you about the printers you plan to use and how they are connected. You can change your mind later. Here's an overview of the concepts and the process:

ABOUT PRINTER DRIVERS

Like cars, different printers have different *features*. Some laser printers have dual trays or envelope feeders, for instance. And *command codes* differ from one printer model to the next. The code used to tell one printer model to print sideways may be different from another's code for the same effect. For these reasons, Windows uses unique printer *driver software* for each different type of printer. Hundreds of printer driver files are shipped on your Windows installation disks. Moreover, some printer makers ship their own drivers with their printers. To save hard disk space, Windows only installs the drivers for printers you've specified. If you later want to add support for a different printer, or need to update a printer driver to a newer version, you'll need to follow the steps outlined in "Installing Printer Drivers," later in this chapter.

ABOUT PRINTER PORTS

The back of your computer probably looks like part of a space shuttle. There are numerous connectors back there, some of them possibly un-labeled. Chances are, at least one is a serial port (often labeled COM1, COM2, etc.) and another is a parallel port (often named LPT1, LPT2, and so on). You may or may not have a network connector back there as well.

Some printers are designed to connect to serial ports, others to parallel ports, and some to either kind. In large organizations, printers are some-times shared over network connections. Windows can work with all three arrangements, but you need to tell it which port to use for which printer.

Before setting up Windows for printing you need to know the following:

- Your printer make(s) and model(s)

- Printer interface type (parallel, serial, or network)

- Port(s) you plan to use (COM1, LPT1, etc.)

- Serial data rate settings for serial printers

- Font cartridges and other printer options to be used

Be certain that each printer is connected to an appropriate connector on your computer with a proper cable. Be aware that connectors and cables that look alike can be *very* different. Get technical help if you are at all uncertain at this point. *Using the wrong cable and/or port can damage your hardware.*

Check printer manuals for information about things like switch settings and setup procedures. For instance, printers that support both serial and parallel connections sometimes need to be set for one or the other.

INSTALLING PRINTER DRIVERS

Have your original Windows installation disks (or copies of them) handy before you start. With your printer(s) properly wired and configured, double-click on the Control Panel icon in the Program Manager's *Main* win-dow. Find the *Printers* icon in the *Control Panel* Window and double-click on it. Then click on the *Add>>* button in the *Printers* window. You'll see a list of printers. Figure 5.1 illustrates this process.

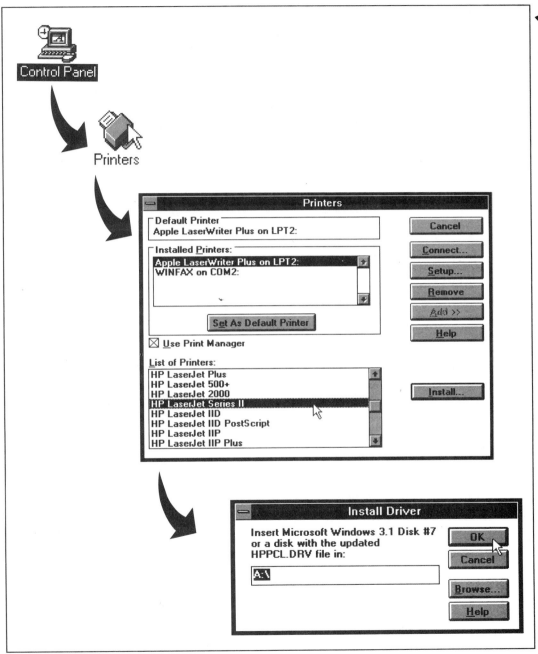

FIGURE 5.1 *Get to the printer installation window via the Control Panel's Printers icon.*

Scroll through the list to find the name of each printer driver you want to install. Double-click on the desired driver name, or click once on the name to highlight it, then click OK. You will probably be asked for a disk, as illustrated in Figure 5.1. Follow the on-screen directions. Soon the new printer driver will be added to the list of installed printers in the Printers window.

SPECIFYING THE DEFAULT PRINTER

With the Control Panel's *Printers* window on screen (see Figure 5.1), examine the list of Installed Printers. Click on the one you want Windows to use as your everyday printer, to highlight the driver name. Then click on the *Set As Default Printer* button. Close the Printer window.

FOR MORE PRINTER INSTALLATION INFORMATION

Don't feel bad if you have trouble installing printers. Computer consultants make a nice living scratching their heads over this subject. Start by checking Windows' on-line help as you work. Next, try reading your printer manual and calling your dealer or printer maker. If all else fails, contact Microsoft. Make notes as you work.

ABOUT FONTS

A font is a named collection of characters (letters, numbers, and symbols) having a similar appearance. Fonts for computer printers come in hundreds of different sizes and thousands of styles. The huge variety of fonts available today makes it easy to add impact and a professional look to your documents. Most Windows applications (including Word and Excel) let you pick fonts from a menu list. You can also change the size of characters and embellish them (italicize, underline, etc.). Windows ships with some fonts of its own, and you can purchase additional fonts. If you create a document on one computer and try to display or print it out on another, it is desirable to have the same fonts on both computers. There's plenty more to know about fonts, much of it beyond the scope of this book. So here's the *Reader's Digest* version of Windows font facts.

Windows supports three font technologies: *bitmap* fonts (also called raster or screen fonts), *vector* fonts (sometimes called plotter fonts), and *outline* fonts (also called TrueType).

BITMAP FONTS

Bitmap fonts are stored on your computer as collections of dots. Examples of Windows bitmap fonts include *Courier*, *MS Serif* (from Windows version 3.0), and *System*. Bitmap fonts look fine at their original size, but do not scale (resize) very well. Resized bitmap characters often look jagged and block-like.

VECTOR FONTS

Vector fonts are collections of instructions (definitions of lines and points, actually) that your computer uses to draw the shapes of characters. Vector fonts scale (resize) fairly well and are often available in large sizes. They're a good choice when printing to plotters. Windows 3.1 vector fonts include *Modern*, *Terminal*, *Roman*, and *Script*.

TRUETYPE FONTS

TrueType support is a new Windows feature. Windows 3.1 comes with a number of free TrueType fonts. Examples include *Courier New* (notice the word *New*), *Arial*, *New Roman*, *Symbol*, and *Wingdings*.

The beauty of TrueType fonts is that, theoretically at least, if you display and print only TrueType fonts, your screen and printer will always agree. That is to say, your document's line and page endings will be the same on screen as on paper. This phenomenon is often referred to as WYSIWYG (pronounced *whizzy wig*). As any bureaucrat will tell you, WYSIWYG stands for "What You See Is What You Get" (almost).

WHICH FONT TYPE IS IT?

When choosing a font to use on a project, you normally pick from a drop-down font menu. You can usually tell TrueType from bitmap from vector fonts by looking at the icons next to font names in font menus. For example, in Figure 5.2, Script is a vector font, Courier New a TrueType font, and Modern a bitmap font.

WINDOWS

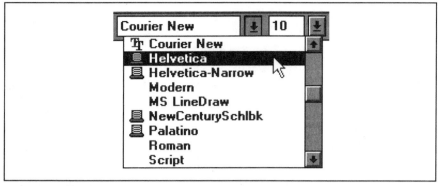

FIGURE 5.2 *Choose fonts from a drop-down menu.*

PRINTER VS. SCREEN FONTS

To add to the confusion, frequently the fonts used to display things on your screen are different from the fonts used by your printer. For example, some printers have built-in fonts, others use plug-in font cartridges, and sometimes your computer sends (or downloads) fonts to your printer.

Subtle differences between screen fonts and printer fonts can cause problems with line and page endings. If an on-screen font is slightly smaller than a built-in printer font, for instance, your finished document may contain more pages when printed than it does when viewed on the screen. This can be a real problem if you've created a table of contents and index, or if you care about keeping certain document elements on the same page.

For the best chance of reaching WYSIWYG nirvana, use TrueType fonts both on screen and for printing. You may need to ask your dealer or printer maker for assistance, since many older printer manuals predate TrueType.

INSTALLING AND REMOVING FONTS

If the fonts you purchased come with an install program and/or installation instructions, use them. Otherwise, to install new fonts on your computer, place the disk containing the font(s) of interest into a floppy drive. Then, from the Program Manager's Main window, double-click on the *Control Panel* Icon. When the Control Panel window appears, double-click on the *Fonts* icon and you'll see something like Figure 5.3.

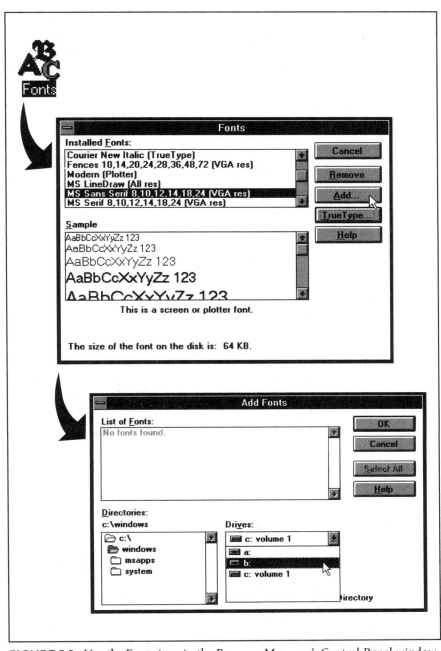

FIGURE 5.3 *Use the Fonts icon in the Program Manager's Control Panel window to add or remove fonts.*

Click the *Add* button. You'll see an *Add Fonts* box like the one at the bottom of Figure 5.3. Use the drop-down *Drives* menu to indicate which disk drive has the font(s) you want to load. When you see fonts listed in the *List of Fonts* menu, click to select one, or Ctrl-click to select several. Or use the *Select All* button to select all the fonts. Click OK to install the selected fonts.

To remove fonts, pick them from the Installed Fonts list. Then use the Remove button.

PRINTING FROM WINDOWS APPLICATIONS

Most Windows-savvy programs (including Word and Excel) use the same commands and similar techniques for common tasks like printing. For example, you will find a Print... choice on most applications' File menus. Frequently, the keyboard shortcut for printing is Ctrl-Shift-F12.

When you execute the Print... command, you'll usually get a Print dialog box that looks something like either of the ones in Figure 5.4.

The two Print dialog boxes in Figure 5.4 have things in common. They both let you specify multiple copies, and they both let you specify a range of pages to print with From and To boxes.

But, as you can see, even print dialog boxes from the same software company have different features. Microsoft Word's Print dialog box (at the top of Figure 5.4) has a Collate Copies check box; the Excel Print dialog box does not. Sometimes the same feature is labeled differently. Word's Setup... and Excel's Page Setup... do essentially the same thing, for instance. Sometimes the appearance of Print dialog boxes changes when you select different printer models. Check out your printer and application software's documentation, and request on-line help for more assistance with your particular configuration and printing options.

SWITCHING PRINTERS
IF YOU HAVE MORE THAN ONE

If you are lucky enough to have more than one printer, use the Print Setup... choice found in the File menu of most Windows programs to display the Print Setup dialog box shown in Figure 5.5.

You will see a list of printer drivers. Hopefully, this list will match the printers that are actually connected to your computer, although it may not. Click on any valid printer driver, then either click OK to choose the printer,

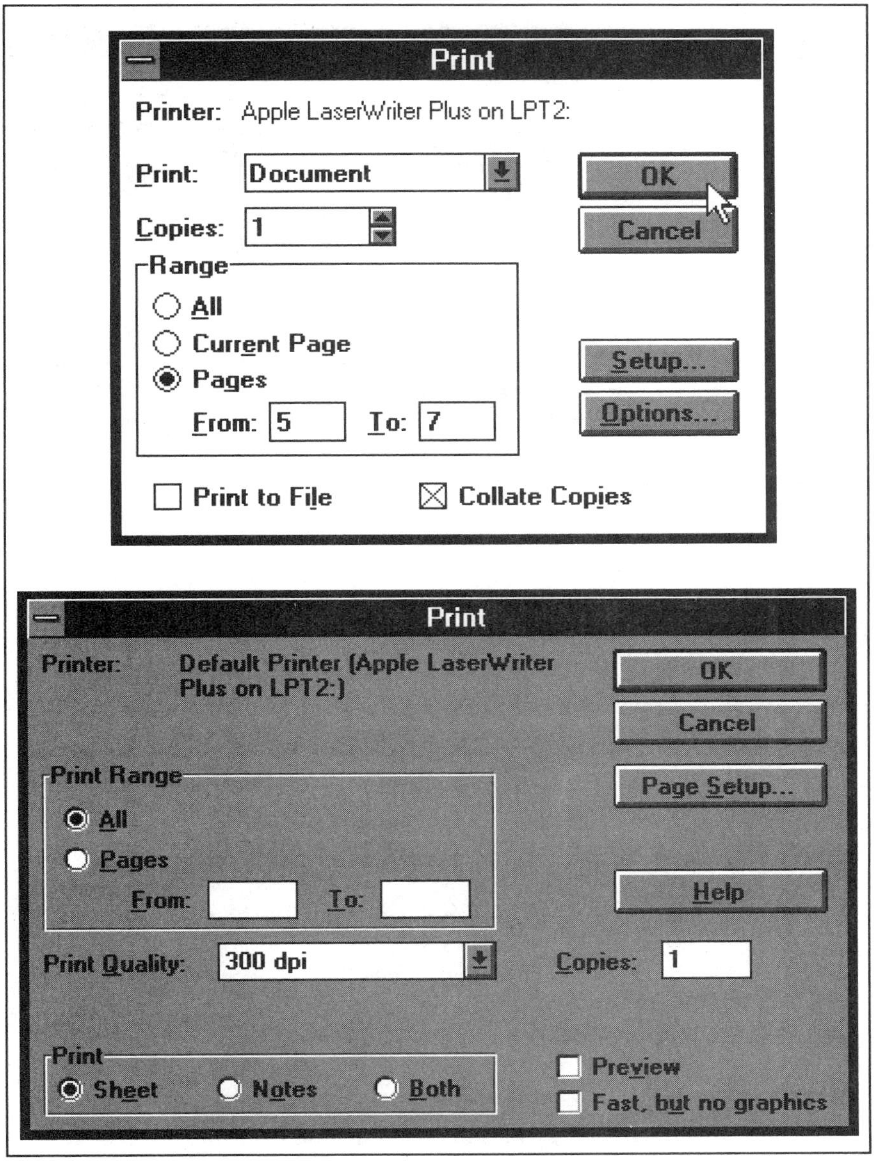

WINDOWS

Print

Printer: Apple LaserWriter Plus on LPT2:

Print: Document   [OK]

Copies: 1   [Cancel]

Range
  ○ All
  ○ Current Page
  ● Pages   [Setup...]
     From: 5   To: 7   [Options...]

☐ Print to File   ☒ Collate Copies

Print

Printer: Default Printer (Apple LaserWriter   [OK]
            Plus on LPT2:)
                                                      [Cancel]
Print Range
  ● All   [Page Setup...]
  ○ Pages
     From: To: [Help]

Print Quality: 300 dpi   Copies: 1

Print
  ● Sheet   ○ Notes   ○ Both   ☐ Preview
                                     ☐ Fast, but no graphics

FIGURE 5.4 *Most Windows applications have similar-looking Print dialog boxes. The top one is from Microsoft Word, the other from Excel.*

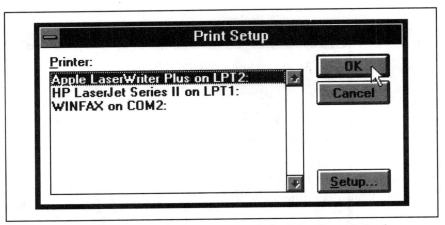

FIGURE 5.5 *Choose from multiple printers with the Print Setup dialog box, reached from the File menu's Print Setup... command.*

or first click Setup... to visit the printer's Option dialog box (the purpose of which is described in a moment).

If you have multiple printers, get in the habit of choosing the printer you plan to use right when you start the project. Then your on-screen indications of margins, line endings, and other printer-related specifications will be accurate.

PRINTER OPTIONS

Most printer drivers also provide options-setting windows for specifying paper size, tray, orientation, and so forth. Figure 5.6 shows some of the many options for a Hewlett-Packard LaserJet Series II printer.

Notice that this Options dialog box has yet another Options... button, which will take you to additional printer choices. Ahh, technology.

PRINT MANAGER'S ROLE IN PRINTING

Unless you disable Print Manager with the Control Panel, Windows automatically runs it whenever you print. Print Manager acts as an intermediary between your application (Word, for instance) and your printer. Among other things, this can sometimes let you get back to work on other projects while your printer prints. If you share a printer with others on a network,

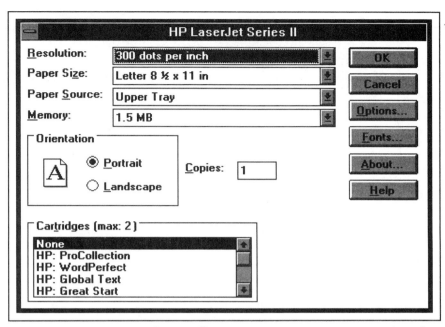

FIGURE 5.6 *Most printer drivers offer numerous printer setup options. Consult your printer manuals and on-line help to learn more about each option.*

Print Manager will help you stack printing jobs in queues and show you where your job is in line.

To bring Print Manager to the forefront while printing, use the Task List or Alt-Tab tricks described in Chapter 2. You can also run Print Manager without printing by double-clicking on its icon in the Program Manager's Main window. Print Manager's primary window looks like Figure 5.7.

PRINTING FROM
NON-WINDOWS APPLICATIONS

When you run non-Windows programs under Windows, they print as they always did. That is to say, you will not see any of the Print dialog boxes described earlier in this chapter, and non-Windows programs will not print through Print Manager.

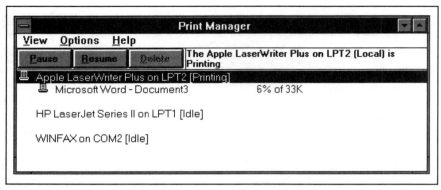

FIGURE 5.7 *Print Manager lets you see and control the status of your printing jobs and printers.*

NETWORK PRINTING

If you have installed a Windows-compatible network, and have configured Windows to run on the network, you can use Print Manager to help you select and use network printers. The level of network printer support depends on your network.

In addition to consulting your network documentation and network manager, read the file called NETWORKS.WRI shipped with Windows 3.1. It can usually be found in your WINDOWS subdirectory. Use the Write Accessory to read and print it.

QUITTING PRINT MANAGER

Unless you've displayed the Print Manager window, Print Manager quits automatically when finished printing. This frees up RAM. To force Printer Manager to quit before printing is complete, double-click on its Control box and either choose Exit from the View menu, or Close from the Control menu. If there are still things to be printed, you'll be given a chance to change your mind about quitting.

6

Personalizing Windows

Windows 3.1 lets you personalize your computer's look and feel. If you have a color or gray-scale monitor, you can pick color or shading combinations for borders, menus, and other windows elements. If your computer contains an audio board, you can change the standard alert beep to chimes or other lifelike, often amusing sounds. Even if you don't have a color-equipped, multimedia-capable computer, Windows lets you fine-tune the behavior of your mouse, keyboard, and other tools. It also makes it easy to set your computer's internal clock/calendar. If you create international documents, there are date, time, and measurement-formatting settings designed to make you look like you know your way around the world. Portable computer users will find settings designed to improve life on the road. This chapter explores the many options found in the Windows Control Panel and elsewhere.

SYSTEM-WIDE CHOICES
WITH THE CONTROL PANEL

Double-click on the Control Panel icon found in Program Manager's Main group. The Control Panel window contains a dozen or more icons representing small programs called *drivers* used to modify your computer's configuration. The exact number and mix of icons varies depending on the type of computer you have (286, 386, 486). You may see additional icons if your computer is connected to a network, or if you use special pointing devices, and so on. A typical Control Panel is shown in Figure 6.1.

To make changes, either pick an item from the Control Panel's Settings menu or double-click on the icon of interest. Either way, you will see one or more Settings windows where you use buttons, check boxes, menus, and other tools to observe and alter settings. The changes you make with the Control Panel are automatically stored in your WIN.INI file.

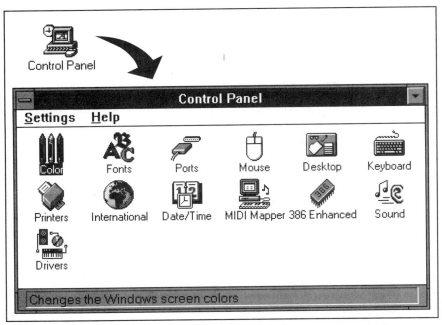

FIGURE 6.1 *Reach the Control Panel by double-clicking on its icon in the Program Manager's Main window.*

SETTING YOUR
COMPUTER'S CLOCK AND CALENDAR

As you probably know, your computer has a battery-operated clock/calendar chip that maintains the correct time and date even when the computer is turned off. Your computer uses the chip to time-stamp and date-stamp files. Many applications programs (including Word and Excel) use the clock/calendar chip as a source of date and time information as well.

Occasionally, your clock chip needs setting (in spring and fall, for instance). Do this with the Date & Time window shown in Figure 6.2. It can be reached by double-clicking on the Control Panel's Date/Time icon, or by choosing Date/Time... on the Control Panel's Settings menu.

Click-and-drag to choose (highlight) the item you want to change (day, year, hour, whatever). Type the new number or click on the appropriate arrows to increase or decrease the setting. Click OK to make the changes.

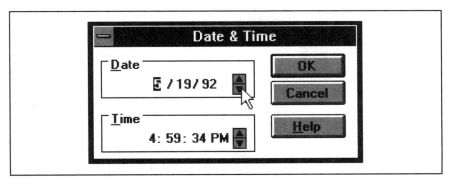

FIGURE 6.2 *Use these controls to set your computer's internal clock and calendar.*

CHANGING THE APPEARANCE OF YOUR DESKTOP

You can alter the color and patterns used to decorate your desktop (the Windows workplace) and many of its elements (window borders, menu highlighting, and the like). Use the *Desktop* and *Color* icons shown in Figure 6.3 to accomplish this.

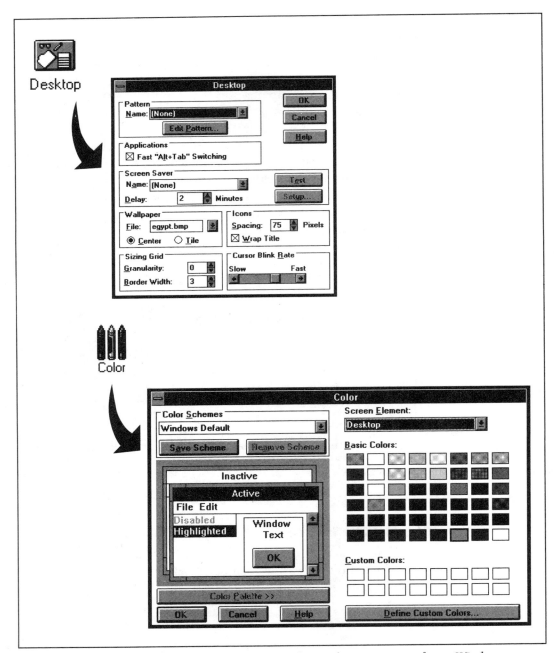

FIGURE 6.3 *Use the Desktop and Color settings to change the appearance of your Windows desktop.*

Desktop Patterns

When you first install Windows, the background is a solid pattern. You can pick one of a dozen or more alternative patterns with names like Waffle and Scottie. These add texture and interest to the Windows background that you see when windows are minimized.

The Control Panel's *Desktop* icon gives you control over the Windows background. Double-click on it to see choices like the ones in the top part of Figure 6.3. Pick a pattern from the drop-down pattern menu, then click OK to change the pattern. Minimize enough windows to admire your work and make any adjustments. If, after spending an hour playing with the patterns provided by Microsoft, you want to design your own, click the Edit Pattern... button and use your mouse to add or subtract blocks to build a pattern. Click OK to save your work.

Wallpaper

You can display bitmap graphics on your desktop, including your own logos, geometric designs, and just about anything else that can be scanned or drawn with a paint program. The actual color and shading of wallpaper images will depend upon your hardware's capabilities. Wallpaper graphics can cover the whole desktop or just a small part (typically the center). Microsoft provides some samples to get you started. Wallpaper images should be stored in your Windows directory and must end with the extension .BMP.

To pick the desired wallpaper, open the *Desktop* window just as you would to change a desktop pattern, then visit the *Wallpaper* drop-down menu to make your choice. Choose *Center* by clicking on the circle to center small wallpaper images. The *Tile* button arranges multiple copies of small wallpaper images to create quilt-like arrangements that cover the screen. Just for fun, check out all of Windows' standard images, but consider settling for something simple as your everyday wallpaper (the Windows logo tiled, for instance). Otherwise you will have trouble seeing icons on your desktop.

Some of the more gaudy wallpaper patterns (256COLOR.BMP, for instance) may be hazardous to your health when tiled. If you plan to display these for long periods of time, consider keeping an air sickness bag next to your computer.

Desktop Color Schemes

Here, too, available choices will depend upon your hardware. The most capable video adapters and monitors can display an amazing range of solid and nonsolid colors. On some screens you'll only see a few solid colors or even just black-and-white (or orange-and-black, perhaps.)

Microsoft provides two dozen standard color (and gray-scale) schemes with names like *Black Leather Jacket*, *The Blues*, and *Hot Dog Stand*. You may also create your own.

In the Control Panel window choose *Color* either from the Settings menu or by double-clicking. You will see a foreshortened version of a window like the one in the bottom of Figure 6.3.

Pick a standard Microsoft color scheme from the drop-down Color Schemes menu. Windows will demonstrate the schemes for you in the Color window sample screen as you pick them from the menu.

To create your own schemes, click on Color Palette to reveal the right half of the window containing color choices. Specify the element whose color you want to modify from the Screen Element drop-down menu. Click on the color sample you desire, or create custom colors by clicking on the Define Custom Colors... button and clicking on the Custom Color boxes. Experiment. You can name and save your schemes. Click OK to apply your new scheme.

CHANGING THE BEHAVIOR
OF YOUR MOUSE OR OTHER POINTER

As you read in Chapter 1, it is possible to change the way your mouse, trackball, or other pointing device responds to your hand actions. Lefties often switch the functions of their left and right mouse buttons. Some people want Windows to wait longer for them between clicks when they double-click. Others want to change the distance the on-screen pointer moves in response to their hand movement.

Double-clicking on the Mouse icon in the Control Panel window reveals the standard Mouse dialog box shown in Figure 6.4.

Experiment with these settings to find a combination that feels right for you. Drag the sliding controls left or right to adjust tracking and double-click settings. When it comes to double-clicking, use the slow setting at first. On some computers, it is almost impossible to double-click fast enough to

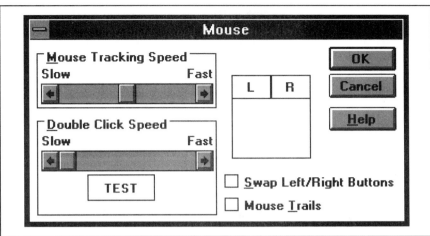

FIGURE 6.4 *The standard Microsoft mouse driver lets you change the way your mouse responds. Other companies provide their own drivers for pointing devices; look for them in your Control Panel.*

satisfy Windows if you use the fastest setting. Double-click on the Test button to see whether Windows recognizes your double-clicks. If the button changes color, Windows recognizes your double-click. If it doesn't change color, decrease the double-click speed.

If you use a pointing device that is Microsoft Mouse–compatible (Kensington's Expert Mouse trackball, for instance), you may be able to use the standard Microsoft Mouse driver. Its control window is shown in Figure 6.4. Otherwise, read the instructions that came with your pointer, or see if the installed driver has its own on-line help.

Incidentally, chances are that changes you make here (such as swapping buttons) will *not* affect the way your mouse performs in non-Windows programs that support a mouse. This can be more than a little disorienting at first.

FEATURES FOR PORTABLE USERS

The *Mouse Trails* box in the standard Microsoft Mouse window (see Figure 6.4) causes Windows to display multiple images of the mouse pointer as you drag it. (Microsoft insiders inelegantly call these "mouse droppings.")

Mouse trails help you find your pointer on sluggish LCD displays where pointers sometimes disappear or "submarine" when in motion.

Portable computer users will want to check out the LCD and Plasma Screen color settings. There are three LCD schemes and one called Plasma Power Saver for plasma display owners. Chances are, at least one of them will improve the appearance of Windows programs on your portable.

CHANGING YOUR KEYBOARD'S BEHAVIOR

Touch typists, rejoice! Windows also lets you customize the repeat response of your keyboard. Double-clicking on the Keyboard icon in the Control panel reveals a window like the one shown in Figure 6.5.

As you have probably discovered, when you hold down a key long enough in most programs, the same character will appear on the screen over and over until you release the key. The *Delay Before First Repeat* slider determines how long you need hold down a key before this starts. The *Repeat Rate* setting determines how many repeating characters are inserted per second.

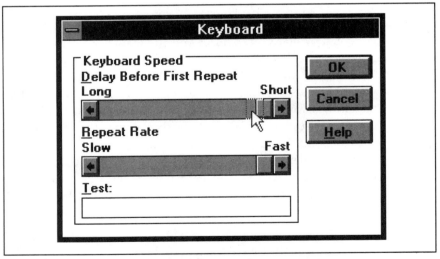

FIGURE 6.5 *The Keyboard controls let you adjust repeat rate.*

WINDOWS

CHANGING YOUR COMPUTER'S SOUNDS

If you have an MPC-compatible sound board whose sound drivers are properly installed, you can assign fascinating sounds to various events like starting and quitting Windows, or error alerts. Windows and most sound boards come with sound files on disk that can be used this way. Examples include CHIMES.WAV, CHORD.WAV, DING.WAV, and TADA.WAV. You can also purchase sound files, or even create your own. Sound files should be stored in your Windows folder and should end with the extension .WAV.

If you are set up for sound, double-click on the Sound icon in the Control Panel. You'll see a window like the one in Figure 6.6.

Highlight an event of interest, then highlight a corresponding sound file. You can hear (preview) sounds by highlighting them and clicking on the *Test* button.

Be sure you have compatible speakers or headphones connected to your sound board. To disable the sounds, remove the check mark from the *Enable System Sounds* box by clicking on it.

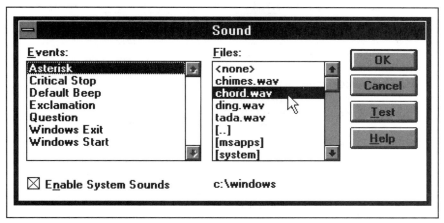

FIGURE 6.6 *If your computer has a compatible sound board, you can set Windows to make different noises whenever certain events occur.*

USING INTERNATIONAL SETTINGS

Many Windows applications (including Word and Excel) are able to use international settings for things like measurements, dates, and currency formats. Bring up the International window by double-clicking on the

International icon (the globe) in the Control Panel. You'll see something like Figure 6.7.

Most of the choices are self-explanatory or easy to understand by experimenting. And there is the usual excellent on-line help available. The *Language* choice may be a little tougher to figure out. It does not change the language used for word menus, windows, and the like; rather, it determines how programs like Word and Excel *sort* alphanumeric lists. Picking the proper language will ensure that lists containing accented characters (such as umlauts and tildes) sort properly.

The country drop-down menu is a quick way to change date, time, number, currency, and paper size options with a drag and a click. Scroll through the list from Australia to the United States, and pick the country and language of your choice. If you don't see the one you want, create your own, then name and save it.

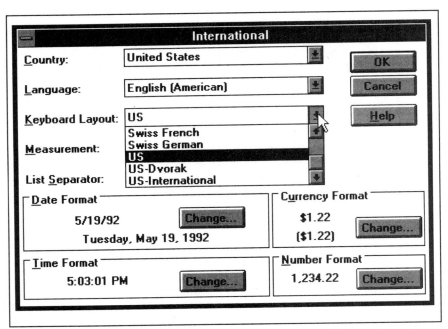

FIGURE 6.7 *Windows can help make you look worldly by adjusting date, time, and other formats to meet a variety of international standards.*

PICKING ENTERTAINING SCREEN SAVERS

These days, *screen saver* is a misnomer of sorts. Older monitors sometimes had images burned into them if you displayed the same thing in the same area of the screen for too long—when away from your computer, for instance. Screen saver programs provide constantly changing images designed to prevent this. (It is pretty difficult to damage a modern computer display this way.)

Many people love screen savers anyway, primarily for their entertainment value. You can turn your computer into a window on the *Enterprise* or a Microsoft billboard or a piece of animated art. Here's how:

The Screen Saver choice can be found in the Control Panel's *Desktop* window (see Figure 6.3 if you've forgotten what it looks like). Windows comes with a number of animated shows that start automatically if your computer sits idle for a period of time you define.

Drop down the list of available screen savers (the list is labeled Name). Pick one and test it by clicking on the Test button. Move the mouse or press a key to return to the Desktop window. Most saver choices have additional setup options used to change speeds, colors, number of items on the screen, and so on. (You could spend the better part of a rainy Saturday fiddling with this, and why not?)

When you find a combination you like, pick a delay time (two minutes is the default). Thereafter, if you ignore your computer for the specified amount of time, it will run the animation until you move the mouse or type something.

You may find that the simplest savers are the best. Check out Marquee, for instance. It scrolls text across the screen. Click the setup button to define your own text. You can also change the text size, color position, and more.

Starfield Simulation will hypnotize Trekkies. *Flying Windows* will make Microsoft's marketing department smile.

OTHER CONTROL PANEL FEATURES

Your Control Panel may have drivers not discussed in this chapter. For instance, some peripheral manufacturers (like makers of multimedia hardware) provide their own drivers. When in doubt, double-click on a driver and check its on-line help, or refer to the documentation that came with the driver.

ADDING AND REMOVING
CONTROL PANEL DRIVERS

When you get hardware that needs a new driver, follow the manufacturer's instructions. If by remote chance there are none, or if you want to update an existing driver, choose (double-click) the Drivers icon in the Control Panel. You will see a list of installed drivers and buttons for installing, deleting, and changing the setup of drivers.

The Add button will show you a list of Microsoft-supplied drivers that are probably gathering dust on one of your installation disks. You will be prompted to put the appropriate floppy in drive A if you try to install one of these. Another choice you will see is Unlisted or Updated Driver. Use this choice with update disks, or with disks from other manufacturers.

STARTING APPLICATIONS
WHEN YOU START WINDOWS

There are other ways to personalize Windows besides playing with the Control Panel. For instance, if you always want to see the Calculator accessory on your desktop, or if you always want to use Word when you start your computer, you can drag program icons (or duplicates) into the Windows StartUp group as illustrated in Figure 6.8.

CHANGING THE APPEARANCE OF ICONS

Many programs (including most non-Windows applications) have boring-looking program icons. You can change these! Here are the steps:

1. In the Program Manager, click once on the ugly icon to select it.

2. Choose *Properties* from the Program Manager's File menu.

3. Click Change Icon.

4. You will see a window containing a sideways-scrolling collection of icons like the one in Figure 6.9.

5. Slide and double-click on a replacement icon.

6. Click *OK* and show someone your handiwork.

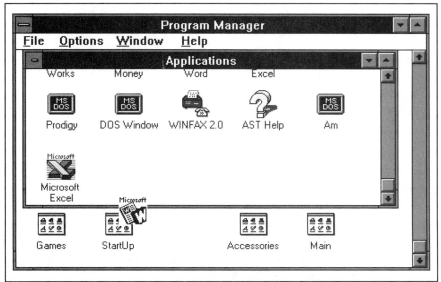

FIGURE 6.8 *If you drag applications (or copies of applications) into the Program Manager's StartUp group, the programs will run automatically each time you start Windows.*

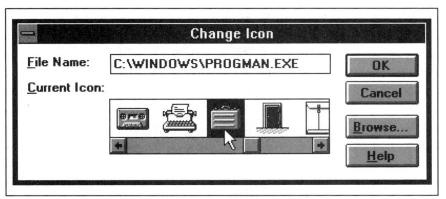

FIGURE 6.9 *Replace icons with one more suited to your needs.*

TURNING OFF FILE
MANAGER'S CONFIRMATION MESSAGES

If you like to live life on the edge, and if you hate those messages like "Do you really, *really* want to delete C:\COMMAND.COM?," a trip to the Confirmation... command on File Manager's Options menu may be in order. You will see a collection of check boxes like those shown in Figure 6.10. Remove check marks from items you don't want to confirm. For instance, if you don't want to be warned when you are about to replace an existing file, remove the check from that box.

If you share a computer with others, either leave these alerts enabled, or put a BIG sign on your computer to warn others of the changes you've made.

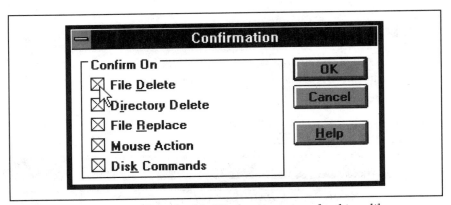

FIGURE 6.10 *It is possible to disable Windows warnings for things like duplicate file names. If you share your computer with others, be sure to tell them you've done this.*

Running
Non-Windows
Applications

Chances are, you purchased Windows 3.1 primarily in order to run *Windows* applications like Word and Excel for Windows, covered in Parts II and III of this book. But you may also need to run programs that were not specifically designed for the Windows environment—at least, until you can purchase Windows versions or upgrades. There are several ways to do this. The "cleanest" is to simply quit Windows (from the Program Manager), then run your non-Windows programs normally from the DOS prompt. This approach frequently offers the best performance, while minimizing memory shortage problems.

Sometimes you will find it inconvenient to quit Windows. Or you may want to run both a Windows program and a non-Windows program simultaneously. Moreover, Windows offers tools like the Clipboard, File Manager, and Accessories that can be helpful even when running non-Windows programs.

This chapter will look at several ways to run non-Windows programs from within Windows itself. It also explores special files called PIF files, which Windows uses to optimize performance of your non-Windows programs.

READ BEFORE YOU CLICK-AND-DRAG

Many vendors of non-Windows programs have created their own special installation procedures that may differ from those you are about to read here. A few programs will not run at all, or will run poorly, under Windows 3.1. Start by reading the documentation and any README files shipped with your non-Windows programs.

Remember, too, that you will probably need to first use a non-Windows program's installation procedures and tools *before* running the Windows installer. For instance, many non-Windows programs are shipped as "compacted," or compressed, files on multiple disks. You will need to use the MS-DOS program's installation software to decompress and install the files on your hard disk before you can run the Windows Setup program. If you have questions, consider calling the program's manufacturer to ask for assistance with Windows installation. This can save you hours of frustration.

SETTING UP NON-WINDOWS APPLICATIONS

When you first install Windows, the installer normally looks for and "installs" your non-Windows programs so that Windows can take a crack at reconfiguring and running them. In the process, PIF files are created for each program, along with icons that normally appear in your Applications windows. If you add new MS-DOS programs after running the Windows Setup program, you can run Setup again to install them. It is also possible to set up programs via Program Manager or File Manager. Let's look at Setup first.

USING THE WINDOWS SETUP
PROGRAM FOR NON-WINDOWS APPLICATIONS

Start the Windows Setup program by double-clicking on its icon in the Program Manager's Main window. You can see this icon in the top of Figure 7.1.

Choose *Set Up Applications...* from the Windows Setup *Options* menu. If you click OK at this point, Windows will seek out and list all Windows and non-Windows applications. To selectively install programs, click to choose them, then click the Add button.

If you only want to add a single program and you know its name and path, click the "*Ask you to specify an application*" button as shown in Figure 7.1.

You will be asked to type the path and file name for the desired program. Don't forget to type the file name's extension (.**EXE**, or whatever). Enter an optional group name if you want the program to be installed with a specific group of programs.

If all goes well, you will see a new icon with the program's name either in your Program Manager window or in the group window you've specified. Sometimes this will be a custom icon; other times it will be a generic-looking MS-DOS icon. (See Chapter 6.) Double-clicking on the new icon *should* run the non-Windows program.

Once in a while, however, Windows will not be able to install your new program, in which case you will be informed of the problem and shown a suggestion or two. Write down (or screen-print) these messages. This is also a good time to call the program manufacturer or Microsoft for assistance.

USING PROGRAM MANAGER
TO SET UP NON-WINDOWS APPLICATIONS

If you don't like using Windows Setup, or if you see a dead-end message like the one at the bottom of Figure 7.1, try using the Program Manager to install your non-Windows applications.

Choose *New* from the Program Manager's File menu, then click the *Program Item* button as shown in Figure 7.2. Then click the OK button and you will see the Program Item Properties window, also illustrated in Figure 7.2. Type the icon name you want to use in the *Description* box. Tab or point to the *Command Line* entry box and type the *path* and *program name*, complete

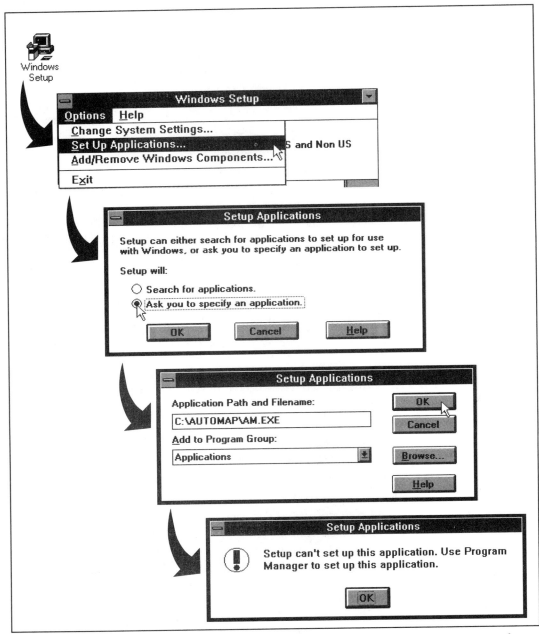

FIGURE 7.1 *Double-clicking on the Windows Setup icon in the Program Manager's Main window is one way to start installing a non-Windows application.*

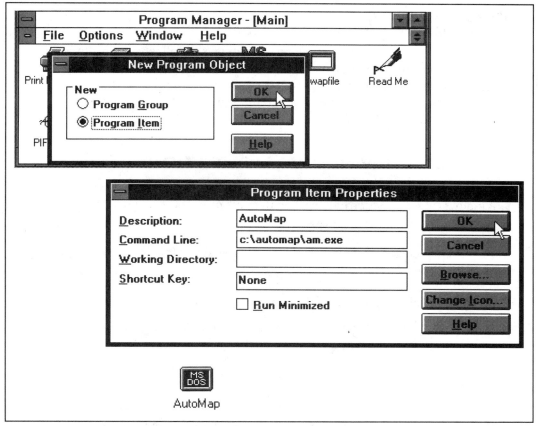

FIGURE 7.2 *You can use the Program Manager to install non-Windows applications.*

with extension. A check mark in the *Run Minimized* box will start the program as an icon rather than filling your screen with it. Normally, you will want to leave the Working Directory field blank unless the software maker suggests otherwise.

Incidentally, Program Manager searches for a PIF file when you install this way. (PIF files will be described shortly.) If it can't find a PIF file, it uses DEFAULT.PIF.

USING FILE MANAGER
TO SET UP NON-WINDOWS APPLICATIONS

Arrange your desktop (open and resize windows, scroll, and so on) in a way that you can see File Manager and the applications group where you want to place the application icon. Select the file of interest in File Manager (point-and-click), then drag the icon into the group where you want it. Windows will create a PIF file, if necessary.

STARTING NON-WINDOWS APPLICATIONS

There are many ways to start non-Windows applications from within Windows. Since they don't all work with every program, you'll need to experiment. The possibilities include:

- Double-clicking on a program icon in Program or File Manager

- Double-clicking on an associated document icon

- Double-clicking on a PIF file icon

- Using the Run… command from the Program Manager File menu, then typing a path and file name

- Using the MS DOS prompt reached from the Windows MS-DOS icon

ABOUT THE MS-DOS ICON IN THE MAIN GROUP

If your computer supports the 386 Enhanced mode (most 386 and 486 computers do), you can run an MS-DOS program in a Windows window. Figure 7.3 illustrates this.

You can move, resize, and minimize the MS-DOS window like any other. It is sometimes even possible to use your Windows Clipboard to share information with non-Windows programs this way.

Double-click on the MS-DOS Prompt icon shown at the top of Figure 7.3. You will see a window running DOS like the one shown in this figure. Start

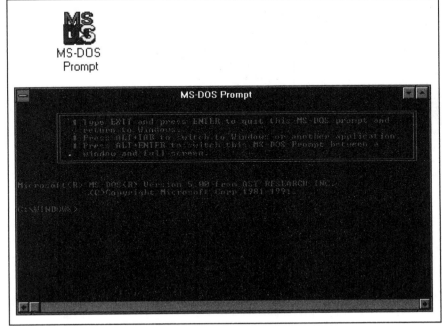

FIGURE 7.3 *Your 386 or 486 computer can often run MS-DOS programs in a Windows window. (You must be in Enhanced, not Standard, mode for this to work.)*

your program from the DOS prompt just as you did in the good old days. When you are done, quit the application as usual, then type **EXIT** at the DOS prompt to close the MS-DOS window. Remember to exit to Windows and then exit it properly before shutting your system down.

While running in a DOS window, you should be able to switch to Windows applications, the File Manager, accessories, and so on by using the Alt-Tab key combination.

You can switch between a window and full-screen MS-DOS by pressing the Alt-Enter key combination. This toggles between a window and the full screen.

WINDOWS

USING A MOUSE
WITH NON-WINDOWS PROGRAMS

Your mouse or mouse-compatible pointing device may work with non-Windows programs that are mouse-savvy. Generally, this requires setting up the mouse driver (in DOS) before starting Windows. Follow the instructions that came with your pointing device. If you are unsure whether your application program supports a mouse, check the documentation that came with the program.

FONT SIZES IN 386 ENHANCED MODE

Non-Windows programs can sometimes be run in different font sizes and styles when run under Windows in 386 Enhanced mode. For example, you may be able to choose a smaller font size to reduce the dimensions of the DOS window on your desktop.

To try it, visit the Control Panel and choose Fonts. Select the desired font size and check the Save settings on the Exit box. Click OK. This may cause problems in some programs, so experiment.

PRINTING FROM NON-WINDOWS APPLICATIONS

When you print from a non-Windows application while in Windows, the printing is sent directly to the printer, bypassing the Print Manager. Therefore, use the standard DOS facilities to set up printer ports.

MEMORY CONSIDERATIONS
WITH NON-WINDOWS PROGRAMS

Since the first computer was built, users lament, there has never been enough of the right kind of memory. Conventional DOS RAM—the so-called first 640K used by DOS—always seems in short supply. It is chewed up by DOS itself, by pop-up (TSR) programs, by network drives, and by heaven knows what all. There are, however, ways to juggle program demands and work around the shortage of conventional RAM. Entire books have been written on this subject. Here are a few tips for managing RAM when running non-Windows programs under Windows.

- Close or minimize applications you are not using.

- Note that full-screen DOS uses less RAM than running DOS in a window. (Press Alt-Enter to toggle between them.)

- Don't use wallpaper. (Turn it off with the Control panel's Desktop settings.)

- Turn off Background execution (see "The PIF Editor" below).

- Keep the Clipboard empty.

- Try to avoid using unnecessary TSRs, network drivers, and the like.

- Make sure your computer's CONFIG.SYS file is properly set for the available RAM.

- Explore the use of memory enhancement programs like those offered by Quarterdeck.

TERMINATE-AND-STAY-RESIDENT PROGRAMS AND WINDOWS

Terminate-and-stay-resident (TSR) programs are supported under Windows. Set them up as usual under DOS. Remember that TSR programs do not usually release RAM when they are not being used. This can sometimes cause unnecessary Windows "Out of Memory" messages, and may even prevent running certain Windows and non-Windows applications. If you encounter this problem, consider setting up batch files that load Windows *without* unneeded TSRs, then when you want the TSR just load it at that time.

POP-UP PROGRAMS AND WINDOWS

Although many of these have been made obsolete by such Windows accessories as Calculator and Calendar, you may have a few favorites (like SideKick) that you want to squeeze into RAM.

The general approach is to run TSRs under Windows as though they were regular applications. You may need to create PIF files for these programs. Switch to them using the Alt-Tab key combination or the Task Manager.

PROGRAM INFORMATION (PIF) FILES

Windows looks for PIF files whenever you run a non-Windows program. Normally, the PIF file has the same name (often abbreviated) as the program itself. A program called AM.EXE would typically have a PIF file called AM.PIF, for instance. If Windows can't find an appropriate PIF file, it uses DEFAULT.PIF, which may or may not be suitable. It's a good idea to place all PIF files either in the *Windows* directory or in the directory containing the program. Usually the program's installer does the right thing for you.

PIF files tell Windows about the program's memory requirements, display needs, reserved keyboard shortcuts, and more. Knowledgeable users can modify PIF files or even create new ones. (See your program documentation.)

THE PIF EDITOR

A program called PIF Editor (found in the Program Manager's Main window) can simplify editing PIF files. If you have a 386 or 486 machine, double-clicking on the PIF Editor icon reveals the first window shown in Figure 7.4. Clicking on the *Advanced...* button (when in 386 Enhanced mode) reveals the second window shown below it.

If you plan to experiment with PIF settings, it's a good idea to save a copy of your working PIF file first. Use the PIF Editor's on-line help and the information provided with your non-Windows programs.

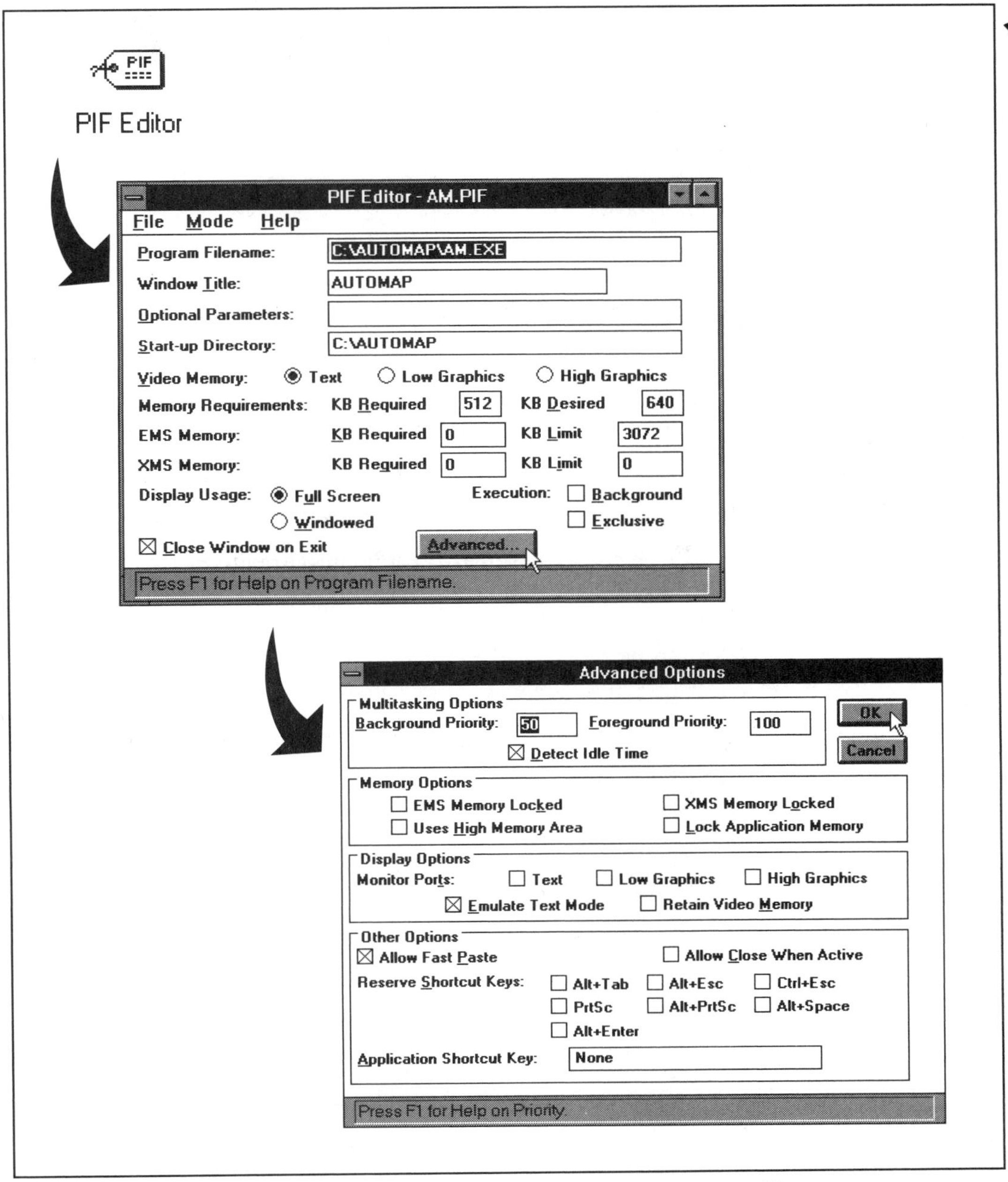

WINDOWS

PIF Editor

PIF Editor - AM.PIF

File   Mode   Help

Program Filename: C:\AUTOMAP\AM.EXE

Window Title: AUTOMAP

Optional Parameters:

Start-up Directory: C:\AUTOMAP

Video Memory: ● Text   ○ Low Graphics   ○ High Graphics

Memory Requirements: KB Required   512   KB Desired   640

EMS Memory: KB Required   0   KB Limit   3072

XMS Memory: KB Required   0   KB Limit   0

Display Usage: ● Full Screen   Execution: ☐ Background
                ○ Windowed   ☐ Exclusive

☒ Close Window on Exit   Advanced...

Press F1 for Help on Program Filename.

Advanced Options

Multitasking Options
Background Priority: 50   Foreground Priority: 100   OK
                       ☒ Detect Idle Time   Cancel

Memory Options
☐ EMS Memory Locked   ☐ XMS Memory Locked
☐ Uses High Memory Area   ☐ Lock Application Memory

Display Options
Monitor Ports: ☐ Text   ☐ Low Graphics   ☐ High Graphics
                   ☒ Emulate Text Mode   ☐ Retain Video Memory

Other Options
☒ Allow Fast Paste   ☐ Allow Close When Active
Reserve Shortcut Keys: ☐ Alt+Tab   ☐ Alt+Esc   ☐ Ctrl+Esc
                         ☐ PrtSc   ☐ Alt+PrtSc ☐ Alt+Space
                         ☐ Alt+Enter

Application Shortcut Key: None

Press F1 for Help on Priority.

FIGURE 7.4 *Program Manager's PIF Editor simplifies making changes to PIF files.*

8

Windows sans Mouse

You need a mouse or other pointing device to use Windows efficiently. But once in a while you'll be without. Perhaps the little bugger just dropped dead in its tracks. Or maybe you find yourself at 30,000 feet with a computer that's bigger than your tray table and a neighbor that won't let you use hers for your mouse. Or maybe you prefer keeping your hands on the keyboard and find it annoying to reach for your mouse when doing certain tasks. There are ways to work around most of these problems most of the time. Unfortunately, these tricks won't work with all applications. Let's take a look.

APPLICATION SWITCHING FROM THE KEYBOARD

To flit from one Windows application to another, *hold down* the Alt key and *tap* the Tab key while watching the center of your screen. Each time you press Tab, the name of a different (running) application will be displayed. When you see the one you want, release the Alt key and you will be taken to that application.

MENU BAR HOPPING

If you learn nothing else about mouseless Windows computing, learn how to get to menus and execute commands on menus sans mouse. Then if your mouse pointer stubbornly refuses to move (it will someday), you will at least be able to save your work and restart your computer. Alas, you'll use different key combinations for different window and menu types. Here are the tricks:

1. Press Alt-Esc to reach the window containing the Menu bar of interest, making it the *active* window.

2. Press either the Alt or F10 key (the first menu name in your menu bar will become highlighted—File, typically).

3. Use the left or right arrow keys if necessary to highlight a different menu.

4. Use the down or up arrow keys to reveal the chosen menu and highlight the choice of interest.

5. Press Enter to execute your choice.

Incidentally, if you enter this menu mode by mistake, or want to leave it without making any choices on the menu, tap Esc or Alt or F10 a second time. The menu will disappear. (This trick works with most keyboard menus.)

MENU CHOICES WITH LETTER KEYS

Some mouseless menu tricks can often save you time even if you have a working mouse. For instance, after you tap the Alt key to enter the Menu mode, you can usually tap a letter key or two to make a menu choice. This is often quicker than mousing around if you know what you are doing. Take a look at Figure 8.1.

Figure 8.1 shows a typical Help menu. The menu name itself (Help) has an underlined letter H. Each menu command has a unique underlined letter (I for Help Index, G for Getting Started and so on).

You can reach menus and their commands from the keyboard alone by pressing the right combination of keys. For instance, pressing Alt, then **H**, then **W** would get you WordPerfect help in this example. (Incidentally, lowercase letters work just fine.)

Try learning a few shortcuts for commands you use a lot (like Alt **E G** for Word's GoTo command). If you like this approach, try adding one new shortcut to your subconscious each week. Regrettably, different programs often use different shortcuts.

CONTROL MENU—GATEWAY TO MOUSELESS WINDOW MANIPULATION

As you probably recall, the *Control menu* gives you a way to move, size, and close windows. By necessity, the keystrokes used to open Control menus differ for *Windows windows*, *document windows,* and Windows running non-Windows (MS-DOS) programs. (Nobody said you'd *like* working without a mouse...)

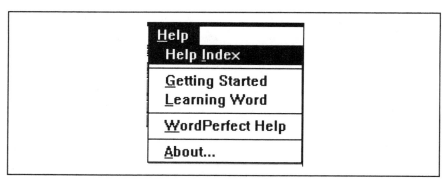

FIGURE 8.1 *The underlined letters are keyboard shortcuts for choices.*

Mouseless Control Menus in Windows Windows

I. Press Alt-Esc to reach the Windows window containing the Control menu of interest (making it the active window).

2. Press Alt-spacebar to open the Control menu for the active window. (The menu will drop down.)

3. Use the down or up arrow keys to reveal the chosen menu and highlight the choice of interest.

4. Press Enter to execute your choice.

Mouseless Control Menus in Windows Document Windows

I. Press Ctrl-Tab or Ctrl-F6 to reach the document window containing the Control menu of interest (making it the active window).

2. Press Alt-hyphen to open the Control menu for the active window. (The menu will drop down.)

3. Use the down or up arrow keys to reveal the chosen menu and highlight the choice of interest.

4. Press Enter to execute your choice.

Mouseless Control Menus in Windows Running MS-DOS

When running MS-DOS applications in Standard mode, use the Alt-Esc key combination to switch from the MS-DOS application to Windows. Press Alt-spacebar to open the Control Panel.

When running MS-DOS applications in Enhanced mode, use the Alt-Esc key combination to switch to the MS-DOS window, if necessary. Press Alt-spacebar to open the MS-DOS window's Control Panel.

MOUSELESS WINDOW MOVEMENT

1. Use the appropriate combination of steps described previously to activate the window of interest and reveal its Control menu.

2. Choose *Move* from the Control menu (with the down arrow and Enter keys).

3. After you've pressed Enter to activate the move command, you can use the arrow keys to move the window up and down, left and right.

4. Tap Enter again to tell Windows you are happy with the new window position.

MOUSELESS WINDOW SIZING

You can use keystrokes to resize windows. It works a lot like mouse dragging to resize. The Control menu's Minimize and Maximize choices are also useful. To resize a window by dragging it with keystrokes:

1. Select (activate) the window to be resized.

2. Open the Control menu.

3. Choose *Size*.

4. The on-screen pointer becomes a four-headed arrow.

5. Use the *up*, *down*, *left*, and *right* arrow keys to reshape the window's outline.

6. Press *Enter* to resize the window and leave the size mode.

As you might have guessed, it is possible to minimize and maximize windows by picking the appropriate Control menu command for any selected window. Simply open the window's Control Panel, pick Minimize or Maximize, and mash the Enter key.

WINDOWS

ICONS AND KEYSTROKES

Nearly anything you can do to windows with keystrokes you can also do to icons. They can be selected from the keyboard, their Control Windows can be displayed, icons can be moved or maximized, and so on. Try it.

THE MOUSELESS DIALOG BOX

You can employ most of the tricks you've learned so far to navigate and operate dialog boxes. Generally, you start by activating the control you want to use (a button, list, check box, etc.); then you make your desires known (you type some text, place a check mark in a box, and so on). Finally, when you've made all the necessary choices, you OK the changes and close the dialog box. All of this is easier said than done without a mouse.

ACTIVATION OF DIALOG BOX CONTROLS

Tabbing moves you from place to place within a dialog box. (Holding down the Shift key when you Tab moves you backwards.) It sometimes takes the eye of an eagle to figure out where you are in a dialog box. Take Figure 8.2, for instance.

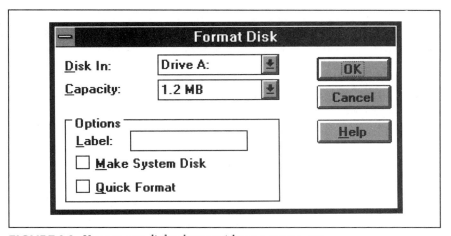

FIGURE 8.2 *You can use dialog boxes without a mouse, too.*

When you first open this dialog box, the OK button is the active control. Look closely and you will see that it has a slightly darker (thicker) border than the other buttons.

Since OK is the active control, pressing Enter at this point would accept all of the default settings shown in Figure 8.2 and would attempt to format a 1.2MB disk in drive A. There would be no disk label, it would not be a system disk, and it would not be "Quick formatted." To change choices in dialog boxes, you must tab to the appropriate control (thereby activating it), then use it. Here are the techniques for dialog box controls.

EDITING TEXT BOXES

Text boxes often change color when you are in them. Other times you will simply see a small flashing insertion point (a stick) when you have activated a text box. Enter and edit text as usual, using right and left arrow keys and the Del key in place of the mouse for selecting text and moving the insertion point. (See "Text and the Single Finger" later in this chapter for details.) Tab to leave the text box when you are finished editing.

OPERATING BUTTONS WITH KEYSTROKES

Buttons are outlined when they are ripe for picking. Tab to outline the button of interest, then tap Enter to use the button. (This is the equivalent of pointing-and-clicking with a mouse.) Some buttons also have keyboard shortcuts. In Figure 8.2, pressing **H** is the same as pointing-and-clicking the Help button. It will bring up on-line help.

OPERATING CHECK BOXES WITH KEYSTROKES

The labels next to check boxes (like Make System Disk in Figure 8.2) are outlined as you tab to select them. Pressing the spacebar checks and unchecks selected boxes. Frequently, single keystrokes work here too. **M** will check and uncheck the Make System Disk box in our example. **Q** will check and uncheck Quick Format.

WINDOWS

LISTS FROM THE KEYBOARD

After you tab to a drop-down list, use the down arrow key to reveal the list, then use the up and down arrow keys to scroll through the choices in the list. Tab out when you see what you want. Sometimes you can type in list windows if you know the exact name of the desired choice. The Home key moves you to the first item in a list. End takes you to the last item in a list. When it is possible to select all the items in a list, Ctrl-/ (Control-slash) will select them all for you.

ENTER KEY SAYS YOU ARE FINISHED—USUALLY

Tapping the Enter key ordinarily executes the selected button. Since the OK button is often the (default) selected button, tapping Enter is often (but not always) a quick way to close a dialog box and execute your specified changes. Get in the habit of checking to see which button is highlighted before tapping the Enter key. Otherwise, you may accidentally activate a Cancel button or some other unwanted button choice.

CANCELING A DIALOG BOX

To close a dialog box without making any changes, press the Esc key. The Alt-F4 key combination will do the same thing, but is longer and is harder to remember.

CURSOR (INSERTION POINT) MOVEMENT WITHOUT CURSING

The following cursor (insertion point) tricks work in most places:

The up and down arrow keys move the insertion point up or down one *line*. Right and left arrow keys move you right or left one *character*. If you hold down the Ctrl key, the right and left arrows move you a *word* at a time.

Home and End take you to the *beginning* and *end* of a line, respectively. Holding the Ctrl key while you do this usually takes you to the *extremes* of the text.

The Page Up (or PgUp) and Page Down (PgDn) keys frequently move you to the *next* or *preceding screenfull* of text. (To use PgUp or PgDn, Num Lock must be off.)

TEXT AND THE SINGLE FINGER

Selecting text without a mouse can differ from application to application. For starters, try these tricks:

The Shift up and Shift down arrow keys often select one *line* up or down. Shift right and Shift left arrow keys select one *character* to the right or left of the insertion point. If you hold down the Ctrl key, these tricks often work on *whole words*.

Home and End highlight (select) from the insertion point to the *beginning* and *end* of a line, respectively.

The Page Up (or PgUp) and Page Down (PgDn) keys frequently highlight the *next* or *preceding screenfull* of text. (To use PgUp or PgDn, Num Lock must be off.)

MORE KEYBOARD SHORTCUTS

Additional shortcuts that will expedite your work when using the keyboard are listed on the inside covers.

9

Improving
Windows Performance

"If the darn thing works at all," my dad used to say, "leave it alone." That may be good advice where Windows is concerned, particularly if you are not a "computer person." The Windows 3.1 installer does a fairly decent job of inspecting your computer and making the necessary setup decisions based on what it finds. But there are things you can do to tweak Windows, and if you use reasonable care you may be able to improve its performance noticeably under some circumstances.

If you don't know what you are doing, however, you can degrade its performance, or even bring things to a grinding halt. If you do decide to experiment, make notes as you work, be sure you've backed up any files you decide to alter, and don't start fiddling when a deadline is looming. If you've never successfully altered an AUTOEXEC.BAT or CONFIG.SYS file, for instance, you may want to have a knowledgeable assistant looking over your shoulder. There are also several good books on this subject, including Robert Cowart's *Mastering Windows 3.1* (SYBEX, 1992).

Things that affect Windows performance fall into five general categories:

- Your computer's processor and processor speed

- The amount of RAM you have, its speed and type

- Disk space, speed, and utilization

- CONFIG.SYS settings

- The applications you run under Windows

PROCESSOR TYPE AND SPEED

Windows 3.1 requires a great deal of processor horsepower. Be aware that older 286 machines will never reach the performance levels of today's 386 and 486 machines, no matter how much money you throw at them. Chances are, by the time you drop in a "coprocessor board," improved display adapter, and other enhancements, you will have spent close to what it would cost to purchase a brand-new 386 or 486 machine. If you are unhappy with Windows performance on an older 286 machine, think long and hard before upgrading rather than replacing your hardware. That said, many of the suggestions that follow will improve Windows performance on a 286 computer, only not as noticeably as on some newer 386 and 486 systems.

RAM, VIRTUAL MEMORY, AND WINDOWS PERFORMANCE

Perhaps the most dramatic (and often the most cost-effective) improvements are RAM-related. Windows runs best when it has lots of random access memory. This is particularly true if you like to run more than one program at once and tend to switch between them regularly. There are three

WINDOWS

categories of RAM memory: *Conventional*, *Extended*, and *Expanded* or *EMS*). In addition, with a certain disk drive trick you can work around a shortage of RAM. It is called *virtual memory*.

To see how much Conventional, Extended, and Expanded memory your computer *thinks* it has, quit Windows and type **mem** at the DOS prompt. You will get a breakdown that looks something like this:

```
C:\>mem

    655360  bytes total conventional memory
    655360  bytes available to MS-DOS
    426816  largest executable program size

   1048576  bytes total EMS memory
   1048576  bytes free EMS memory

   3407872  bytes total contiguous extended memory
         0  bytes available contiguous extended memory
   1048576  bytes available XMS memory
            MS-DOS resident in High Memory Area
```

It shows you how much RAM of each type is available. Your computer might actually have more memory than is shown in the report. It is possible, for instance, for a computer to have RAM installed but unavailable because of a problem with your memory management software or other setup issues. If you think you have more memory than the amount you see in this memory report, consult your hardware manuals, and possibly your computer dealer, for assistance.

CONVENTIONAL MEMORY

Today's computers generally have the maximum possible 640KB (about 655,360 bytes, or 640×1024 bytes per kilobyte) of Conventional RAM. Older machines may have as little as 256KB. MS-DOS uses some of your Conventional RAM, and so do many of the drivers and memory-resident programs installed by your AUTOEXEC.BAT and CONFIG.SYS commands. Whatever is left, Windows can employ. Obviously, if you have less than 640KB bytes of Conventional RAM installed, you should consider installing the full complement.

One way to free up whatever Conventional RAM has already been installed is to remove things from the AUTOEXEC.BAT and CONFIG.SYS files that you no longer need. When experimenting, be sure to keep a copy of your working AUTOEXEC.BAT and CONFIG.SYS files that you can reinstall if your changes cause problems. (You might even make a printout of their contents each time you change them.) The best bet is to start by preparing a system disk, then placing copies of your known-good AUTOEXEC.BAT and CONFIG.SYS files on that disk. Then test to see if you can use the newly created system disk to boot your computer and access your hard disk *before* you do any experimenting with AUTOEXEC.BAT and CONFIG.SYS files on the hard disk!

At that point, try removing (or temporarily disabling) unnecessary memory-resident programs, unused hardware drivers, etc. Reboot from your hard disk and run the memory test again to see if you have freed up significant Conventional RAM.

You can either delete unwanted lines or "REM them out" (disable them) by inserting the Remarks abbreviation (REM) as the very first characters in a line. For instance, in the excerpt from an AUTOEXEC.BAT file below, the DOSSHELL command has been REMed out:

```
C:\DOS\DOSKEY /INSERT
C:\DOS\SHARE.EXE
rem C:\DOS\DOSSHELL
```

To reenable the DOSSHELL command (or other things you've REMed out), simply delete the REM and the wordspace. This technique has the advantage of preserving the order of your batch and SYS files. And it gives you an easy way to undo mistakes. If you are using a DOS version earlier than 4.0, you will get error messages each time DOS encounters a REM in your CONFIG.SYS file, but the REM trick still works. Once you are happy with your modifications, you might want to delete REMed out lines to avoid seeing the error message(s) each time you boot.

You can use a text editor like the Windows *Notepad* desk accessory to make changes to your AUTOEXEC and CONFIG files, or you may prefer to use the DOS EDIT or EDLIN commands. Do *not* use regular word processors like the Write Desk accessory for this task, as they might add nonstandard ASCII characters to your .SYS and .BAT files when you save your changes, preventing them from running.

BUFFER AND FILES SETTINGS

Among other things, your CONFIG.SYS file contains a line like
BUFFERS=30 and another like FILES=30, as shown below:

```
DEVICE=C:\WINDOWS\HIMEM.SYS
DOS=HIGH
FILES=30
BUFFERS=30
STACKS=9,256
DEVICE=C:\UTIL\MOUSE\MOUSE.SYS
```

These refer to the amount of RAM reserved for hard disk buffers used to
improve disk access time under certain circumstances, as well as the number
of files that can be opened simultaneously.

Buffers

With MS-DOS version 5.0 or later, buffers can be changed to as high as 30
without depleting Conventional RAM. With earlier versions of DOS, settings in excess of 20 may decrease available RAM. Microsoft recommends
settings between 10 and 20 unless you have a non-Windows program that
requires more than 20 buffers.

Incidentally, if your CONFIG.SYS file contains a line that reads something
like DEVICE=C:\WINDOWS\HIMEM.SYS, do not delete or defeat it. Windows added this line at installation if needed.

Files

If you plan to run non-Windows programs under Windows, be sure your
CONFIG.SYS files setting is at least 30 (the Windows default). Make it
higher if any of your programs require more than 30 files when running
under DOS.

EXTENDED MEMORY

Extended memory is RAM above 640KB in 286, 386, and 486 computers.
Windows 3.1 needs at least 256KB of extended memory to run in the Standard mode on 286 systems, and a minimum of 1MB (one megabyte or
1,048,576 bytes) to run in Enhanced mode on 386 and 486 computers. The

HIMEM Extended memory manager that comes with Windows 3.1 coordinates the use and availability of this RAM. Adding extra, often inexpensive Extended RAM can dramatically improve Windows performance.

EXPANDED MEMORY

Expanded memory is not used by Windows, but it may be required by other programs that you own (like some versions of Lotus 1-2-3). If you have applications that require Expanded memory, you may be able to use them under Windows 3.1, thanks to a Windows feature called *Expanded memory emulation*. You'll need a 386 or 486 processor and sufficient Extended memory to use the emulator.

At installation, Windows copies a file called EMM386.EXE into your Windows directory. You'll need to add the line **device=c:\windows\emm386.exe 512**, or something like it, to your CONFIG.SYS file to use the emulator. You can replace **512** (the Expanded memory amount) with any value from 16 to 32,768 (kilobytes), but only up to to the amount of Extended RAM you have available to use as Expanded memory. There are other options to consider when using Expanded memory. Consult your Microsoft Windows 3.1 documentation for details.

VIRTUAL MEMORY (SWAP FILES)

Virtual memory is a Windows feature that sets aside part of your hard disk to use whenever you run out of RAM. Normally, it does all of this automatically.

Suppose, for instance, you want to use two applications that each required a megabyte of RAM, but you have only one megabyte available. Windows will let you switch back and forth between the programs by temporarily moving the contents of RAM to your hard disk and back. This approach is much slower than having sufficient RAM to hold both programs, and it takes up precious disk space—but it does work, and is usually quicker than quitting and restarting programs each time you need to switch from one to another. Windows does this by creating things called swap files.

Whenever you run Windows, it can automatically establish a temporary swap file (called WIN386.SWP) on 386 and 486 machines, disk space permitting. The size of this swap file is based on available disk space, and it can

shrink and grow automatically as needed. Or you can specify the maximum amount of available disk space to use for swapping.

It is also possible to establish quicker, permanent swap files, named SPART.PAR and 386SPART.PAR. These are hidden files. Once they've been created, Microsoft strongly recommends that you not delete, rename, or move them from your disk.

To display and change your virtual memory settings, double-click on the *386 Enhanced* icon in the Control Panel. Click the *Virtual Memory...* button in the resulting 386 Enhanced window. Click on Change>> to expand the Virtual memory window. Help is available here. Figure 9.1 illustrates the route to the virtual memory settings.

In the example, there is a permanent 11,758KB swap file located on drive C. You could either change the size of the permanent file by typing in the New Size box, or switch to a temporary file (or no file) by using the Type drop-down menu; but Microsoft recommends that you leave these settings alone.

GETTING THE MOST FROM YOUR HARD DISK

Windows requires a lot of disk space. So do many Windows applications. While the best way to optimize disk performance and space is to purchase the biggest, fastest drive and controller board you can afford, there are other, cheaper things to try first. Start by deleting unnecessary files and lost clusters. Then consider using a disk tune-up program (like Norton Utilities) to regroup fragmented files.

DELETING UNNEEDED FILES

Windows probably installed some files that you can live without. For instance, you may want to delete *games* and associated *game help* files (like SOL.EXE, SOL.HLP, WINMINE.EXE, and WINMINE.HLP). If you don't use accessories (CALC, CALENDAR, CARDFILE, CLOCK, TERMINAL, or RECORDER), delete them and their help files.

The Windows Program Manager's *Windows Setup* icon offers an option called *Add/Remove Windows Components...* that can help you quickly remove more than 2MB of README files, games, accessories, wallpaper, etc. Reach it as shown in Figure 9.2.

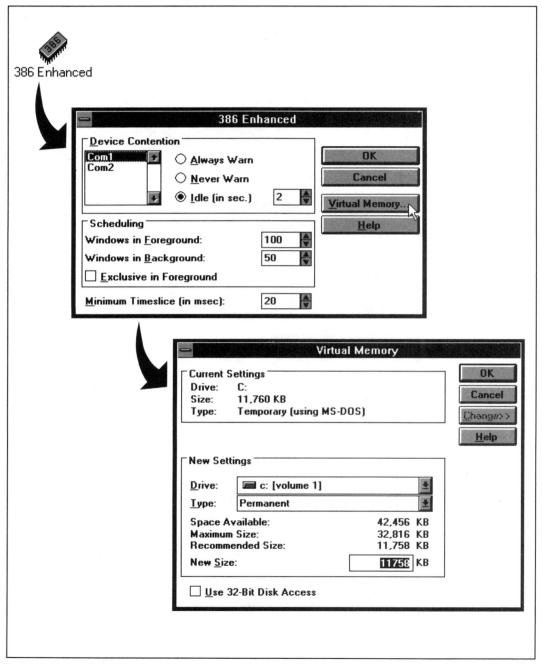

FIGURE 9.1 *It's possible to view and change the virtual memory settings found in the Control Panel.*

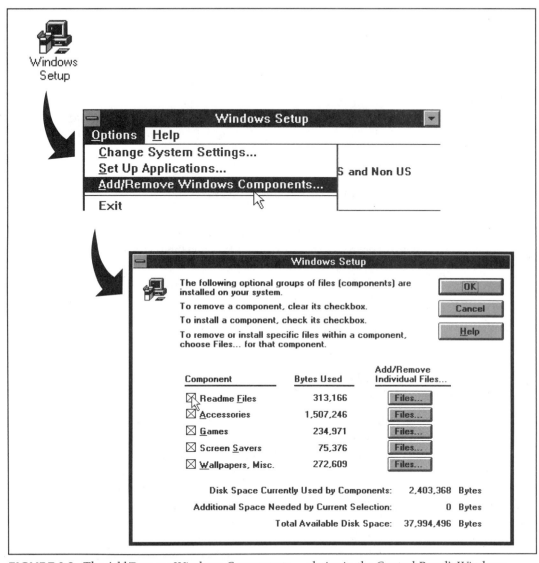

FIGURE 9.2 *The Add/Remove Windows Components… choice in the Control Panel's Windows Setup menu can be used to quickly free up more than 2MB of hard disk space.*

You can have Windows delete all files of a particular kind (all README files, for instance), or you can pick and choose from a list—*selected* README files, for example.

Be considerate when doing this. If others will be using your computer, ask before deleting things like accessories. Consider using Write to print out README files on paper before you delete them, and so on.

While you are cleaning things up, realize that nearly everyone has old documents that should be copied to floppies, then deleted from their hard disks. Do you?

DELETING LOST CLUSTERS—A CAUTION

Lost clusters occur when a program quits unexpectedly or has trouble saving a file. You may already be in the habit of locating and deleting lost clusters (freeing up disk space) by using the DOS CHKDSK /f command. But there is one important caution now that you are a Windows 3.1 user. Never, *never,* NEVER run CHKDSK /f with Windows running! Quit Windows before running CHKDSK. Then, from the plain old vanilla DOS prompt, type **CHKDSK /f**. Generally, you will not want to convert lost clusters to files, so answer **N** to the resulting conversion question.

APPLICATIONS AND WINDOWS PERFORMANCE

If an application runs sluggishly under Windows, check the documentation that came with it or contact its maker for recommendations. Sometimes changing the display mode or having Windows set aside more RAM for the application will speed things up. Some non-Windows applications run noticeably faster directly from DOS (not from the Windows DOS prompt). This requires quitting Windows. Some non-Windows programs run faster under Windows in full-screen mode than they do in a Windows window. Experiment. Take notes. Read. Make sure you have the most recent versions of applications programs and PIF files designed for Windows 3.1. Feel free to call software vendors and Microsoft for specific assistance.

PART TWO

WORD
Processing
and
More

Word Overview

Microsoft Word for Windows is one of those rare programs that you can start using successfully in an hour or two but never outgrow, even if your needs become quite sophisticated. This chapter will give you an overview of the Word workplace and Word's many features. If you've used other word processing packages before, you might find enough information here to begin creating documents almost immediately. The three chapters that follow this one (Chapters 11 through 13) contain a first word processing exercise for beginners and other readers wanting to take things a step at a time. Even if you are an experienced computer user, you will want at least to skim these three chapters, since they also contain helpful tips and techniques. Chapters 14 through 23 are so arranged that you can quickly find additional information about the Word features and concepts that you need to become more productive at word processing, regardless of the kind of work you do. Let's get to it…

THE WORD WORKPLACE

One easy way to start Word for Windows is to double-click on the Microsoft Word icon in Window's Program Manager or the WINWORD.EXE icon in File Manager. When you start Word, an untitled document window automatically appears. Like other Windows windows, Word document windows can be resized and moved. Figure 10.1 shows a typical Word window.

WORD WINDOWS

You'll notice familiar Windows tools including a title bar, scroll bars, a menu bar, and a Control Menu box. While it is possible to run Word without a mouse, the use of one makes things much easier.

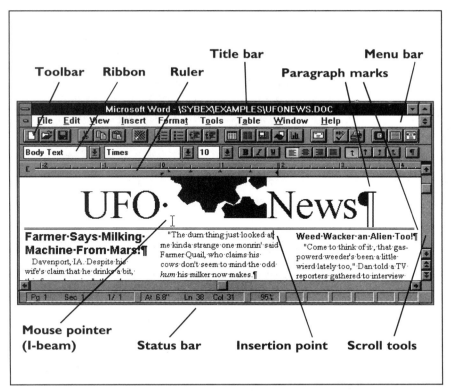

FIGURE 10.1 *A typical Word document window shows menu choices, tools, a ruler, and other features.*

Some Windows devices (like the mouse pointer) look a little different in Word. And Microsoft has provided some new tools you may not have seen before, like the ribbon, ruler, Toolbar, and paragraph marks. We'll look at these things shortly.

TYPING BASICS

You can start typing immediately in a new Word window. The Backspace key deletes one character to the left each time you press it. When you reach the right margin while typing, there is no need to press the Enter key. Word, like most contemporary word processing programs, will automatically "wrap" words (push them down to the next line) when they won't fit on the current line.

THE WORD MOUSE POINTER

In Figure 10.1 the mouse pointer looks like (and is called) an *I-beam*. In Word the mouse pointer changes shape and size when it is able to do different things. For example, when it can be used to *drag-and-drop* text it looks one way, when it can be used to resize window parts it looks another way, and so on. Get in the habit of watching the mouse pointer as you move it around in Word.

THE INSERTION POINT

The insertion point shows you where text or graphics will be placed. In Figure 10.1, the insertion point lies just after the letter "t" in the top of the second text column. If you were to start typing in this example, text would be inserted between the "t" in "at" and the space following the letter "t".

Here's an important tip: People often confuse the *insertion point* (a straight stick) with the *mouse pointer*. These are different tools! You *move* the insertion point by pointing to a new location with the *mouse pointer* (I-beam), then *clicking* once with the *primary mouse button* (usually the left button). It is the *click* that moves the insertion point. If you point with the mouse, but forget to click, things will be inserted at the *old* location, not the new one.

PARAGRAPH MARKS

Much to the chagrin of your English teachers, in Microsoft Word, *paragraphs* need not be two or more sentences on a related topic. The newsletter title "UFO News" in Figure 10.1 counts as a Word paragraph. So does the nonsentence "Weed Wacker an Alien Too." Even a single *blank line* can be a paragraph in Word. Paragraphs always end with paragraph marks like those at the ends of the aforementioned Word paragraphs.

Each paragraph mark "stores" formatting information like margin, line spacing, and indentation settings for the paragraph that precedes it. For instance, if you accidentally (or intentionally) deleted the paragraph mark at the end of the "Weed Wacker" heading, the words would take on the characteristics of the text that follows it. That is to say, the heading text would no longer be bold, the font would change, it would be indented like the body text, and so on. The moral is, use care when deleting paragraph marks. Realize that they contain hidden information used to format the words that precede them.

MOVING AROUND IN A DOCUMENT

You can move from place to place in a document by scrolling, or by using your computer's navigation keys (PgUp, PgDn, Home, End, and so forth). Word's Go To... choice on the Edit menu lets you move to specific pages and bookmarks.

SELECTING TEXT—THE BASICS

You *select* (highlight) text to modify, delete, or overwrite it. Word offers a variety of selection techniques, described in more detail in Chapter 11. Here are a few examples:

- Dragging with the mouse selects text (hold down the primary mouse button while you drag).

- Double-clicking on words selects them.

- While holding down the Ctrl key, point anywhere in a *sentence*, then press the left mouse button to select the entire sentence.

- Point to the left of a line (the I-beam will change to an arrow), then click *once* to select the whole *line*.

- Point to the left of a paragraph (the I-beam will change to an arrow), then *double-click* to select the whole *paragraph*.

- Hold down the Ctrl key and press **5** on your numeric keypad to select an entire Word document.

THE UNDO COMMAND (CTRL-Z)

Word's Edit menu contains a powerful command worth mentioning at this point. If you make a mistake (like deleting a paragraph mark, or typing with the insertion point at the wrong location), the *Undo command* can often return your work to the way it was prior to your mistake. Word watches what you do and can usually undo your most recent action. If the last thing you did was type something, Word will ordinarily be able to undo the typing. If you just reformatted something, Word might be able to restore the old formatting. The exact name of the Undo command on the Edit menu changes to tell you what can be undone. You must, however, catch your mistakes before starting something else. For instance, if you type something, then reformat what you've typed, Word can undo the formatting, but not the typing. The keyboard shortcut for Undo is *Ctrl-Z*.

WORD HELP

Word provides loads of on-line help. The *F1 function* key brings up a help window that behaves as you'd expect. You can search for subject matters of interest, see a list of recent topics you've read, and so on.

There is also a *Help menu* on the right end of the Word menu bar. This menu will let you get the same help available with the F1 key, plus much, much more. Assuming that you let Word install them, there are several tutorial choices and an intriguing feature for experienced WordPerfect users. The *WordPerfect Help* menu choice will demonstrate and help you understand Word's versions of your favorite WordPerfect techniques.

If the tutorial and WordPerfect choices aren't on your help menu, you can use Word's installer to add them.

THE TOOLBAR, RIBBON, AND RULER

We'll leave complete descriptions of the ribbon, ruler, and Toolbar (shown in Figure 10.2) to upcoming chapters. For now, it is useful to know that

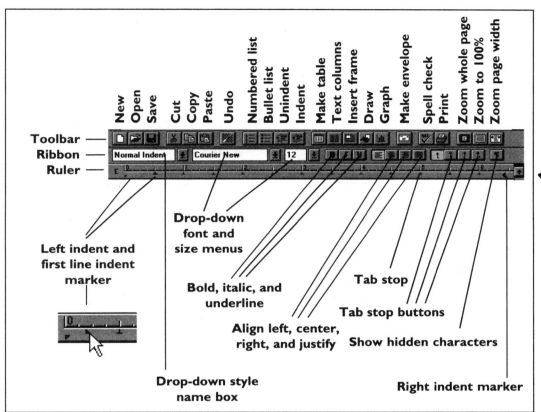

FIGURE 10.2 *The Toolbar, ribbon, and ruler let you activate principal features with your mouse.*

these are tools you use with your mouse. You can choose to display or hide the Toolbar, ribbon, and ruler with the *View menu*. (Sometimes, if you make a Word window too small, you won't see all of the available buttons.)

Toolbar

The *Toolbar* gives you quick access to commonly used commands like Print… and Save and Spelling…. For instance, to print a Word document, you can simply click on the Toolbar button that looks like a printer. It is possible to add, delete, and rearrange buttons on the Toolbar. See Chapter 23 for details.

Ribbon

Use the ribbon and your mouse to quickly change any selected text. For example, if you select (highlight) plain text and then click on the B button with your mouse, the selected text will become bold. The I button italicizes, and the U button underlines text.

The paragraph alignment buttons will affect either the paragraph containing the insertion point, or all selected paragraphs. For example, clicking the center button centers all selected text. (This is the preferred method of centering. Use it instead of typing spaces to center things. Then if you change margins or indents, your text will recenter itself automatically.) The other alignment buttons will move text to the right or left. The justify button makes the right edge of your text even, by adding space within selected text.

The ribbon also contains drop-down menus used to pick fonts and sizes. A third drop-down menu in the ribbon lists available styles (collections of formatting decisions). These styles can be applied to one or more paragraphs. See Chapter 15 for details.

Finally, the ribbon makes it easy to pick the appropriate tab stops for tabular typing projects. See Chapter 17 for more about tabs.

Ruler

The ruler lets you specify *indents*, *margins*, and *tab stops* in a Word document. Ruler measurements can be displayed in inches, centimeters, points, or picas by picking the desired unit of measurement in the *Options window* reached from the Tools menu. (Points and picas are typograhic terms. There are 72 points to an inch, 6 picas to an inch, thus 12 points to a pica.)

Don't confuse *indents* with *margins*. Margin settings are usually (but not necessarily) document-wide. Indents are usually set for individual paragraphs or groups of paragraphs. To change an indent using the ruler, place the insertion point in the paragraph of interest (or select multiple paragraphs), then drag the right and/or left indent markers with your mouse.

Notice that the left indent mark has a top and bottom part. Dragging the top part to the right lets you indent the first line of each affected paragraph.

Dragging the top part of the marker to the left lets you create hanging "out-dents." To learn more about margins and indents, read Chapter 14.

THE WORD STATUS BAR

The Word status bar (at the bottom of the Word window) displays information about the insertion point and the text containing it. For instance, in Figure 10.1 the insertion point is in page 1 (Pg 1) of section 1 (Sec 1). The "1/1" indicates that this is page 1 of a 1-page document.

The next area of the status bar tells you that the insertion point is 6.8 inches from the top edge of the page, on the 38th line of the document. The Col statistic (31 in this example) is the number of characters between the insertion point and the left margin. The 95% indicates the current size of the page view. The next part of the status bar shows the status of keys like Num Lock and Caps Lock. Sometimes you will see messages from other Word features like Print Merge Helper here too.

DOCUMENT VIEWS

Word lets you see your work in varying levels of detail using different *views*. Choices include *Normal*, *Outline*, *Page Layout*, and *Print Preview*. They all have advantages and disadvantages. You choose three of the four views on the View menu as shown in Figure 10.3.

Normal View

Figure 10.3 shows a document in Normal view. You'll probably spend most of your time working in Normal view. The screen updates the fastest in Normal view, making scrolling smoother.

But sometimes it is difficult to visualize the finished appearance of a document while working in Normal view. You *will* see where pages break, and how lines will end, for instance, but you *won't* see marginalia like page numbers, headers, and footers. Nor will you have a really good understanding of the white space surrounding your text in Normal view. Page Layout and Print Preview can help with this.

Incidentally, if you switch to Normal view and still find scrolling too slow, choose the Draft mode (also on the View menu). This temporarily displays all text in a single font, speeding screen updates considerably. Removing the

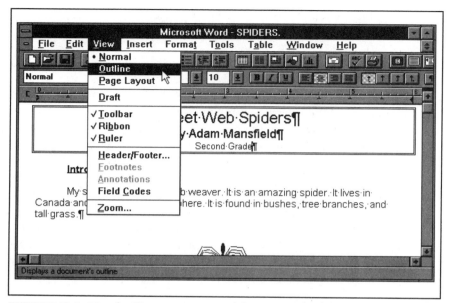

FIGURE 10.3 *Use the View menu to switch between Normal, Outline, and Page
Layout views. Visit the File menu to pick Print Preview.*

check mark from the Draft item on the View menu restores your document's
on-screen appearance.

Outline View

The Outline view is more than a view, it's a way to get a bird's-eye view of
lengthy documents. It will help you organize your thoughts and quickly
rearrange text and graphics. Take a look at Figure 10.4.

Figure 10.4 shows an entire two-page document compressed to six lines,
thanks to Outline view. In this illustration, only paragraph headings are displayed, making it easy to move many sentences by simply dragging a paragraph heading to a new position. For instance, to make all of the
"Appearance" information in Figure 10.4 come after the "Eating habits"
paragraphs, you could simply use your mouse to drag the "Appearance"
heading between "Eating habits" and "Their webs." All the associated text
will follow. The buttons labeled 1–9 and All correspond to heading styles.
They hide and reveal different levels of document detail.

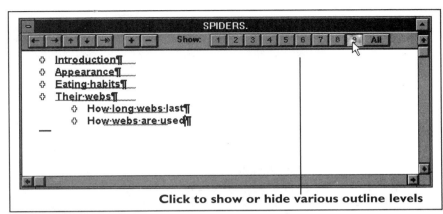

FIGURE 10.4 *Outline view lets you "collapse" a document to see the big picture or to reorganize things.*

You need to understand and use *Heading Styles* to use the Outline view effectively. See Chapters 15 and 20 for assistance with outlining.

Page Layout View

As you can see in Figure 10.5, the Page Layout view displays page margins, as well as header and footer contents. Page layout scrolling can be a little sluggish, particularly on slower computers.

Print Preview

Print Preview is reached from the *File* menu (not the *View* menu). As you can see from Figure 10.6, it can display one or two pages and give you a good idea of how your finished product will look, even though you may not be able to read the words.

This view is particularly useful when creating documents with complex odd and even, mirrored headers or footers.

Margins are represented by dashed lines as illustrated in Figure 10.6. Turn them on and off with the *Margins* button. *Margin handles* let you drag margins to increase or decrease white space. For instance, the text on the two-page document in the illustration might fit onto one page if the white space surrounding the text were reduced by dragging the margin handles.

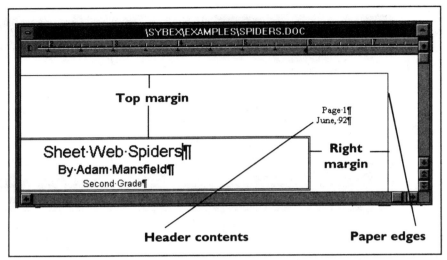

FIGURE 10.5 *Page Layout view shows page edges, margins, headers, and footers, but sometimes scrolls slowly.*

Print Preview also provides a Print button that takes you directly to the Print dialog box.

Multiple Windows

Word lets you simultaneously open and work with up to nine document windows. You can copy things from one window to another via the Clipboard as illustrated in Figure 10.7. Text from the *bottom* document window (titled Document2) has been selected and is ready to be copied to the Clipboard, then pasted into the UFONEWS.DOC window above it.

You can only have one *active* window at a time. The active window has a highlighted title bar. (Document2 is the active window in Figure 10.7.) The Windows menu in the Word menu bar lists all of the available windows. To activate a window, either click anywhere in the desired window or choose its name from Word's Window menu. Word document windows can be resized, moved, and scrolled as you would expect.

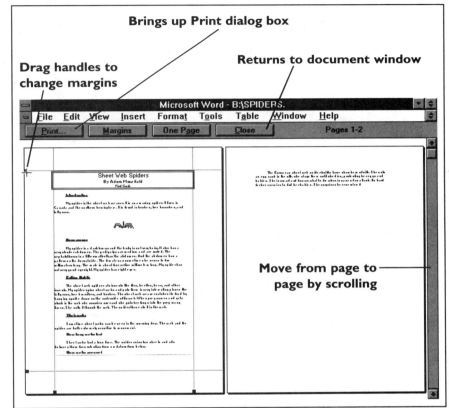

FIGURE 10.6 *Print Preview lets you see reduced representations of one or two pages. It can be a real paper saver.*

Splitting Your Document Screen

You can also split a single Word document window into two parts. This makes it easy to see two views of the same document, or to scroll to two different parts of a large document at once. In Figure 10.8, for instance, the top part of the window is in Outline view while the bottom part is the same document in Normal view. Notice that both window halves contain their own scroll bars. You can scroll the top without affecting the bottom and vice versa.

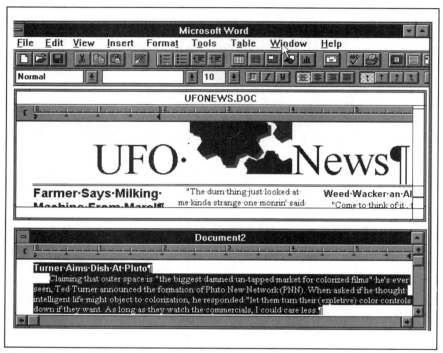

FIGURE 10.7 *Windows lets you have up to nine different document windows
open at the same time.*

To split a window, use your mouse to drag the split bar to the desired
position (see Figure 10.8). To remove the split bar from a window, simply
double-click on the split bar.

Zooming for Different Perspectives

You can use either the zoom buttons on the Toolbar or the Zoom... choice
on Word's View menu to enlarge or reduce the size of things on your screen.
For instance, in Figure 10.9, the *Whole Page* choice reduces an entire page
so that it fits in a Word window.

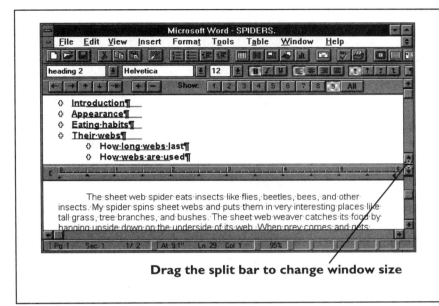

Drag the split bar to change window size

FIGURE 10.8 *A split window shows a document in both Outline and Normal views.*

On-screen text and graphics can be blown up or reduced either by using the preset choices (50%, 75%, 100%, or 200%) or by typing a custom value like the 95% shown in Figure 10.9.

The Zoom features only change the way things *look* on your monitor. They will still *print* at the normal size regardless of the zoom setting.

STYLES, TEMPLATES, GLOSSARIES, FIELDS, AND MACROS

Word contains a number of powerful tools designed to help you store, retrieve, and reuse collections of formatting decisions, saving you a great deal of time and labor. These include *templates*, *styles*, and *glossaries*. Read about styles and glossaries in Chapters 14 and 15. Templates are described in Chapters 13, 15, and 19.

Word's *Insert Field...* command (on the Insert menu) will quickly place in your documents things like today's date, a document author's name, or the current time. Read about this feature in Chapter 14.

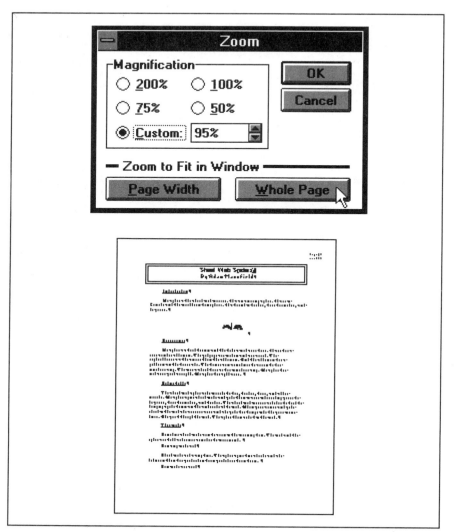

FIGURE 10.9 *Use Word's zoom features to magnify or reduce the size of on-screen images. There are three zoom buttons on the Toolbar. Moreover, the Zoom… choice on the View menu reveals a zoom dialog box.*

Finally, Word can watch you do complex steps and repeat them on demand, thanks to a built-in *macro* capability. Chapter 21 shows how to create and use Word macros.

TABLES

Word's *table* features make quick work of things like price lists and other documents that are a pain to type using tabs. While it takes some practice to get the hang of tables, once you've done it you'll wonder how you ever did without them. Chapter 17 has the details. You can place a variety of different *borders* around items in a table, and even *sort* table contents.

MULTIPLE COLUMNS

Multiple, snaking "newspaper-style" *columns* are a mouse click away in Word. You easily control their width, position, and appearance. See Chapter 17.

MATH FEATURES

While you will probably want to use Excel for many of your budgeting and other math-intensive projects, Word has surprisingly rich mathematics features that can help you create invoices, budgets, personalized mail, and more. Read about these features in Chapter 17.

GRAPHICS TOOLS

Chapter 18 will show you how to import graphics (drawings, photos, organizational charts, logos, and the like) from other programs and clip art disks. Word also comes with its own drawing capabilities so that you can draw your own art. Once you've learned a few simple tricks, you'll be able to create desktop-publishing-like documents in no time.

Word makes it easy to add borders and shading to paragraphs. Chapter 14 shows you how. (Figures 10.6 and 10.7 contain examples of borders.)

PRINT MERGE HELPER

If you've ever tried to send personalized mailings (aka junk mail) to people, you know how difficult that can be with most word processors.

Word's Print Merge features are easier to use than those of most other programs, and perhaps even more powerful. Word also features a Print Merge "Helper" that leads you through the steps necessary to set up a new merge document and configure the data to use with it. See how this all works in Chapter 22.

AUTHOR'S TOOLS

Word offers a number of features that make writing and proofreading almost anything a pleasure. For instance, *Find...* and *Replace...* commands on the Edit menu help you locate and change text, styles, and more. Read about these capabilities in Chapter 20.

Use Word's built-in *Thesaurus* (on the Tools menu) to find exactly—or should I say *precisely?*—the right word. Chapter 20 shows you how.

Word's *Book Marks*, *hidden characters*, *revisions marks*, and *Annotation* features let you make notes to yourself or others that can be printed or suppressed. See Chapter 20 to learn more.

Word's *pagination* and *hyphenation* and *"keep with"* features give you control over how pages end. The *Spelling Checker* (also located on the Tools menu) can verify entire documents or just help you look up the occasional tricky word. It works with industry-specific and non-English dictionaries if you have them, and will let you add your own words whenever you like. See Chapter 20.

A click of Word's *Bullet list* or *Numbered list* buttons on the Toolbar makes short work of list typing. Try them!

Speaking of automating frequent tasks, check out the envelope button on the Toolbar. It will search for an address in the active document, then insert it in an envelope format for quick printing. It will even add a return address if you like. Chapter 19 reveals all.

If you wish you had someone around to spot that dreaded passive voice, or verbs in the wrong place, or long sentences like this one, check out Word's *Grammar Checker*, detailed in Chapter 20. Incidentally, the Grammar Checker found nothing *wrong* with the preceding sentence, but found it a tad long, and eighth-grade reading.

Word's *Equation Editor* is a special version of MathType, shipped free with Word. Use it to create technical documentation, research reports, dissertations, and other documents requiring complex formulae.

While you'll probably want to paste Excel charts into your Word documents, it is also possible to create charts using *Microsoft Graph*. It's a painless way to bring a boring table full of numbers to life.

Finally, if you write long documents, chances are that from time to time you will create (or wish you could easily create) a table of contents and an index. Word can create simple or fancy ones, as you'll see in Chapter 20.

FILE MANAGEMENT TOOLS

Word contains a number of practical features that help you organize and find document files. The *Summary Information* feature lets you classify and quickly search for documents by author, subject, etc. Lawyers love this, since they can enter case numbers, legal issues, and other summary information whenever they create Word documents, then later do a quick search. You too might find this feature useful if you can get in the habit of filling in the Summary Information when you save new documents. If the Summary Information feature annoys you, it can be disabled by visiting the *Save category* option, reached with the *Options…* command on Word's *Tools* menu.

Word's *Find File…* feature (on the *File* menu) will quickly search your disks, looking for documents that meet your search criteria. For instance, you could find all documents written by Bob Dylan that contain the word "rain." Now there's a cheery thought… Chapter 11 shows how Find File works.

Incidentally, don't confuse the Find File… command on Word's File menu with the Find… command on Word's Edit menu. They are different.

There are two other file-related features worth mentioning. *Save All* will save all open Word documents with a minimum of intervention on your part. *Save As…* lets you save an existing document under a different *name* and will also let you save a document in a different *format*. See the information in the next few paragraphs, as well as Chapters 11 and 13, for details.

FILE CONVERSION TOOLS

Chances are, you have a number of documents on floppy disks or your hard disk that have been created with something other than Word for Windows. They may be things you've written using different word processors like WordPerfect or Word for DOS. They may be documents from a friend's or business associate's Macintosh. Or they might even be collections of data from a database or miscellany you've downloaded from CompuServe. Word for Windows comes with conversion utilities that can convert non–Word for Windows documents with little or no effort on your part.

The Word installer placed the converter software on your hard disk (unless you told it to do otherwise). So you can simply attempt to load non-Word documents with Word's Open command (on the File Menu). If the document you specify was not created by Word for Windows, you'll see a Convert File dialog box like the one in Figure 10.10.

Pick the appropriate format, then click OK. Scroll through the resulting Word document to see if the conversion went well.

You can also save Word documents in non-Word formats. There should be a README document called *convinfo.doc* in your WINWORD directory. It contains useful conversion tips, techniques, and trivia. This is recommended reading if you work with non-Word documents!

NEW WAYS TO SHARE INFORMATION

You can't own Word and Excel for Windows without at least trying *object linking and embedding* (OLE, pronounced *oh-lay*). It's a powerful way to keep documents updated when data in other documents change. Chapter 40 demonstrates OLE and suggests some ways to use it.

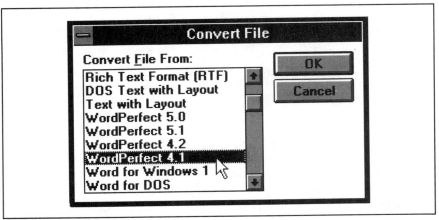

FIGURE 10.10 *Word can convert documents from a variety of non–Word for Windows formats.*

PERSONALIZING WORD

Like Windows itself, Word for Windows lets you make decisions about its look and feel. For instance, you can change the appearance and contents of the Toolbar.

You make choices like these in the Options window, reached with the *Options...* command on Word's Tools menu. There are 11 *category windows* available from the Options... command. They are reached by clicking on icons in the Options window. Figure 10.11 shows 2 of the 11 categories—View and Toolbar.

You'll learn more about options throughout the Word portion of this book. The spelling options are discussed in Chapter 20 along with the Spelling Checker, for instance. Additional information about Options is presented in Chapter 23.

WORD'S PRINT DIALOG BOX

As you can see in Figure 10.12, Word offers a modified Windows Print dialog box when you choose the *Print...* command on Word's File menu. This is how you initiate printing. You use the box to specify the number of copies you wish to print. If you don't want to print the entire document, you can specify page ranges. In addition, you can use this dialog box to print information about a document's styles, glossaries, and other traits. (These printing options will make more sense when you understand Styles, Glossaries, etc.)

HEADERS, FOOTERS, AND FOOTNOTES

Word lets you print things in margins. Typically this is done using *headers* and *footers*. If your documents require footnotes, Word can simplify their creation as well.

HEADERS AND FOOTERS

You create headers and footers in special windows reached with the *Header/Footer...* command on the View menu. The header and footer windows contain buttons you click to insert automatic date, time, and page number entries.

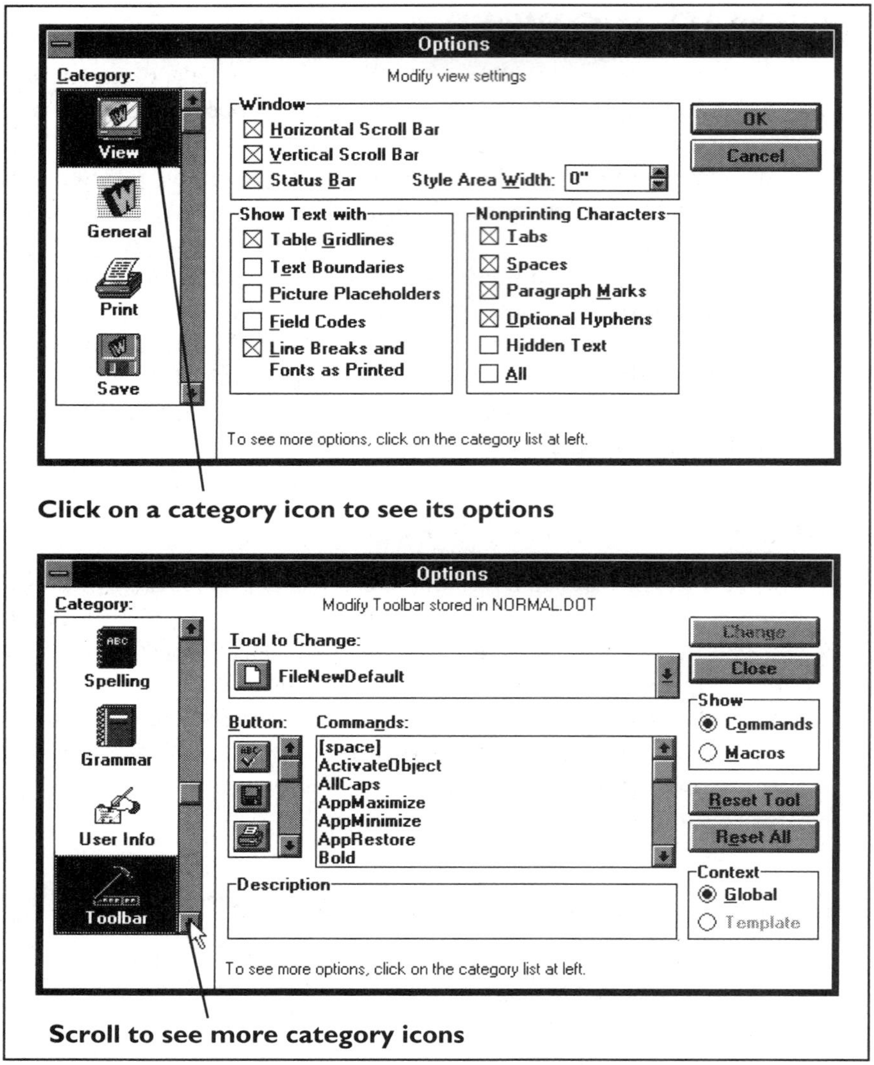

Options

Category:

View

General

Print

Save

Modify view settings

Window
☒ Horizontal Scroll Bar
☒ Vertical Scroll Bar
☒ Status Bar   Style Area Width: 0"

Show Text with
☒ Table Gridlines
☐ Text Boundaries
☐ Picture Placeholders
☐ Field Codes
☒ Line Breaks and
   Fonts as Printed

Nonprinting Characters
☒ Tabs
☒ Spaces
☒ Paragraph Marks
☒ Optional Hyphens
☐ Hidden Text
☐ All

OK
Cancel

To see more options, click on the category list at left.

Click on a category icon to see its options

Options

Category:

Spelling

Grammar

User Info

Toolbar

Modify Toolbar stored in NORMAL.DOT

Tool to Change:
FileNewDefault

Button: Commands:
          [space]
          ActivateObject
          AllCaps
          AppMaximize
          AppMinimize
          AppRestore
          Bold

Description

Change
Close

Show
● Commands
○ Macros

Reset Tool
Reset All

Context
● Global
○ Template

To see more options, click on the category list at left.

Scroll to see more category icons

FIGURE 10.11 *The Options... command reveals a window with a scrolling list of category icons. Click on an icon to see and change its option settings.*

You can type and format text in both headers and footer windows. The usual Word formatting tricks (Toolbar text alignment, ribbon type style selection, etc.) work in headers as well as footers. Headers and footers can

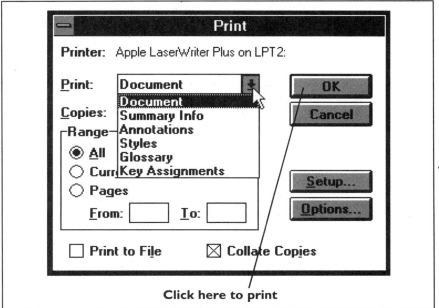

FIGURE 10.12 *The Print dialog box controls many aspects of printing.*

be identical on all pages, or you can place different headers and footers on odd- and even-numbered pages. This is particularly useful when doing two-sided printing. Figure 10.13 shows an example.

It is also possible to print a different header and footer (or none) on the first page of documents or at the beginning of sections in documents. This is one way to suppress margin printing on cover pages. Read more about headers and footers in Chapter 16.

FOOTNOTES

Word's *Footnote…* command on the Insert menu simplifies the entering of footnotes. Word will take care of numbering and positioning footnotes, even when you insert or delete some. Standard and custom footnote formats are possible. Learn more in Chapter 16.

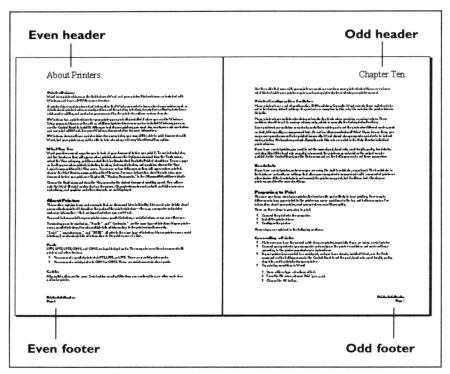

FIGURE 10.13 *Different odd- and even-numbered headers and footers improve the appearance of two-sided documents.*

GETTING MICROSOFT WORD PRODUCT SUPPORT

There are several Word README files in your WINWORD folder. Topics include Document conversion, Word graphics issues, and helpful printer compatibility news.

In addition, you can get Microsoft Product Support as described in Chapter 2.

WHERE TO GO FROM HERE

Now that you have gained an overview of Word's numerous features, you can either try the exercises in the next three chapters or start your own project and bounce around Chapters 11 through 23. Either way, you'll be impressed with Word for Windows.

Typing, Selecting, Editing, and Moving Things

In this and the next few chapters, we'll explore Word's principal text editing features, using the program's default settings and a short quotation from Thomas Edison. You'll type, edit, save, recall, stylize, and print it. Obviously, Word for Windows 2.0 must be properly installed on your computer if you plan to try these exercises.

STARTING WORD

To get started, turn on your computer. Run Windows (by typing **WIN** at the DOS prompt, if necessary), then locate the *Microsoft Word* icon in a Program Manager window or in the File Manager window, as shown in Figure 11.1.

If you are going to start Word from the File Manager, look for the file called WINWORD.EXE in the WINWORD directory. If you can't see the program's name, use Find Manager's Search... command. Look for WINWORD.EXE, searching all your subdirectories starting with C:\. When all else fails, ask someone for assistance.

Once you've located the icon, point to it using your mouse (or trackball), then click on it twice quickly (double-click) to launch the program.

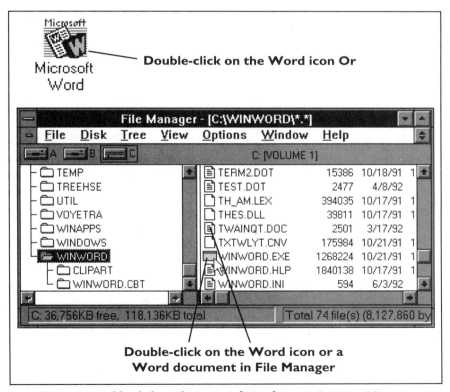

FIGURE 11.1 *Double-click on the Microsoft Word icon in Program Manager, or use File Manager to find the Word program (WINWORD.EXE).*

You will see a new document window similar to the one in Figure 11.2. Its exact size and shape may be different, depending on your monitor and other factors.

You might see part of your Windows desktop in addition to the Word window. This is normal. If it annoys you to see the desktop, click on the Word window Maximize button in the upper-right corner of the Word window.

An active Word window has the standard Windows scroll bars, title bar, size controls, a menu bar, and so on. (If you are unfamiliar with these terms and concepts, take a few moments to review Part I, the Windows section of this book.)

In addition to the usual Windows tools, you'll see a Word ruler, ribbon, Toolbar, and a flashing insertion point. (The insertion point denotes where text will go when you type.) You'll also see a paragraph symbol and the end-of-file marker.

Your mouse pointer should look like an I-beam and move freely about the screen. The status bar at the bottom of your Word window will give you additional information about your project as you work.

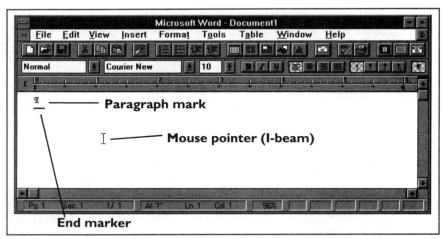

FIGURE 11.2 *A new Word document window will appear when Windows starts.*

OTHER WAYS TO START WORD

Besides double-clicking on the Word icon in Program Manager or File Manager, you can start Word by double-clicking on a Word *document* icon, or on an icon for any document type that has been *associated* with Word for Windows. (See Chapter 4 for more about Associating documents.)

Or you can also use the Run… commands found on Window's Program Manager and File Manager File menus to start Word for Windows.

TYPING TEXT

Once you have Word running, type the following quotation (intentionally type **can can** rather than simply **can**). Don't worry if you also make unintentional typing mistakes, for you'll learn how to fix them in a moment. Watch the screen as you type. Notice that Word automatically moves text down to the next line if it runs out of room near the right edge of the screen. This is called automatic word wrap. Do *not* press Enter until you've typed the period after the word "candles":

"I shall make electricity so cheap that only the rich can can afford to burn candles." (Press Enter here.)

Finish by typing Thomas Edison's name, then press Enter. When you are done, your screen should look something like Figure 11.3.

SELECTING THINGS

Word enables you to do a lot with text after you've typed it. You can change its appearance, move it around, copy it, delete it, and on and on. The first step is to tell Word which text you want to work with. This is done by *selecting* it. Word has many ways to select text. For instance, you can drag your mouse pointer over text while holding down the primary mouse button. There are shortcuts for selecting individual words, lines, sentences, and so on. There is even a Select All menu choice in the Edit menu.

One handy text editing trick is simply to double-click on a word. Try clicking on the second occurrence of "can" in the practice exercise. The

Microsoft Word - Document1
File Edit View Insert Format Tools Table Window Help
Normal
Courier New
10
I·shall·make·electricity·so·cheap·that·only·the·rich·can·can·afford·to·
burn·candles.¶
Thomas·Edison¶
¶
Pg 1 Sec 1 1/1 At 1.5" Ln 4 Col 1 96%

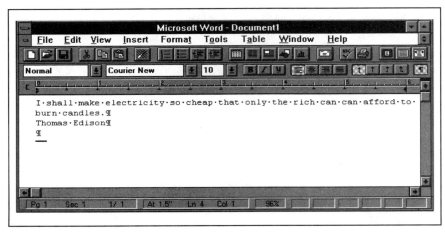

FIGURE 11.3 *Type this quotation, including the "can can" typo.*

word "can" should highlight, along with the space following it. Depending on your system configuration, the selected text will either change color, or be surrounded by a gray or black or white background. That's how you know what you have selected, as you can see in Figure 11.4.

If you are a new mouse user, practice selecting other words, sentences, and single characters with your mouse or trackball. It's only frustrating at first. You'll soon find yourself reaching for the mouse even when using a computer that doesn't have one. Here are some selection shortcuts:

SELECTING WITH A MOUSE

Use the following mouse moves to select text that you wish to manipulate. Some moves require that you hold down keys while pointing or dragging.

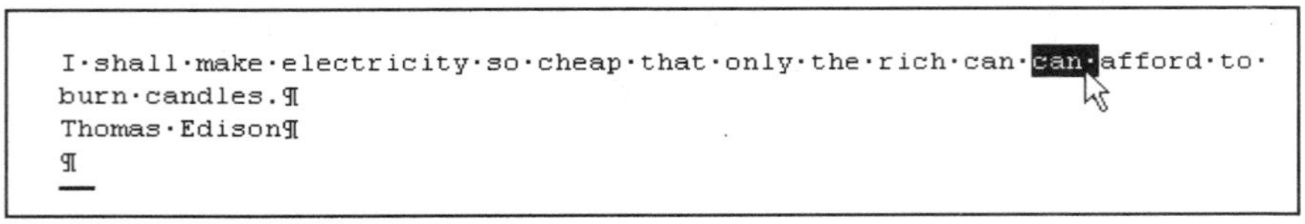

I·shall·make·electricity·so·cheap·that·only·the·rich·can·can·afford·to·
burn·candles.¶
Thomas·Edison¶
¶

FIGURE 11.4 *Selecting text highlights it.*

Selecting Characters with a Mouse

Dragging with the mouse selects text (hold down the primary mouse button while you drag). Changing directions when you drag increases or decreases the selected area. If you drag at the edges of a window, Word will scroll the window to include previously unseen areas in your selection.

Selecting Words with a Mouse

Double-clicking on words will select them. Dragging immediately after you double-click will select words as you drag.

Selecting Lines with a Mouse

Point to the left of a line (the I-beam will change to an arrow). Click *once* to select the whole line.

Selecting Sentences with a Mouse

While holding down the Ctrl key, point anywhere in a sentence, then press the left mouse button to select the entire sentence.

Selecting Paragraphs with a Mouse

Point to the left of any part of a paragraph (the I-beam will change to an arrow). *Double-click* to select the whole paragraph, including its paragraph mark.

Selecting All Text with a Mouse

Point to the left of any part of a document (the I-beam will change to an arrow). Hold down the Ctrl key to select the whole document. This does *not* select text in headers or footers.

Selecting Irregular Areas with a Mouse

Place the insertion point at the beginning of the desired area. Scroll, if necessary. While you hold down the Shift key, point-and-click at the end of the area you want to select. Everything between the insertion point and where you Shift-click will be selected.

To adjust a selection (make the selected area larger or smaller), hold down the Shift key as you drag.

Canceling a Selection with a Mouse

To cancel a selection, click where you want to begin typing next. This simultaneously moves the insertion point and deselects.

KEYBOARD SELECTION SHORTCUTS

Even though mouse selection is often the most efficient method, some touch typists prefer not to move their hands from the keyboard. Others like to use a combination of mouse and keyboard techniques. If that sounds like you, try these key combinations to make selections without reaching for your mouse. You can use either your mouse or the arrow keys to move the insertion point before using the following keystrokes for selecting.

Selecting Characters with Keystrokes

Position the insertion point at the beginning of the desired text. Then, hold down the Shift key and press the right or left arrow keys to highlight characters to the right or left of the insertion point.

Selecting Words with Keystrokes

Holding down the Ctrl-Shift combination while you press the left or right arrow keys extends your selection to the beginning or end of words.

Position the insertion point at the beginning of the desired text (either with the arrow keys or your mouse). Then hold down the Shift key and press the right or left arrow keys to highlight words to the right or left of the insertion point.

Selecting Lines with Keystrokes

Press Shift-End to select from the insertion point to the end of the current line.

Press Shift-Home to select from the insertion point to the beginning of the current line.

Press Shift-down arrow to select from the insertion point to the same column in the line below.

Press Shift-up arrow to select from the insertion point to the same column in the line above.

Selecting Paragraphs with Keystrokes

Use combinations of Ctrl-Shift with the up or down arrow keys to select paragraphs. This is most effective if you position the insertion point at the beginning or end of a paragraph first.

Extending Selected Areas with the F8 Function Key

Repeatedly pressing the F8 function key incrementally increases the selection area, and Shift-F8 reduces the area selected. Your status bar will show the "EXT" message when in this mode. Pressing Esc cancels the Extend mode. You may need to experiment to understand this somewhat confusing feature.

The first time you press the F8 function key, you enter the Extend mode. If nothing is selected when you enter the Extend mode, the next time you press F8 the *word* nearest to the insertion point is selected. The second press enlarges the area to a *sentence*, the next to a *paragraph*, and the next selects the entire *document* (except for headers and footers if you have them). If you've already selected some text before entering the Extend mode, the mode uses the selected text as its starting point. For instance, if you've selected a word, the first extension will be a sentence, and so on. The Shift-F8 key combination reduces the selected area.

Remember, you must press Esc to leave the Extend mode. Check the status bar to see if the mode is off or on.

Selecting All Text or Text in Tables with Keystrokes

To select an entire Word *document*, hold down the Ctrl key and press **5** on your numeric keypad. Alt-5 on your numeric keypad selects an entire Word *table*.

Selecting Unusual Areas with Keystrokes

The Shift-PgUp and Shift-PgDn keys select about a screenful of text below or above the insertion point. (Experiment with this curious and sometimes unpredictable feature.)

Ctrl-Shift-End selects from the insertion point to the bottom of your document.

Ctrl-Shift-Home selects from the insertion point to the top of your document.

DELETING

There are several ways to delete unwanted text like the extra "can" you typed earlier. If you had spotted your mistake right after typing it, pressing the Backspace key three or four times would have removed the unwanted characters and space(s).

Even though you did not make the correction earlier, it is easy to go back now, select the undesired text, and remove it.

Try deleting the extra "can." With the text selected, simply press Delete once to eliminate the unwanted word and its unnecessary space.

UNDOING ACTIONS

Word keeps track of the things that you do, and can often undo your most recent change or changes. This is particularly useful when you've made a major mistake and spot it immediately. If you are following along with the example, point to the Edit Menu with your mouse, then choose the *Undo Typing* command as shown in Figure 11.5.

In this case, the Undo menu choice will be Undo Typing. It will replace the word and space you just deleted. If you haven't already done so, try it. (The keyboard shortcut is Ctrl-Z.)

After you've tried Undo the first time, visit the Edit menu again, and notice that the Undo Typing command has been replaced with a new Undo Undo command, which would, in effect, restore your mistake.

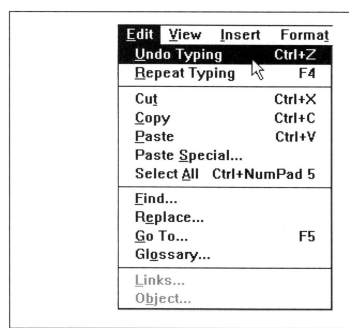

FIGURE 11.5 *The Edit Menu's Undo command changes to tell you what it
can undo.*

INSERTING TEXT

Word offers several ways to insert new text into an existing document.
The most straightforward approach is to move the insertion point to the
desired location, then start typing. Word accommodates the new text by
pushing the existing text to the right and down as necessary.

Suppose you wanted to add the word "darn" between "so" and "cheap" in
Edison's quote. You would start by placing the mouse pointer (the I-beam)
where you want to begin inserting text—between the space and the "c" in
"cheap" for this example. Next, press the mouse button to move the insertion point to the desired position.

Beginners sometimes forget to press the mouse button after pointing with
the I-beam. *Don't confuse the I-beam with the insertion point.* First you must
use the I-beam to point to the location where you want the insertion point
to be placed. Then you must press the primary mouse button to actually
move the insertion point.

Place the insertion point properly and insert the word "**darn** " including the space that follows it. Your screen should look something like Figure 11.6.

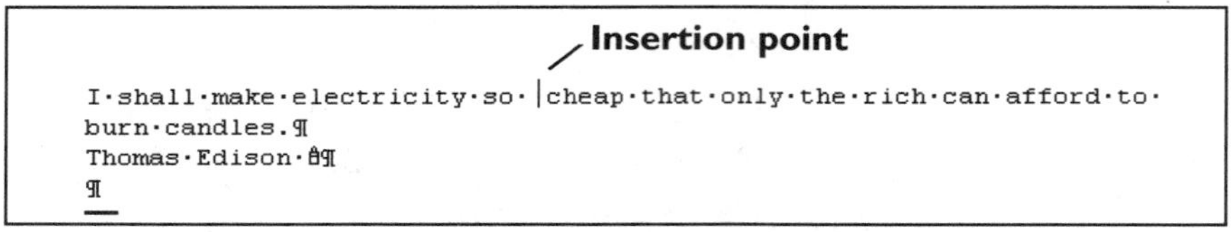

/**Insertion point**

```
I·shall·make·electricity·so·|cheap·that·only·the·rich·can·afford·to·
burn·candles.¶
Thomas·Edison·ô¶
¶
```

FIGURE 11.6 *Position the insertion point before inserting text.*

REPLACING TEXT

Word also makes it easy to *replace* text. It combines the steps of deleting unwanted text, positioning the insertion point, and inserting replacement text. Simply highlight the unwanted text then start typing. The old text disappears and the new text snakes across the screen as you type it.

For example, watch the screen while you highlight the word "rich" (double-click on it), then type "well heeled". Sorry, Mr. Edison.

COPYING AND MOVING THINGS

Word supports all of the usual Windows techniques for copying and relocating things. It also provides two unique move features that leave your Clipboard undisturbed. One is called the *Move Text* function key. The other move feature is called *Drag-and-Drop*, a handy one-step mouse-assisted mover.

Incidentally, you can move text *or* graphics using the techniques described here.

CUT OR COPY AND PASTE

The traditional way to move or duplicate things in a Windows-savvy program is to select the item(s) of interest, Cut or Copy them to the Clipboard, move the insertion point to the desired new position, then Paste. For example, suppose you wanted to move the second paragraph (Edison's name) in Figure 11.7 up to just before the preceding paragraph.

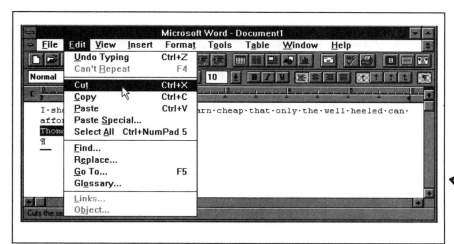

FIGURE 11.7 *One way to move things is to cut and paste them.*

You would start by selecting the entire paragraph (and possibly the ending paragraph mark).

Next, you might use either the Cut command found under the Edit menu or the Ctrl-X shortcut.

The selected text will disappear from the screen and be placed on the Clipboard. Text on your screen below the cut paragraph will move up.

Once the item to be moved is on the Clipboard, place the insertion point at the desired location, as illustrated in Figure 11.8.

Next, paste, using either the Paste choice on Word's Edit menu or the Ctrl-V shortcut. Text will flow to the right and down as the Clipboard contents move into place. In our example, the resulting move would look like Figure 11.9.

Insertion point

I·shall·make·electricity·so·darn·cheap·that·only·the·well·heeled·can·
afford·to·burn·candles.¶
¶

FIGURE 11.8 *Position the insertion point before pasting. Notice that Edison's name has disappeared. It is on the Clipboard.*

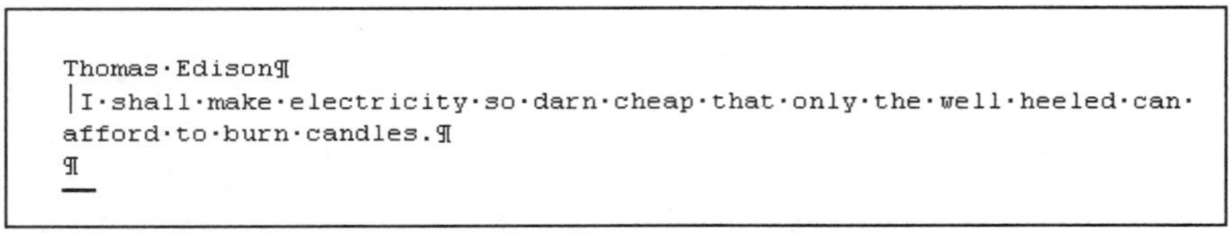

```
Thomas·Edison¶
|I·shall·make·electricity·so·darn·cheap·that·only·the·well·heeled·can·
afford·to·burn·candles.¶
¶
```

FIGURE 11.9 *The Paste was a success.*

REMINDERS ABOUT THE CLIPBOARD

It is important to remember that when you either Cut or Copy to the Clipboard you will replace whatever was previously stored there. If you do this by accident, and spot your error immediately, the Edit menu's Undo command (or Ctrl-Z shortcut) will restore the Clipboard contents.

The Clipboard can store text and graphics. While you normally don't need to see the Clipboard to use it, you can view the Clipboard by using the Windows Clipboard Viewer accessory.

Remember, also, that the contents of the Clipboard disappear when you turn off your computer or quit Windows. If you want to permanently save something from the Clipboard, consider pasting it in a Word document and saving it, or use the Clipboard Viewer's Save As... feature.

DRAG-AND-DROP—
MOVING THINGS WITH YOUR MOUSE

This Word drag-and-drop feature lets you highlight text or other movable objects, then drag them to a new location. For instance, in Figure 11.10, Edison's name has been highlighted with Drag-and-Drop enabled.

With the mouse button depressed while pointing to the highlighted text, the mouse pointer changes appearance slightly. Notice the small rectangle

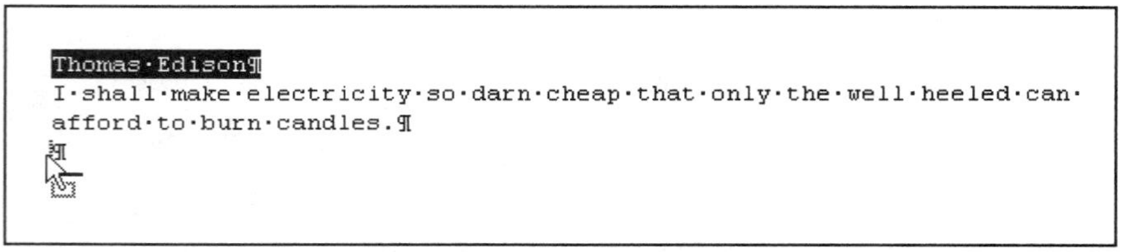

```
Thomas·Edison¶
I·shall·make·electricity·so·darn·cheap·that·only·the·well·heeled·can·
afford·to·burn·candles.¶
¶
```

FIGURE 11.10 *Drag-and-Drop speeds the movement of items you've selected. Notice the pointer's shape.*

near the arrow. Notice, also, the long insertion point. The arrow, box, and insertion point move as one when you move the mouse with the button held down. Once you release the mouse button, the selected item(s) will be inserted at the Drop-and-Drag insertion point. In Figure 11.10, Edison's name would be inserted on a new line. Try it!

To turn Drag-and-Drop off or on, choose Options... from the Tools menu. You will see the General Preferences category. If necessary, click in the appropriate box to place an X there and enable the feature, or click to remove the X and disable it. See Chapter 23 to learn more about changing Word settings. If you wish to turn Drag-and-Drop off and on from the menu bar, Chapter 23 will show you how to add a Drag-and-Drop menu item.

MOVING WITH THE MOVE KEY (F2)

The other way to move things without disturbing your Clipboard's contents is to use the F2 Move key. Start by placing the insertion point where you want the text to be placed after the move. Press the F2 function key. The status bar will ask "Move From Where?" Select the material you want to move, scrolling if necessary. Word marks the things to be moved with a dotted underline. Press the Enter key. Your selection will be moved and the screen will scroll to the insertion point if necessary.

You can reverse the process, if you like, by selecting text before you press F2. Then the status bar will ask you where to move the selected item(s). Pressing Esc cancels the Move process.

COPYING WITH THE MOVE KEY (SHIFT-F2)

Copying with the Move key works like moving with the Move key, except you use the Shift-F2 key combination, and text is copied rather than moved. And the status messages ask about copying.

Start by placing the insertion point where you want the text to be placed after you copy it. Press the Shift-F2 key combination. The status bar will ask "Copy From Where?" Select the material you want to move, scrolling if necessary. Word marks the things to be moved with a dotted underline. Press the Enter key. Your selection will be moved and the screen will scroll to the insertion point if necessary. Pressing Esc cancels the Copy process.

MOVING THINGS BETWEEN PROGRAMS

The contents of your Clipboard usually stay the same when you switch from program to program as long as you do not quit Windows. Thus, you can copy items from a spreadsheet, quit the spreadsheet program, launch Word, and paste the spreadsheet information into your Word document. There are often better ways to do this, however. Read about OLE in Chapter 40, for instance.

INSERTING THE CONTENTS OF OTHER FILES

It is possible to insert the contents of other files directly into your Word documents using the Insert File... command found on Word's Insert menu. This is a great way to "assemble" large documents (say, a newsletter) from a collection of smaller ones (individual articles). The documents you insert don't even need to be Word documents.

Start by placing the insertion point where you want to insert the other document's contents. Then choose Insert File... from Word's Insert Menu. You will be presented with a File dialog box. Use it to tell Word which file you want to insert. (You'll learn how this dialog box works in Chapter 13.)

Word will attempt to load the chosen file at the insertion point. Inserting files this way can affect styles, glossaries, and other characteristics of the document into which you are inserting. (You'll learn more about this in Chapter 15.)

If the file being inserted was not created by Word for Windows, Word will attempt to convert it.

TYPING SYMBOLS
AND SPECIAL CHARACTERS

Have you ever wished there were an easy way to type special symbols like the © for copyright? There is. Do you sometimes type words containing international accent marks like umlauts or tildes? Word's Insert Symbol... command (found on the Insert menu) can help. It brings up a window like the one in Figure 11.11.

Place the insertion point where you want the special character(s), or highlight text you want to replace. Choose the Symbol... command and scroll through the drop-down Symbols From list to choose the *symbol set* you want

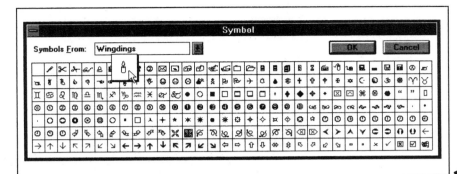

FIGURE 11.11 *Use the Symbol... command in the Insert menu to type special characters and symbols.*

to use (Wingdings, for instance). Use your mouse to point to symbols of interest. You will see an enlarged view of each as you point and press the left mouse button. Double-clicking on a symbol either inserts it at the insertion point in your document or uses it to replace selected text.

Try adding the candle Wingding to your Edison quote, as shown in Figure 11.12. Use Figure 11.11 as your guide. Explore the other symbol choices provided in the Symbol window's Symbol From drop-down list.

Since we'll be using this short text for some future exercises, you might want to take a moment now to restore Edison's actual words using the text editing tricks you've learned so far. Then it will be time to save and print your work.

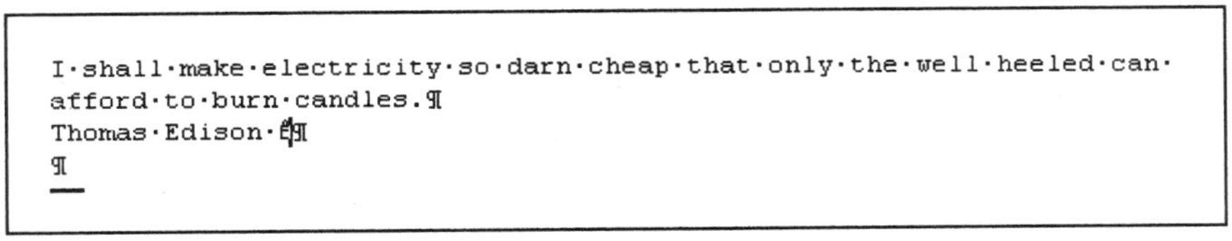

```
I·shall·make·electricity·so·darn·cheap·that·only·the·well·heeled·can·
afford·to·burn·candles.¶
Thomas·Edison·🕯¶
¶
```

FIGURE 11.12 *Try adding a candle symbol and moving Edison's name with Drag-and-Drop. Notice how the pointer's shape changes when you drag-and-drop.*

Saving and
Printing Documents

The quotation you've typed and rearranged exists only on your screen and in your computer's volatile RAM (random access memory). That is to say, if you quit Windows, or switched off the computer at day's end, or experienced a power failure or other malfunction right now, your work would be forever lost. By saving your work to disk as you go, you can pick up where you left off the next day or after a malfunction.

SAVE EARLY AND OFTEN

Many experienced computer users save every 15 minutes or whenever they are interrupted by phone calls, visitors, and so on. That's a good habit to establish.

SAVING A DOCUMENT FOR THE FIRST TIME

Once you are happy with the appearance of the Edison quote, select Save from Word's File menu, or use the Shift-F12 keyboard shortcut. You will see the Save As dialog box illustrated in Figure 12.1.

Among other things, this box is telling you where Word currently plans to store your work. It is also asking for a legal file name (a maximum of eight

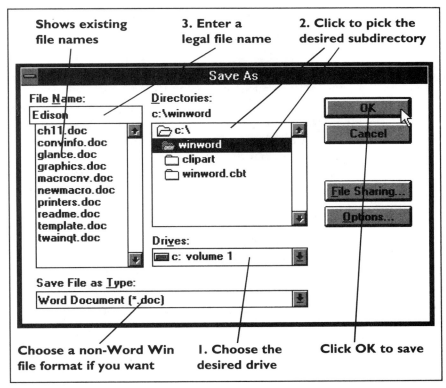

FIGURE 12.1 *This is the Save As dialog box.*

characters and an optional three-character extension). You'll see several other save options as well.

The drop-down Drives menu lets you specify a disk drive (don't forget to put a floppy disk in your floppy drive before saving).

To specify the directory and optionally the subdirectory where you want to store your document, click your way through the folders shown in the scrollable Directories window.

For instance, to store a file in the *winword* folder in Figure 12.1, you would start by clicking on the *C:* folder icon. This would reveal a scrollable list of other folders. When you scroll to find the *winword*, you'd click on it. As you open folders this way, Word lists the resulting path above the scrollable window. In Figure 12.1 the path listed is **c:\winword**. This means if you clicked OK at this point, the Edison document would be saved in the *winword* subdirectory on drive *c*. If you wanted to save the quote in the clip art subdirectory instead, you could click on it next.

If you are following along with the Edison exercise, keep things simple for now by using Word's default Save options. Start by noticing where Word is proposing to put your document. This is a very important habit to establish. If you do not think about *where* you and Word save documents, you will likely misplace them. When saving to a floppy disk or your own small, uncluttered hard disk, this can be a minor annoyance. If you work on a far-flung network with multiple servers and gigabytes of storage space, it can take hours or days to locate lost files.

In Figure 12.1, Word is proposing to store our new document in a subdirectory called **winword** on the C: hard drive. You can tell this from the path listed under the Directories title.

Look at your screen. Take a moment to see where Word plans to save your work. Chances are you will see something slightly different from the folder location shown in Figure 12.1. If you think you might forget the location, write down that directory name or other location information.

If you haven't already done so, type a name for your document and click OK. There is no need to add the .DOC file extension; Word will add it for you.

Word will save your document and, assuming you are using Word's default settings, you will see a summary information dialog box that will help you mark the file in several ways for future retrieval.

SUMMARY INFORMATION

Once you are happy with the appearance of the Edison quote, and save it for the first time, you will see the Summary Info dialog box illustrated in Figure 12.2.

Things you type in its optional boxes can help you find files quickly even on crowded hard disks and huge network servers. Enter one or more keywords, the subject matter, author name(s), and miscellaneous comments. Word's Find File... command (described in Chapter 13) lets you look for this summary information.

Word only asks you to enter summary information *once* (at the time you start a new document). If you never plan to use the Find File... command to search for summary information, and if you are annoyed by the appearance of this dialog box, you can turn it off from the Save category of the Options dialog box. (See Chapter 23 for details.)

The Summary Info can be called up, viewed, and edited at any time in the future with the Summary Info... command on Word's File menu command.

Notice the Statistics... button on the Summary Info dialog box, which reveals some additional information about your project. Figure 12.3 shows an example of this.

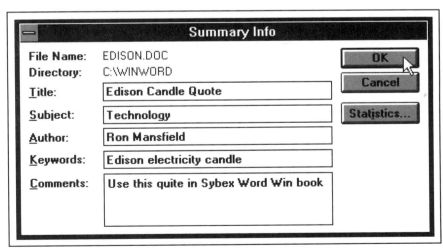

FIGURE 12.2 *Enter optional summary information here to help Word's Find File feature locate the document later.*

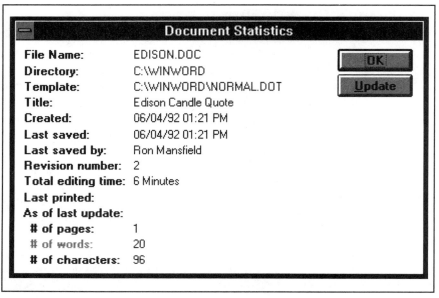

FIGURE 12.3 *The Document Statistics button on the Summary Info dialog box
tells you all sorts of things about a document's history and content.*

SAVE OPTIONS

Word gives you considerable control over how and where documents are
saved. You can save in non-Word file formats, have Word periodically save
automatically for you, and more. Most but not all of these options are turned
on and off from a dialog box reached with the Options… button in the Save
As dialog box.

Saving in Different Formats

The drop-down *Save File as Type* menu in the Save As dialog box lets
you convert your work into non–Word for Windows formats. This makes it
possible to give to colleagues compatible file copies that use different
word processing programs like WordPerfect or Word for DOS. It also lets
you create plain ASCII files and Word templates. (Templates are explained
in Chapter 15.)

Before you save in a non–Word Win format, pick the desired format from the drop-down Save File as Type list as illustrated in Figure 12.4. For normal everyday work, use the Word Document (*.DOC) type.

Saving on Different Disks

To save to a different disk, pick it from the drop-down Drives menu before you save. The Drives menu is shown in Figure 12.1. This is how you save to floppies, to different hard drives, and to network servers.

Automatic Backups

The *Options...* button in the Save As dialog box brings up the series of Save options shown in Figure 12.5.

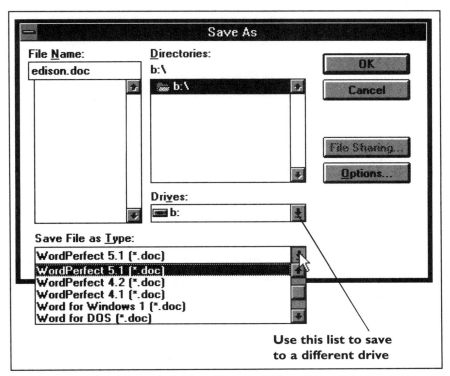

FIGURE 12.4 *Scroll through the drop-down Save File as Type list to save in different formats.*

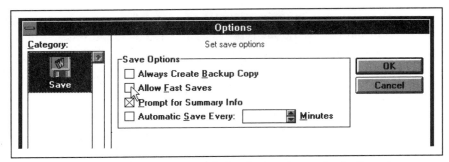

FIGURE 12.5 *Reach these options with the Options button in the Save As
dialog box.*

Incidentally, you can also reach these save choices with *Save category*,
reached with the Options... command in the Tools menu. Chapter 23 explains that approach. For now, let's look at the options and their use.

Always Create a Backup Copy

An X in this box causes Word to make backups, starting with the *second
time you save.* This is a confusing feature, worth understanding so that you
don't expect too much from it. Even with the box checked, Word does *not*
make a backup the first time you save a new document. If you save for the
first time, then find that your original file is damaged, you will not have a
backup.

The second time and every subsequent time you save, Word creates a
backup file with the same name as your original and the extension .BAK.
This copy will not contain your most recent changes. Rather, it is a copy of
your document *before* you started making changes. So, if you open an existing document, make a lot of changes, and save just once when you quit, you
will not have a backup of all of those changes. What you will have is your
primary document file containing the changes and an older version with the
.BAK extension. The older version will not have your latest work. This is less
serious if you get in the habit of saving early and often as you work, since
the backup feature replaces the .BAK file each time you save. Thus, if you
save every 15 minutes, and just seconds before the next save you experience
a problem with your document file, the backup will contain all but the last
15 minutes worth of changes.

However, since Word normally saves these backup files on the same disk with the original files, a hardware failure—or a fire—can leave you without your primary or backup files.

Word's automatic backup feature is no replacement for a routine backup to floppies, tape, a network file server, or some other media. Hard disks fail. Count on it.

Allow Fast Saves

The Allow Fast Saves option speeds the saving process by saving just changes most of the time. Occasionally Word will still make you wait for it to save the entire document from beginning to end if you enable Fast Saves. But sometimes it won't. Many experienced users disable Allow Fast Saves since it uses more memory, can be a little finicky, and may cause problems if you ever need to recover a damaged document file. Disable Fast Saves and take a break every 15 minutes. It's better for you *and* your files.

Prompt for Summary Info

Removing the check mark from this box prevents Word from automatically asking you for summary information. You can still enter it on a case-by-case basis with the Summary Info... command on the File menu.

Automatic Saves

Word will save automatically for you at intervals you specify. Since you can't undo saves, realize that this feature can deprive you of earlier versions of your work if you really screw up and don't reload an earlier version before Word replaces it with your current work.

Many experienced users switch this off and use their own brains as timers. They also save whenever they are interrupted by visitors or phone calls. Try it.

PRINT PREVIEW SAVES TIME AND PAPER

Let's take a look at the Print Preview feature before you actually print your first Word document. You *can* bypass Print Preview and simply print immediately to paper, but previewing of all but the simplest document is advised.

It lets you see a screen representation of one or more entire pages before you print them, often saving paper and time. (As you'll see in a moment, Print Preview has other uses as well.) Pull down the File menu and choose Print Preview. Your screen will look something like Figure 12.6.

Print Preview will give you an excellent idea of *where* the text will print on the paper. It will allow you to visualize margins and the overall page balance as well. If your document contains headers, footers, line numbers, and other embellishments, you will see them represented here. You probably won't be able to read text in this view, however, nor can you edit here.

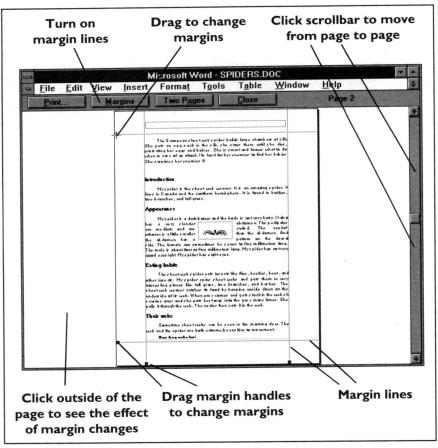

FIGURE 12.6 *Print Preview lets you spot layout mistakes and change margins without wasting paper or time.*

Notice the buttons at the top of your screen in Print Preview. Print... takes you to the Print dialog box (discussed in a moment). The Margins button turns margin lines on and off. They are on in Figure 12.6. The third button from the left switches between one- and two-page view; its name changes with the view. The Close button takes you back to Normal or Page Layout view, depending on which you were using when you switched to Print Preview.

CORRECTING THINGS YOU SEE WHEN PREVIEWING

If you spot a problem in your work, you can click on either the Page Layout or Close buttons near the top-right of the screen to quit previewing. Then you might fix the errors and preview again until you get your page just right.

ADJUSTING PAGE BREAKS
AND MARGINS WHILE PREVIEWING

You can drag margin lines by their handles (squares). After you've dragged margins to new positions, click outside of the preview page. Word will repaginate and display the effects of your changes.

PRINTING DOCUMENTS

Finally, it is time to print. Be certain that your printer is turned on and ready to go. Most laser printers need to warm up, so if you are using one and have just turned it on, wait for the ready light before attempting to print. It is always a good idea to save your work before you print. This way, if there is a system or printer malfunction that "locks up" your computer, you will not lose work when you reboot your computer or restart Word.

QUICKLY PRINTING AN ENTIRE DOCUMENT

The fastest way to print one copy of an entire document is to use the Print button on your Toolbar. Not surprisingly, it looks like a miniature printer. One click will send your document to the printer.

SWITCHING PRINTERS

If you have more than one printer, use the Print Setup... command on the File menu to select the desired printer. (Normally, you will want to choose the correct printer right when you begin a new project.) A typical Print Setup dialog box is shown at the top of Figure 12.7.

PRINTING MULTIPLE COPIES

To print multiple copies of a document, choose the Print... command on Word's File menu. You'll see a dialog box like the one at the bottom of Figure 12.7. Enter the desired number of copies in the Copies box, then click OK or press Enter to print.

PRINTING RANGES OF PAGES

To print ranges of pages, enter starting and ending page numbers in the From and To boxes. (If your document has multiple sections with page numbers starting at 1 in each section, see Chapter 16.)

CANCELING PRINTING

Canceling printing can be very easy, or a living hell. When you print, you'll see a Printing dialog box containing a Cancel button. Clicking it or pressing the Escape key (Esc) will stop the job. However, because Word sends your document to Print Manager, the Cancel button often disappears long before the printing is finished. When this happens, the only way to cancel a job is to get to the Print Manager dialog box shown in Figure 12.8, select the job to kill from the list of files queued up, and click the Delete button.

This is often much easier said than done. Print Manager frequently hogs most of your computer's resources, putting the screen, mouse, and keyboard in extreme slow motion. Be prepared to wait and fidget while Word gets around to your request while printing. Or take a mental health break. You may find it easiest to power down your printer or take it off-line to get Print Manager's attention and bring the dialog box to the foreground. Disrupting printing this way can be risky business and may even lock up your computer. That's why it is a good idea *always* to save before you print.

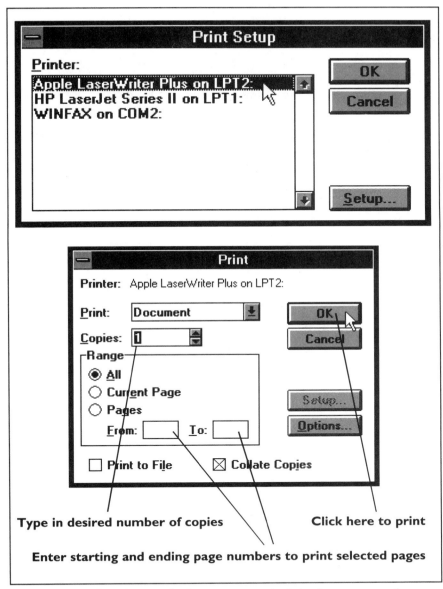

WORD

FIGURE 12.7 *If you have multiple printers, use the Print Setup command on Word's File menu to choose the appropriate one before printing.*

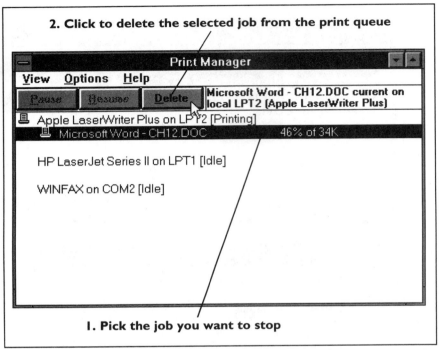

FIGURE 12.8 *Cancel long jobs from the Print Manager dialog box.*

13

Working with Documents

You must *open* a document (place it in your computer's RAM and on your screen) before you can work with it. You can either work with existing documents stored on your disk(s) or start new ones. You start new documents by using the *New...* command on Word's File menu. (When you start Word it also automatically opens a new document for you.) Word's *Template* feature makes it easy to start new projects without needless repetition of standard things like margin settings, typestyle selections, line spacing choices, and so on. To resume working on an *existing* document that you've previously saved to disk, you use the *Open...* command found on Word's File menu. This loads a copy of the disk-resident document into RAM and displays it on your screen.

The last four documents you've saved to disk are conveniently listed at the bottom of the Word File menu, making it a snap to reload and continue working on any of them.

If you've misplaced a document on your disk, or if you want to locate several related documents, Word's *Find File...* command can help you round up and load them.

Figure 13.1 shows the File menu features used to create new documents, as well as to locate and load existing ones. After you've read this chapter, try locating and opening your Edison quote using the techniques shown here.

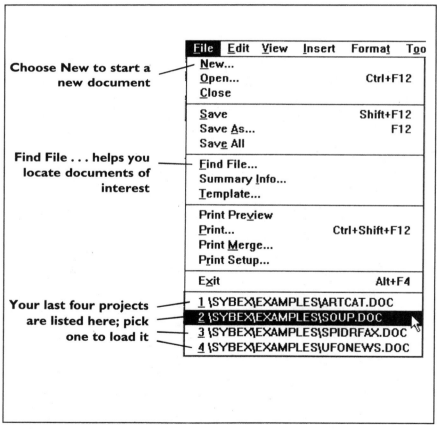

FIGURE 13.1 *Use New... to create a new untitled document. Open... places copies of disk-resident files in RAM and on your screen. Find File... rounds up lost or related documents. Word lists the last four files you've used, for quick reloading.*

You can open and convert documents saved by programs other than Word. This makes it possible to edit documents created by WordPerfect or other word processors, as well as ASCII text files and more.

As you already know, it is possible to have more than one Word document open at once. You can only work in one document at a time, however. This is called the *active* document. Use Word's *Window* menu to make a document active. Clicking in a document window with your mouse pointer also activates a document.

It is also possible to insert one document in another, thereby constructing long, complex documents from a series of simple, short ones. Use the File... command on Word's Insert menu to do this.

This chapter explores the process of creating new documents, opening existing ones, finding lost files, and converting non-Word documents for use with Word.

STARTING WORD
CREATES AN UNTITLED DOCUMENT

When you start Word, you are presented with an empty, "untitled" document window based on Word's default *Normal* template. Untitled documents have the temporary title "Document" and a sequential number in their title bars (Document1, Document2, or Document3, for instance). You can start typing immediately.

CREATING NEW DOCUMENTS
WITH WORD ALREADY RUNNING

If Word is already running, choose the New... command on Word's File menu or press Alt, then F, then N to begin the process of opening a new untitled document. (This is the "mouseless" way to reach menu choices.) But before you begin typing, you'll need to decide which template to use. For many projects, that's as simple as clicking the OK button to accept Word's NORMAL (default) template.

WORD'S TIMESAVING TEMPLATES

Templates are "patterns" for the common document types you routinely create. They are files that store formatting decisions like margin settings, header and footer designs, page numbering setups, typestyles, and so on. But they can also store much more. Templates often include boilerplate text, fields that automatically insert today's date and the author's name, and the like. Templates can also temporarily "redesign" the Word workplace by loading custom glossaries, modified Toolbars, macros, and more. Some templates ask you for, then insert, additional information whenever you use them. As you can see, these are powerful, sometimes confusing, tools.

Microsoft provides many standard, predefined templates for things like business memos, proposals, overhead transparencies, press releases, and so on. You can use them as they stand or personalize them. It is also possible to create your own templates either from scratch or based on Microsoft's. These standard templates are explored in Chapter 19, since you'll need to know more about Word before you can fully exploit and modify them.

For now, it is enough to know that many everyday typing projects can begin with Word's NORMAL template. When you Choose New… on Word's File menu, you will see a New dialog box like the one in Figure 13.2.

The *New* window contains a scrollable list of available templates. The template named in the *Use Template* box will be used for your next project. When the box first opens, "NORMAL" appears in the Use Template box. Clicking the OK button selects that choice and opens an untitled document for you to use for your project.

To choose a different template, scroll (if necessary), then click on a template name to move it to the Use Template box. Finish by clicking OK to open a new document using the chosen template. (*Hint*: Double-clicking on the template name in the scrollable list will save you a trip to the OK button.)

When you pick most of Word's templates other than NORMAL, they display a dialog box or two with questions that must be answered before you can create a new document based on the template. Figure 13.3 shows what you'll see if you choose the FAX template.

Some templates have certain window sizes or other specific requirements. If you accidentally choose the wrong template, you may need to click one or more Cancel buttons, then close the resulting, unwanted new document before continuing.

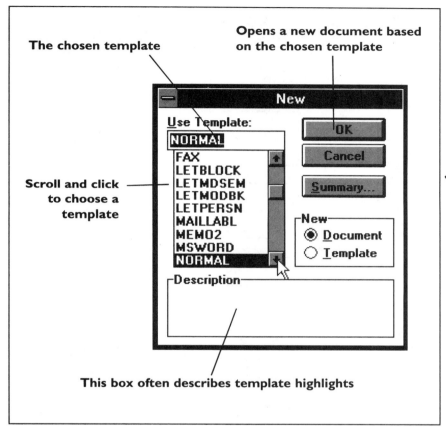

The chosen template

Opens a new document based on the chosen template

Scroll and click to choose a template

This box often describes template highlights

FIGURE 13.2 *Start your first few typing projects by using Word's NORMAL template. Learn more about the others in Chapter 19.*

OPENING PREVIOUSLY SAVED WORD DOCUMENTS

There are a number of ways in which you can open existing Word documents to view or edit them. You can open documents from within Word itself, or from Window's File Manager.

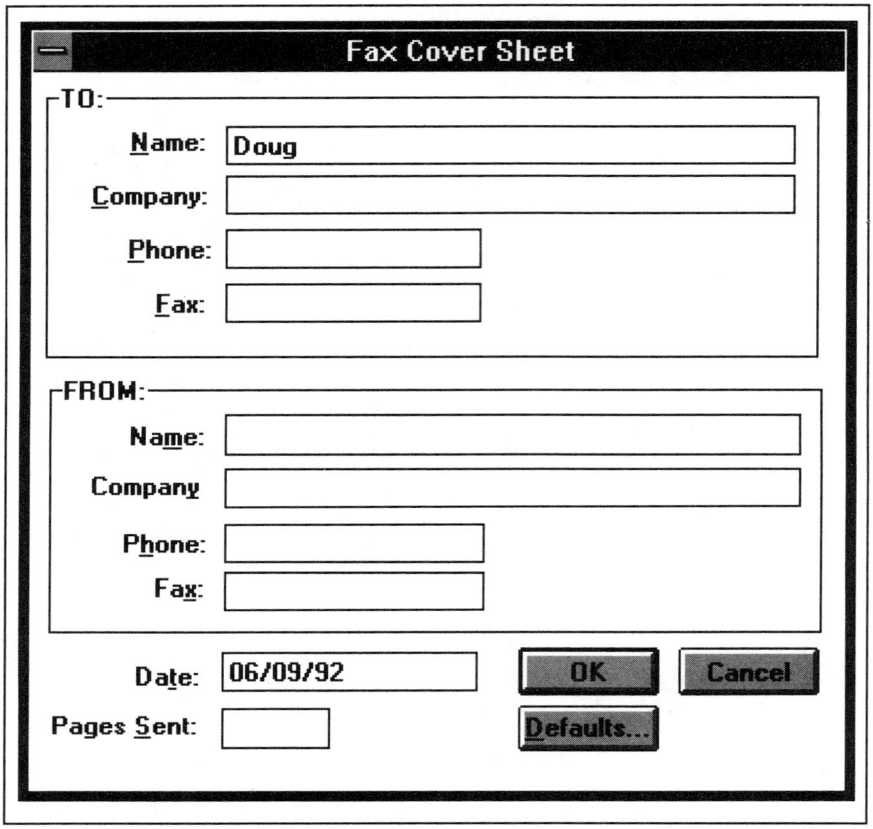

FIGURE 13.3 *Many templates such as this Fax Cover Sheet ask you for additional information. Use Cancel buttons and the Close... choice on Word's File menu to abort accidental template selections.*

OPENING WORD DOCUMENTS FROM FILE MANAGER

From Window's File Manager, you can simply double-click on a Word document's icon. If Word is already running, File Manager will open the document and return you to Word, where your chosen document will be the active window. If Word is not running when you double-click on a document icon, Windows will first run Word, then load and display the chosen document instead of an untitled one.

OPENING WORD DOCUMENTS FROM WORD ITSELF

With Word running as the active window on your screen, Choose Open…
on Word's File menu, or use the Ctrl-F12 keyboard shortcut.

You will see an Open dialog box like the one in Figure 13.4.

Start by choosing a disk drive if the one shown in the Drives box is not
the one you want. Click on the box to reveal a drop-down list, then pick the

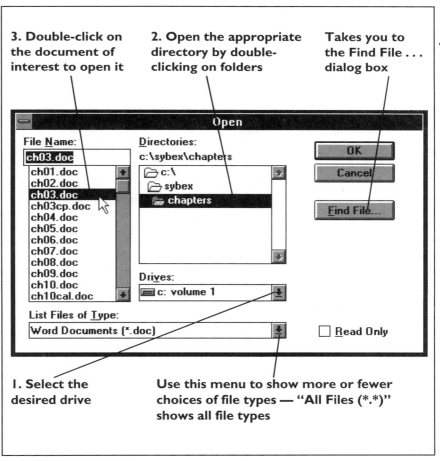

FIGURE 13.4 *Use the Open dialog box to pick the appropriate drive, directory,
and file. The List Files of Type drop-down list can help restrict the file list.*

drive of interest. If the file you want is on a floppy disk, insert the floppy before clicking on the chosen drive icon.

If the desired file is buried in subdirectories, click on as many folders in the Directories list as necessary to open the subdirectory containing your file. Watch for the file name of interest to appear in the File Name scrollable list at the left of the Open dialog box as you open directories.

Clicking once on a file name in the scrollable File Name list will move the name to the File Name box at the top of the list. Clicking OK opens the file named in that box. As is often the case in scrollable lists, double-clicking on a name will save you a trip to the OK button.

SHORTENING FILE LISTS WITH FILTERS

As you probably know, Word document file names normally end with the extension .DOC, while Word's backup files usually end with .BAK, and so on. Other programs like WordPerfect may use different file name extensions.

And, some users try to give meaningful, consistent names to their files (LTRBOB1.DOC, MEMOSUE2.DOC, and so on). When trying to find the right file to open in a crowded directory, you will often find it useful to limit, or *filter*, the number of files you see in the scrollable File Name list. You might want to see only Word backup files or just memos or whatever. Other times you'll want to see and open files even if they were not created by Word. You can do these things by editing the "filter" choice in the List Files of Type drop-down menu and/or by entering filter criteria in the File Name area at the top of the Open dialog box.

For instance, to see files of all types, rather than just Word files, pick the All Files (*.*) choice on the drop-down menu or simply use the asterisk wild card. Type *.* in the File Name box before picking a directory to examine. Whenever you change the filter, you will need to click on the appropriate directory icon to update the list.

If you use a naming scheme for your files, you can sometimes limit lists by "filtering" file names. For instance, if you consistently name your files containing business letters with the prefix Ltr and prefix all files containing memos with the prefix Memo, then the filter **LTR*.DOC** would list only your Word business letters found in the selected directory while **MEMO*.*** would find just memos, regardless of whether they were created by Word or another program.

As you will see in a moment, Word's Summary feature and Find File... often prove to be better tools for this type of hunting and gathering.

Take note of one caution when using filters like those just described. It is possible to be tricked into thinking that files have disappeared when they are still right where they belong. Suppose, for instance, you just finished using filters to help you search for only files that end in the extension .BAK. Unless you remember to remove that filter from the File Name box, you won't be able to see Word file names ending in .DOC the next time you use the Open dialog box. So, if you can't see files that you think are in the directory you are searching, check the File Name box. It should usually say *.DOC when attempting to look for and load original Word documents, or *.* when looking for documents with unknown names or extensions.

FIND FILE—THE FINDER OF LOST DOCUMENTS

The Find File... feature (located on Word's File menu) is a powerful tool for locating and loading specific files. For instance, you can use it to search for documents that were created or modified within specific date ranges. Or, if you've entered author, subject, keyword, and other information using Word's Summary Info feature, you can search for documents based on these criteria. Find File... even lets you look for words and phrases contained *within* files. For instance, if you wanted to round up all of the documents you've created pertaining to budgets, you might use Find File... to locate all word processing documents, spreadsheets, and database files that contain the word "budget." (Don't confuse Find File... with Find...; read about Find... in Chapter 20.)

STARTING A FIND FILE... SEARCH

The first time you choose the Find File... command in a Word session, Word will search the current directory (the one you last used with Open... or Save...). It makes a list of all files and opens a window something like the one in Figure 13.5.

If you see the file you think you want in the File Name list, you can select it by clicking on its name in the scrollable list. Once selected, a file can often be viewed in the Content area of the Find File window, plus it can be loaded as a Word document, copied, deleted, or even printed by choosing the appropriate button in the Find File window.

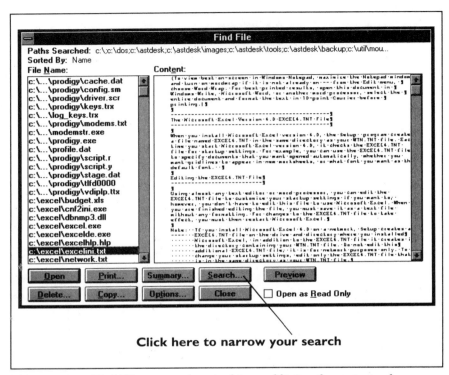

Click here to narrow your search

FIGURE 13.5 *Find File... starts by searching and listing the contents of your current directory. You can often see the contents of files and load them as Word documents. Use the Search... button to limit (filter) the file list.*

If you try to load a non-Word document, Word will give you several file conversion options (see "Opening and Converting Non-Word Documents" later in this chapter). You may or may not be pleased by the results. Some files open and convert nicely, while other files (like programs and sound files) will be meaningless when opened by Word. (As a rule, there is no good reason for you to open a program file that ends with an .EXE or .COM extension.)

NARROWING YOUR SEARCH

Frequently, the initial file list will be inconveniently long to deal with. Use the Search... button in the Find File menu to restrict the list. You'll see a new dialog box like the one in the top of Figure 13.6.

In the example, the word "spider" was placed in the Any Text box. The resulting search list shows only files containing the word "spider" within them. Clicking the Preview button after selecting a file of interest often lets you see its contents.

You can combine search filters to narrow your search even further. For instance, you could search for spider files where Adam was the author and the creation date was within a specific time period. The trick is to use selection criteria that net all files of interest without flooding you with irrelevant documents. When in doubt, use fewer filters, then sort the resulting list. Here's how that works:

Sorting Your List of Found Files

The Options... button on the Find File window brings up a dialog box that lets you change the way files are listed and described. Figure 13.7 shows you how it looks. Use the Sort Files By options buttons to rearrange the document list.

The List File Names With buttons reveal things like document statistics. For example, choosing Statistics displays things like the template used to create the document, its author, number of revisions, word count, and so on. (Word count comes in handy if you are a writer requested to write an article with a specified number of words.)

Some of these options (like Title) require time-consuming passes through your listed files. Be patient.

OPENING AND
CONVERTING NON-WORD DOCUMENTS

Assuming that you let Word install its converters when Word itself was installed, whenever you try to open a non-Word for Windows document with Word you will see a *Convert File* dialog box like the one in Figure 13.8.

Pick the appropriate converter from the drop-down list and click OK. With luck, you'll soon see a new document that resembles the original.

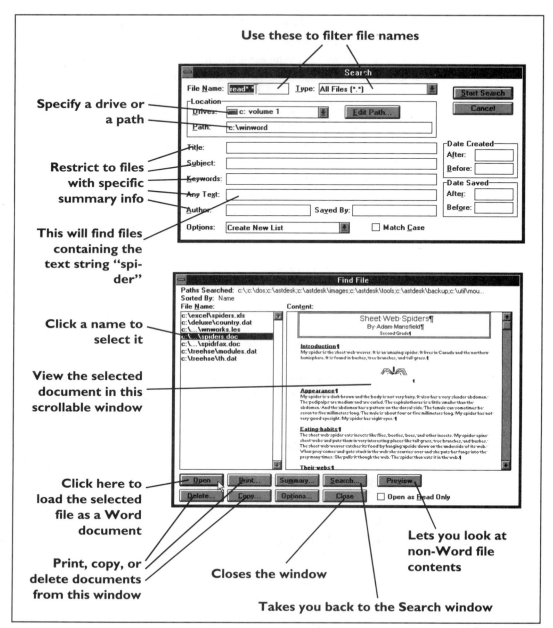

FIGURE 13.6 *The search criteria in the top of this figure narrowed the File Name list down to seven files. Each file listed in the Find File window at the bottom contains the text string "spider" somewhere within it.*

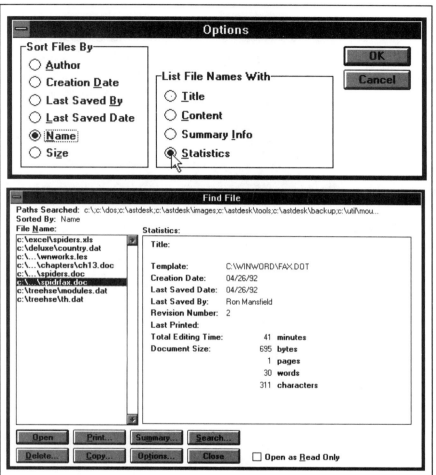

FIGURE 13.7 *Use Find File's Options… to sort and further filter lists of found files. Here the Statistics option displays information about the highlighted file's history and size.*

Conversion from one document type to another can sometimes be a frustrating process. For instance, if you create a document on a computer with different fonts than the one you use to convert the document, there will almost certainly be differences in typestyles, as well as line and page endings.

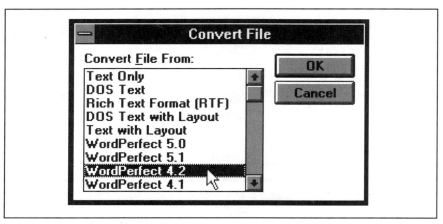

FIGURE 13.8 *Word will offer you several conversion choices when you try to load a non–Word for Windows file.*

Moreover, some document attributes won't always convert properly. For example, if you open a WordPerfect document in Word, underlining will be preserved, but the type of underlining may change (continuous underlining might become word underlining, and so forth). To learn more about conversions, use Word to read and possibly print the CONVINFO.DOC file located in your WINWORD directory.

If you haven't already done so, use the techniques in this chapter to find and open your Edison quote. We'll use it to explore formatting techniques in Chapter 14.

14

Word Formatting
Tools and Tips

If you are accustomed to typing line after line of 66 boring-looking, typewriter-like characters day after day, you are in for a pleasant surprise. Word for Windows offers a mind-boggling collection of document, paragraph, and character formatting options. In this chapter you will learn a number of tricks to make your documents come alive. Experiment as you read along. Get in the habit of switching to Print Preview or Page Layout view when necessary to admire your work in progress. There's a lot to cover here. Let's get to it.

TYPING HABITS TO BREAK

If you learned how to type on a typewriter or an old word processor, chances are you have established habits that will slow you down when using Word. Scan these tips, then read on to learn how to format the "Word way":

- When you indent paragraphs, don't use the Tab key or spaces. Instead, use Word's Indent marker. (It's the top half of the split triangle at the left side of the ruler.)

- Don't use the spacebar to center text. Use the Center button on the ribbon instead. Then, when you change margins or indents, text will recenter properly.

- Use tabs or Word's Table features rather than typing multiple spaces to create columns of text and numbers. Word's special decimal tab feature really simplifies typing columns of numbers. (Read about tabs and tables in Chapter 17.)

- Consider using Word's "Space Before" and "Space After" paragraph features rather than pressing Enter repeatedly to put white space between paragraphs.

- Don't press the Enter key repeatedly to start a new page. Use Word's Insert Page Break feature instead.

QUICK CHANGES WITH THE RIBBON, RULER, AND TOOLBAR

While complex formatting can require visits to a number of menus and dialog boxes, you can accomplish quite a bit with a few quick mouse clicks and a drag or two. Consider the Edison quote in Figure 14.1.

If you've been following along with the previous exercises and want to reproduce Figure 14.1, load your Edison quote and follow these steps.

1. Select all of the text by dragging (or Shift-clicking).

2. Use the drop-down Font menu to change all of the text to Times New Roman or a substitute, if necessary.

3. With all the text still selected, change the font size to 24 points using the drop-down Font Size menu.

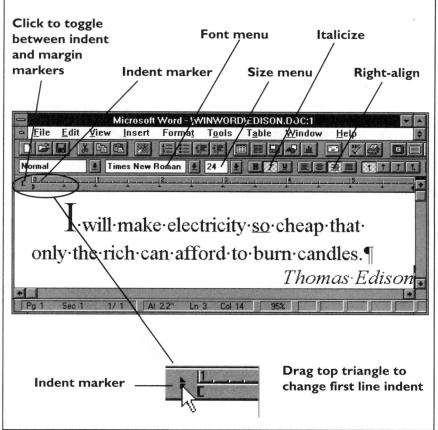

FIGURE 14.1 *The formatting you see here was done using only the ribbon, ruler, and Toolbar.*

4. Click anywhere in the quote itself to deselect the text and place the insertion point in the first paragraph (the insertion point should be in the quote, not Edison's name).

5. Drag the top of the indent marker about $1/2$" to the right, indenting the first line of the quote.

6. Select just the "I" and increase its size to 48 points.

7. Select Edison's whole name (either click at the left edge of that line or double-click and drag across the name itself).

8. Italicize the name with the Italic button.

9. Right-align with the appropriate alignment button on the ribbon. (If you look closely, you'll notice that the Italic and Right-alignment buttons are depressed on the ribbon in Figure 14.1.)

That's all there is to it! In the rest of this chapter, we'll learn more about these formatting tools and others.

A SYSTEMATIC APPROACH TO FORMATTING

Because Windows can show you how your document will look before you print it, it's a good idea to make some of the important, document-wide formatting decisions right when you start a project. For instance, if you have more than one printer, choose the one you will be using when you start the project. If you know you will be printing on an unusual paper size, tell Word about that up-front too. If you want nonstandard margins, set them early on. If you will be adding multiline headers or footers, it's a good idea to design those at the start also. When possible, enter text in the type sizes and styles you plan to use when printing.

With those decisions out of the way, you will have a better idea of how many pages your document will contain as you work. And you will have a good idea of its overall appearance.

Always make all of your formatting changes before creating a table of contents or index, since altered margin settings, type sizes, and a myriad of other things affect how much text will fit on a page, and thus which pages contain specific items.

PAGE SETUP

If you have only one printer, you can go directly to the Page Setup… command on Word's Format menu. (If you have multiple printers, use the *Print Setup…* command on the File menu to pick the printer you will use for your new project before visiting Page Setup on the Format menu.) The Page Setup dialog box looks like the boxes shown in Figure 14.2.

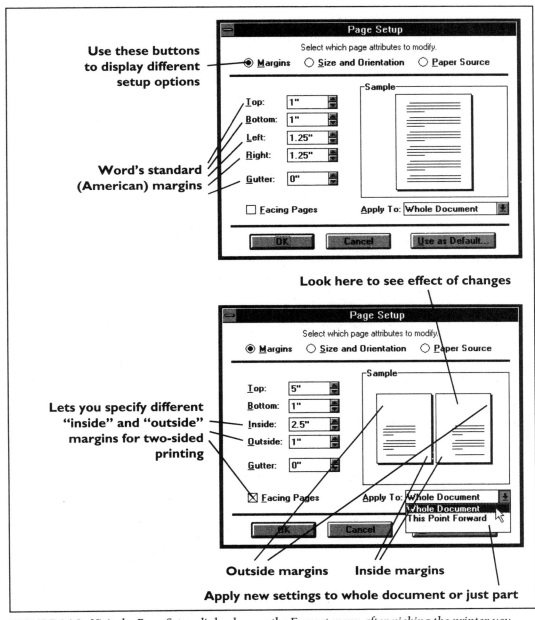

FIGURE 14.2 *Visit the Page Setup dialog box on the Format menu after picking the printer you will use.*

This is where you can define margins, paper size, and paper orientation. If your printer has multiple trays, you can use Page Setup to specify the tray(s) used.

Notice the three option buttons along the top of the dialog box. Use them to display different lists of setup options (margins, paper sources, or paper sizes and orientation). Usually, you will want to start with the Margins option as illustrated in Figure 14.1. Margins are white space surrounding your text.

You can either use Word's default settings (in America they are 1" top and bottom, 1.25" left and right) or enter your own margin preferences. Checking the Facing Pages box lets you specify different inside and outside margins for two-sided printing. In the bottom part of Figure 14.2, notice how the nonstandard margin settings look in the sample area.

PAPER SIZE

While still in the Page Setup box, choosing the Size and Orientation option button displays completely different options, as you can see in Figure 14.3.

A drop-down list lets you choose from a number of standard paper sizes compatible with your printer. It's also possible to specify nonstandard sizes here. Check your printer's documentation to discover its paper size limits. Type **in** or " for inches or **cm** to specify centimeters.

PAPER ORIENTATION

The orientation buttons let you specify long, skinny paper (Portrait printing) or wide, shallow paper (Landscape, or sideways printing). The sample area illustrates the two different options.

You can specify these choices for the entire document or just for selected pages.

PAPER SOURCES

If your printer has more than one paper tray, you may be able to specify different trays for all or parts of a document. For instance, if you have a dual-tray printer, you might be able to load letterhead in one tray and second sheets in the other. Then use the Paper Source dialog box to specify which

Available sizes vary with printer

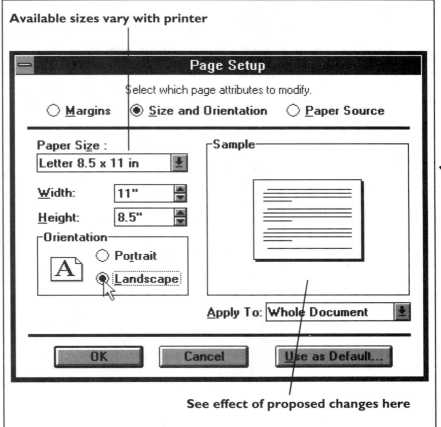

See effect of proposed changes here

FIGURE 14.3 *Use the Size and Orientation options in the Page Setup dialog box, reached from the Format menu, to specify paper size and orientation.*

tray to use for different parts of your document. Figure 14.4 shows a typical Paper Source dialog box. Check your printer manual for details.

DIFFERENT SETUPS FOR DIFFERENT PAGE RANGES

Normally, you'll use the same Page Setup information for all the pages in your document. But you can restrict most setup changes to specific pages or ranges of pages. For instance, if you have a three-page document, and want the first and last pages to print in portrait orientation and the middle page

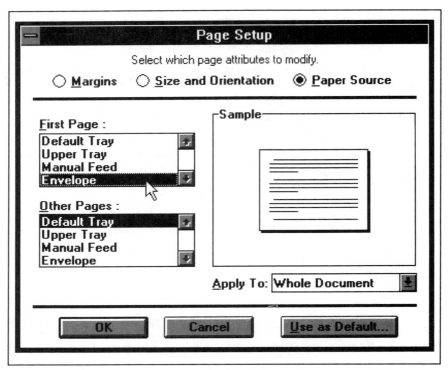

FIGURE 14.4 *Check your printer manual for information about multiple tray features supported by Word for Windows.*

in landscape, you can start with the whole document in portrait orientation. Then place the insertion point in page 2 at the point where you want landscape orientation to begin. Use Page Setup to switch to landscape. Use the "This Point Forward" choice on the Apply To menu. Then place the insertion point in page 3 of your document where you want to switch back to portrait, and use Page Setup to switch back, using the "This Point Forward" option once more. Use Print Preview to check your work.

The same general trick works with margin settings and many other document-wide formatting choices. Word will insert the necessary section marks to separate different portions of your document. They look like double, dark page-ending lines. If you delete a section mark, you will also delete the formatting information saved with them (page orientation, unusual margins, etc.). See Chapter 16 for more about sections.

DEFINING A DEFAULT PAGE SETUP

Clicking the Use as Default... button in a Page Setup dialog box will modify the template you are using to create your document. *Use this feature with care.* If you start a document using the NORMAL template, then set an oddball collection of margins, paper sizes, and page orientations as the default, the next document you start with the NORMAL template will have those same characteristics.

MARGINS, INDENTS, AND GUTTERS

By now you should know that margins are white space around the edges of your document. Ample margins enhance readability and increase a document's attractiveness. Besides specifying margins with the Page Setup dialog box, you can change them by dragging the Margin handles in Print Preview. It is also possible to change them by displaying, then dragging the margin mark on the ruler.

Generally, you will want to use the same margin settings document-wide, or at least for entire sections of a document. When you want to make temporary changes—to set off a paragraph or two, for instance— use indentations.

Indentations are additional white space added to margins. For instance, if you had 1" left and right margins on an 8.5"-wide page, there would be 6.5" left for text. If you indented selected paragraphs .25" on the right and left, the text in those paragraphs would be only 6" wide. You change indentation by selecting the paragraph(s) to be indented, then either dragging the indent markers on the ruler or specifying indent measurements in the Paragraph dialog box (described in a moment). The first line of each paragraph can have a different indentation than the remainder of the paragraph.

Gutters are additional white space added to the left margin in single-sided documents or added to the inside margins of two-sided documents. Ample gutters facilitate binding without obscuring the text. You specify gutters in the Margins portion of the Page Setup dialog box as shown in Figure 14.5. (You might find it just as easy to increase the left or inside margins, instead.)

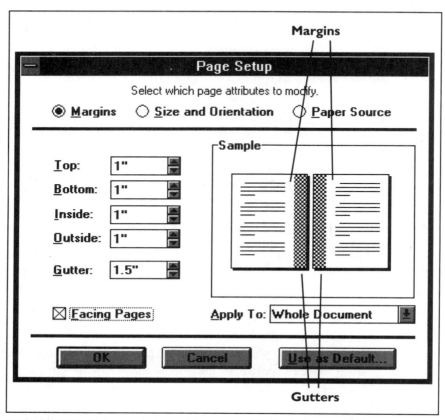

FIGURE 14.5 *Gutters are extra white space added to left or inside margins to facilitate binding.*

NEW LINES WITHOUT PARAGRAPH MARKS

Sometimes you will want to start a new *line* without starting a new *paragraph*. (You will see why in a moment.) This is done by holding down the Shift key when you press the Enter key. Instead of seeing the traditional paragraph mark at the end of lines entered this way, you will see a left-pointing arrow. But why bother?

Many users type all four or five lines of a letter's inside address this way. It makes it easier to move or reformat the address, since you need only place the insertion point anywhere in the address, rather than selecting all the lines. It's a handy tool in table entries, as you will see later. And, as you'll learn when we get to paragraph numbering and bulleting in a moment, there are other reasons to have Word treat multiple lines as a single paragraph.

Turn down the corner of this page or tuck away the Shift-Enter tip in a handy portion of your brain. Remember—to keep short lines together in the same paragraph, use Shift-Enter.

THE PARAGRAPH FORMATTING DIALOG BOX

While you can accomplish many paragraph formatting tricks with the Toolbar, ruler, and ribbon, you will occasionally need to visit the Paragraph dialog box illustrated in Figure 14.6. Reach it with the Paragraph... command on Word's Format menu.

There are drop-down menus for text alignment (left, center, etc.) and for line spacing (single, double, and so on). Check boxes let you specify pagination and line numbering requirements. You can also enter precise decimal indentation and spacing measurements in inches (**in**), centimeters (**cm**), points (**pt**), or picas (**pi**).

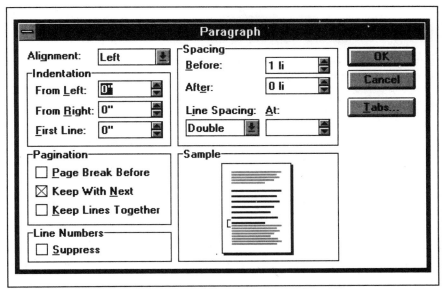

FIGURE 14.6 *Use the Paragraph dialog box for complex paragraph formatting.*

REMEMBER THE IMPORTANCE OF PARAGRAPH MARKS

The choices that you make in this dialog box are stored either with the paragraph mark at the end of the paragraph containing the insertion point, or with all the marks in paragraphs you've selected prior to making the changes. When you delete a paragraph mark, the paragraph settings disappear with it. A quick Undo can often cure this.

WHITE SPACE ABOVE AND BELOW PARAGRAPHS

Use the Spacing Before and After boxes to specify the amount of space above and below paragraphs. This is often a better way to add white space between paragraphs than pressing the Enter key, since it gives you a wide range of control over the amount of space. You specify space in lines, inches, centimeters, points, or picas.

LINE SPACING IN THE SAME PARAGRAPH

You can adjust the spacing between lines in the same paragraph with the *Line Spacing* and *At* choices in the Paragraph dialog box. By default, Word using single spacing that provides about six lines per inch. Unless prevented from doing so, it adjusts this interline spacing to accommodate large characters or graphics inserted in a line. For instance, if you double the size of one character in a paragraph, the spacing above and below that line in the paragraph will normally change to accommodate it.

It is possible to type spacing measurements in the At box within the Paragraph dialog box to specify your own custom line spacing dimension. And you can use the drop-down Line Spacing menu to tell Word if that's the minimum desired line spacing, or the exact desired line spacing.

The Line Spacing menu also offers the choices Auto, Single, 1.5 Lines, and Double.

Auto permits Word to change interparagraph line spacing as necessary to accommodate odd-sized characters or graphics. Word will also adjust spacing this way with single, double, and 1.5 line spacing selected. The Exactly choice overrides automatic spacing.

KEEPING LINES OR PARAGRAPHS TOGETHER

Sometimes it is important to keep lines or paragraphs together, or to force them to start them on a new page. Select the paragraphs of interest, then check the appropriate boxes to keep lines and/or paragraphs together on the same page. It is also possible to use this dialog box to force a paragraph always to start on a new page.

PARAGRAPH BORDERS

Word's border and shading features can add visual impact to a document, as you can see in Figure 14.7. These tools are also great for creating forms.

Start by selecting one or more paragraphs needing borders. Then reach the Border dialog box from the Border... command on Word's Format menu. Either choose one of the Preset borders like the Shadow choice used for the Edison quote, or construct your own border design by clicking in the border diagram.

For instance, the message form at the bottom of Figure 14.7 was created by selecting all of the paragraphs (with narrow margins) used to label the form (While You Were Out, To:, and so on). A medium-thick line was chosen by clicking in the Line area. Then the Preset Box choice was used to surround the form with the chosen medium-thick line. Before clicking OK, the thinner horizontal lines were added by choosing a thin line in the Line box, then clicking in the *center* of the Border diagram. This takes some practice—practice that will bear fruit in future Word operations. To remove border elements, click on them a second time. To completely remove borders, click on the *None* preset. Experiment. Practice. When you find combinations you like, they can be saved as Styles—something you'll learn about in Chapter 15.

PARAGRAPH SHADING

Notice the shaded "While You Were Out" portion of the form in Figure 14.7. It was added by clicking the *Shading* button in the Border Paragraphs dialog box.

When the Shading dialog box appears, specify the shading percentage or color choice you want, and click OK to apply it to selected paragraph(s). You'll need to experiment to find shades and colors that reproduce well on your printer. Just because they look good on your screen doesn't mean they

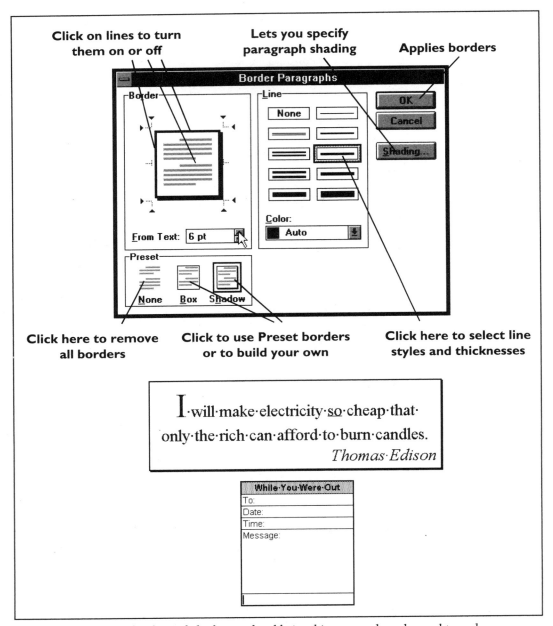

FIGURE 14.7 *Word's border and shading tools add visual impact and can be used to make drop-shadow box quotes and to construct forms.*

will look good when you print. Test before committing to shading choices. Light (10–40%) is often better than dark (50–90%).

Sometimes, combinations of character colors and shading can produce interesting results. For instance, if you flip ahead to Figure 14.13 you'll see an example of solid black paragraph shading with white lettering (the words "Effect" and "Shortcut"), producing "reverse" text.

CREATING BULLETED PARAGRAPHS (LISTS)

The bullet button on Word's Toolbar is a quick way to turn selected paragraphs into bulleted lists for emphasis, as illustrated in Figure 14.8.

This feature works best on paragraphs that are not already indented, since Word does its own automatic indenting. Notice how Word automatically inserts tabs when it makes bullet lists.

To change the size and shape of bullets, reach the windows shown in Figure 14.8 from the Bullets and Numbering... command on Word's Tools menu. Pick a bullet style that appeals to you, or click the New Bullet... button to pick a different one from the Symbol dialog box. When you get to the Bullets and Numbering dialog box, be sure to click on the Bullets option button to see the available bullet options.

PARAGRAPH AND LINE NUMBERS

There are several ways to number lines and paragraphs. It can be fairly frustrating to unnumber something that is improperly numbered, and the results of numbering will sometimes surprise you. Save your work immediately *before* you try any of the numbering techniques described here, and don't save again until you are absolutely certain that the numbering is correct. (If it is *not* correct, you can reload an unnumbered copy from your disk and try again.) Immediately after you've numbered, check your work! Undo (Ctrl-Z) can often rescue you if you spot the problem before doing anything else.

THE NUMBERED LIST TOOLBAR BUTTON

The Numbered list button on your Toolbar promises simple numbered lists. And it delivers, within reason. In theory, all you need do is select (highlight) multiple paragraphs that you want to number, then click the button.

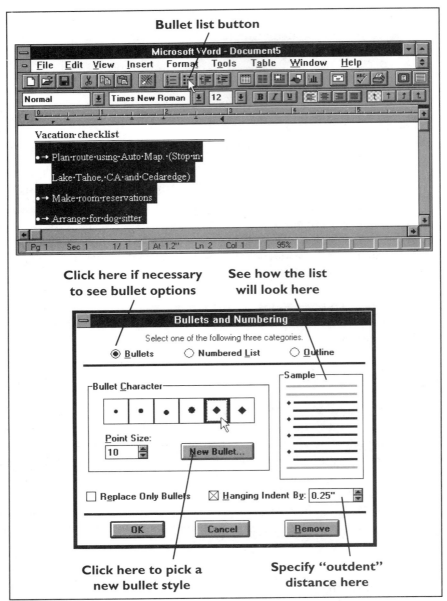

FIGURE 14.8 *Select multiple paragraphs and click the Toolbar's bullet button to create bullet lists. The resulting dialog box, reached with the Bullets and Numbering command on the Tools menu, lets you change bullet styles.*

As the top part of Figure 14.9 shows, Word automatically indents, numbers, and tabs selected paragraphs.

Unfortunately, it numbers *all* selected paragraphs, sometimes creating unexpected results. Notice what happened to the indented list of seafood within the selected paragraphs. Because there is a paragraph mark after "instance:" the shrimp line was numbered. The same goes for the clams and white fish lines. In fact, the quantities were treated as line numbers and *changed!* Those ingredients need to be listed on their own short lines, but treated as part of the paragraph above them.

If you use the Shift-Enter key combination after "Instance:," "shells," and "clams" instead of pressing the Enter key, the ingredients would still appear on separate *lines*, but they would be treated as part of the same *paragraph*. The bottom part of Figure 14.9 shows how this works.

While the "Shift-Enter" approach solves the numbering problem, you will still need to use tabs to *indent* the seafood list, since all lines in the same paragraph must use the same indentation settings.

Oh, yes. One other tip is in order here: Let the chowder simmer uncovered for at least 45 minutes, then add garlic plus other spices to taste, and simmer a minimum of 2 hours.

THE BULLETS AND NUMBERING DIALOG BOX

When the Toolbar number and bullet buttons leave you wanting more, the Bullets and Numbering dialog box often gives you improved control. Reach it from the Bullets and Numbering... command on Word's Tools menu. It looks like Figure 14.10.

Clicking the option buttons at the top of this box reveals one of three groups of options. You've probably already read about the Bullets options, and you will learn about Outline options in Chapter 20, so we'll concentrate on the Numbered List options here. If necessary, click on the Numbered List button to reveal the options shown in Figure 14.10.

The Format menu offers a variety of numbering styles, including traditional Arabic numerals, Roman numerals, letters, and so on.

The Separator menu lets you specify periods, dashes, brackets, and other characters to set off your numbers from the text. Watch the sample box as you work. Square brackets are shown in Figure 14.10.

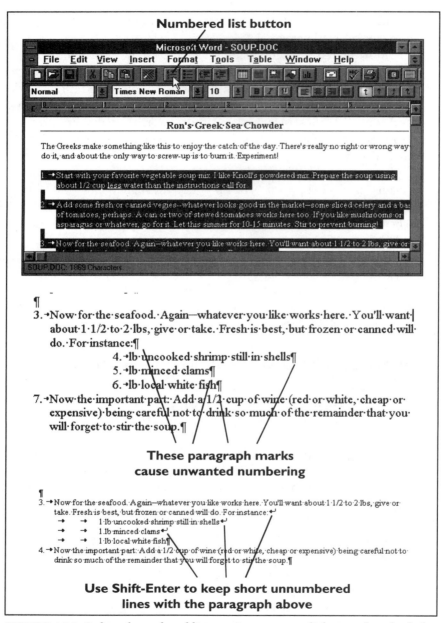

FIGURE 14.9 *Indented, numbered lists are just a mouse click away, but check the results carefully!*

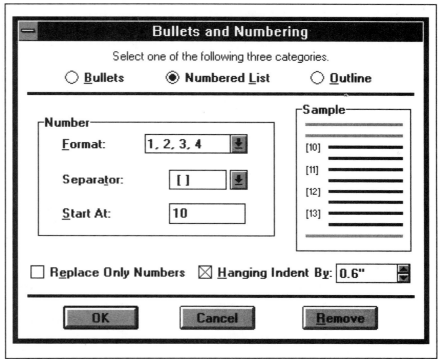

FIGURE 14.10 *Reach this box from the Bullets and Numbering... command on the Tools menu.*

You can specify a starting number on the Start At box. If you open the Bullets and Numbering dialog box with a numbered list selected, you will see the number of the first paragraph in the Start At selection.

It's possible to specify the hanging indent amount either by typing it in or using the up and down arrows on the Hanging Indent By box. If you remove the check mark, your numbered paragraphs will not have hanging indents.

REMOVING BULLETS AND PARAGRAPH NUMBERS

To remove bullets or numbers from paragraphs, select the text to be purged, then visit the Bullets and Numbering dialog box shown in

Figure 14.10. Pick the appropriate option button (Bullets, Numbered List, or Outline), then click the Remove button. If the lists were indented, and you want to remove the indents, remove the check from the hanging indent box.

UPDATING BULLETS AND PARAGRAPH NUMBERS

To update text containing bullets or numbered paragraphs (after inserting new items, for instance), select the text to be updated, then visit the Bullets and Numbering dialog box shown in Figure 14.10. Pick the desired option button (Bullets, Numbered List, or Outline), then click the OK button. With the Replace Only Numbers box checked, Word will only update paragraphs that previously had numbers or bullets—good to know if you have numbered and unnumbered paragraphs intermixed and want to keep things this way.

LINE NUMBERING

If you type legal documents, radio scripts, or other things that need line numbering, Word has a workable solution to most problems. Unfortunately, you'll need to flip to Print Preview or actually print your document to see line numbers, as they are not visible in Normal, Page Layout, or Outline views. They are quite easy to produce, however. The line numbering dialog box is reached via the Line Numbers... button, which is well hidden in the Section Layout dialog box. Start your journey at the Section Layout... choice on Word's Format menu.

When you click the Line Numbers... button, you will see a dialog box like the one at the top of Figure 14.11.

The choices are pretty much self-explanatory, except for From Text. That's where you specify the amount of space between the numbers and your text. The Continue button is used to number consecutively when connecting large documents that have been saved in chunks in several different files.

The bottom of Figure 14.11 shows a typical Print Preview of a line-numbered page. Incidentally, legal typists will be glad to learn that the double vertical lines between the numbers and text were easily added with the Border command.

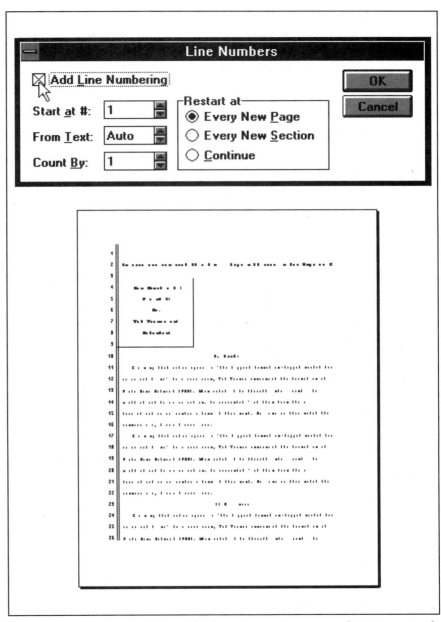

FIGURE 14.11 *Line numbering only shows in Print Preview and on your printed pages. Word provides many line numbering options.*

HYPHENATING TEXT

Hyphens are used to tie words together and to even out ragged line endings by overruling Word's desire to wrap entire words that don't fit to the next line. It's best to even-out line endings only after your document is otherwise perfect. Check that spelling. Fiddle with the margins. Get line and paragraph spacing the way you like them. Then and only then, before you create a table of contents or index, hyphenate. "Measure twice, cut once," Grandpa used to say.

MANUAL HYPHENATION

To force Word to print a hyphen (called a *hard hyphen*) in text—Corky Sherwood-Forest, for instance—press the unshifted minus key next to the zero key on your keyboard. To type a hyphen that also forces both words to stay on the same line (nonbreaking hyphens), press Ctrl-Shift-hyphen. The hyphen will look too big and will float above the words on-screen, but it will print properly and force the words to stay on the same line.

AUTOMATIC HYPHENATION
TO EVEN OUT RIGHT MARGINS

Assuming you've let Word install the necessary files for automatic hyphenation (it does so by default), you will be able to use the Hyphenation… command to even out your raggedy right margins and tighten up justified text.

When you issue the Hypenation… command (found on the Tools menu), you'll see a Hyphenation dialog box. Click the OK button to start. Beginning at the insertion point, Word will then scan your text looking for places to insert *optional* or *soft hyphens* (ones that will print only if needed to break the word at line's end).

Word proposes spots to hyphenate, which you can either accept or overrule. Word uses a large internal hyphenation dictionary, but occasionally breaks a rule or two. (There are international hyphenation dictionaries available. Contact Microsoft for details.)

As you can see from Figure 14.12, Word suggests a place to split the word both in the dialog box and in the text itself. Choose the Yes button to accept the suggestion and continue. Or move the hyphenation point with the right or left arrow keys, then press Enter to hyphenate and continue. The No button leaves a word as is. Cancel quits hyphenating.

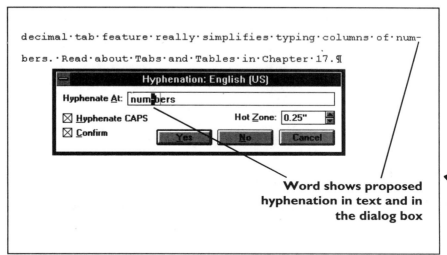

decimal·tab·feature·really·simplifies·typing·columns·of·num-
bers.·Read·about·Tabs·and·Tables·in·Chapter·17.¶

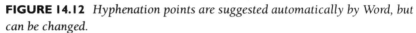

**Word shows proposed
hyphenation in text and in
the dialog box**

FIGURE 14.12 *Hyphenation points are suggested automatically by Word, but
can be changed.*

If you don't start hyphenating with the insertion point at the very beginning of your document, Word will ask if you want to continue when it
reaches the bottom.

REMOVING UNWANTED OPTIONAL HYPHENS

Even though optional (soft) hyphens won't print unless they can improve
a line ending, some people hate looking at them, particularly if their document is littered with extraneous ones caused by numerous revisions after
hyphenating. If you decide to remove a few, just delete them like any other
characters. To delete all optional hyphens, use the Replace... command
described in Chapter 20. (Replace optional hyphens with nothing.)

CHARACTER FORMATTING

Characters are the letters, numbers, and symbols you enter from the
keyboard, then see on the screen and print. Word lets you use a wide variety
of typestyles and also permits you to easily alter the appearance of characters. You do this by selecting characters of interest and altering them with

the ribbon, various keyboard shortcuts, and the Character dialog box reached with the Character... command on Word's Format menu. You can do the following:

- Select from a variety of fonts (type designs)
- Increase and decrease the size of characters
- Make characters bold
- Italicize characters
- Strike through characters
- Underline or double-underline words and, optionally, spaces
- Change words to all caps or small caps
- Change the color of characters
- Make superscript or subscript characters
- Expand or compress the spacing between characters
- Designate characters as hideable
- See the effect of your decisions on-screen

Figure 14.13 shows examples of many of the character formatting changes you can make. The figure also lists the keyboard shortcuts for character formatting. Additional shortcuts are listed on the inside covers of this book.

REMOVING CHARACTER FORMATTING

Most character formatting keyboard shortcuts and Toolbar buttons toggle. That is to say, the first time you press Ctrl-B or click the Bold button, text will become boldface. Pressing Ctrl-B or clicking a depressed Bold button while bold text is selected will remove the bold formatting. This also works with italics, underlines, and so on.

The keyboard shortcut Ctrl-spacebar will often remove added character formatting, returning it to the appearance called for by the style of the text. (See Chapter 15 for more about styles.)

Effect	Shortcut
Bold	Ctrl+b
Italic	Ctrl+i
Single (continuous) underline	Ctrl+u
Word underline	Ctrl+w
Double underline	Ctrl+d
all caps off ALL CAPS ON	
Small Caps Off SMALL CAPS ON	
Super script	
Sub script	
~~Strikethrough~~	
Colors	
Spacing: E x p a n d e d Condensed	

FIGURE 14.13 *Characters can be formatted in many ways.*

COMBINING CHARACTER FORMATS

Character formats can be combined. For instance, it is possible to make bold, underlined, italicized characters. Frequently, character formatting can be used with other Word features to create unusual effects. For example, the reversed top line in Figure 14.13 was made by changing the color of the characters to white and using the paragraph shading feature to create a black (100%) background.

While you can do a great deal of character formatting with keyboard shortcuts and the ribbon, sometimes you'll need to visit the Character dialog box shown in Figure 14.14. Reach it with the Character... command on the Format menu.

FONTS AND SIZES

The fonts available to you will depend on your chosen printer and on which fonts you've installed under Windows. If your printer uses plug-in font cartridges, they too will affect your available choices. Most newer printer documentation includes tips for Windows printing. If you have an

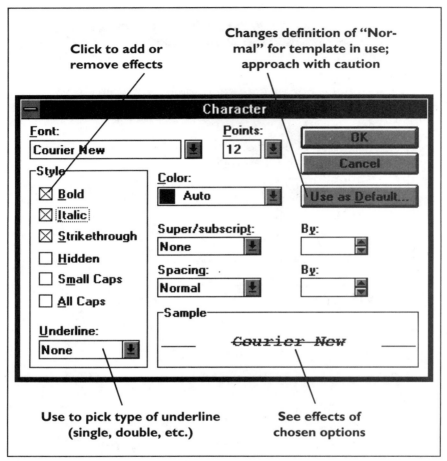

FIGURE 14.14 *The Character dialog box offers many formatting options.*

older printer, contact its maker; the company may have published tip sheets for Windows users.

Which Fonts Can You Use?

Word can use any fonts your printer supports, assuming you've properly installed the fonts in Windows. Usually you can see and print Modern,

Roman, and Script fonts on most printers. You can purchase and install additional fonts in Windows. When you use Word's pull-down ribbon Character dialog box font menus, you may see additional printer fonts (indicated by small icons of printers). Figure 14.15 shows five printer fonts. TrueType fonts, if installed, are also supported by most printers. These have TT next to them in font lists.

Screen vs. Printer Fonts

There are actually two kinds of fonts—screen fonts and printer fonts. If you have both installed, you will see the fonts listed in Word font lists. And your on-screen document and a printed copy of it should be nearly identical. That is to say, a paper document will usually have the same line and page endings as you see on-screen. You stand the best chance of producing identical screen and paper documents when using TrueType fonts.

It's a good idea to have the "Line Breaks and Fonts As Printed" option checked in the View Category of the Options dialog box. (This is the Word default setting.)

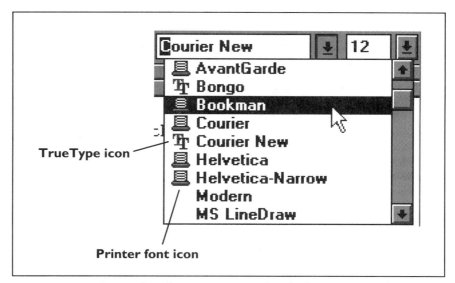

FIGURE 14.15 *Printer fonts have printer icons beside them. TrueType fonts are indicated with TT.*

Font Differences on Different Computers

When using a second computer to edit or print a document that was created on another, you will need to make certain that both have the same fonts installed if you expect identical page and line endings. This often means that you will also need identical or similar printers at both ends, as well.

Font Sizes

Word's drop-down size lists indicate the available sizes for the chosen font and printer. Sizes are indicated in a traditional typographic unit, points (**pt**). A point is $1/72$nd of a vertical inch. Thus, a 72-point "Q" is 1" tall, from the top of the letter to the bottom of the "tail" stroke. Word supports point sizes from 4 to 127 in half-point increments. (You will probably not have all these point sizes for most fonts on your computer.)

You can change point sizes by first selecting text, then choosing a new size from a size menu (either on the ribbon or in the Character dialog box). You can also enter the desired size into the size box with your keyboard (select the type size box on the ribbon and type **12**, for instance).

You can increase or decrease the size of selected text using keyboard shortcuts, as well. To increase to the next available size, press Ctrl-F2. Use Ctrl-Shift-F2 to decrease the size.

CHARACTER SPACING

To increase or decrease the amount of space between characters, select the characters you want to affect, then visit the Character dialog box (pick Character... on Word's Format menu). Pull down the spacing menu. Choose Expanded to add space between characters or Condensed to push characters closer together. Word will propose a point size to use for expanding or condensing. You can accept or change the amount of space. Watch the Sample portion of the dialog box. It will demonstrate the effect as you experiment with different settings.

SUPERSCRIPTS AND SUBSCRIPTS

To place some characters above or below the baseline, select the characters you want to affect, then open the Character dialog box (pick Character... on

Word's Format menu). Pull down the Super/subscript menu. Choose Super-script, Subscript, or None. Superscript pushes characters up, Subscript pushes them down. Word will propose a point size to use. You can accept or change the proposed height. Watch the Sample portion of the dialog box. It will demonstrate the effect.

COLOR

Even if you can't display color, you can print it on color-capable printers, plotters, and film output devices. Word supports 16 colors. Select characters to colorize, then visit the Character dialog box and pick the desired color to be displayed and printed.

HIDDEN TEXT

By formatting text as hidden, you can choose whether or not to display or print it. (Think of it as "hideable" text, if that helps.) Use hideable text to make notes to yourself or others that you might not want to print, or want to print sometimes and suppress other times. Hidden text is also used when creating index and table of contents entries, as you will see later.

Select text and format it with the *Hidden* box in the Character dialog box, or use the Ctrl-H keyboard shortcut. When visible on screen, hidden text is indicated with light dotted underlines.

To display and hide on-screen hideable text, use the Hidden Text check box in the View category of the Options dialog box. (Reach it with the Options... choice on the Tools menu.) This check box is overridden by the View All check box.

Hideable text can be printed or not, regardless of whether you can see it on your screen. Use the Options... button on the Print dialog box to reach printing options. Then place a check mark in the Hidden Text option box to print hideable text. Remove the X to suppress printing.

Hideable text will affect page and line endings—*and* your index, *and* your table of contents! Therefore, it's best to remove it or convert it to regular text before final pagination, index creation, and so on. Word's Replace... command can help you remove or modify hidden text. (See Chapter 20.)

Don't accidentally format page breaks or section breaks as hidden text. This can cause mysterious page and section breaks.

ALL CAPS AND SMALL CAPS

The All Caps character format causes Word to display and print characters as uppercase letters regardless of how they were typed. The Small Caps feature converts lowercase letters to uppercase letters in a slightly smaller point size, while leaving uppercase letters in their original size and case—a very hip effect these days.

ESTABLISHING DEFAULT CHARACTER SETTINGS

Approach this button with caution, particularly if you are a beginner. The *Use as Default...* button in the Character dialog box will look at the character formatting decisions you've made in this dialog box, and will change the definition of "normal" characters for whichever *template* you are using at the time. If you happen to be using the NORMAL template and define bold, italic, double-underscored Wingdings as the new default, thereafter any new documents you start typing with the NORMAL template will use the Wingdings font and will exhibit the bold, italic, double-underscored attributes you've specified.

YOUR TURN

Even if you didn't make the Greek sea chowder described in Figure 14.9, you've been give a lot to digest in this chapter. It is critical that you understand paragraph and character formatting before you can use and understand styles, glossaries, and the other tools described from here on. Take some time to practice what you've learned so far. Then see how to further automate your work when we explore styles and glossaries in the next chapter.

15

Styles, Glossaries, and Templates for Speed and Consistency

You may find that you can use Word without knowing a lot about its styles or glossaries or templates. But they can make you much more productive. Learning about *styles* and *style sheets* and Word's *standard styles*, as well as how to apply *normal* and *base styles*, can save you hundreds or even thousands of hours. And, if you work with other people on large, complex projects, or if your organization wants a "uniform" look for all of its printed documents, styles and templates are essentials. Consume this chapter a little at a time. Try a few style experiments when you are not working on a rush project. Some of the concepts may seem confusing and frustrating at first. It will all make sense sooner than you think.

STYLES AND STYLE SHEETS

Styles are collections of paragraph and character formatting decisions that you make and save, using meaningful names. Styles make it easy for you to reuse complex paragraph formats without laboriously recreating them each time. Each *document* has its own collection of styles. A document's collection of styles is called the document's *style sheet*.

You need not use all available styles in a document. The promotional piece in Figure 15.1 contains eight *styles*, but only four are used.

All of the available style names for a document appear in the drop-down list at the left edge of the ribbon. When you place the insertion point in a paragraph, the name of the style that has been used to format that paragraph appears in the style name box.

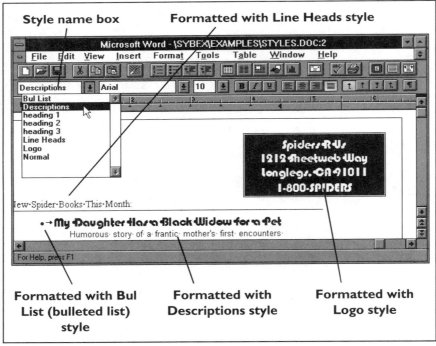

FIGURE 15.1 *This letter contains eight styles.*

Some styles in this example are very simple. For instance, the style *Line Heads* is just like Word's normal default style (flush left, single-spaced text in the 10-point Times Roman font), but it also has a thin line under the text. This was accomplished first by using Word's Border command to modify the paragraph style, then by naming and saving the resulting new style.

The most complex collection of formatting tricks in Figure 15.1 was used to create the Logo style. It started out as normal text. The Font was changed to Bingo. Characters were changed from black to white. The left and right indents were changed to place part of the text in the right margin and to indent the text and paragraph borders about 4" from the left margin. Border and border shading changes were also made to the paragraph. Then this whole laundry list of steps was saved as a style called Logo.

You can have up to 220 styles per document. Word comes with a number of built-in styles. You will find creating and naming your own styles to be very easy, though developing clever style strategies takes more forethought. Here's how it all works.

DEFINING STYLES FROM THE RIBBON

With the ribbon in view (pick Ribbon from the View menu if necessary), you can quickly define new styles. Create a sample paragraph with the desired characteristics. Place the insertion point in this formatted paragraph, then double-click in the style box (the name portion of the drop-down style name list). As shown in Figure 15.2, the text in the style box will be highlighted, indicating that you can type a replacement style name. Type a meaningful style name and press Enter. Word will save the style information and add the new name to the style sheet. From then on you will see the new style on the drop-down style list for the current document.

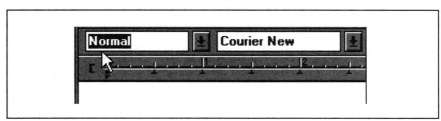

FIGURE 15.2 *To define styles from the ribbon, place the insertion point in the properly formatted paragraph of interest, then double-click in the style box. Type a new style name and press Enter.*

STYLE NAME CONSIDERATIONS

Style names can be up to 24 characters long and contain any characters except the backslash (\). Spaces are permitted. Word for Windows ignores upper- and lowercase differences in style names.

Try to be consistent when naming similar styles in different documents. You'll learn more about this later in the chapter.

APPLYING STYLES FROM THE RIBBON

Once you've defined styles, you can easily apply them to one or more paragraphs. Either place the insertion point in a paragraph or select multiple paragraphs, then scroll through the drop-down style list to pick the desired style. Your text will be reformatted using the selected style. That's all there is to it.

APPLYING STYLES FROM THE KEYBOARD

Instead of pointing to style names on the drop-down list with your mouse, you can apply styles by pressing the Ctrl-S keyboard shortcut. The style box will be highlighted. Either type a style name or use the up and down arrow keys to highlight the one you want. Press Enter. Your paragraph(s) will be reformatted. (If you like this technique, assign short style names to speed your keyboard entries.)

The Repeat function key (F4) works when applying styles. After you apply a style once, you can immediately move the insertion point to random paragraphs, pressing the F4 function each time to apply the new style only where needed.

Assigning Keyboard Shortcuts to Styles

To assign keyboard shortcuts to your favorite styles, place the insertion point in the style. Open the Style dialog box by selecting Style... from the Format menu and specifying the key combination you want to use (like Ctrl-Shift-N for Normal). Use the Ctrl + Shift + Key boxes shown in Figure 15.3.

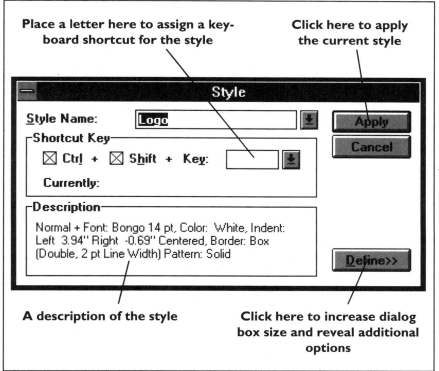

FIGURE 15.3 *Reach the Style dialog box from the Format menu or use the Ctrl-S shortcut.*

THE STYLE DIALOG BOX

As is often the case with Word, there is a dialog box for styles, which contains powerful features not found on the ribbon. Pick Style… from the Format menu to reach the Style dialog box. You will see something like Figure 15.3.

This dialog box lets you define new styles, as well as rename, explore, list, or delete existing styles. It serves other purposes, too, as you will soon see.

DEFINING STYLES IN THE STYLE DIALOG BOX

To define a style via the Style dialog box, place the insertion point in a paragraph containing the desired format, then open the Style dialog box.

Click the *Define>>* button to expand the dialog box, revealing the extra options shown in Figure 15.4.

Enter a legal style name. In Figure 15.4 a new style named Line Heads has been defined and is described. You can also bring up other dialog boxes from this one by clicking on the appropriate button (Character..., Border..., and so on). This makes it possible for you to modify style elements before you finalize the style. You will learn more about the *Based On* and *Next Style* lists in a moment.

PRINTING OUT A STYLE SHEET

It is often useful to have a printed list of styles and their descriptions. This can help you (and others) keep things consistent in a large organization, and

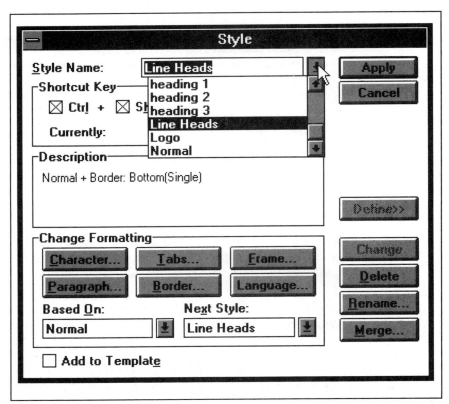

FIGURE 15.4 *Click the Define>> button to expand the Style dialog box.*

it can help in troubleshooting formatting problems in complex documents. To print style information, choose Print… from Word's File menu and use the drop-down Print menu to select *Styles*, as shown in Figure 15.5.

WHEN AND WHERE STYLES ARE SAVED

Styles are saved with your document, and they are only saved when you save the document. The collection of styles for a document is called a *style sheet*. It is not a separate file, but rather an integral part of your document's file.

BASING ONE STYLE UPON ANOTHER

This time-saver is often a source of bewilderment for newcomers. It occasionally catches old pros off-guard too. Word lets you "build" upon styles, or "base" one upon another. You've seen examples of this in the promotional piece at the beginning of the chapter. The Line Heads style is built by starting with the Normal style and adding instructions to create a custom paragraph

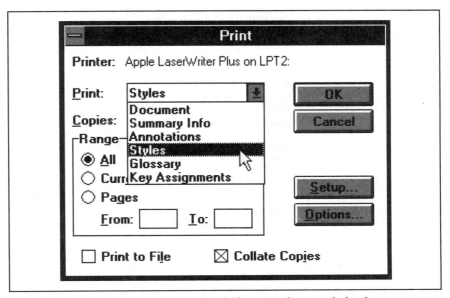

FIGURE 15.5 *You can print Styles details from Word's Print dialog box.*

border. In other words, the style Normal is a *base style*, on which you can base a Line Heads style.

If you change the Normal style so that it uses the Helvetica font instead of Times Roman, any paragraphs formatted with the Line Heads style will change to Helvetica, too. That's the good news and the bad news.

Word "watches" you as you develop new styles and bases new styles on the style you modify. Unless you are careful, you can create quite a chain reaction this way. Experienced users try to create one or two "base styles" and tie most of the rest of their styles to those base styles, rather than basing each new style on the previous style.

What's the appropriate base style? That will vary with your project. At first, you may find it less confusing to base all of your styles upon Normal. Then experiment and observe carefully, perhaps printing out the results for review and refinement. You will soon learn from experience which combinations work best for you. Newcomers, beware: play with *copies* of important documents, especially if it is ten minutes before the Federal Express deadline.

The Style dialog box lets you force specific styles to be based upon other styles of your choosing. Pick the appropriate base style from the drop-down Based On menu, found near the bottom of the Style dialog box. Figure 15.6 shows a style based on Bul List.

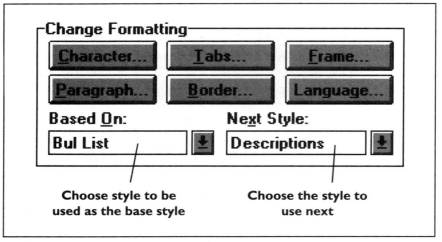

FIGURE 15.6 *Word lets you specify which style each other style is based upon. You can also determine which style is applied next.*

SWITCHING AUTOMATICALLY TO DIFFERENT STYLES

Frequently, you can predict the order in which styles will be used. If you always place descriptions under headings, for instance, you might specify a style called Descriptions as the Next Style. Then, whenever you finish typing a heading (by pressing Enter), Word will switch to the Description style.

The Style dialog box lets you specify which style Word will "flip to" when you finish typing a paragraph and press Enter. Frequently, you want the next paragraph to be in the same style as the one preceding. This is the default condition when creating styles.

But, as you can see in Figure 15.6, it is possible to specify different "next styles" by choosing a style in the style list and picking a next style from the drop-down *Next Style* list. In our example, Word will switch to the Descriptions style when you press the Enter key after typing in the style being defined.

If you've defined a style this way, then need to type multiple identically-formatted paragraphs or short lines like the seafoood list in Chapter 14, you should override the automatic switching by using Shift-Enter to terminate all but the last line in the paragraph you are typing. This way, Word treats all of the lines as one continuous paragraph and doesn't prematurely switch styles.

WORD'S STANDARD STYLES

Word's designers have created many "standard" styles that are used by its features that automatically generate footnotes, outlines, indexes, tables of contents, page numbers, headers, and footers. You will read about these special styles in other chapters of this book. Most of them do not normally appear in your style sheet until you use the associated features in a document.

It is possible to view such styles and to force Word to place them in your style sheet by using this trick: open the Style dialog box, then press Ctrl-Y and scroll through the Style Name list in the Style dialog box to see and use the styles.

MODIFYING WORD'S STANDARD STYLES

You can *modify* standard styles, change their base styles and, with few exceptions, otherwise treat them like the custom styles you create. However, you cannot *delete* standard styles, and you cannot *rename* them. Standard styles are all based on Normal, therefore changes to the Normal style (or your Word default font) will affect all standard styles.

MANUAL FORMATTING AND STYLES

It is possible to override or embellish styles with additional character formatting. You already know how to make these character-based changes from the ribbon, keyboard, and Format menu commands.

REAPPLYING/REDEFINING STYLES

If you make any style changes to a paragraph, then ask Word to apply the exisiting style to that same paragraph (applying Normal to an already Normal paragraph, for instance), you will be visited by a strange and powerful dialog box. It is shown in Figure 15.7.

This box serves two purposes. First, it lets you reapply a style to a paragraph that you have inadvertently messed up. Suppose you accidentally dragged the first-line-indent marker in a Normal paragraph, and as a result the paragraph no longer looks like the others. By choosing the Normal style again from the ruler, you will get a chance to "reapply" your Normal style and *repair* the errant paragraph.

The second use of this dialog box is to let you quickly *redefine* a style. Suppose you hate the flush-left first-line indent that Word uses for Normal text. Solution: change the indent in any one Normal style paragraph, then pick Normal from the Style list. Click on the Redefine button, and click OK. Word will redefine the Normal style using the new indent from your sample

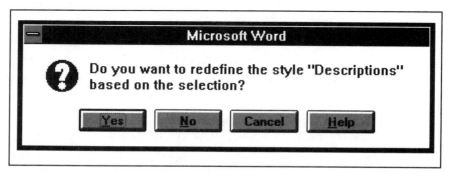

FIGURE 15.7 *Word wants to know if you indeed wish to modify the paragraph or the style itself.*

paragraph. All of your Normal paragraphs and all paragraphs *based on* Normal will be changed. This is why it is advisable to make very few changes to the Normal style. If you like text with indented first lines, for instance, consider creating a style called Body rather than changing the Normal style to include an indent.

DELETING STYLES

You cannot delete Word's standard styles, but you can remove the custom ones you've created. Unwanted styles can be deleted by selecting them in the Styles dialog box's drop-down list and clicking on the Delete button, located in the big version of the Style dialog box. All paragraphs formatted with a deleted style will revert to the document's Normal style.

RENAMING STYLES

Styles can be renamed in the big version of the Style dialog box. (Choose Style... from the Format menu, then click the Define>> button.) Select the style name you want to change from the drop-down Style Name menu. Click the Rename... button. You'll be asked for a new name. Click OK when you've changed the name. Click Apply and OK to apply the change. The style name changes, but the style remains intact.

FINDING AND REPLACING STYLES

Style-change junkies, rejoice! Word lets you search for and replace styles. For instance, you can change all Heading 1 paragraphs to Heading 2. Word's Replace feature is fully described in Chapter 20.

USING THE SAME STYLES IN DIFFERENT DOCUMENTS

After you've spent time setting up complex styles, it would be nice to be able to reuse them in new projects. Word provides several ways to do this. For repetitive tasks, consider setting up templates containing styles, glossary entries, and other reusable items. (Templates are discussed later in this chapter.)

If you have just a style or two you want to copy from one document (the source) to another (the destination), select some text from the paragraph(s) containing the style(s) of interest, *being sure to include the paragraph mark* associated with that text, and paste it into the destination document needing the new style(s). In fact, all you really need to copy and paste is the paragraph mark. The style information will follow. Be aware, however, that if the destination document has a style name identical to the style being copied from the source, the destination document will reformat the incoming text rather than take on the new style. Moreover, if you copy more than 50 styles at once, the source document's entire style sheet will be automatically copied to the destination document.

Other Word commands that exchange style information will bring over styles as necessary. For instance, Subscribe, Link, Glossary, and Paste Special all attempt to bring styles with them.

It is also possible to "merge" different style sheets, a process that copies unique styles from one document to another and modifies styles with identical names. There are a few land mines to tiptoe around.

First, you must save any changes to the source document before attempting a merge. This "records" the current styles for the source document. Next, inspect the source and destination documents for possible style name problems. Consider printing out both style sheets and comparing them before you merge.

When you merge, styles on the *destination* style sheet with names identical to those on the *source* style sheet will take on the characteristics of the source style sheets. Styles not found on the destination style sheet will be correctly imported from the source style sheet.

Here's how to do it. With styles properly named and saved, work in the destination document. Open the big version of the Styles dialog box and then click Merge…. Select the source document from the resulting Open dialog box, and click it open. Word will update the destination document as described above.

When you are sure that the desired results have been achieved, save the destination document to record the changes to its style sheet.

STYLE TIPS

- Establish organization-wide style sheets and style-naming conventions. This will make it easy for you and others to work on projects together.

- Use the "Space Before" and "Space After" paragraph features, along with the Shift-Enter key combination, rather than creating white space by pressing Enter several times.

- When experimenting with styles, work on document copies. This is particularly important for new users working on complex documents that contain interrelated styles.

- Combine styles with the power of Word's glossary and template features.

- Establish one or two base styles for complex documents. They need not be based on Word's Normal style, particularly if the look of the document is radically different from your usual work.

- Assign keyboard shortcuts to your favorite styles, and print a list.

- Don't mess with the Normal style too much, particularly if you have based a number of other styles upon it.

GLOSSARIES

Imagine the ease of simply pressing a couple of keys to call up and insert entire paragraphs, or full mailing addresses, or properly formatted letter closings including your signature. Those are just a few of the things Word's glossary feature will help you do. It can also save and recall graphics, memo distribution lists, tab settings, and just about any element of a Word document. Creating new glossary items is quick and easy. Each saved item is called an *entry*. Collections of entries are called *glossaries* or *glossary files*. Glossary files are saved to disk. You can have different glossaries for different tasks, and switch between glossaries as necessary. It is also possible to *merge* entries from different glossary files.

DEFINING YOUR OWN GLOSSARY ENTRIES

To create glossary entries, simply select (highlight) all of the things in a document that you want to define as a glossary entry, then call up the *Glossary dialog box*. Use the Glossary... command on Word's Edit menu. Your screen will look something like Figure 15.8.

In this example, an entire letter closing has been selected. It contains three lines of text, a severe left indent, and a scanned signature that has previously

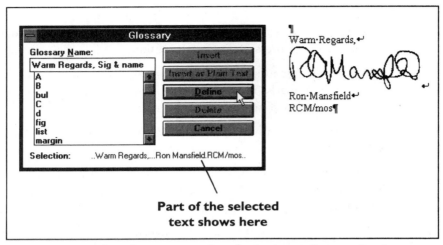

**Part of the selected
text shows here**

FIGURE 15.8 *Define glossary entries by selecting items, then opening the
Glossary dialog box from the Edit menu.*

been pasted from the scrapbook using Word's graphics capabilities. All of
these elements will become one glossary entry that can be quickly recalled.

Assign a meaningful name of up to 31 characters and spaces (**Warm
Regards, Sig & name**, in the example), then click on the Define button to
add the entry to your glossary.

If the document you are working on was based on the NORMAL template,
your entry will simply be saved at this point.

If, however, your document is based on a template other than NORMAL,
you will see a dialog box like the one in Figure 15.9.

You'll learn about templates in a moment. For now, remember that
choosing Global makes glossary entries available in all of your documents.
The Template option restricts the availability of glossary entries to specific
documents.

INSERTING GLOSSARY
ENTRIES IN YOUR DOCUMENTS

Once an item is in your glossary, there are several ways to paste it into *any*
document you are working on.

The obvious method is to place the insertion point where you want the
glossary item to appear, then open the Glossary dialog box. Highlight

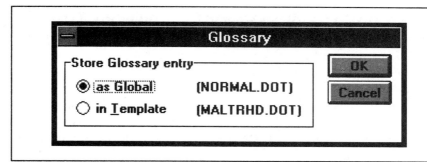

FIGURE 15.9 *Word lets you use glossary entries globally or just in selected documents.*

the glossary entry of interest (scroll first, if necessary), then click the Insert button, or simply double-click on the entry name.

The desired entry will appear at the insertion point in your document and the Glossary dialog box will vanish. The entry will contain the formatting used when the entry was originally created and saved.

If you click the Insert as Plain Text button, instead, Word will insert unformatted text, which will take on the style of the paragraph receiving the text.

INSERTING GLOSSARY ENTRIES FROM THE KEYBOARD

There's a time-saving keyboard trick for inserting glossary entries. Place the insertion point where you want it. Type the glossary name and press the F3 function key. The glossary entry will replace its name in your document.

CHANGING AND DELETING GLOSSARY ENTRIES

To delete glossary entries, open the Glossary dialog box, highlight the undesirable entry, and click the Delete button.

To modify an entry, insert the item needing work into your document, make the necessary changes, and select it. Open the Glossary dialog box, highlight the corresponding entry name, then click Define. A dialog box pops up, asking "Do you want to redefine the glossary?" Click yes. Your modified entry will *replace* the old one.

HOW AND WHERE GLOSSARY ENTRIES ARE STORED

Glossary entries aren't saved until you quit Word (ugh!). If you've spent a long time creating valuable entries, consider quitting and restarting Word to ensure that the entries are properly saved before a power failure or other malady.

If the document you are working on was created using the NORMAL template, new and edited glossary changes will be saved with the same template (the file name is NORMAL.DOT), making the glossary items available to all new documents.

If you created a document with a template other than NORMAL, you will see a dialog box like the one in Figure 15.9 whenever you create a new entry.

This dialog box lets you make the glossary entry globally available or lets you restrict it to a particular template. You'll learn more about templates shortly.

COLLECTING ITEMS WITH THE SPIKE

The spike is a special glossary feature that lets you cut and collect multiple chunks of text and graphics, then insert them all at once at the designated insertion point. Think of it as a Clipboard that does not get overwritten each time you place something new on it.

Select an item you want to add to the spike and press Ctrl-F3. The selected item will disappear. Select another item and spike it (Ctrl-F3). Continue until you have everything you want on the spike. Move the insertion point to the desired location and do one of the following. To place a copy of the spike's contents at the insertion point, type **spike** and press the F3 function key; the spike's contents will replace the word "spike," and remain available on the spike for later use. To paste the spike's contents and empty it, position the insertion point and press Ctrl-Shift-F3.

GLOSSARY ENTRIES AND STYLES

Remember that all global glossary entries are available, regardless of what document you are working on. Thus, glossary entries you've *created* in one document may use styles that do not exist in the document you are currently working on. When this happens, Word will add the necessary style to the current document's style sheet.

The usual cautions apply regarding different styles with the same style name and the importance of basing one style on another when you insert glossary entries containing style information. See Chapter 17 for details.

PRINTING GLOSSARY ENTRY LISTS

It is possible to print glossary items for review and ready reference. Choose Glossary from the drop-down Print menu in Word's Print dialog box.

TEMPLATES

As you probably know by now, Word templates are document files saved to disk with the file extension .DOT. Think of them as partially-completed documents that can eliminate most of the repetitive clerical steps you do regularly. In fact, it is impossible to create a new Word document without using a template. That's why you always see the Template dialog box when you start a new project. Beginners usually opt for the NORMAL template for early projects.

Templates contain their own Page Setup information, as well as glossaries and style sheets. It's possible to have templates change the Word workplace as well. For instance, templates can bring modified Toolbars and macros with them. Microsoft provides a number of templates that you can use as is or can modify. You can also create your own. Let's start by looking at the Microsoft-provided NORMAL template you've already used.

THE NORMAL TEMPLATE

This is where Word stores all "Globally" available features, like glossary entries that you want to make available for every document. It is also where Word gets its standard Toolbar configuration, the Normal style, and so on.

MAKING YOUR OWN TEMPLATES

To make your own templates based on the NORMAL template, use the New... command on Word's File menu. Choose the Template option button. When you click OK, Word opens a new untitled document called Template1 (or Template2, or whatever).

Start your new document. Create and import any necessary styles, boilerplate text, page setup specifications, and so on. Create and test macros if you wish. You can even use the Options… command on the Tools menu to change things like tools on the Toolbar.

When you are satisfied with your work, use Word's Save command. Word will add the .DOT extension to your document name for you.

You can also open existing documents and save them (or variants of them) as templates. Open the document, make desired changes, and use Word's Save As… command. Pick Document Template (*.DOT) from the Save File as Type drop-down menu.

EDITING TEMPLATES

You can open templates as if they were documents, then change and save them. Use Word's Open command with the *List Files of Type* drop-down list displaying *Document Template (*.DOT)*. Templates are usually stored with WIN.EXE, typically in the WINWORD directory. Make the changes to your template and use the regular Save command. Word will add the .DOT extension and save the template properly.

ASSIGNING A DIFFERENT TEMPLATE TO A DOCUMENT

You can always see which template a document is attached to by choosing Template… on Word's File menu. You'll see a dialog box something like that shown in Figure 15.10.

You can change the template that a document is attached to by picking a different template from the drop-down list. What happens next depends upon a number of factors.

If the new template you choose has different tools in the Toolbar—different glossary items, and keyboard shortcuts, for instance—you will see these changes when you click OK.

The appearance and content of your document will not change, however. For instance, if the new template contains text or headers or footers, they will not be added to your current document. Page Setup information (margins, page orientation, and the like) also remains unchanged.

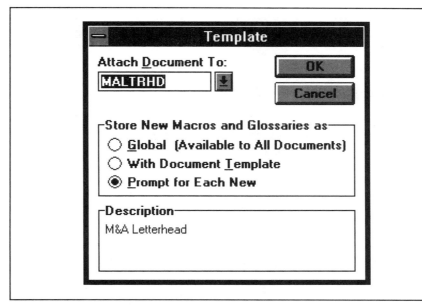

FIGURE 15.10 *The Template... command lets you see and change template attachments.*

MICROSOFT-SUPPLIED TEMPLATES

Chapter 19 describes and demonstrates many of the powerful templates shipped and installed with Word. You can base your own new templates on modified versions of these, if you like.

Now, let's turn to headers, footers, sections, page numbers, and footnotes.

16

Headers, Footers, Sections, Page Numbers, and Footnotes

Headers and footers are places to put repetitive information in a document's top and bottom margins. (Don't confuse *footers* with *footnotes*, which are quite different.) When you think of *sections*, you probably imagine traditional book sections—collections of several related chapters, for instance. As you'll soon see, Word's section features can help you organize large projects this way, of course, but they do much more. Word sections are designed to let you change major formatting features at places you decide in your document. Adding *page numbers* to Word documents can be as simple as a click. Other powerful numbering features take more time and effort, but produce impressive results. Word's *footnote* features make the program popular in legal, academic, and technical communities. Here, too, a simple mouse click or two gets the basic job done, while other features let you fine-tune your work.

HEADERS AND FOOTERS

You can have headers and footers print something simple on each page like your name, using the document's default style, or something complex like a graphic. Stylized text, dates, and automatically generated page numbers can all be included in headers or footers.

Headers and footers can be identical on all pages in your document, or you can specify different contents for each section of the document. Odd- and even-numbered pages can have different-looking designs if you wish. The first page of each document or each section can be unique.

Editing takes place in special Header and Footer windowpanes, opened from the View menu. It is possible to apply virtually any paragraph or character style in these panes using ribbons and rulers. Once headers and footers have been added to a document, you can see and edit them in the Page Layout view. They are also displayed in Print Preview, but not in Normal view.

CREATING HEADERS AND FOOTERS

To enter a header that repeats on all pages in your document, choose Header/Footer... from the View menu. You'll see a dialog box like the one shown in Figure 16.1.

Double-click on Header. A new *header windowpane* will open as shown in Figure 16.2. Create and edit header text as you would in any other Word window. You can also paste graphics here, insert fields, apply styles, and otherwise format your work as usual. Do not place table of contents or index entries in headers or footers, however, for that would prevent their being gathered automatically when you generate the contents or index.

Figure 16.2 shows an example of a header containing right-aligned title-and-author text, bold characters, a thick paragraph border, and an automatic page number preceded by the word **Page**.

EDITING HEADERS AND FOOTERS

You can edit headers and footers in Page Layout views or in header and footer panes. They cannot be edited in Print Preview.

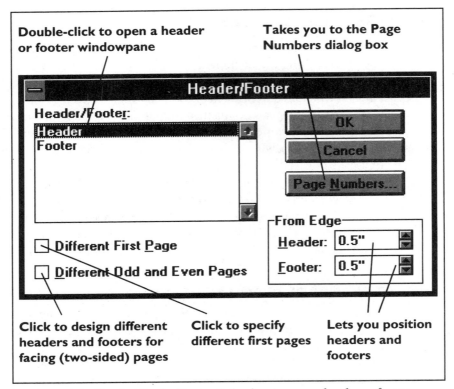

FIGURE 16.1 *Use the Header/Footer dialog box to open a header or footer windowpane.*

Repositioning Headers and Footers

Use Print Preview to fine-tune header and footer page positions. Switch to Print Preview. Turn on margin handles (click on the margins button). Drag margin handles or the headers and footers themselves.

Click the Margins button again to turn off the lines and handles. The headers and/or footers will be repositioned. Not all printers can print at the extreme tops and bottoms of pages. Don't place things closer to the page edges than your printer can print.

The Header/Footer dialog box shown in Figure 16.1 also lets you specify the distance from headers and footers to the page edges.

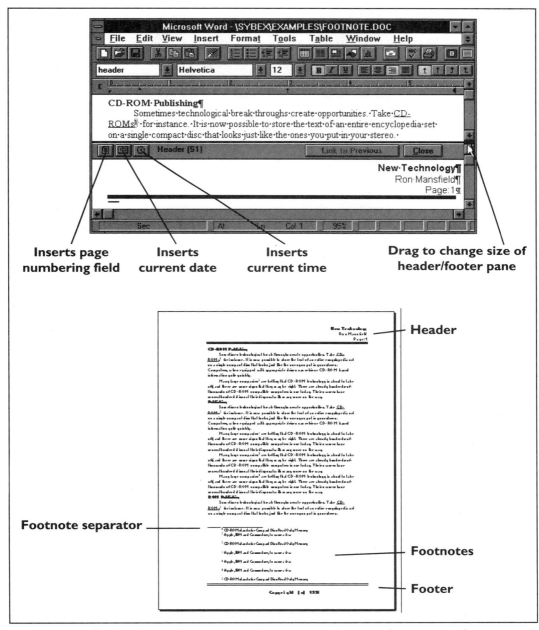

Inserts page numbering field

Inserts current date

Inserts current time

Drag to change size of header/footer pane

Footnote separator

Header

Footnotes

Footer

FIGURE 16.2 *This header window uses several character and paragraph settings. It also contains automatic page numbering.*

Inserting Page Numbers

The quickest way to insert page numbers in headers or footers is to open a header or footer pane, place the insertion point where you want the page number to print, and click the Page Numbers... button shown in Figure 16.2. You can use the Word ruler, ribbon, and Toolbar to format and position page numbers inserted this way. Page numbers will print, and can be seen both in Page Layout view and in Print Preview.

Embellished Page Numbering

For additional control over page numbers, use the Page Numbers dialog box reached from the Page Numbers... command on Word's Insert menu. As shown in Figure 16.3, it gives you control over number formats, alignment, and position.

Specifying Starting Page Numbers

You can also specify starting numbers for whole documents or sections. The *Continue from Previous Section* button lets you link separate, short document files to create a single long one with continuous numbering when you print. Use this when you print your Great American Novel.

Different First-Page Headers and Footers

There are two useful option buttons on the Header/Footer dialog box (reached with the Header/Footer... command on the View menu). One button lets you specify a different first page for headers or footers. For instance, you might want to turn off page numbering on the first page of a document or section.

Headers and Footers for Even and Odd Pages

The second button in the Header/Footer dialog box lets you set up different odd and even headers and footers. This will be of interest if you want to have left-justified headers and footers on even-numbered pages, plus right-justified headers and footers on odd-numbered pages in two-sided documents (as shown in Figure 16.2).

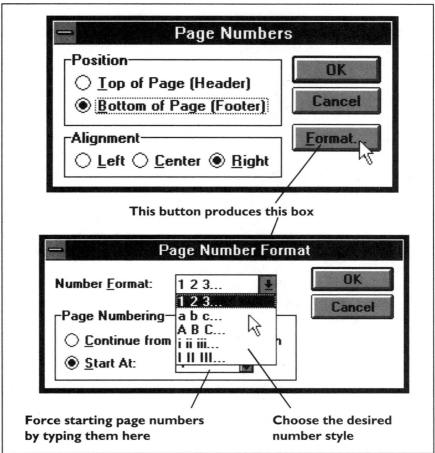

This button produces this box

Force starting page numbers
by typing them here

Choose the desired
number style

FIGURE 16.3 *Position your page numbers and specify their formats in these dialog boxes.*

Different Headers and Footers in Sections

It is often desirable to design different headers and footers for different sections of a document. For instance, if you are writing a book or long report, you can create a new section for each chapter, then have headers and footers that contain chapter names or chapter-specific page numbering schemes (1-2, 3.3, etc.). You might also want to have a different style of page numbering for the first section of a document (such as i, ii, iii, for the preface), then 1, 2, 3 for the main text. You'll learn how to break a document into sections later in this chapter.

Once you have created a multisection document, you can create different headers and footers for different sections by simply placing the insertion point in the section of interest, then opening header and/or footer panes. Then use the header, footer, and page numbering tools in combination, just as you would in a document with only one section.

FORCING PAGE BREAKS

Sometimes you want to force something to the top of a new page. For instance, you may want to start a new topic or place a table at the top of a new page. Rather than pressing Enter a number of times to force text to the following page, either press Ctrl-Enter to force a break, or use the Break... command found on Word's Insert menu. If you use the menu command, you'll see a dialog box like the one in Figure 16.4.

Choose Page Break and click OK. Whether you inserted a page break with the dialog box or the Ctrl-Enter shortcut, in Normal view you'll see a line that is darker than Word's automatic page break lines, but lighter than section break lines (discussed in a moment). Figure 16.4 shows what a manually inserted page break looks like.

Incidentally, be careful not to format page or section breaks accidentally as Hidden text. Hidden breaks can cause very confusing page numbering and pagination problems.

It is best to wait until you are completely done formatting, checking, and editing your document before inserting manual page breaks. You *will* want to insert them before you create a table of contents or index, however, for obvious reasons.

REMOVING FORCED PAGE BREAKS

Simply highlight unwanted forced page breaks, then cut or delete them as you would any other text. If you want to delete many such breaks, consider using Word's Replace... command to replace all or selected page breaks with nothing. (See "Finding and Replacing Special Characters" in Chapter 20.)

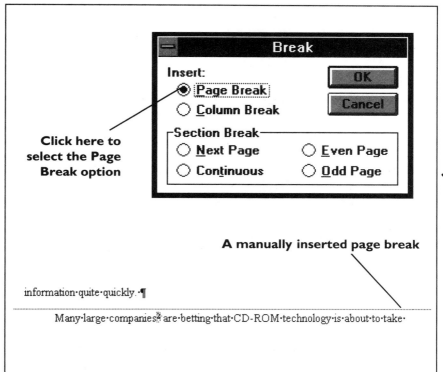

FIGURE 16.4 *Insert forced page breaks with the Break dialog box, or use the
Ctrl-Enter keyboard shortcut. Forced break lines appear darker on your screen
than automatic breaks, but lighter than section breaks.*

SECTIONS

Sections need not be used only for lengthy books or reports. It is a shame
that sections aren't called "zones" or something less specific. You can start a
new section whenever you want to change the format or position of a page or
the progression of page numbers. Sections can be used to turn line numbering on and off. Since footnote positioning can be different in each section, sections are sometimes used for this purpose. Last, but by no means least,
sections can be used to change the number of columns in a document. There
are no hard-and-fast rules about when to create new sections. Experienced
Word users often create multiple sections in a one-page document. Others
use a single section for an entire 100-page report.

INSERTING AND REMOVING SECTION BREAKS

Use the Break... command on Word's Insert menu to open the Break dialog box illustrated in Figure 16.4. Use it to choose one of the Section Break options.

Next Page breaks your work right at the insertion point and starts a new page immediately. *Continuous* uses the remaining white space on the page containing the section break. In other words, if you inserted a continuous break in the middle of page 3, the rest of page 3 would contain text from section 2. (Word would not start a new page first.) Continuous breaks are often used to change the number of columns in multicolumn documents.

The *Odd Page* option forces Word to start the new section on an odd-numbered page. This is how to get new sections always to start on right-hand pages when doing two-sided printing, even if it means leaving an entirely blank preceding page. *Even Page* has the same effect, but always starts sections on even-numbered (left-hand) pages.

SECTION FORMATTING

Each section can have its own margins, page orientation, number of columns, line numbering options, and so on. Place the insertion point in the section you want to format, then visit the appropriate dialog boxes including Page Setup, Columns, Header/Footer, Page Numbers, and Section Layout. Figure 16.5 illustrates the process for defining sections.

PAGE NUMBERS AND SECTIONS

Unless you tell Word otherwise, it will number pages continuously regardless of the number of sections in your document. To overrule this, place the insertion point in the section where you want to change the numbering. Open the header or footer containing the page numbers and visit the Page Numbers dialog box. (See Figure 16.3 if you've forgotten how this looks.) From there, open the Page Number Format dialog box and choose the desired number style (i ii iii; I II III; 1 2 3; and so on). Specify a new starting page number if you like. For instance, if you were in section 2 and you wanted page numbers to start over at 1, enter **1** in the Start At box.

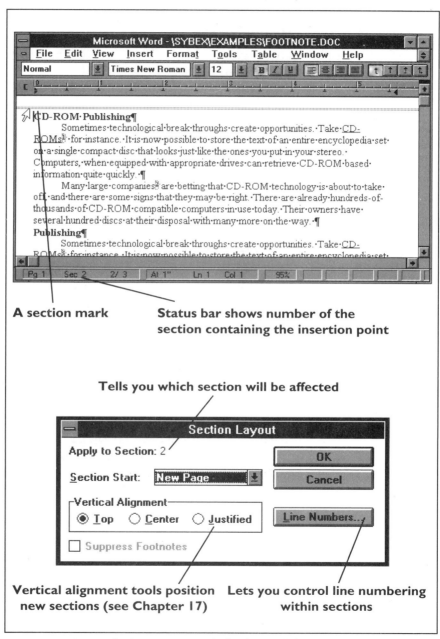

A section mark

Status bar shows number of the
section containing the insertion point

Tells you which section will be affected

Vertical alignment tools position
new sections (see Chapter 17)

Lets you control line numbering
within sections

FIGURE 16.5 *Use the Section Layout dialog box to define key section features.*

PAGE NUMBERS CONTAINING
SECTION OR CHAPTER NUMBERS

There are at least two ways to add chapter or section numbers to page numbers (as in 2.1, 2-1, and so on).

The low-tech way is to open each section's header or footer pane where you want page numbers and manually type section or chapter numbers and separators (such as periods or hyphens) just before inserting the automatic page numbers. For instance, you might type **Chapter 2.** or **Section II Chapter 3 Page-**, then click on the page number button in the open pane.

USING FIELD CODES FOR CHAPTER NUMBERING

A fancier way to include chapter or section numbers automatically with page numbers requires the use of a named SEQ, or *sequence* field, and something called *field codes*. While more complex than our low-tech trick, sequence numbering will let you see and print sequential chapter (or section) numbers in your table of contents and index. The general field code skills you learn here can also be used to number other things sequentially, such as illustrations within your documents.

In general, what you do is define a field name for something you want to count (chapters, or illustrations, or whatever), then insert a named field code in your document wherever you want Word to increment the counter. For instance, if you wanted to count chapters, you might name a field code "chapter" and insert the code at the beginning of each chapter.

Then you'd place a similar (but slightly different) code in each header or footer where you wanted the chapter number to print. Each time Word encounters the chapter code in *text*, it will increment the chapter count. Since you've also set up each header or footer to display and print the current chapter count, headers or footers will show a 1 for Chapter 1, a 2 for Chapter 2, and so on. Like so many things, the best way to understand this is to try a simple example. Study the figures as you read and experiment.

Here's an overview followed by numbered steps that take you through the field coding.

Overview

Start by breaking your document into the separate sections you desire. Then define a hidden sequence code name and add it to the beginning of each section (chapter, in our example). Create additional sequence entries for headers and footers where you want the numbers to print, but don't hide these codes. Check your work in Page Layout view or Print Preview. You'll need to make field codes visible while you create and edit them, then hide the codes to see the results of your work.

Steps for Automatically Numbering Chapters

Here's a step-by-step example of chapter numbering:

1. Break the document into sections.

2. Make field codes visible by picking the Field Codes choice on Word's View menu. (There should be a check mark next to the menu choice.)

3. Position the insertion point at the beginning of your first chapter (or section, or whatever).

4. Press the Insert Field key combination (Ctrl-F9). Word will insert two field characters {} and place the insertion point between them.

5. Type **seq** plus a name of your choosing for the sequence (**chapter**, for instance). You can use any field name you like here; just be consistent later. For instance, **ch** or **chptr** would work instead of **chapter**.

6. Finish by typing **\h**. This backslash command tells Word to hide the command and not print it. (In our example, we've typed the hidden sequence {**seq chapter\h**}.) Figure 16.6 illustrates this.

7. Press the F9 function key to update the count.

8. While in Normal View, open the first header or footer of interest.

9. Position the insertion point where you want the chapter number to print.

10. Use Ctrl-F9 to insert a SEQ field in the header or footer.

11. Type the same sequence as before, but end it with **\c** so that the results will print—{**seq chapter\c**}, for instance.

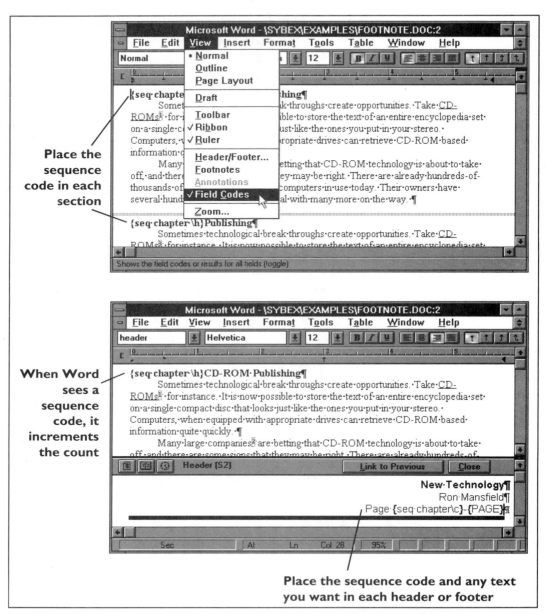

FIGURE 16.6 *Place sequence codes at the beginning of each chapter or other thing you want to count. Word will increment the counter each time it encounters the code.*

12. If you want to include page numbers along with the chapter numbers, add a special page number field {**PAGE**}, or click on the page number button and Word will insert the page field for you. Add text and spacing, if you like. The finished header or footer entry might be:

Page {seq chapter\c}-{page}

Figure 16.6 illustrates this.

13. From the View menu turn off Field Codes.

14. Switch to Page Layout view and examine your headers or footers. They should include chapter numbers that change properly at the beginning of each chapter as illustrated in Figure 16.7.

15. If it works, shout "hallelujah!" and show a friend. If not, check your spelling of code names.

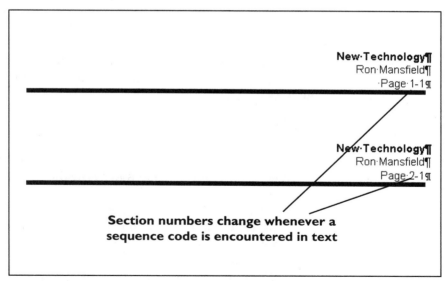

FIGURE 16.7 *Chapter numbers increment automatically whenever Word encounters the hidden SEQ code in text.*

PRINTING SELECTED SECTIONS

In multisection documents, you need to specify section numbers when printing selected ranges of pages. For instance, to print pages 5 through 10 in section 3 of a document, you need to enter **5s3** in the Print Dialog From box (indicating page 5 of section 3), and **10s3** in the To box. To print across multiple sections, enter different section numbers in the From and To boxes (from **4s2** to **3s3** would print parts of sections 2 and 3, for instance).

FOOTNOTES

Choosing Footnote... from the Insert menu or pressing the Alt, **I**, **N** key combination puts Word's standard footnotes feature to work in an eye blink.

Footnotes consist of in-text *footnote markers* (usually, but not necessarily, sequential numbers), the *footnotes* themselves, and footnote *separators*— that is, lines that separate footnotes from the document text. When footnotes are long and spill onto other pages, you may want to include Word's footnote *continuation notices*. Figure 16.8 shows Word's default footnote markers and the automatically numbered footnotes they help you create.

Since footnote text can be embellished (italicized, made smaller, etc.) just like other Word text, you already know how to modify the appearance of footnotes. Positioning, inserting, editing, and deleting footnotes and separators and markers is equally painless.

EASY, AUTOMATIC FOOTNOTES

Figure 16.8 shows an automatic (default) Word footnote. It should take you less than 10 seconds to add your first footnote to existing text.

Start by placing the insertion point where the footnote marker is needed (after the word ROMs in the first line of our example). Next, either choose Insert Footnote... or press the Alt, **I**, **N** key combination. You can dismiss the *Footnote dialog box* by clicking OK, when using Word's defaults.

The document window automatically splits into two panes, then a footnote reference number (1 in this case) appears both at the insertion point and in the footnote area of the split document window.

The insertion point automatically moves to the footnote area where you can type the footnote.

To return to the main document, move the insertion point with the mouse or press Alt-Shift-C.

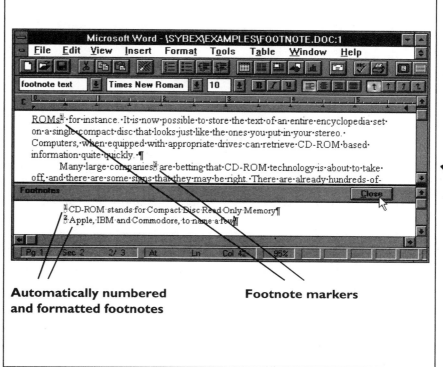

**Automatically numbered
and formatted footnotes**

Footnote markers

FIGURE 16.8 *Footnote markers are clearly visible in text. Read and edit footnotes in the footnote window.*

VIEWING FOOTNOTES

Footnotes are *always* displayed in both Page Layout view and Print Preview. If they are not visible in Normal or Outline view, and you want to see them, choose Footnotes from the *View* menu. If you are constantly entering or referring to footnotes, you can leave the footnote pane visible while you work. Use the footnote scroll bars if necessary to view notes. Resize the footnote area to suit your taste and screen size. Drag the bar separating the two areas the same way you resize other Word split screens (point to the split box and drag).

To hide the footnote window, choose Footnotes a second time from the View menu or click the Close button in the footnote pane.

Double-clicking on a footnote marker in your document will display the footnote. If necessary, Word will open the footnote pane and scroll to the appropriate note. There may be a slight delay. Be patient.

INSERTING, COPYING, MOVING, AND DELETING FOOTNOTES

Whenever you insert footnotes, Word renumbers the existing notes properly. You can copy, move, or delete entire footnotes as easily as you would a single character. Select the footnote *marker* of interest in the *document text*. (This can take a steady hand, particularly if you have Drag-and-Drop enabled.) Cut, copy, and paste (or drag-and-drop) the footnote *mark*.

Word does the rest. If you have footnote numbering turned on, numbers will update in your text and in the corresponding footnotes. If you copy and paste a mark, a corresponding new footnote will magically appear in the right spot in your footnotes. Deletion works as you would expect.

To edit footnote text, use Page Layout view or open the footnote pane itself. Type, format, cut, paste, or drag-and-drop away to your heart's content.

CHANGING FOOTNOTE APPEARANCE

Word lets you modify many footnote parameters via the Footnote Options dialog box shown in Figure 16.9. You make other footnote-related decisions in the dialog boxes reached from this one.

This dialog box comes up automatically the first time you insert a note. Alas, there is no other *obvious* way to bring it up again without unintentionally inserting a footnote marker. Fortunately, though, there *is* a way. Choose Footnote... from the Insert menu, then click the Options button.

CONTROLLING FOOTNOTE NUMBERING

You can specify the starting number for footnotes in the Footnote Options dialog box. Only Arabic numbers are permitted.

Footnote numbering can restart in each section if you check the Restart Each Section button in the Footnote Options dialog box.

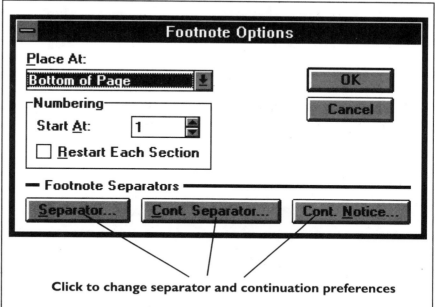

FIGURE 16.9 *Personalize footnote appearance using the Footnote Options dialog box (via the Options... button on the Footnote dialog box). Reach it with the Insert menu's Insert... command.*

Tabs, Tables, Columns, Sorting, and Math

This chapter explores ways to organize and format lists and other columnar material. While typing tabs can help you set up simple columnar lists, you'll often find that tables are more flexible for involved typing projects. Word also lets you create multiple snaking text columns like those you see in newspapers and magazines. Finally, Word's sorting and math features let you rearrange and perform calculations on portions of your text.

TABS AND TAB STOPS

To understand tabs, you need to know about *tab characters* themselves and *tab stops*. Tabs are characters you type from the keyboard with the Tab key. When you press the Tab key, it moves the insertion point and therefore the position of the next text you type. A small arrow is displayed on-screen, indicating the tab character.

Tab *stops* are the places to which the insertion point moves. Stops can be moved. The Microsoft standard settings specify tabs every half-inch (0.5"). Different kinds of tab stops have differing effects.

TYPES OF TAB STOPS

Word offers four specialized tab stop types. They each work with tabs to help align text, and are particularly useful for making simple columnar lists like the one in Figure 17.1.

Left Tab Stops

Left tab stops are like the plain vanilla ones you find on your old Smith-Corona. Text typed at these tab stops bumps up against the left edge of the stop. Left tab stops were used to align the album names and play times (columns 2 and 3) in Figure 17.1.

Center Tab Stops

Center tab stops position your entry *between* the neighboring tab stops, indent markers, or margins on either side of the center tab stop. In Figure 17.1, the song titles (in column 2) are aligned with a center tab stop.

Right Tab Stops

Right tab stops push whatever you type to the right. As you can see in column 1 of Figure 17.1, this is a great way to type long lists of numbers of varying length.

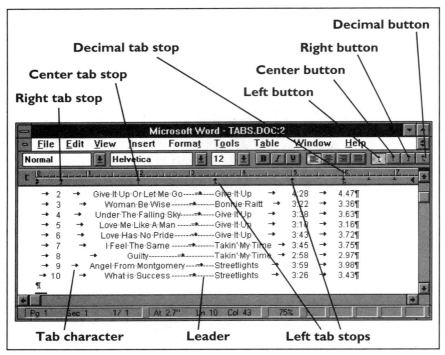

FIGURE 17.1 *Word provides Left, Center, Right, and Decimal tabs.*

Decimal Tab Stops

Decimal tab stops behave as you'd expect. As shown in column 5 of Figure 17.1, they align columns of numbers containing decimal points, and are perfect for simple financial reports.

SETTING TAB STOPS

Tab setting is easiest with both the ribbon and ruler in view. If that's not the case, choose ribbon and/or ruler from the View menu.

Tab *stops* are stored with the paragraph mark for each paragraph, thus all of the rules about paragraph markers apply. If, for example, you set tab stops once and type returns at the end of each typing line, each new line (actually a paragraph) will use the same tab stops as the preceding one until you tell Word otherwise.

SETTING TAB STOPS WITH THE RULER

With the ruler in view, point to the button with the picture of the desired tab stop type. It will become depressed. Click and drag a new tab stop onto the lower portion of the ruler as shown in Figure 17.1. If you make a mistake, drag the stop off the ruler and try again.

USING THE TABS DIALOG BOX

The Tabs dialog box shown in Figure 17.2 is reached from the Tabs... command on the Format menu. Use it to see, modify, and delete tab stop settings.

Compare the tab stops listed in Figure 17.2 with the tab stops on the ruler of the example in Figure 17.1. The dialog box shows you each tab stop's position, alignment, and leading characters, if any. For instance, the third tab stop in Figure 17.1 is 3.5" from the left margin, is left-aligned, and has leading dashes.

To change a tab's position from the dialog box, select it in the list and type a new position. Use the option buttons to change alignment and leaders for chosen stops.

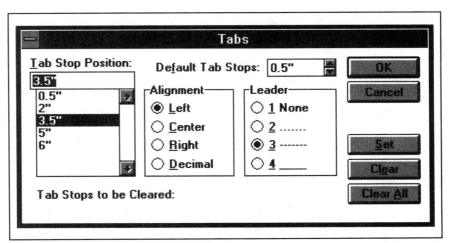

FIGURE 17.2 *Reach the Tabs dialog box with the Tabs... command on the Format menu.*

CLEARING TAB STOPS

You can drag the occasional tab off the ruler if you don't need it. The Tabs dialog box (see Figure 17.2) provides facilities for clearing selected tab stops or all tab stops at once. Default stops remain. This can make an absolute mess of your pride and joy.

Undo should work if you accidentally clear all custom tabs, but it is always a good idea to save your work before experimenting with major changes like these. Remember, these features only work on paragraphs you have selected.

ENTERING TABULAR INFORMATION

Once you have set up tab stops, simply press the Tab key to reach the stop and begin typing. Word will position the text as you type. If you are typing at a center tab stop, or a right stop, text will flow appropriately as you type. When you type at decimal stops, the insertion point sits at the decimal position.

To leave an entry blank, simply "tab past it" by pressing the Tab key.

MOVING TAB STOPS

To move tab stops before you've entered text, point to the stop of interest and drag away. If, however, you have already entered text that uses the tab stop(s) you want to move, first select *all* of the text that uses this stop before moving the tab stop(s).

For instance, if you had already typed the lines in Figure 17.1 and wanted to move the left tab stop, you would need to highlight all of the lines before moving a tab stop. Otherwise, some lines (paragraphs) would have different tab stops than others. Incidentally, you'd also want to highlight the *paragraph mark* beneath the last line if you ever plan to enter more items using the tab stops. Otherwise the last paragraph marker won't "know" about the tab stop change.

If you highlight paragraphs with different tab stop settings, the stop markers on the ruler will turn gray. Only the stops for the top paragraph will be displayed.

TABLES

You insert tables anywhere you need them in Word documents. They can be used in place of tabs for lists of items or to place paragraphs of information side-by-side. You can embellish tables with borders and shading, making it possible to create complex forms, price lists, and so on. Figure 17.3 shows a two-column table being used to create a resume.

PARTS OF A TABLE

Word tables consist of horizontal *rows* and vertical *columns*. You do the typing in areas called *cells*.

Cells can contain *text*, *numbers*, or *graphics*. Text is edited and embellished as usual in cells. For instance, Word's ribbon and ruler features are available while typing and editing in tables.

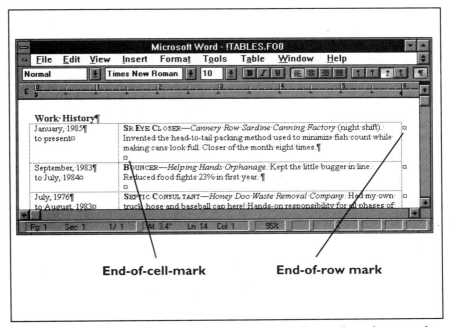

FIGURE 17.3 *You can see three rows, two columns, and six cells in this example. The dotted cell gridline does not print. Use Word's border commands to add printable lines.*

The light dots around each cell create nonprinting table gridlines. (You can add printing table and cell borders with Word's Border... command.) The little dots are end-of-cell and end-of-row marks. Click on the Show ¶ button in the ribbon if you can't see them on your screen.

A number of table-specific features let you control the size, shape, and appearance of cells. Border and shading features are available. Other table features help you insert and delete rows and columns.

Tables can be created from existing text without needless retyping. Or you can use Word's table feature to organize information, then convert your table to text. The table feature can even be used to import and export spreadsheet data.

CREATING TABLES WITH THE TABLE DIALOG BOX

Place the insertion point at the place in your Word document where you want to insert a table. Choose the Insert Table... item from Word's Table menu.

The Insert Table dialog box will appear. Enter the desired number of columns and rows for your table. Don't worry if you are uncertain about the exact number of columns or rows you'll need. You can always add or delete them later. Figure 17.4 shows the dialog box entries for three two-column rows.

Unless you tell it to do otherwise, Word computes an automatic column width, taking into consideration the available text area in your document and the number of columns you've specified. Initially, all table columns are the same width. You can change column widths using techniques described later in this chapter.

CREATING TABLES WITH THE TOOLBAR

Instead of using the Insert Table... command, you can click on the table button in the Toolbar and drag to select the desired number of rows and columns. Figure 17.4 illustrates this too.

ENTERING INFORMATION IN TABLES

You navigate, enter, and edit table text just as you do any other Word text. Use your mouse or arrow keys to position the insertion point, then type normally. Think of the cell borders as margins. Word will automatically wrap

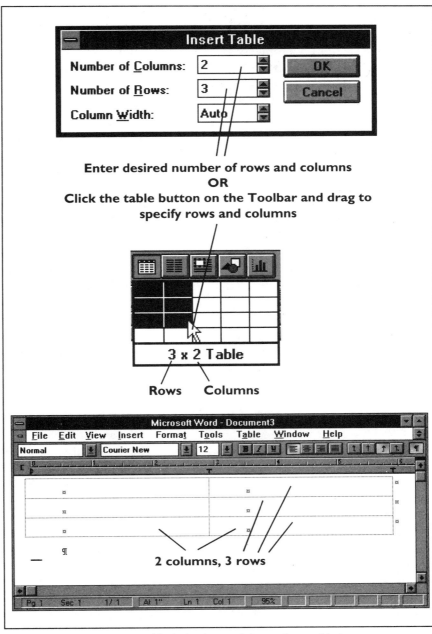

FIGURE 17.4 *The Insert Table dialog box and the resulting table it creates.*

text as you reach the right edge of a cell. Rows will automatically grow taller as necessary to accommodate your typing.

To move from cell to cell within a table, either use your mouse, or use the *Tab* key to go forward and *Shift-Tab* to go backward. The insertion point will move *left and down* to the next row when you press Tab in the last column on the *right* side of a table (don't press Enter till done with the table), and it will move *right and up* one row when you *Shift-Tab* past the *left*.

Here's an important tip: Since you use the Tab key to navigate in tables, you cannot simply press Tab to enter tab characters in cells. Instead, you need to hold down the Ctrl key while pressing Tab.

You can apply the usual character formatting to all or selected characters in a table. In Figure 17.3, for instance, several font sizes, as well as bold and italic embellishments, have been used in portions of some cells. The familiar ribbon, ruler, and menu features all work here.

First-time table users are sometimes unaware of the important role that *paragraphs* play in tables. Each *cell* in your table can contain *more than one* paragraph. Create paragraphs in the usual way: while typing in a cell, press the Enter key.

You can apply all of Word's *paragraph formats* to paragraphs in cells. Since cells can contain multiple paragraphs, they can also contain multiple paragraph *formats*. Thus, within a *single cell*, you can have several different indent settings, tab settings, line spacing specifications, and the like.

SELECTING THINGS IN TABLES

You can select characters, words, rows, columns, and other items in tables using either mouse or keyboard techniques, or a combination of both. In addition, Word also provides table-specific selection tools enabling you to choose whole cells, entire rows, columns, or areas, as Figure 17.5 illustrates.

SELECTING SINGLE CELLS

The area between the first character in a cell and the left edge of the cell is called the *cell selection bar*. Clicking on it selects the contents of the entire cell.

You can also select an entire cell by dragging with the mouse. Just be sure that you include the end-of-cell mark in your selection.

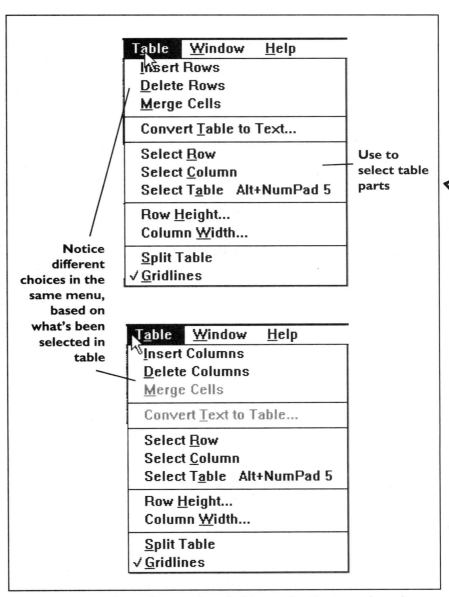

Notice different choices in the same menu, based on what's been selected in table

Use to select table parts

WORD

FIGURE 17.5 *Word provides a number of table-specific selection tools on the Table menu. The choices change, based on what parts of a table you've selected.*

SELECTING ROWS

Double-clicking in any cell selection bar will select the entire row. Pointing to the left-most or right-most cell in a row and then dragging will also work.

SELECTING COLUMNS

To select a column, move the mouse pointer to the invisible area at the top of a column called the *column selection bar*. You'll know you've arrived when the pointer changes into a large, down-pointing arrow like the one in the last example in Figure 17.6. Click to select the entire column. Selecting the bottom or top cell in a column and dragging up or down will also work.

SELECTING ADJACENT GROUPS OF CELLS

To select groups of adjacent cells, either drag through the cells or click in one cell and Shift-click in another. For instance, to select everything but the headings in Figure 17.6 you could *click* in the *Billie* cell, then *Shift-click* in the cell at the opposite corner containing the number *450*. All but the table's top cells would be selected.

SELECTING THE WHOLE TABLE

To select an entire table, place the insertion point anywhere in the table and use the Select Table command from the Table menu. The keyboard shortcut for this is Alt-NumPad 5 (press the 5 on the numeric keypad).

MODIFYING TABLE LAYOUTS

While Word's default table settings may be fine for simple typing tasks, you will eventually want to change column widths, overall table width, cell spacing, and so on. You'll want to insert, delete, and move rows and columns.

Creating complex tables can be a little frustrating at first. As always, it is a good idea to save your work before you experiment with new table formats. Beginners should consider working on copies of important documents. That said, let's look at a number of ways to modify standard table designs.

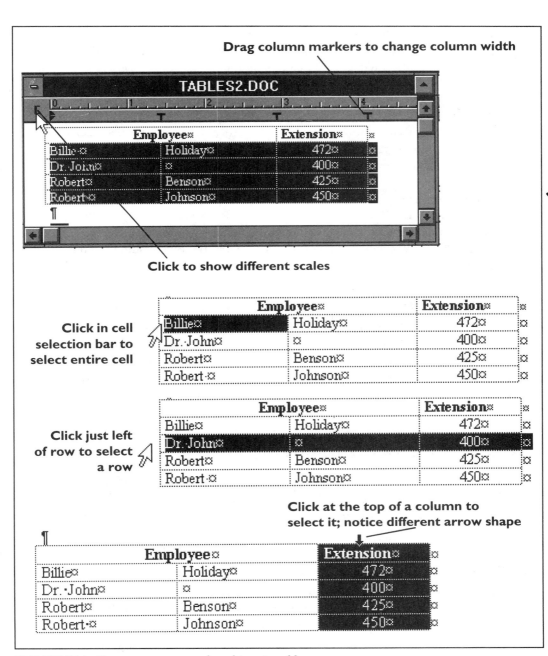

FIGURE 17.6 *Use your mouse to select things in tables.*

Table rulers have three different scales: table scale, indent scale, and margin scale. Click on the marker at the left end of the ruler to switch scales. When in table scale you'll see "T" markers on the ruler.

MERGE CELLS

Use the Merge Cells feature to combine the contents of multiple cells. This is a great way to make a heading that was typed in one cell span an entire table or selected columns. In Figure 17.6, the Employee heading was created by merging two cells.

Employee was typed in the first cell of a three-column table, then the first two cells of the first row were selected and the Merge Cells command (from the Table menu) was used to combine their contents. An unnecessary paragraph mark was removed and the characters of the two headings were made bold.

TABLE BORDERS THAT PRINT

An easy way to dress up (and often clarify) a table is to add printable borders. Select the cell or cells you wish to surround, then choose Border... from the Format menu. The Border choices will look a little different than the ones you see when the insertion point is not in a table. Pick the desired combination of line thicknesses and apply the borders just as you would add them to Word paragraphs.

ADDING ROWS AT THE END OF A TABLE

To add a row at the *end* of an existing table, place the insertion point anywhere in the *last cell* (the one in the *lower-left corner* of your table) and press the Tab key. Word will insert a new row, using the corresponding styles of the cells immediately above.

INSERTING ROWS IN THE MIDDLE OF A TABLE

To insert a single row in the middle of a table, select the *entire row* below where you want the new row. When you visit the Table menu, it will now contain an Insert Rows command (remember to select a row first). Then use the Insert Rows feature found in the Table menu. To add multiple rows, either repeat Insert Rows command as many times as you need rows, or try this alternate approach.

Select as many existing rows as you want to insert new ones *before* making the insertion. In other words, if you want to add three rows, select the three existing rows beneath the desired insertion point, *then* use Insert Rows command. Word will insert three rows.

CHANGING ROW HEIGHTS

Normally, Word sets the height of each row *automatically* to accommodate the cell containing the tallest entry. For instance, if *one* cell in a row needs 2" to accommodate the text or graphic it contains, *all* of the cells in that row will be 2" high. All cells in a row *must* be the same height, but different rows can (and often do) have different heights.

You can overrule Word's automatic row-height settings via the Table menu's Row Height... command. You can specify minimum or exact dimensions. This is one way to create forms with fixed-size entry areas.

Place the insertion point anywhere in the row whose height you wish to specify. If you want multiple rows to share the same height, you can select them.

DELETING ROWS

Delete one or more selected rows with the Table menu's Delete Rows command. You can also delete selected rows with the Edit menu's Cut command or the Ctrl-X shortcut.

CHANGING SPACING BETWEEN ROWS

To change the *white space* between rows, you must change the spacing in the text in the first and/or last paragraphs in the cells. (Don't confuse this with the *height* of rows, which is something else entirely.) Use the same techniques you use to add space between nontable paragraphs. Choose the Paragraph... command on the Format menu and specify before and after spacing.

INSERTING COLUMNS
AT THE RIGHT EDGE OF A TABLE

To insert a column at the right edge of a table, place the insertion point over the end of row marks at the right edge of the right-most column. Click to select all of the end of row marks.

Visit the Table menu and choose Insert Columns. Word will add a new column but will not change the width of the earlier columns to accommodate it. To make the now enlarged table fit on your page, you may need to adjust margins, column widths, or page orientation. New columns will contain rows with formats identical to the old right-most column.

INSERTING COLUMNS IN THE MIDDLE OF A TABLE

To insert a single column in the middle of a table, place the insertion point in the column *to the right of* where you want the new column to appear. (You must highlight the entire column, or the Table menu will read "Insert Cells." Then you must select Insert Entire Column from the Insert Cells dialog box.) Then, use the Insert Columns feature found on the Table menu.

To insert multiple columns, either repeat the process (perhaps using Repeat Insert... from the Edit menu), or *select* as many existing columns as you want to insert new ones *to the right of* the desired location of the new columns. In other words, if you want to add three columns, select the three existing columns to the right of the desired insertion point, then visit the Table menu. Word will inset three columns.

All new columns initially will contain rows with formats identical to the column to the right of the new ones.

DELETING COLUMNS

To delete columns, select the column or columns to be removed, then use the Table menu's Delete Columns command.

CHANGING COLUMN WIDTHS

You can change the widths of entire columns or selected cells within columns. Most changes can be made by dragging column markers on the table scale in the ruler. You can also use the Table Menu's Column Width... command.

Using the Ruler to Change Column and Cell Widths

To change column or cell widths from the ruler, drag either column borders or the column markers ("T") on the ruler. Changing column widths can be problematic at first, so save your work before experimenting.

To drag the width of an *entire column*, select the column of interest. This is an important step! If you fail to select the entire column, your changes will affect only one cell. If you want to make multiple columns the same new width, select them all and change them simultaneously.

With the column selected, display the *table scale* on the ruler. To do this, click on the *scale button* at the left edge corner of the ruler once or twice slowly until you see a square bracket ([).

The table column markers ("T") will be displayed on the ruler and are ready for dragging. When you drag this way, markers to the right of the mark you drag will also move, changing the overall size of the table. To maintain the table size, hold down the Shift key when dragging column markers.

It is possible to change the size of just one cell by highlighting the cell, then dragging. Here, too, holding the Shift key while dragging will preserve the table's overall width.

Undo Formatting is available if you need it. Visit the Edit menu or use the (by now familiar?) Ctrl-Z shortcut.

When you are just learning, it's pretty easy to mess things up while dragging cell and column borders around this way, particularly if you change cell widths when you meant to change column widths. If Undo can't fix the problem, and if you don't have a better previously saved version, perhaps the Column Width... command and its resulting dialog box can help.

The Column Width Dialog Box

The Column Width dialog box, shown in Figure 17.7, can be used to define cell and column widths. This is also where you can adjust space between columns.

Reach it with the Column Width... command on the Table menu. Type spacing measurements, or use the arrows to increase or decrease spacing. Select the columns of interest and specify new widths. Use the Previous and Next Column buttons to move from column to column. To change the widths of multiple columns simultaneously, select them before visiting this dialog box.

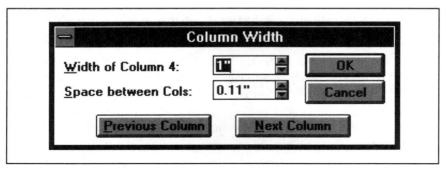

FIGURE 17.7 *Use the Column Width dialog box to specify column widths and space between columns.*

If your table is a mess, consider selecting all of the columns and using the Column Width dialog box to change all columns to the same width. Then try modifying individual columns again.

CHANGING THE SPACE BETWEEN COLUMNS

Word assigns initial cell widths based on the available text area and the number of columns you request. In the process, it sets aside a small amount of unprintable space between (actually within) each cell. This space takes away from the usable cell space. For instance, a 1.5" column with .25" column spacing would have 1.25" of usable space in each cell.

To change the space between columns, select the column(s) of interest, then type a new specification in the Space between Cols box found in the Column Width dialog box.

TABS TO TABLES AND BACK

Sometimes you'll start a project using tabs and wish you'd created a table—or a co-worker will give you some tabbed text. Other times, you will want to export things you've typed with Word's table feature into databases and other programs that expect tab- or comma-separated input.

Word makes it fairly easy to convert back and forth. You may need to do some cleanup before or after conversion. Always work on *copies* of your documents when you do this!

CONVERTING FROM TEXT TO TABLES

Highlight the text in your Word document that you want to turn into a table. Pick Convert Text to Table... from the Table menu. Word may ask if the columns are indicated by paragraph marks, tabs, or commas, then will attempt to convert the text into a new table based on your answer.

Converting Tab-Delimited Text

Click the Tabs button in the Convert Text to Table dialog box. Lines of text separated by paragraph marks or line breaks will become *rows* in your table. Tab-separated strings of text *within* those lines will become cell entries in the row. Word will automatically create the necessary number of columns based on the maximum number of tabs in a line.

For instance, *Sony Corporation (Tab) 800-222-7669 (Enter) SYBEX, Inc. (Tab) 510-523-8233 (Tab) Publisher (Enter)* would create two rows with three columns even though the last cell in the first row will be empty. You may need to change column widths to make the table look right.

Converting Comma-Delimited Text

Click the Commas button in the Convert Text to Table dialog box. Lines of text separated by paragraph marks or line breaks will become *rows* in your table. Comma-separated strings of text *within* those lines will become cell entries in the row. Word will automatically create the necessary number of columns based on the maximum number of commas in a line.

For instance, *Sony Corporation (Comma) 800-222-7669 (Enter) SYBEX, Inc. (Comma) 510-523-8233 (Comma) Publisher (Enter)* would create two rows with three columns even though the last cell in the first row will be empty.

Beware of commas that might create unintentional cells like the one between SYBEX and Inc.

Moreover, if cells contain multiple paragraphs, the paragraph marks in cells may cause problems.

Converting from Paragraphs

Click the Paragraph marks button in the Convert Text to Table dialog box. If you ask Word to convert paragraphs, it will propose a single column and create as many rows as you have paragraphs. Changing the number of columns will distribute paragraphs among the columns from left to right. In other words, in a two-column layout the first paragraph would end up in the top-left cell of the new table, the second paragraph in the top-right cell, the third in the left-cell of row 2, and so on.

CONVERTING FROM TABLES TO TEXT

Select the Word table cells you wish to convert. Choose Convert Table to Text... from the Table menu. Word will provide a Table to Text dialog box that asks if you want the table converted to *Tab*, *Paragraph marks*, or *Comma separated* text. Pick one. If you pick the Comma or Tab options, Word will convert each row of your table into one line (a paragraph, actually). *Cells* in your old tables will become tab- or comma-*separated items* on the lines.

Remember that commas in text (like the one in SYBEX, Inc.) will confuse Word. If you choose tab text, you will probably need to set new tabs after the conversion.

Choosing the Paragraph marks option will convert each old table cell into at least one paragraph. If cells contain multiple paragraphs, the paragraph marks are retained during the conversion, so some cells will create more than one new paragraph.

MOVING CELL CONTENTS

To move the contents of cells, first find or create new empty destination cells in the appropriate quantity and configuration to hold the items you plan to move. For instance, if you plan to move a 4-row-by-6-column collection of cells, you will need the same number of available cells in the same configuration (4×6) to receive the moved items.

Copy or cut the items of interest by highlighting them and either using Copy or Cut from the Edit menu or using keyboard shortcuts (Ctrl-C or Ctrl-X).

At this point you either can *select* the exact same cell configuration at the destination (4 rows of 6 columns, in our example) or you can try a shortcut. Simply place the insertion point in the upper-left destination cell. (If you use this shortcut, do *not* select the cell.) Be sure to place the insertion point before the end of cell mark, then paste. All of the cells will flow into their new destinations, bringing their formatting information with them.

Undo Paste works here if you spot trouble immediately. Delete the old columns using Delete Columns if necessary.

STYLES, TEMPLATES, AND TABLES

Word will use the current style (at the insertion point) when creating a new table. You can change the style of the whole table or apply different styles to different portions of the table.

Consider creating multiple *styles* if you plan to play with table formatting. For instance, you might have a style for table headings, another for standard text, another for decimal-aligned numbers, and so on. Set up paragraphs in cells with desired line and paragraph spacing, tab settings, etc., then, with the insertion point in a paragraph, choose Style… from the Format menu.

Apply the new style(s) to all appropriate paragraphs in your table by selecting the paragraphs and using the ribbon's Style menu. From then on, simply changing a style will change all table text formatted with the changed style.

MULTIPLE COLUMNS

Most people find short lines of text easier to read than long ones. That's one reason newspapers and book designers frequently use side-by-side *snaking columns*. Text flows from the bottom of one column to the top of the next until a page is filled, then it flows onto the next page. Word makes it easy for you to arrange your text in columns like these. The *Toolbar buttons* let you choose up to six columns. Moreover, the *Columns* command on the Format menu lets you specify up to 100 columns. It also provides a way to adjust the amount of *white space* between columns and lets you place a line (rule) between columns.

In a single-section document, all of your pages must have the same number of columns. But, by breaking a document into multiple sections, you can have as many different column designs as you have sections.

Word automatically adjusts column widths to accommodate your chosen page size, orientation, and document margins. You can overrule these decisions.

It is possible to use indents within columns. You can edit columnar text just as you do any other. When you work in Page Layout view you will see *side-by-side* columns as they will print. When working in Normal view you will see text in the appropriate column *width*, but you will not see the columns in position next to each other.

SIMPLE COLUMNS WITH THE COLUMNS BUTTON

The easy way to create columns is to place the insertion point in the section of interest, then click on the Text Column button in the Toolbar. Drag to the right, across the little pictures of columns, to highlight them, selecting the number of columns you want as shown in Figure 17.8.

CHANGING COLUMN WIDTHS AND SPACING

When you use Word's columns feature, Word makes all of the columns in a section the same width. Thus, changing the width of one column always

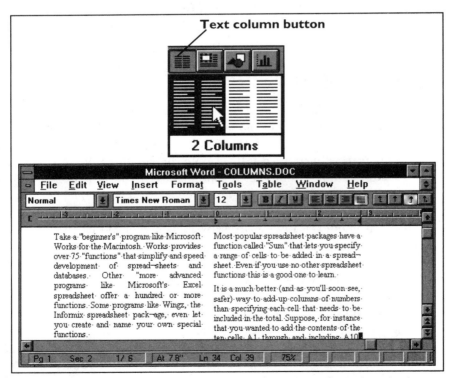

FIGURE 17.8 *Use the Text Column button on the Toolbar to specify multiple columns. View the results with Page Layout view or Print Preview.*

causes identical changes in the others. (Use tables for side-by-side columns of different widths.) Incidentally, while it is possible to indent paragraphs, then turn these indented paragraphs into columns, you may end up with smaller columns than you'd expect this way. It's better to create columns first, *then* indent them.

Changing Column Widths with the Ruler

To change column widths with your mouse, display the ruler and switch to Page Layout view. Place the insertion point in a column whose width you want to change. Be sure the column margin markers ([and]) are displayed on the ruler, above the columns. (Click on the marker at the left edge of the ruler if necessary to display the column margin markers.) Drag one of the column's margin markers to change the widths of all columns.

Changing Column Characteristics with the Columns Command

The Columns... command on the Format menu reveals the dialog box shown in Figure 17.9. With it you can change the number of columns in a section, their width, and the amount of white space between them. And you can specify a vertical line between columns to enhance legibility.

The settings in Figure 17.9 created the dual columns shown in Figure 17.10. Notice that a line was specified between the two columns. It doesn't show in Page Layout view, but displays in Print Preview and prints properly. Notice also that a section break separates the single-column text from the dual columns. Figure 17.10 also shows the Column margin markers clearly.

CONTROLLING COLUMN BREAKS AND LENGTHS

Word automatically places column breaks to fit as much as possible on each page. If you want to keep things together that Word wants to split up, use Word's Keep With Next feature in the Paragraph dialog box.

You can force column page breaks of your own to control the length of columns and to force them to start where you want. Place the insertion point where you want a column break, then press Ctrl-Shift-Enter, or use the

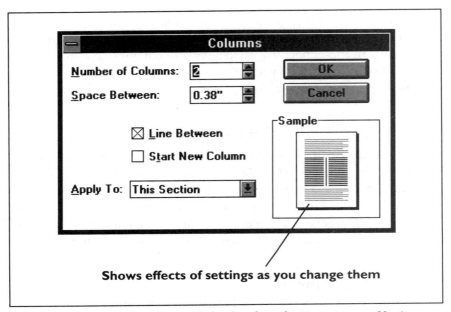

FIGURE 17.9 *Reach the Columns dialog box from the Format menu. Use it to design and alter column specifications.*

Column Break options in the Break dialog box (reached from the Insert menu). Column breaks look like page breaks in Normal view, which is the easiest place to see, select, and delete them. While you can't see the breaks themselves in Page Layout view or Print Preview, you do see their effect in these views.

SORTING INFORMATION WITH WORD

Have you ever created things like an *alphabetical list of employees* and their phone extensions, then needed a list of *phone extension* assignments sorted by extension number? Most of us have a variety of lists like these, and they always seem to be in the wrong order.

You could retype the old list or cut-and-paste, but Word's Sorting... command found under the Tools menu might be a better solution.

Word can sort lines of tabular text, items you've entered in tables, or even whole paragraphs in a document. The sort command can be quite helpful

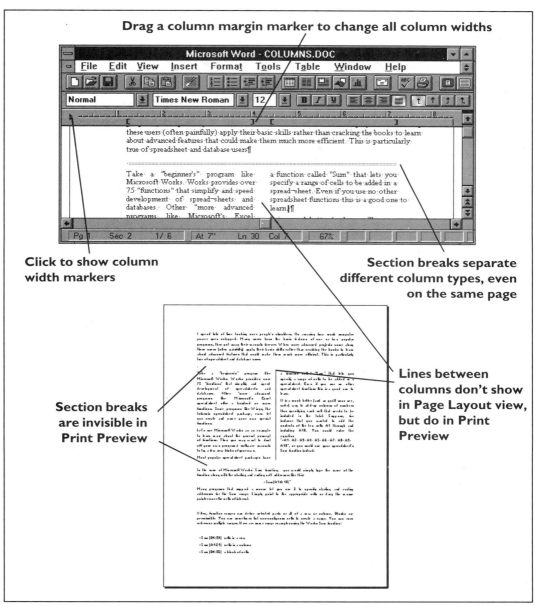

Drag a column margin marker to change all column widths

Click to show column width markers

Section breaks separate different column types, even on the same page

Section breaks are invisible in Print Preview

Lines between columns don't show in Page Layout view, but do in Print Preview

FIGURE 17.10 *The two-column section of this document was created using the settings shown in Figure 17.9. Notice that the line between columns only shows up in Print Preview.*

when preparing data files for Word's Print Merge feature (discussed in Chapter 22).

As with some other powerful Word features, Sorting... can make substantial changes to your document, so it is best to save before you sort. Consider practicing on *copies* of important files. Word's sort feature will attempt to sort any selected text alphabetically, chronologically, or numerically. Take the list of employee names, phone extensions, and birthdays in Figure 17.11, for instance.

First select *all* the text you want to rearrange (and nothing else). Unselected text will not sort. Next, pick Sorting... from the Tools menu. Choose the sort order, key field, and any case options you desire. Then click OK to sort the text. Be aware that if you only select the last names in Figure 17.11, the contents of all the other cells will remain unchanged, thereby giving people different last names. To sort properly, you'd need to select everyone's full names, phone extensions, and birthdays, but *not* the column headings.

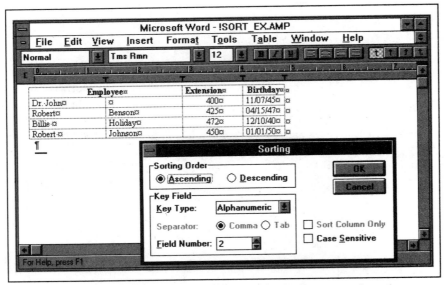

FIGURE 17.11 *Highlight text to be sorted, then choose Sorting... from the Tools menu.*

SORT ORDER

Normally, Word sorts *alphanumerically* in *ascending order* based on each character's *ASCII code*. That is to say, the default sort would start with numbers 0–9, then progress from uppercase A to lowercase z.

The *descending* alphanumeric sort will progress from lowercase z to uppercase A, then from 9 to 0 (zero). Lines beginning with punctuation marks or symbols (*, =, etc.) will appear at the top of ascending sorts and the bottom of descending sorts. Uppercase letters come before lowercase letters.

Accented characters are treated like their nonaccented equivalents. Thus ñ and n are the same for sorting purposes.

You can also choose to sort on date order if your text contains dates in recognizable formats, including these and others:

11/07/47

11-07-47

November 7, 1947

7-Nov-47

November-47

SPECIFYING THE FIELD USED FOR SORTING

Word will sort text separated into columns or separated with commas or tabs. Take the table in Figure 17.11, for instance. There are four fields—one containing first names, another with last names, and so on. To sort the table by last name, you would highlight all the names, numbers, and dates in Figure 17.11, then specify field number 2 to have Word sort on last names.

This same basic approach works when things are separated by tabs or commas instead of being placed in tables. Count each tab or comma as the beginning of a new field. For instance, in the string **Benson, Robert, 425, 04/15/74**, Robert would be field 2.

WORD'S MATH FEATURES

Word has several interesting math capabilities. For instance, if you type the expression **2+2**, then select it and choose Calculate from the Tools menu, the answer (4) will be briefly shown on the status bar. The expression

10(2) would yield 8, since Word treats numbers in parentheses as negative numbers. Multiplying by a percentage yields the correct answer, too. For instance, 200*25% yields 50. Complex expressions like 2400-(2400*10%) are also possible.

Every time you calculate like this, answers are automatically placed on your Clipboard, enabling you to paste them into your text. Reasonably complex mathematical expressions can be computed this way, and it is possible to highlight and sum columns of numbers either to provide answers or to check for typographic errors when typing numbers.

You can also use Word's math features to set up simple spreadsheets (tables, actually) in Word documents. But since you probably own Excel, your time would be better spent learning how to create and integrate Excel spreadsheets with Word documents.

Check Word's on-line help and documentation for more about Word's intriguing math features.

18

Working with Graphics in Word

Because Word for Windows harnesses the graphics power of Windows, you can use a variety of drawing programs to create your own artwork, plus you can incorporate other people's art in your Word documents. Word lets you place, resize, reposition, and embellish graphic images. You can work with drawings, charts from spreadsheet packages, photos from scanners, and just about any other computer-compatible art form. You can simply *paste* graphics, or you can place them in *frames*. As you'll soon see, the use of frames makes it easier for you to reposition and work with graphics. There are plenty of new graphics-related buzzwords and standards to learn. Indeed, another book the size of this one could be written just on those subjects. But this chapter contains all you'll need to start creating your own art and using free or low-cost *clip art*—that is, collections of graphic images stored on disk that can be copied and pasted into drawing programs such as Microsoft's Draw.

IMPORTING GRAPHICS

Like text, computer art can be stored in disk files. Unfortunately, different drawing packages, scanners, and other graphic tools create files in their own unique formats. Word comes with a number of built-in translation utilities (called *filters*) that can convert graphics from many sources, enabling you to insert them in Word documents. At a minimum, you will be able to work with the following graphic formats (whose usual file extensions are listed after their names):

AutoCAD 2-D (DXF)

AutoCAD Plotter (PLT)

Computer Graphics Metafile (CGM)

DrawPerfect (WPG)

Encapsulated PostScript (EPS)

HP Graphic Language (HGL)

Lotus 1-2-3 (PIC)

Micrographx Designer 3/Draw Plus (DRW)

PC Paintbrush (PCX)

TIFF (Tagged Image File Format) (TIF)

Windows Bitmap (BMP)

Windows Metafile (WMF)

If you don't see the format you need here, contact Microsoft technical support. They may be able to provide you with new filters, give you some work-around tips, or refer you to makers of graphics conversion programs.

USING THE INSERT PICTURE COMMAND

The easiest way to get hooked on graphics is to try importing a picture or two. Start by opening a new or existing Word document. Place the insertion point where you want the picture to appear, then choose Picture... from Word's Insert menu. You'll see a dialog box something like Figure 18.1.

Chances are, you have some graphic images on your hard disk already. For instance, your Windows directory probably has nearly a dozen bitmapped

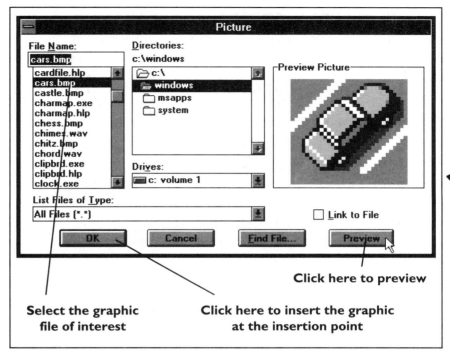

FIGURE 18.1 *Use the Insert Picture command to preview and insert disk-resident graphic files.*

files (files ending in .BMP). Use the scrollable lists to find files of interest. When you see one, click on the name to highlight it, then click the Preview button to get an idea of what it will look like. Figure 18.1 shows an example of this.

When you find a graphic you like, click OK and it will be pasted into your Word document. (If you are having trouble finding bitmapped or other graphics, use Word's Find File... command to search your whole disk for files ending with the graphics extensions listed previously.)

USING YOUR CLIPBOARD TO INSERT ART

If you already have a drawing program that you use to create and edit artwork, it is possible to copy your work to the Clipboard, then paste it into a Word document.

USING MICROSOFT DRAW

Word's installer also places on your hard disk a small but useful drawing program called Microsoft Draw. You can use it to draw new pictures or edit existing ones. When you exit Microsoft Draw, the resulting graphic is pasted into your Word document at the insertion point. You'll need a mouse to use it. (Trying to draw with a keyboard instead of a mouse is like trying to paint a house with a toothbrush.)

Starting Microsoft Draw

There are three ways to start Draw. The easiest is to place the insertion point where you want your new art to be placed, then click on the Toolbar's Draw button—the button with the square, circle, and triangle.

Or, if you have a Word document containing a graphic you want to modify, double-clicking on the graphic will often run Draw.

Finally, you can use the Object... command on Word's Insert menu. From the resulting dialog box shown at the top of Figure 18.2, scroll to the Microsoft Draw choice and double-click on it.

Using Draw

Regardless of how you start Microsoft Draw, you will see a drawing window like the one in Figure 18.2. Here you use a series of buttons, menu commands, and your mouse to draw, resize, and rearrange shapes, lines, and text. Here's an important tip: you may need to resize or maximize the Draw window to see all of the buttons on the left! Draw has on-line help. Undo works in Draw.

Drawing Things

First, click on a shape button or line button (line, ellipse, circle, or whatever), then use your mouse to create lines or shapes. For instance, to create rectangles like those shown in the organizational chart in Figure 18.2, you would click on the rectangle button, then drag with your mouse to create a rectangle of the desired shape and size. (Holding down the Shift key while you do this creates squares.) Use the ellipse tool for ovals and circles. (The Shift key helps you make precise circles.)

Double-clicking here is one of
3 ways to start Microsoft Draw

The Microsoft Draw window

Click then use your mouse to
move and resize things

Click to enlarge your view of
things. Shift-click reduces.

Drag for lines. Shift-drag to
draw horizontal, vertical or
45-degree lines.

Drag for an ellipsis. Shift-drag
for circles.

Drag for rounded rectangles.
Shift-drag for rounded squares.

Draw arcs with this tool

Click-and-drag repeatedly with
this tool for irregular shapes

Turn on grid lines to help align items

If necessary, drag to increase window size
or click maximize button to show all
draw tool buttons

When you exit Draw, your
picture is placed at the insertion
point in the active document

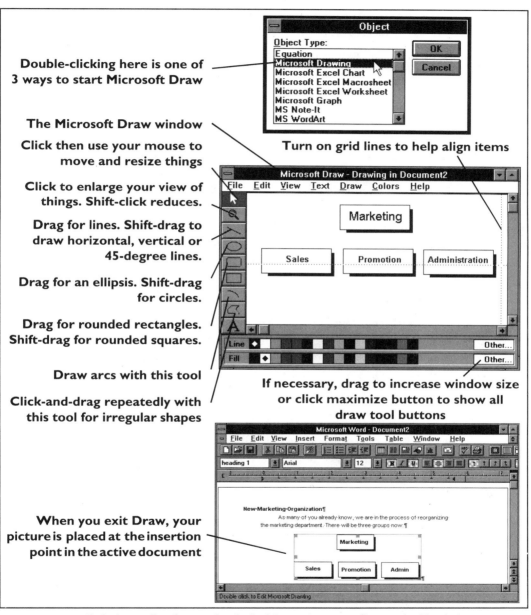

FIGURE 18.2 *Click the Toolbar button that looks like an American flag, or double-click on Microsoft Drawing in the Object Type dialog box to start the Draw program.*

To create polygons, choose the polygon tool, then click-and-drag repeatedly until you are done. For example, to make a triangle, you would click once to anchor the first point and drag for the first side; click again to anchor the second point and drag again; click to anchor the third point and drag back to the starting point; then click one last time to complete the triangle.

Selecting Things

To select rectangles or other drawing elements (lines, text, and so forth), you would click on the arrow button at the top of the drawing tool stack, then point to the item you want to move. This selects it. Holding down the Shift key lets you select multiple objects. The Edit menu contains a Select All choice that selects every item in your drawing. Selected objects are surrounded by small handles. Click outside of any selected object to deselect all selected objects.

Multilevel Menus in Draw

The Draw window contains multilevel menus that let you specify different line styles and patterns, among other things. For instance, the *Line Style* choice on the Draw menu lets you pick different line widths and specify solid or broken lines. The drop-shadow effect around the org chart boxes in Figure 18.2, for example, was created by drawing thick lines on two sides of each box.

It takes three clicks to use these multilevel menus. First, click on the Menu name (Draw, for instance); then click the command (Line Style, perhaps); then click on the choice in the resulting list.

The choices you make affect items you've selected just before making the menu choices, as well as any new items you create. For instance, if you select a line then choose the Dash-dot line style, the selected line will change to a Dash-dot line. If you've selected things constructed of visible lines (circles, squares, etc.), the lines used to construct them will change. Moreover, new lines and objects constructed of lines will use the new style until you change it again.

Text in Microsoft Draw

You create text objects by first selecting the Type size and attribute from Draw's multilevel Text menus (font, size, alignment, etc.), then creating an empty text object by clicking on the text tool (the A button). Type text as usual, realizing that you are limited to one line of 255 characters per text object. Obviously, you can create multiple text objects and place them near each other to create multiple lines. Text does not word wrap. Press Enter when you've finished typing.

To edit text, select the text *object* of interest, then select and edit text *within* the object. You can embellish text (make it bold, italic, and so on), plus you can combine the effects, but the entire object will have all of the characteristics. (In other words, you can't make just one of several words in an object bold.)

Moving Things

Select the item or items to be moved, then point to one of the selected items with your mouse pointer, avoiding the object's handles. Drag with your mouse and watch as an outline of the object(s) proposes a new location. Releasing the mouse button completes the move.

Draw has optional, "invisible grid lines" that make it easy to align things. This makes dragging a little jerky when the Snap To Gridlines feature is enabled. The grid lines act like magnets, and moved objects migrate to them no matter how hard you try to prevent this. For precise, smooth moves, turn the *Snap To Grid* feature off from the Draw menu.

Resizing Things

You resize objects by selecting them and dragging the handles that appear at the corners of the objects. Holding the Shift key while you drag diagonally retains the object's overall proportions and reduces or enlarges the same percentage in both dimensions. Holding the Shift key while you drag horizontally maintains an object's original height. Holding the Shift key while you drag vertically maintains an object's original width.

Draw does not automatically resize text in objects. Use the Text Size submenu to do this.

Layers and Groups

You can construct objects from multiple elements placed near, on top of, or beneath each other. (The org boxes in Figure 18.2 consist of a rectangle, two lines, and a text box, for instance.) Things piled on top of each other are said to be *layered*. Obviously, you would not be able to read the text in the organization chart if it were hidden behind the boxes, so you would normally want to create the text *after* you draw the boxes. Alternately, you can select items and use Draw's *Bring To Front* or *Send To Back* commands on the Edit menu to arrange layers to your liking.

Sometimes you'll want to turn multiple drawing parts into a single object. This makes it easier to move and resize complex elements (an org box with its shadow lines and text, for instance). Simply select all of the elements of interest and use the *Group* choice on the Draw menu. Henceforth, all of the items will act as a single item until you select the group and choose Ungroup from the Draw menu.

Reorienting Objects

To flip objects, select them and choose Rotate/Flip from the Draw menu. Choose one of the four choices on the resulting submenu. Undo works if you use it before doing something else.

Duplicating Objects

Once you've created an object (say, an org chart box), you can select, copy, and paste it to save time. Consider grouping complex collections of lines and shapes and text before duplicating them.

Leaving Draw

To quit Draw for Word, where you want to polish a document that will contain drawings or clip art, click on Exit and Return to Document from Draw's File menu. This will close Draw and paste your drawing at the insertion point.

SOURCES OF CLIP ART

If you don't have the time or inclination to draw your own art, you can purchase compatible clip art disks from mail-order firms and retail computer dealers. Many companies and nonprofit groups also distribute low-cost (or free) shareware and public domain clip art. Check local computer user groups and on-line art libraries like the ones provided by CompuServe. If you have a scanner, you can convert printed images to Word-compatible art. Be sure you understand and honor any copyright restrictions when you use other people's art.

SIZING AND CROPPING GRAPHICS WITH YOUR MOUSE

When you click on a graphic in a Word document, it will be surrounded by a light gray box containing eight handles—one in each corner and one on each side of the outline box. To increase or decrease the size of a graphic, drag a *corner* handle diagonally, releasing it when you are happy with the proposed size. Use the handles on the *edges* of the graphic outline to stretch (distort) your graphic horizontally or vertically. Undo works if you act promptly.

To crop a document (hide part of it), hold down the Shift key while you drag any of the handles to create the desired effect.

SIZING AND CROPPING GRAPHICS WITH THE PICTURE COMMAND

The Picture... command on Word's Format menu reveals a dialog box containing information about a selected picture's original size and any cropping or resizing that's been done. You can also use this box to specify new size and cropping dimensions. The Reset button returns a graphic to its original size and uncrops it.

BORDERS FOR INSERTED GRAPHICS

You can use Words Border... command to add and modify borders around graphics, the same way you work with borders around paragraphs.

FRAMES—POWERFUL POSITIONING TOOLS

Frames are a sure source of confusion. Push on, though. It will be worth your while to understand them!

If you simply paste a graphic into a Word document, it is treated like a character. You can then place the graphic between characters, move it from one line to another, copy it, delete it, and so on. But it is a slave to things like line and paragraph specifications, margins, indents, and others. So, to have maximum control over graphics and other document elements, you should place them in *frames*.

Frames let you precisely position objects, virtually anywhere in your document. An extra advantage to using them is that they allow you to tell Word to flow text around them, making your publication or report more distinctive. Frames can contain graphics, Excel charts, Word text, or combinations thereof. In fact, it may be helpful to think of frames as pages within a page that you can move, resize, and embellish.

To use frames, you create them, insert things into them, then size and position them either with your mouse or with the Frame dialog box. Normally, you'll want to work with framed items in Page Layout view so that you can easily see and move them.

INSERTING FRAMES AND FRAMING THINGS

Either you can insert an empty frame and then place something in it, or you can select something *then* frame it. In either case you use the Frame command on the Insert menu *or* the Frame button on the Toolbar. The Frame button looks like an American flag.

Inserting Empty Frames

Start by switching to Page Layout view, if you are not already in it. (When you forget to do this, Word will ask if it can switch views for you.) Click the Frame button or choose Frame from Word's Insert menu. Your pointer will change to crosshairs. Drag to create a frame of the approximate size and shape you desire, located about where you want it to be placed. Shortly after you release the mouse button you'll see a frame surrounded by a black border. It will contain a paragraph mark. You can either type text in the resulting frame (you'll learn how in a moment), or you can paste things from your Clipboard or use many of the Insert menu commands, including the Picture... and Object... commands.

Framing Existing Objects

If you already have something in your document that needs framing, simply select it and use either the Frame button or the Frame command on the Insert menu. If you accidentally frame the wrong thing or too many or too few things, a quick undo should work. If it doesn't, read on.

SELECTING AND DELETING FRAMED ITEMS

While in Page Layout view, it's possible to delete frames *and their contents* by simply *selecting* the frame then cutting (Ctrl-X), or by pressing the Del key. (Select a frame by pointing and clicking with your mouse. Eight dark black handles and a black line will appear around the frame when you've selected it.)

To remove a frame, but *not* its contents, select the frame, then use the *Remove Frame* button in the Frame dialog box (reached from the Format menu). If you remove a frame but not its contents this way, the frame's *border* will remain. Delete it or change it as described next.

DELETING OR CHANGING FRAME BORDERS

Frames are always created with borders, but these can be removed or altered. Select a framed object in Page Layout view by clicking on the object. Use Word's standard Border command to change or remove the border. For instance, clicking on the None icon in the Preset area of the Border dialog box removes a frame's border.

POSITIONING FRAMED ITEMS WITH A MOUSE

The dirt-simple way to position frames is to drag them with your mouse while in Page Layout view. Move the pointer around the edges of the framed object until it turns into a four-headed arrow like the one in Figure 18.3. Press down on the primary mouse button and drag. Soon after you release the mouse button, the frame will take up residence in its new location.

When you position frames this way, they use the left and top edges of the page as reference points. As you add or delete text in your document, the framed item stays right where you dragged it. This is often the desired effect. But what if you want to keep a framed item with specific text?

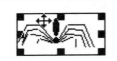

FIGURE 18.3 *When the mouse pointer has four arrowheads, you can move frames with it.*

POSITIONING FRAMED ITEMS WITH THE FRAME DIALOG BOX

For precise frame positioning, or to force a frame always to position itself relative to other things that might move as you edit your document, use the Frame dialog box reached from the Frame... command on the Format menu. Figure 18.4 shows it.

When you select a frame and open this dialog box, you will see the current size and position of the frame. You can specify new size and position settings for the frame in inches (**in**), centimeters (**cm**), points (**pt**), lines (**li**), or picas (**pi**).

ALIGNING FRAMES WITH REFERENCE POINTS

The Frame dialog box also provides a mind-boggling array of positioning and reference options. For instance, you can force a frame always to remain in the exact horizontal and vertical center of a page, even when you change margins or page sizes. Or, you can tell Word to keep a frame a specified distance from margins or columns. Finally, you can anchor a frame to text so that when the text moves, the frame accompanies it. Place a check mark in the Move with Text box to accomplish this.

RESIZING FRAMED ITEMS

To change the size of a frame and its contents, select the frame, then either enter new dimensions in the Frame dialog box or drag the frame with the two-headed arrow as shown in Figure 18.5.

TEXT AND FRAMES

Frames and text can be used together several ways. Besides framing text, you can position frames relative to text, and/or have text flow around frames. Here are a few ways to work with frames and text.

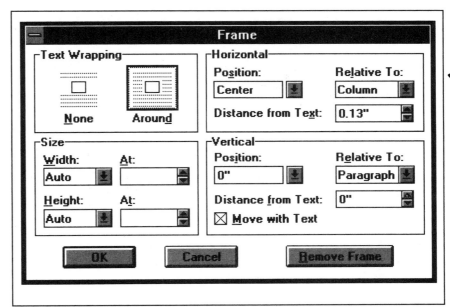

FIGURE 18.4 *Use the Frame dialog box for precise frame sizing and positioning.*

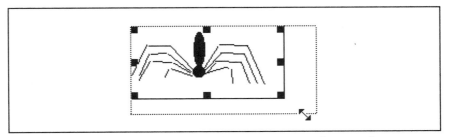

FIGURE 18.5 *Drag with the two-headed arrow to resize a frame and its contents, or enter specific dimensions in the Frame dialog box.*

Placing Text in Frames

You can use frames as small text windows that can be moved anywhere in your document. For instance, in Figure 18.6 Adam's paragraph headings are being framed and moved into his document margin. (You may want to remove the frame borders when you do this.)

When you make sure that the *Move with Text* option is checked in the frame dialog box, the headings will stay with their paragraphs when your document is edited.

A quick way to create lots of marginal headings like Adam's is to create one, then redefine the document's heading style(s) based on the example. All of your headings will be framed and placed in the margin quicker than you can say "arachnid."

When framing existing text, Word will make the frame big enough to accommodate all of the text you've selected. If you paste text into an *existing frame*, make sure the frame is big enough to prevent "weird word wrap," a particular problem when you've specified large line indents or placed long words in narrow frames. If the text you insert changes into a long vertical string of characters, try resizing the frame to make the text legible.

Feel free to use virtually all of Word's text formatting tools in Frames. You can have multiple paragraphs in frames. Word's ribbon and ruler work in frames. You can change type sizes and styles, center, justify, and otherwise fool with text in frames. Even Word's Spelling Checker peeks into them.

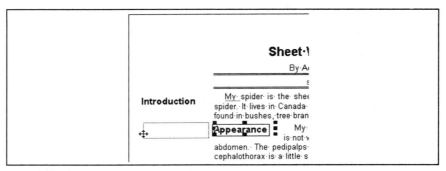

FIGURE 18.6 *Framed text can be used to place headings in margins, among other things.*

Inserting Text in Framed Graphics (Captioning)

If you want to add a caption to a framed graphic, select the frame, then press the Enter key. You'll see a new paragraph mark in the frame. Type the caption. Stylize the text, if you like. The caption will stay with the frame when you move it.

Flowing Text around Frames

As Adam will tell you, Word can flow text around frames. Figure 18.7 shows an example of this.

For this to work, you must have a minimum of 1" between the frame and your margin, column boundary, or another framed item.

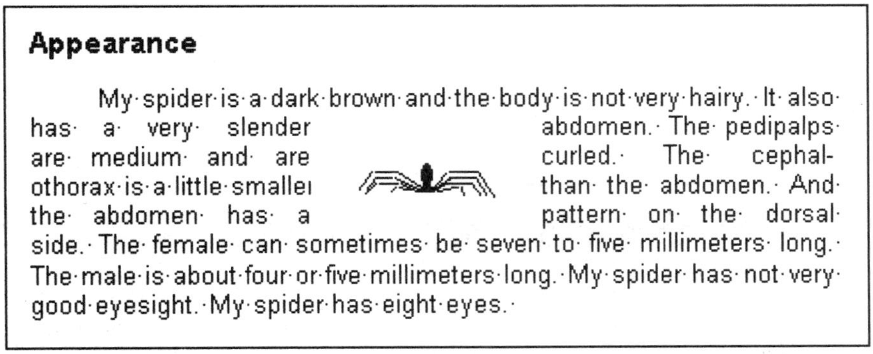

Appearance

My·spider·is·a·dark·brown·and·the·body·is·not·very·hairy.·It·also· has· a· very· slender   abdomen.· The· pedipalps· are· medium· and· are   curled.· The· cephal- othorax·is·a·little·smaller   than· the· abdomen.· And· the· abdomen· has· a   pattern· on· the· dorsal· side.· The· female· can· sometimes· be· seven· to· five· millimeters· long.· The·male·is·about·four·or·five·millimeters·long.·My·spider·has·not·very· good·eyesight.·My·spider·has·eight·eyes.·

FIGURE 18.7 *Text will flow around a frame if there is enough text to accommodate it.*

HOW GRAPHICS APPEAR IN DIFFERENT VIEWS

When you place unframed graphics in a Word document, you can see them with Normal, Page Layout, and Outline views, plus Print Preview. The Draft option hides graphics to speed scrolling.

Framed graphics can be seen where they will print when displayed in Print Preview and Page Layout view. When you switch to Normal or Outline views, framed items will appear within the page boundaries where they will print, but not necessarily in their printing positions. You can easily spot framed items in Normal and Outline views. They have small black boxes in the left margin next to them.

SPECIAL EFFECTS WITH WORDART

There's an intriguing little program installed with Word called WordArt. You can use it to create unusual-looking text objects. From the Insert menu choose Object..., then scroll to MS WordArt and double-click on it. You'll see a dialog box like the one in Figure 18.8.

Either type new text or paste text from your Clipboard. Experiment with the fonts, sizes, styles, alignment, and other options. You'll see a preview as you work. When you are happy with the effect, click OK and WordArt will paste your concoction into the active Word document at the insertion point.

Frame the object if you like, to make it easier to move. Since the fonts supplied with WordArt are bitmapped, they may be hard to read in small sizes and appear jaggy if they get too big. Experiment!

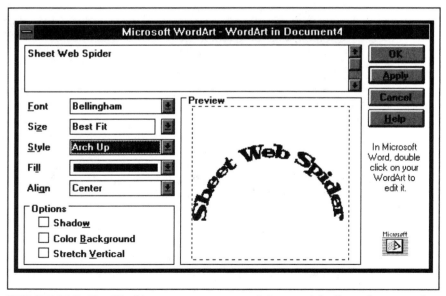

FIGURE 18.8 *Use WordArt to create text containing special effects, then paste it into your Word document and frame it.*

REPEATING FRAMED ITEMS ON MULTIPLE PAGES

To repeat the same framed object on multiple pages, create the framed object and copy it to your Clipboard. Switch to Normal view and open a header or footer. Paste the frame. You won't *see* the framed object in this view; instead, you'll see just the little square black frame marker.

Switch back to Page Layout view and drag the item to reposition it, if necessary. Use your bag of header and footer tricks with items thus placed. You can have different frames on odd and even pages, for instance, or different items in different sections.

It's time to put down the book and grab your mouse. Try a few of the techniques in this chapter. When you're tired of doing all the work, check out the next chapter, where you'll see how templates and macros provided with Word can speed everyday tasks.

WORD

19

Letters, Envelopes, Memos, and Other Everyday Tasks

Microsoft has provided a variety of tools and templates designed to speed production of frequently created documents. These include everything from a simple Envelope button on the Toolbar to complex templates that ask you questions and change the appearance of your menu bar. You can use these tools as they stand or modify them to fit your needs and preferences. Let's take a look.

TEMPLATES SPEED DAILY CHORES

By now you know that Word templates are files you can use as patterns to create similar documents without spending lots of time setting up styles, formats, and other elements. Word comes with letter, memo, report, envelope, mailing label, and other templates.

STORING USER INFORMATION

Many of Microsoft's predefined templates rely upon information that you are asked to enter the first time you use certain templates. For instance, *Enter Sender Information* is required by most of the templates used for correspondence. The first time you pick a template needing sender information, you will see a dialog box like the one in Figure 19.1.

Enter and check the information carefully, since typos made here will appear in all documents you create with a number of different templates. If you spot errors after you've closed the Enter Sender Information dialog box, you can update it later with the Set Letter Options... command found on many template menus.

TEMPLATES CHANGE MENUS

Some predefined templates change Word's menus. For instance, the letter templates have additional items on their Format menus that let you insert saved addresses, create fax cover sheets, and more. Figure 19.2 shows an example of this.

TEMPLATE INSTRUCTIONS

Since some templates can be quite complex, and frequently seem to have a mind of their own, many come with special on-line instructions. As you can see in Figure 19.2, menus often contain Instructions... commands. Figure 19.3 shows the instructions for letter templates. Get in the habit of checking instructions like these when you try a new template.

TEMPLATE OPTIONS

On the theory that even repetitive projects are never exactly the same, many predefined templates include dialog boxes that ask you for desired

```
┌─────────────────────────────────────────────────────────┐
│ ─         Enter Sender Information:                       │
│                                                           │
│  Enter YOUR name and address. It is used in letters and   │
│  envelopes you create. You only need to do this once.     │
│                                                           │
│  ┌Mr.──────┐  Full Name: ┌─────────────────────────────┐  │
│  ├─────────┤             │ Ron Mansfield               │  │
│  │Mr.    ▲ │             └─────────────────────────────┘  │
│  │Ms.      │  Suffix:   ┌──────────┐                       │
│  │Miss   ▼ │           └──────────┘                        │
│  └─────────┘                                               │
│     Position: ┌─────────────────────────────────────────┐ │
│               │ Author                                  │ │
│               └─────────────────────────────────────────┘ │
│     Company:  ┌─────────────────────────────────────────┐ │
│               │ Sybex, Inc.                             │ │
│               └─────────────────────────────────────────┘ │
│   Address 1:  ┌─────────────────────────────────────────┐ │
│               │ 2021 Challenger Drive                   │ │
│               └─────────────────────────────────────────┘ │
│   Address 2:  ┌─────────────────────────────────────────┐ │
│               └─────────────────────────────────────────┘ │
│        City:  ┌─────────────────────────────────────────┐ │
│               │ Alameda                                 │ │
│               └─────────────────────────────────────────┘ │
│       State:  ┌──────────┐   Zip Code: ┌───────────────┐  │
│               │ CA       │             │ 94501         │  │
│               └──────────┘             └───────────────┘  │
│                                                           │
│  Phone Number: ┌──────────────────┐   ┌────────────┐      │
│                │ 510-523-8233     │   │    OK      │      │
│                └──────────────────┘   └────────────┘      │
│    Fax Number: ┌──────────────────┐   ┌────────────┐      │
│                │ 510-523-2373     │   │   Cancel   │      │
│                └──────────────────┘   └────────────┘      │
│ Writer's Initials: ┌──────────────┐                       │
│                    │ RCM          │                       │
│                    └──────────────┘                       │
│ Typist's Initials: ┌──────────────┐                       │
│                    │ mos          │                       │
│                    └──────────────┘                       │
└─────────────────────────────────────────────────────────┘
```

FIGURE 19.1 *Word asks once for information required by some templates, then saves it for repeated use.*

changes. These are often presented to you when you start a new project, and can usually be reached from menu commands as you work. For example, the Letter Options dialog box shown in Figure 19.4 can be reached from the Set Letter Options... command on the letter templates or Format menu.

It shows you the settings and text it plans to use, then lets you change these and other options with buttons.

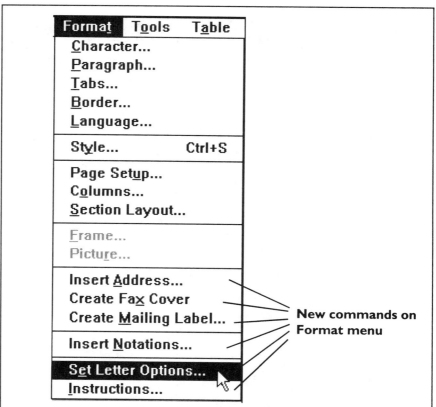

FIGURE 19.2 *Some Word templates change your menus.*

RUNNING TEMPLATES

Once you've entered the necessary information, Word's templates create a new document. This is often accompanied by a frenzy of on-screen activity that may make you think your computer is possessed. And it is—by special macros that construct a document using your input. Figure 19.5 shows the beginnings of a letter based on the choices shown in the prior illustrations.

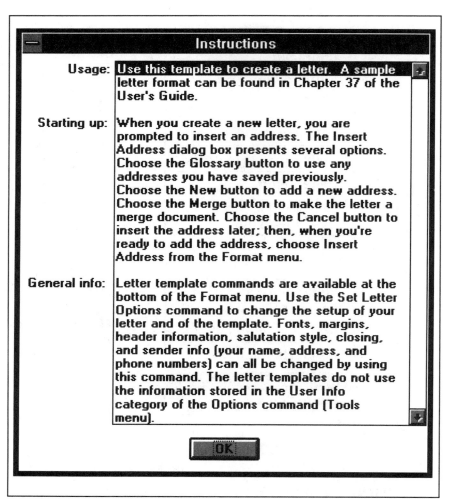

FIGURE 19.3 *On-line instructions are available for Word's letter templates.*

PRINTING ENVELOPES WITH THE ENVELOPE BUTTON

After you've created a letter either with the template or from scratch, an envelope can be a mere mouse click away. By using either the Envelope button on the Toolbar or the Create Envelope... command from the

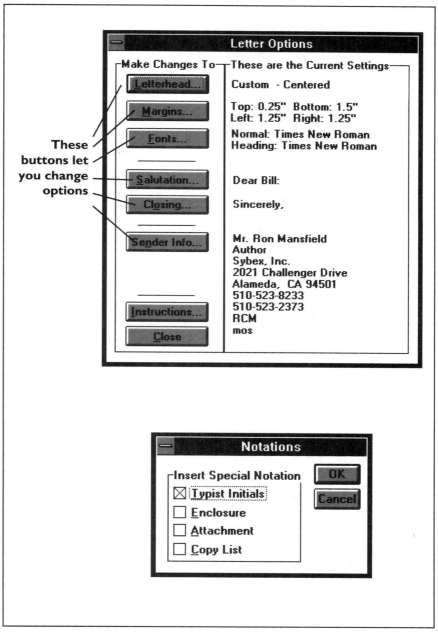

FIGURE 19.4 *Many templates have their own option dialog boxes.*

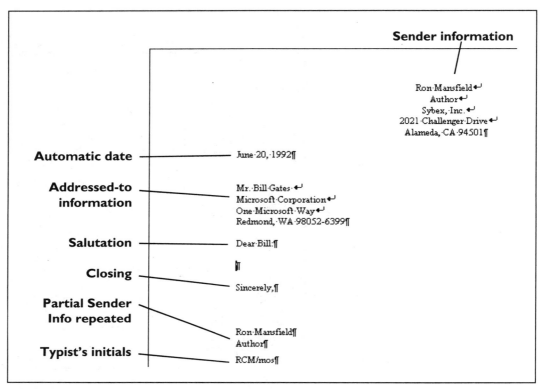

FIGURE 19.5 *The letter templates will automatically insert sender and addressee information, today's date, a salutation, a closing, and the sender's name, among other things.*

Tools menu, you will be presented with a dialog box like the one shown in Figure 19.6.

You are given a choice of envelope sizes and asked about the type of printer you'll be using. You can print just the envelope or just the letter, or both. The *Add to Document* button will place the envelope in your current document as page 0 (zero). Addresses can also be saved as glossary entries to avoid having to retype them in the future.

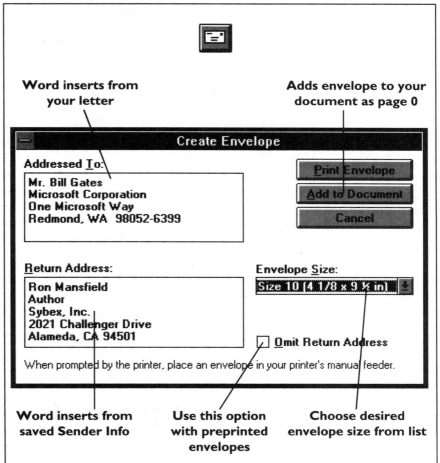

**Word inserts from
your letter**

**Adds envelope to your
document as page 0**

**Word inserts from
saved Sender Info**

**Use this option
with preprinted
envelopes**

**Choose desired
envelope size from list**

FIGURE 19.6 *Speed envelope creation with the Envelope button or the Tool menu's Create Envelope... command.*

EXPLORING THE PREDEFINED TEMPLATES

Many of Word's predefined templates are based on *Webster's Secretarial Handbook* and other recognized authorities. They include:

LETTERS

LETBLOCK—a standard block letter format with flush-left margins, a flush-left date, no first-line indentation, and flush-left second page information (recipient name, company, date, page numbers, etc.)

LETMODBK—similar to LETBLOCK, this modified block letter template has an indented date and signature block; second page information is all placed on one line with the page number centered

LETMDSEM—similar to LETMODBK, but with first-line indents

LETPERSN—similar to LETMODBK, but for use in a personal letter with no author's title or notations after the signature block

MEMOS

The memo template (**MEMO**) is based on *Webster's Secretarial Handbook*. As you can see in Figure 19.7, it is possible to create and use lists of recipients.

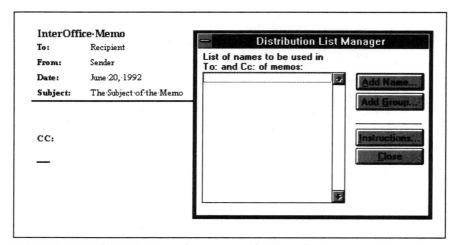

FIGURE 19.7 *The MEMO template prompts for lists of recipients, which can be saved and reused.*

OVERHEAD TRANSPARENCIES

Word's **OVERHEAD** template is a quick way to set up landscape documents complete with major and minor headings. A bullet command quickly adds bullets to lists. Figure 19.8 shows you what the two standard transparency pages look like.

REPORT TEMPLATES

There are three report templates, named **REPSTAND**, **REPLAND**, and **REPSIDE**. These templates set up portrait or landscape reports using report information you enter in a dialog box at the start of the project. Figure 19.9 shows the **REPSTAND** template at work.

The **REPSIDE** template places headings in margins. You'll probably need to use Word's Zoom features to make text big enough to see while you enter and edit in report templates.

MAILING LABELS

The **MAILLABL** template can create single or multiple labels for a number of standard Avery label styles. Pick the Avery product number from a drop-down menu provided by the template.

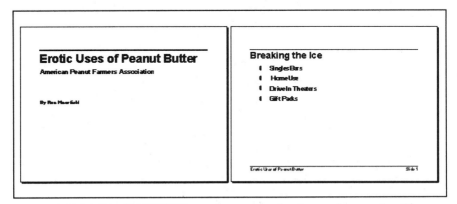

FIGURE 19.8 *The OVERHEAD template creates landscape documents with easily created bullet lists.*

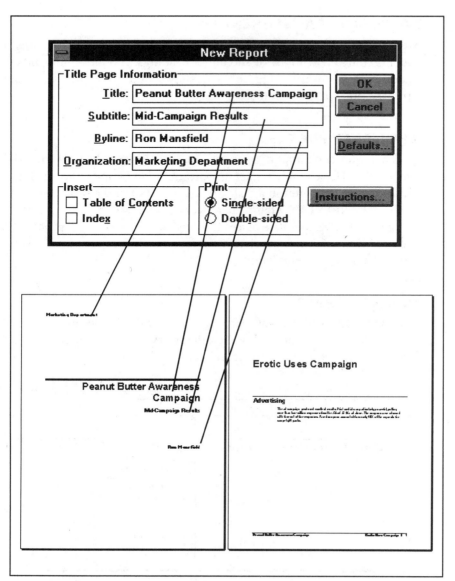

FIGURE 19.9 *Enter title, subtitle, and other information to create impressive-looking reports with any one of Word's three report templates.*

FACSIMILE (FAX) DOCUMENTS

Word's **FAX** template produces facsimile cover sheets. The template automatically enters today's date and sender information. You can also create cover sheets like this from other templates that contain the Create FAX Cover command on their Format menus.

PRESS RELEASES

The **PRESS** template creates news releases in the format recommended by the *Associated Press Stylebook*. It prompts you for a subject and for contact information, which is repeated in your document where necessary.

ARTICLE

Budding authors take note: the **ARTICLE** template helps you create professional-looking editorial submissions. It asks you for a title, contact information, and publication rights, then creates the generally accepted submission format described in a fascinating book called *Writer's Market 1991*.

DISSERTATIONS

The dissertation template (**DISSERT**) formats your work using the guidelines described in Kate Turabian's *Manual for Writers of Term Papers, Theses, and Dissertations* (University of Chicago Press), 5th edition. Read the file called TEMPLATE.DOC in your WINWORD directory before using this template.

TEMPLATES AS TEACHERS

Microsoft's templates are interesting examples of complex Word documents. A great way to learn new Word tricks is to create documents with these templates, then explore the styles, Page Setup information, and other techniques used by the template makers. Technocrats call this process "reverse engineering." We call it self-teaching.

20

Power Tools

If you've read and understand the information in Chapters 10 through 19, you can already create impressive-looking Word documents. This chapter and the ones that follow describe power tools that can make you even more productive, whether you write best-sellers or operate a small business. Some tools help you quickly move from place to place in large documents. Others help polish prose, or automatically create an index and table of contents.

MOVING QUICKLY TO
SPECIFIC PLACES IN YOUR DOCUMENT

Besides the scroll bars and navigation keys (Home, PgUp, PgDn, and End), Word has a number of navigational aids. For instance, the Find... command lets you quickly locate text or formats. And it's possible to mark and quickly locate key parts of your document, thanks to Word's Bookmark features. The Outline view lets you get the big picture, then zoom in on a specific area of interest. You've already seen how to split a window into panes so that you can see widely separated parts of a document at the same time. Let's now look at these features in more detail.

NEXT PANE KEYS

When you split a document into panes, or when you've opened a header, footer, or footnote pane, the *F6* and *Shift-F6* (Next Pane and Previous Pane) keys will move you from pane to pane and back. This makes it possible to work in multiple panes without reaching for your mouse, or accidentally repositioning the insertion point in your open panes.

GO BACK

Word watches as you reposition the insertion point and edit at different places in your document. It remembers the last three locations where you've worked. Word takes you back to the previous editing location, scrolling the screen, if necessary. The insertion point moves at the same time, so that when you arrive back at the old location you can begin working there immediately. You can press Shift-F6 up to three times to cycle through the three preceding work locations. The fourth time you press Shift-F6, you are returned to the spot where you initiated the Go Back requests.

When you close a document, Word also remembers where you were working. If you press Shift-F5 immediately after you open a document, you will be returned to the spot where you were working when you quit.

GO TO WITH THE F5 FUNCTION KEY

To get to a specific place in the document, you can press the F5 keyboard *once*. The status bar asks you to enter the desired location. For instance, to go to page 10 you could press F5, then type 10 and press Enter.

WORD

If you are working in a multisection document where the page numbers restart at 1 in each section, you must specify section and page numbers. Typing **S3P12** would take you to page 12 in the third section, for instance. Figure 20.1 illustrates this.

If you don't know a specific page number, you can enter a percentage to get in the right neighborhood. For example, entering **50%** would take you to the middle of your document, **10%** would position you near the top, and so on.

To go to a footnote, enter an **f** and the footnote number. The entry **f3** would take you to the third footnote. If you have annotated your document (described later), enter the annotation number of interest, preceded by the letter **a**. (Enter **a10** to get to the tenth note, for example.)

NAVIGATING WITH THE GO TO... COMMAND

Pressing the F5 function key twice in a row or choosing Go To... on the Edit menu reveals a Go To dialog box. You use it instead of the status bar to enter navigational requests. But there is a better use for the dialog box. It lets you find bookmarks, which are described next.

CREATING AND FINDING BOOKMARKS

Bookmarks are invisible "pointers" that you can name and insert anywhere you want in your document. Then you can use them to move from place to place. For instance, if you are writing a report containing information about sales, markets, and problems, you can insert pointers with those names, then use the Go To dialog box (or F5 function key) to move to those points in the document. You can have up to 450 bookmarks in a document.

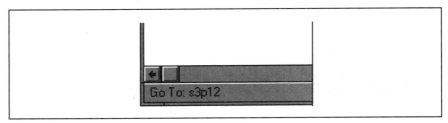

FIGURE 20.1 *Press the F5 function key once and type a navigational request (page number, section number, etc.) in the Go To area, then press Enter.*

Entering Bookmarks

Move the insertion point to the *location* you want to mark, or select a *collection of text* you want to mark, then choose the Insert Bookmark... command from the Insert menu, or press Ctrl-Shift-F5. You'll see a dialog box like the one at the top of Figure 20.2.

Type a unique bookmark name of up to 20 characters with no spaces. You can use letters, numbers, and the underscore character (_). Names must

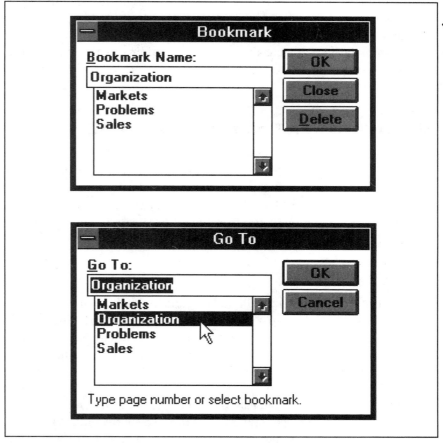

FIGURE 20.2 *Create bookmarks with the Insert Bookmark... command, and find them with the Go To... command. Or use the Ctrl-Shift-F5 shortcut and the status bar to create them or the F5,F5 key sequence to find them.*

start with letters. For instance **Sales_Figures-93** would be permitted, but **93Sales or 93-Sales Figures** would not.

Finding Bookmarks

To move the insertion point to a bookmark, press the F5 function key and type the bookmark name in the status bar (pressing Enter executes the move). If you don't remember the name of the bookmark, reveal the Go To dialog box by pressing F5 twice, or choose the Go To... command from the Edit menu. Then pick the bookmark from the scrolling list of names as shown at the bottom of Figure 20.2.

Happily, if you delete all of the text pertaining to a bookmark, the bookmark disappears with it.

FINDING AND REPLACING TEXT, STYLES, AND MORE

Word offers several options when finding text. You can have it look for strings of text (like all occurrences of "Bob"), or restrict the search to stop only at places where "Bob" is in a heading, or find text in which "Bob" is *not* part of another word like "bobsled." Word either will just point out occurrences of the requested text (scrolling if necessary to display it in context), or will change things that it finds.

FINDING TEXT

The Find... command will find text and highlight it for you. This is a good way to move quickly to a specific place or places in your document.

Choose the Find... command on the Edit menu (don't confuse this with Find File... on the File menu). You'll see a dialog box like the one in Figure 20.3.

Type the text string of interest in the *Find What* box, then click the Find Next button to begin the search. (If you've used Find... since you last started Word, your most recent request will already be in the Find What box. Before searching, highlight and replace the earlier search request, if necessary.)

You can find *all* occurrences of the text string, or be more restrictive. Simply typing **Bob** will find "Bob," "BOB," "bob," "bobcat," and "discombobulate." The *Match Whole Word Only* and *Match Case* options can be used

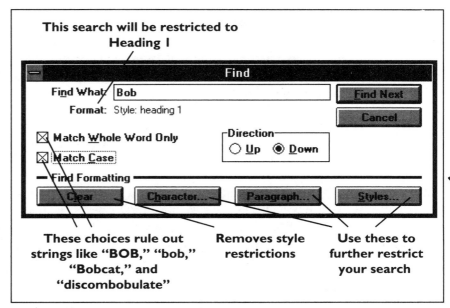

This search will be restricted to Heading 1

These choices rule out strings like "BOB," "bob," "Bobcat," and "discombobulate"

Removes style restrictions

Use these to further restrict your search

FIGURE 20.3 *Find text of interest with the Find... command on Word's Edit menu.*

to find only "Bob" in this example. Searches can be further narrowed by specifying styles or formats. For instance, clicking the Styles... button in the Find dialog box reveals a list of styles. When you pick a style, it is listed beneath the Find What box. Thus, in Figure 20.3 Word will only look for "Bob" in level 1 headings.

You can also specify character and/or paragraph formats when searching. The restrictions can be combined. For instance, you could look for occurrences of "Bob" in only Normal style that have also been embellished with Bold character formatting. Use the Clear button to remove style, character, and paragraph format restrictions.

Searches begin at the insertion point. The Up or Down buttons can be used to tell Word which way to look. If you don't start the search with the insertion point at the beginning or end of a document, Word will ask if you want it to continue after reaching the end of the specified search area. Answering Yes will cause Word to search the whole document.

Once you've found what you want, you can double-click on the Find dialog box's Close box or click on the Cancel button to continue editing.

SIMPLE TEXT REPLACEMENT

Suppose you wanted to change each occurrence of Bob's name to Mary. You *could* find "Bob," then *manually* replace his name with hers. But the *Replace...* command is a better tool for tasks like this. Reach it from the Edit menu. Figure 20.4 shows the resulting Replace dialog box.

The Find portion of the Replace process works like the Find command described previously. But you can also specify replacement text and/or styles. It's even possible to remove things by telling Word to replace something with nothing. At the top of Figure 20.4, Word has been told to replace "peanut" with "goober" everywhere. (You would have a problem here if you had unwittingly typed "Europeanutopia" without a space.) At the bottom of Figure 20.1, Word will change the style of all level 1 headings to level 2.

After you've specified the text and, optionally, the attributes to find and replace, click the *Find Next* button to start the process. Word will highlight the first occurrence it finds, then wait for you to click either the *Replace*, *Replace All*, or *Cancel* button.

Replace will make the change and look for the next occurrence. *Find Next* will leave the first occurrence intact and look for another. Replace All does just that, sometimes with extremely fast and unwanted results. Undo (Ctrl-Z) can help if you act immediately after screwing up. It's a good idea to save your work before using Replace All; you might even want to watch the first few replacements by using Find Next before turning Word loose on your 50-page report.

FINDING AND
REPLACING SPECIAL CHARACTERS

You can use the Find... or Replace... commands to locate, change, or remove tabs, page breaks, paragraph marks, and more. You do this by typing caret marks (^) and letters in the Find or Replace boxes. For instance, to find two consecutive paragraph marks and replace them with one mark, you would type ^p^p in the find box and ^p in the Replace box. To delete all manual page breaks, you would type ^d in the Find box and not enter

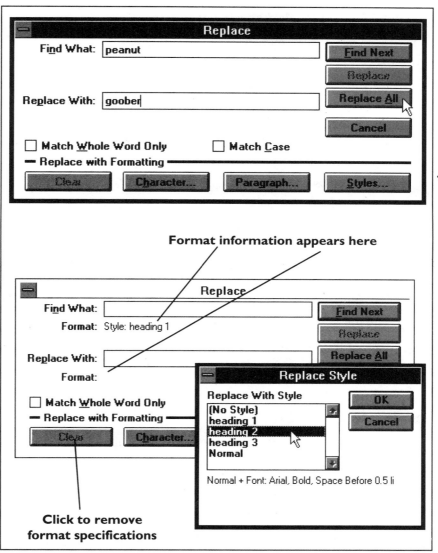

FIGURE 20.4 *The Replace command can replace text, change styles, or even remove things.*

anything in the replace box. Here is a list of the special characters you can replace and their codes:

Tabs	^t
Paragraph marks	^p
Manual page breaks	^d
Line breaks (Shift-Enter)	^n
Column breaks	^14
Section breaks	^d
Footnote reference marks	^2
Annotation marks	^5
White space	^w
Graphics	^1
Optional hyphens	^-
Nonbreaking hyphens	^~
Nonbreaking space	^s
Fields	^19

REVISION MARKS

The Tools menu's Revision Marks… command reveals the dialog box shown in Figure 20.5. Revision marks show readers where you've changed any portion of a document. Start with a draft document and turn on revision marking by checking the *Mark Revisions* option box in the upper-left corner of the Revision Marks dialog box. As you work, Word marks your revisions using embellishments you specify in this dialog box. At this point, you will see old and new text whether you have deleted it or not. In Figure 20.5 newly inserted text is underlined, while deleted text is marked with strikethrough lines, a bit like the way proposed changes to city ordinances are printed in your voter's booklet. Print and distribute your marked-up draft.

After the marked-up version of the document has been reviewed by your peers, you can make any last-minute corrections, then use the *Accept*

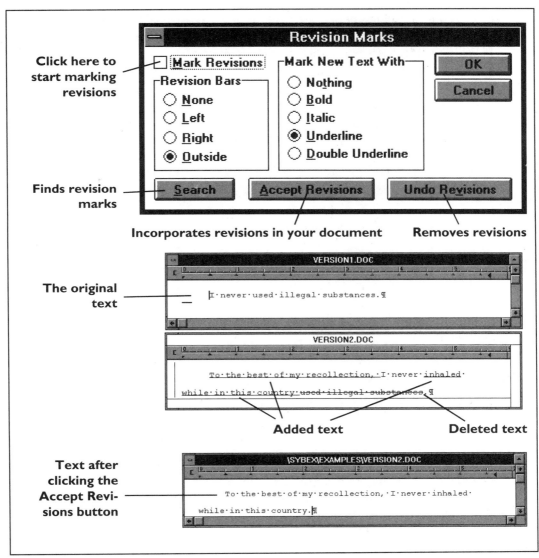

Click here to start marking revisions

Finds revision marks

Incorporates revisions in your document

Removes revisions

The original text

Added text

Deleted text

Text after clicking the Accept Revisions button

WORD

FIGURE 20.5 *Create a draft. Turn on revision marking. Edit the draft, pass it around for review, then click Accept Revisions to make the changes and remove the revision markings.*

Revisions button to incorporate the modifications. The revision marks and deleted text will disappear. Inserted text will take its rightful place.

Clicking Undo Revisions reverts to the previous version of your document. If you want to keep multiple versions of documents, use Save As... to give each version a distinctive name.

CREATING OUTLINES

You've already read about the Outline view elsewhere in this book. It works with Word's heading styles to create collapsible documents that can be easily reorganized. Here's how to outline.

USE HEADING STYLES TO SPEED OUTLINING

Format all of your major and subheadings using Word's heading styles. (You can change the appearance of headings if you don't like the Word defaults.) Use the *Heading 1* style for "top-level" headings, *Heading 2* for the next level down, and so on.

Type text beneath the headings as usual, using Normal or your own "body" style.

VIEWING OUTLINES

Next, switch to Outline view and use the *Show* buttons to hide and reveal different levels of your document. Figure 20.6 illustrates this.

PROMOTING AND DEMOTING HEADINGS

To upgrade a heading, place the insertion point in it, then click on the left-pointing "promote" arrow. For instance, doing this to a Heading 2 line will make it a Heading 1. The right-pointing arrow demotes headings. Use the right-pointing arrow to demote headings (from 1 to 2, for instance).

QUICKLY REARRANGING
DOCUMENTS IN OUTLINE VIEW

With an outline collapsed, you can drag headings and their associated body text to different locations, thereby rearranging the document's organization. Move the mouse pointer near the heading you want to move.

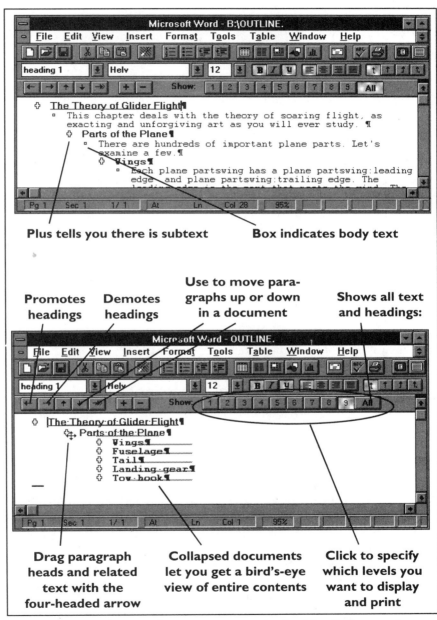

FIGURE 20.6 *Outline view lets you see varying levels of detail. You can also promote or demote headings in this view and move large blocks of text quickly.*

When it turns into a four-headed-arrow pointer, use it to drag the heading. Associated text will follow the heading. Undo works here if you need it.

QUICKLY REARRANGING TABLES IN OUTLINE VIEW

Here's a great tip! You can view *tables* in Outline view and use the same four-headed-arrow dragging trick to rearrange rows.

PRINTING OUTLINES

In Outline view, Word prints only the text you see on screen. Thus, if you compress your document so that just headings show, you can print an outline of your document. Click the All button or return to Normal or Page Layout view to print the entire text of your document.

THESAURUS

The Thesaurus… command can help you add flavor and punch to your documents. Select the word you want to change or are not quite sure about, then open the Thesaurus dialog box shown in Figure 20.7 from the Tools menu or with the Shift-F7 keyboard shortcut.

LOOKING UP AND REPLACING WORDS

The Meanings section of the Thesaurus dialog box lists the various meanings and parts of speech for the word you've selected. If antonyms (words with opposite meanings) are available, an Antonym choice is available at the end of this list.

Pick the meaning of interest, and you'll see a list of synonyms (or antonyms) in the box to the right of the Meanings box. Picking one of these words places it in the Replace With box. If you click the Replace button at this point, the word in your text will be replaced with the word you've chosen.

If you're not satisfied, you can look for still more words by using the Look Up button. It will display synonym and antonym choices for the word you've placed in the Replace With box.

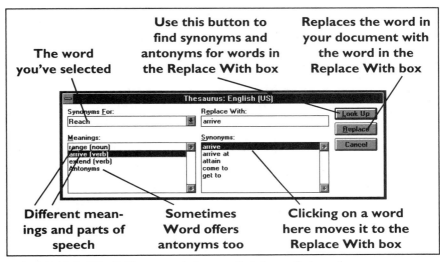

The word you've selected

Use this button to find synonyms and antonyms for words in the Replace With box

Replaces the word in your document with the word in the Replace With box

Different meanings and parts of speech

Sometimes Word offers antonyms too

Clicking on a word here moves it to the Replace With box

FIGURE 20.7 *Word's Thesaurus helps you find the perfect word.*

As you wander around like this, Word builds a drop-down list of words you've looked up. Visit the Synonyms For drop-down menu to see and choose these earlier words.

If the original word you are trying to replace is misspelled or unfamiliar to the thesaurus feature, you will see a list of words close to your word in alphabetical order.

The Cancel button closes the Thesaurus window and leaves your old word intact. Undo also works if you use it immediately.

SPELLING CHECKER

The spelling checker will search your document, looking for unfamiliar words and for repeated words on the assumption that these might be typographic or spelling errors. Word compares all the words in your document with its "standard" dictionary as a starting point and can also look for words in custom dictionaries that you create or purchase. They contain proper nouns, technical terms, medical or legal terms, and so on. British English and non-English dictionaries are also available (contact Microsoft for information about these). When Word finds suspected errors it points them out and suggests changes, then lets you leave things alone, change the first occurrence, change all occurrences, or add the word to your custom dictionaries.

CHECKING SPELLING

Start the Spelling... command from the Tools menu, or click the spelling key on the Toolbar (the ABC ✓ button), or press the F7 function key.

If there is no text selected in your document when you start checking, Word examines the entire document starting at the insertion point. If you've selected a word or words, the checker examines only the selected material.

In either case, the checker compares each text string it finds whose words are separated by spaces. If it can match the string with a word in one of your open dictionaries, it ignores it (approves it) and continues the checking.

When it spots an unfamiliar string (like "lable" in Figure 20.8), it places the questionable word in the *Not in Dictionary* box and makes suggestions.

Frequently the Change To box will contain the properly spelled suggestion. In that case, you can choose to have Word replace just this occurrence of the misspelling with the suggestion, or all subsequent misspellings in the document you are checking.

Sometimes you'll need to pick a different word from the suggestion list as shown in Figure 20.8. Clicking on a word in the list moves it to the Change To box.

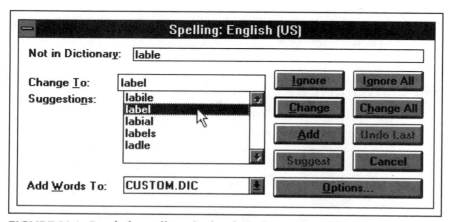

FIGURE 20.8 *Reach the spelling checker from the Tools menu or press the F7 function key. There is also a spelling button on the Toolbar.*

Once in a while, there will be no suggestions. For example, this happens occasionally if the checker encounters the last word in one sentence and the first word of another, not separated with a space (**end.Beginning**, for instance).

You can fix things like this without leaving the spelling checker or retyping the two words. When you click in the *Not in Dictionary* box, its contents will be placed in the *Change To* box where you can edit it (insert a space, or whatever), then click Change or Change All.

Sometimes, the checker will stop on *correctly spelled* words that are not in its standard dictionary (people's names, technical terms, etc.). If you wish, you can either tell the checker to ask you about the same unfamiliar word each time it encounters it (do this by using the *Ignore* button), or you can tell the checker to ignore the word for the rest of the checking exercise by clicking *Ignore All*. If it's a word you use regularly, consider adding it to your custom dictionary.

CUSTOM DICTIONARIES

Word automatically creates an empty custom dictionary the first time you use the spelling checker. It is called CUSTOM.DIC. When you encounter a properly spelled word that you want the checker to ignore in all your documents, use the Add button to place the word (or product part number or whatever) in your custom dictionary. The checker adds words to dictionaries capitalized exactly as they appear when you click the Add button.

Words saved in all-lowercase letters will be recognized regardless of case. Words with capitalization may not be recognized unless the case matches exactly. For instance if you add "VisiCalc," Word will question "visicalc" and "VISICALC." Obviously, you can add these variants to your custom dictionaries if you want.

It's possible to create more than one custom dictionary. This is useful if you write in more than one language, for instance, or if you have a high-tech client and a humanities client who spell words differently. The Add Words To box has a drop-down list of available dictionaries. Use the Spelling Options category (described in Chapter 23) to tell Word which dictionaries to use.

EXCLUSION DICTIONARY

You can create an "exclude" dictionary that will force Word to challenge properly spelled words that you prefer not to use ("dialogue," for instance). This is how to do it. Open a new Word document. Type each exclude word on its own line (press Enter after each word). Use the Save As... command to save the exclusion dictionary as *Text Only*, using the same name as your main dictionary, but with the extension .EXC. The U.S. English dictionary is called SP_AM.LEX, for instance, so its affiliated exclude dictionary would be SP_AM.EXC.

REPEATED WORDS

Have you ever typed "the the" and not spotted it until you were presenting a paper in an important meeting? Repeated words are a common typing mistake. The spelling checker hunts them down for you, as you can see in Figure 20.9.

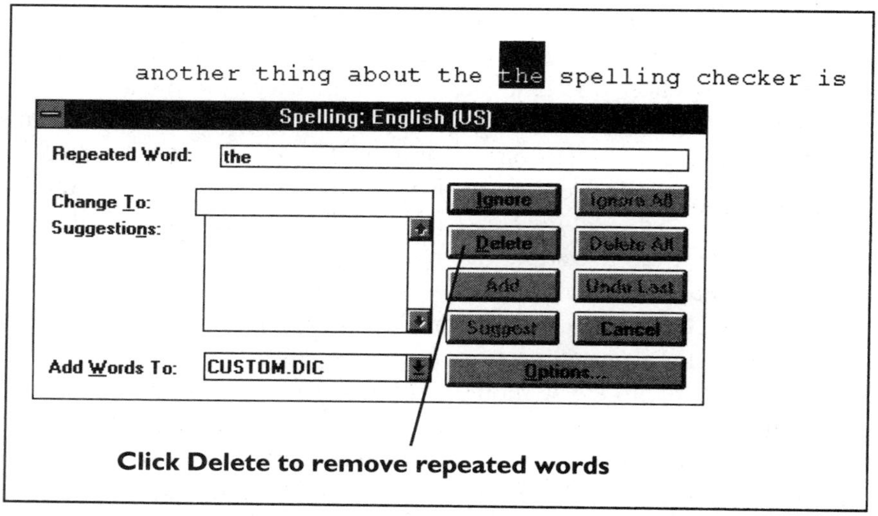

Click Delete to remove repeated words

FIGURE 20.9 *The spelling checker points out repeated words and lets you delete them or leave them alone.*

Occasionally Word will spot repeated words that you want to keep—particularly if you write fiction (Oh. Oh. Yes. Yes!, for instance...). Click Ignore to keep your deathless prose intact.

GRAMMAR CHECKING

Speaking of writing style, to let Word poke its nose further into your composition, choose the Grammar... command on the Tools menu. It will prowl your document looking for grammatical irregularities like pronoun errors and clichés. When it finds them, it points them out and suggests changes. You have some control over the rules used and the severity with which they are applied.

CHECKING GRAMMAR AND STYLE

Sometimes the Grammar... command just spots possible grammatical problems. Other times it can suggest changes, and even make them for you.

To begin, either select text to be inspected, or let the checker work from the insertion point through your entire document. When the grammar checker spots trouble, it highlights the questionable phrase, then displays its observations and suggestions. Figure 20.10 shows an example of this.

When the checker doesn't recognize a word, it launches the spelling checker. Use the spelling checker to fix the problem(s), and the grammar check will continue automatically. (To save time, run the spelling checker *before* you check grammar.)

The Ignore and Next Sentence buttons work as you'd expect. The Ignore Rule button turns off a grammar rule for the duration of the current grammar-checking exercise.

When Word can propose specific changes (like fixing the capitalization in the example at the bottom of Figure 20.10), the Change button can make the change for you.

If the Change button is dimmed, you'll need to click in the actual document to make the change, then restart the grammar checker from the insertion point.

WORD

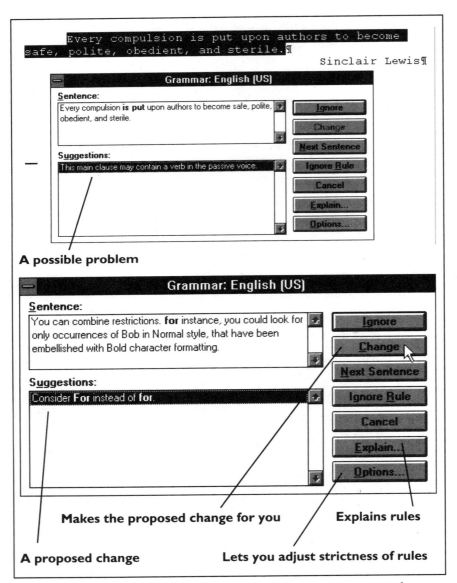

FIGURE 20.10 *At times the Grammar... command merely spots potential
problems. Other times it offers to make changes for you.*

CHANGING GRAMMAR PREFERENCES

The Options dialog box shown in Figure 20.11, and the additional dialog box that its Customize Settings... button reveals, can let you fine-tune the checker's strictness.

Reach the options either from the Options... command on the Tools menu (described in Chapter 23) or with the Options... button in the Grammar dialog box.

DOCUMENT STATISTICS

If you so choose, the grammar checker will display document readability statistics at the end of a grammar-checking exercise. Figure 20.12 shows an example.

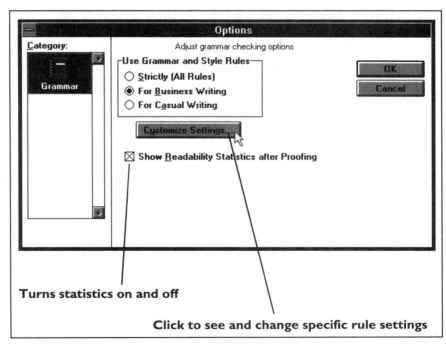

Turns statistics on and off

Click to see and change specific rule settings

FIGURE 20.11 *You can control the grammar checker's strictness.*

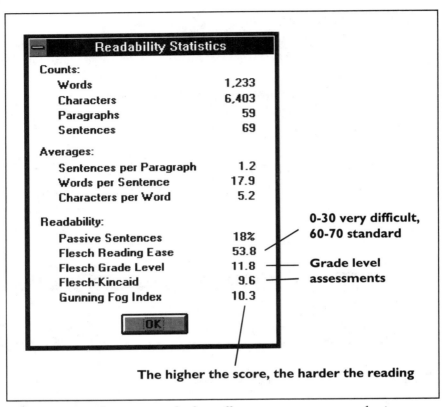

FIGURE 20.12 *The grammar checker will count, sum averages, and voice an opinion about readability, if you let it.*

CREATING A TABLE OF CONTENTS

If you use Word's heading styles, creating a table of contents can be as easy as falling off a log. Make sure your document is complete, proofed, and paginated to your liking before you create the table of contents.

A SIMPLE TABLE OF CONTENTS

Assuming you've used Word's heading styles (heading1, heading2, etc.), the Table of Contents... command on the Insert menu will produce a great-looking table of contents, placing it at the insertion point. The various heading levels are indented. Heading level 1 will comprise the left-most listings, heading 2 lines will be slightly indented, heading 3 notations slightly more indented, and so on. You can specify which heading levels appear. Leading dots are automatically inserted to make it easy to read page numbers.

Figure 20.13 shows the Table of Contents dialog box used for simple projects based on heading styles. If you add or delete text, or make other changes that affect pagination (margins and the like), you will need to re-create your table of contents.

The table of contents will not include headers, footers, footnote annotations, or embedded objects.

COMPLEX TABLES OF CONTENTS AND OTHER LISTS

It is possible for advanced users to employ *field codes* to create a complex table of contents, including entries not formatted with heading styles. For instance, suppose the heading in your document is "Sales Overview," but you want the table of contents entry to read "OVERVIEW—Sales." Field

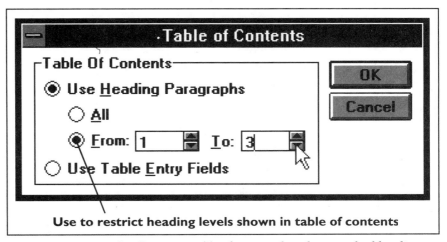

Use to restrict heading levels shown in table of contents

FIGURE 20.13 *Word will create a table of contents based on standard heading styles. You control the heading levels that will show.*

codes can do this because they let you specify the text displayed in the table of contents.

Field codes are also useful if you want several lists in your document— like an illustration list and a table of contents.

Single-Level Table of Contents with Field Codes

The steps for using fields to generate a single-level table of contents are outlined here. (It's a good idea to experiment on a *copy* of a fairly small document when trying this.)

1. Display hidden text with the ¶ Toolbar button.

2. Move the insertion point to *just after* a word or phrase you want to list.

3. Press Ctrl-F9 to insert a field code. Field brackets ({}) will appear.

4. Insert **tc** and the text you want to print, surrounded by quotation marks. (The finished entry might look like {tc "**Introduction**"}, for instance.)

5. Repeat steps 2 through 4 for each entry.

6. Move the insertion point to the place where you want to insert your table of contents.

7. Hide your hidden text and field codes with the ¶ Toolbar button and the Field Codes command on the View menu.

8. Open the Table of Contents dialog box from the Insert menu.

9. Choose the Use Table Entry Fields option.

10. If View field codes is on, Word will insert a TOC field ({**TOC\F**}) at the insertion point.

11. Highlight the TOC field code and press the F9 function key to update the table of contents.

12. Switch to Print Preview or print to inspect the finished table of contents.

Multilevel Table of Contents with Field Codes

To create indented lists (up to eight levels deep), add a backslash (\), a level command (the letter l), and a level number (1–8) at the end of the coded entries. Figure 20.14 shows an example of this.

Chapter Numbers in Your Table of Contents

Remember the Sequence field trick explored in Chapter 16? If you use it for page numbering multisection documents, you can create table of contents containing chapter numbers along with page numbers (2–5, for instance).

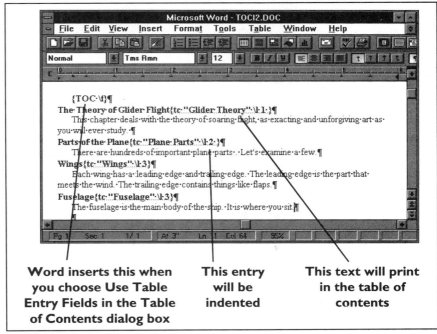

Word inserts this when you choose Use Table Entry Fields in the Table of Contents dialog box

This entry will be indented

This text will print in the table of contents

FIGURE 20.14 *Field codes give you control over what gets printed in table of contents entries.*

If you used **chapter** as the chapter sequence name, creating table of contents entries like {tc \s chapter} will print page numbers with chapter and page numbers separated by a hyphen.

Learn More about Field Codes

There's much more to learn about field codes, although space prohibits more detail here. You may want to refer to a comprehensive Word book like Michael J. Young's *Mastering Word for Windows, version 2.0* (SYBEX, 1992) to learn more about fields and their many intriguing uses.

FORMATTING A TABLE OF CONTENTS

Once you've created a table of contents, you can format it like any other Word text. You can either change the text itself, or modify the Styles Word uses for creating the TOC.

CREATING AN INDEX

Preparing an index is usually the very last step in the publication process. Word will compile simple or complex indexes based on words you identify. You can just list words alphabetically with their page numbers, or you can show page *ranges* and add references like "goobers, *see* peanuts." With effort, you can also create multilevel indexes with subentries.

Index entries are created using hidden text. Word can do much of the work for you, but indexing is a time-consuming task. It is a very good idea to completely polish, proofread, correct, and paginate your document before creating an index. As always, practice on a document copy, not your original.

SIMPLE INDEX ENTRIES

Begin by selecting a word or phrase you want to index. Choose Index Entry... from the Insert menu. An Index Entry dialog box will appear with the selected text placed in a text box as shown in Figure 20.15.

You can edit the text in the Index Entry text box. For instance, you could capitalize "soaring" in Figure 20.15. Use the option boxes to make the index

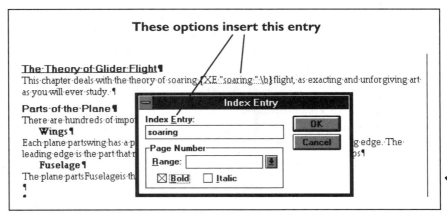

FIGURE 20.15 *Select text to index and choose Index Entry... from the Insert menu. Edit the text if necessary, and pick the desired options. Run Index... from the Insert menu to compile your index.*

entry bold or italic, and enter a page range to be printed next to the entry if you like. When you are satisfied with the entry, click OK and Word will insert a hidden entry like the one shown in Figure 20.15.

COMPILING AND VIEWING AN INDEX

After you've made index entries for all the desired words, move the insertion point to the location where you want the index to print (typically, at the end of your document). Hide the hidden text. Choose Index... from the Insert menu (not Index Entry..., which is on the same menu). You will see a dialog box like the one in Figure 20.16.

Choose the options you want and click OK. The Normal Index option indents multilevel indexes (discussed in a moment). Run-in Index prints entries and subentries on the same line. Indexes always print alphabetically. You can cause a noticeable break in the list whenever the first letter of the main entries changes. This makes it easy to spot where the A's stop and the B's begin. The None heading choice does not create these separate alphabetic groups. The Blank line choice puts white space between the A's and B's. The Letter option precedes each group with its letter (A, B, C, and so on).

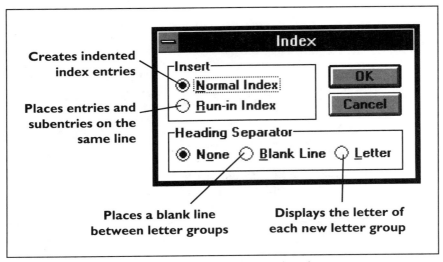

FIGURE 20.16 *Word offers several options for simple indexing.*

When you have made your index option choices, click OK. Word will insert an index code at the insertion point in your document, then compiles your index. Switch to Print Preview or print your document to inspect the index. If you make changes to your document or index entries, use the Update Field (F9) key to recompile the index.

MULTILEVEL INDEXES

You can create multilevel indexes with up to seven levels of subentries—probably far more than you will ever need. For instance, if you wanted to list the words "Wings" and "Fuselage" under the heading "Plane Parts," you could place the insertion point at the end of the word "Wings," and create the index entry **Plane Parts:Wings**. Then move to "Fuselage" and create the entry **Plane Parts:Fuselage**. (See Figure 20.17.) Notice the colons separating the main entries from the subentries. This tells Word you want "Plane Parts" to be the major heading with "Wings" and "Fuselage" beneath it.

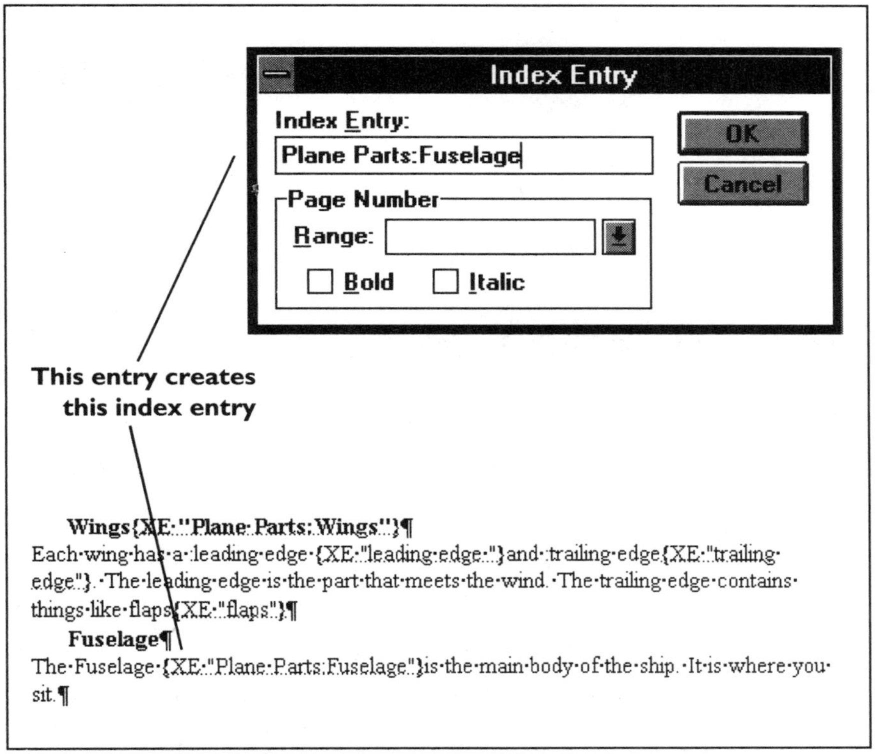

FIGURE 20.17 *Create multilevel index entries with the Index Entry dialog box.*

Introduction to Macros

Word's Template and Glossary and Style features automate many otherwise tedious tasks. But once in a while you find yourself mumbling "There *must* be a better way..." as you do repetitive tasks. For instance, if you use Outline view to print outlines of your documents, you must first switch to Outline view, then specify the outline level you want to print, and finally visit the Print... Command on the Edit menu, where in turn you must wait for another dialog box and click OK to start the printing. You could grow old fast... Like a marvelous mime, Word's *Macro* feature can watch you do all these things once, record the steps to disk, and repeat them for you whenever you ask. Word uses a programming language called *WordBasic* to do this, but you need not become a programmer to create, use, and even edit simple macros that help expedite your work.

CREATING SIMPLE MACROS

Open or prepare a document suitable for the macro you want to create. For instance, if you want to make an outline-printing macro, you'll need to have a document on your screen that has headings formatted with Word's Heading styles. Or, if you want to create a macro that will sort the contents of a table, you'll need to have a table on your screen.

Practice the steps you intend to use once or twice before recording them if you are uncertain of where things are or how they work. When you are ready to record, choose Record Macro… from the Tools menu. You'll see a dialog box like the one in Figure 21.1.

Give your new macro a name, starting with a letter (not a number) and containing up to 26 characters, but no spaces. (When the OK button dims, you've broken a naming rule.)

If you want to assign a keyboard shortcut, do it by typing a character in the Key box. Placing an X in the Ctrl or Shift boxes constructs key combinations (Ctrl+Shift+S, for instance).

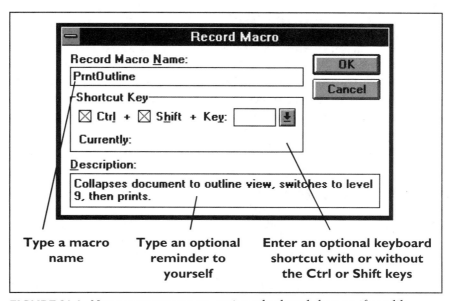

FIGURE 21.1 *Name your new macro, assign a keyboard shortcut if you like, make a note to yourself, and click OK to begin recording.*

The description box can be used to hold a note to yourself about the macro. Type up to 255 characters here. (The description will appear when in the Macro dialog box, discussed in a moment.)

Once you've named the macro (and optionally entered a keyboard shortcut and description), click OK to start recording. Word will watch you work. Take your time. Word will speed things up when it plays back your macro.

If you must move the insertion pointer or select text while recording macros, use the keyboard methods or menu commands to do this, since you can't record mouse movements in a document window. For instance, if you create a table-sorting macro, use the Table menu's *Select Table* command rather than trying to use the mouse to select table cells.

When you've finished your task, choose *Stop Recorder*, the command that replaces Record Macro... on Word's Tools menu. Macros recorded this way are saved with the document template you are using at the time.

RUNNING MACROS

Once you've recorded macros, you can run them either by using their keyboard shortcuts, if any, or by picking them from the Macro Name dialog box shown in Figure 21.2. Reach it from the Macro... command on the Tools menu.

If your macro requires you to do things first (placing the insertion point in a table, for instance), do so. Then visit the Macro dialog box and either double-click on the macro name in the scrolling list, or highlight a name and click Run. Word will run the macro and perform the tasks quicker than humanly possible.

EDITING MACROS

If you are unhappy with a macro because it doesn't do what you intended, you can record over it by using the Record Macro... command with the same name you used previously. Or you can use the *Edit* button in the Macro dialog box (see Figure 21.2) to open a WordBasic editing window like the one shown in Figure 21.3.

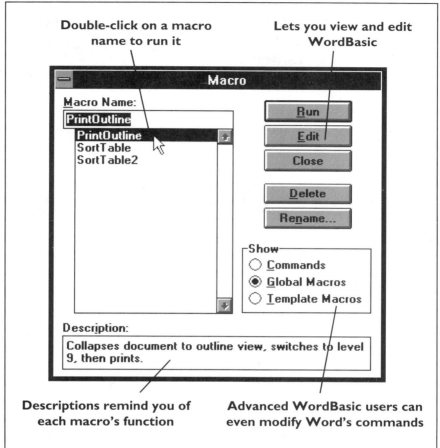

FIGURE 21.2 *Browse and choose macros to run from this dialog box reached
with the Macro... command on Word's Tools menu.*

Figure 21.3 shows a macro that switches to Outline view, sets the view to
show only headings, and prints the outline.

Obviously, you'll need to know a lot more about WordBasic before you can
edit macros this way. But the adventurous can even try a few things on their

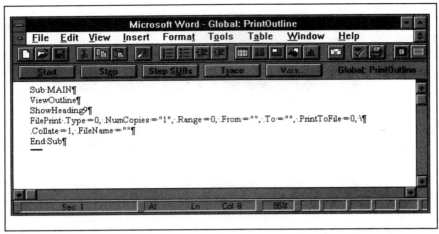

FIGURE 21.3 *WordBasic macros can be explored and edited by advanced users.*

own. For example, Inserting (typing) the command ViewNormal as the line before EndSub will cause Word to switch back to Normal view after printing.

LEARNING MORE ABOUT
MACROS AND WORDBASIC

On-line help is available for WordBasic and its commands. Record and examine your own macros and see how Word constructs WordBasic statements. If you become intrigued by the workings of this programming language, Microsoft sells separate manuals and even runs training courses in many cities on the subject. Contact its product support folks for details.

WHERE MACROS ARE STORED

Macros are saved with templates, not documents. Word can make macros available either globally or with specific document templates. To change where macros are stored, open the Template dialog box shown in Figure 21.4, reached from the Template... choice on the File menu.

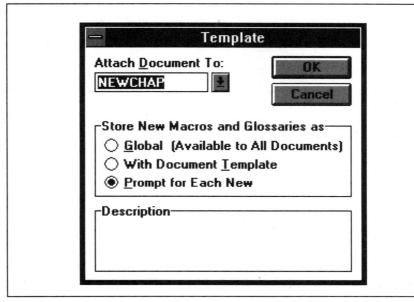

FIGURE 21.4 *Macros are stored with templates. Use the option buttons to tell Word if you want them to be available globally or only with selected templates.*

22

Introduction to Print Merge

Word's Print Merge feature is sometimes referred to as "mail merge," since it is so often used to create personalized (well, junk) mail. But it has other beneficent purposes as well. You can use it to create name tags for conferences, invoices, and much more. Print Merge combines collections of data contained in something called a *data file* with "boilerplate" text that you create in a special Word document called a *main document*. For instance, the data file might contain a list of deadbeat customers, their mailing addresses, and the amounts they owe. The main document might be a final-notice letter that "knows" where to insert information from the data file. When you use the Print Merge command, Word combines the data with the boilerplate text to create a series of unique documents.

The general steps to creating a new Print Merge project from scratch are as follows:

1. Design a data file.

2. Enter data.

3. Design a merge file.

4. Check for errors.

5. Print the merged documents.

You can sometimes do the steps out of order, and you may be able to use existing documents as data files (Word tables or Excel worksheets, for instance). Let's look at a sample project starting from scratch.

CREATING A SIMPLE PRINT MERGE PROJECT

Begin by either retrieving an existing Word document that you want to use as a main document, or opening a new document. Then choose the Print Merge... command from the File menu. You'll see a dialog box like the one in Figure 22.1.

When you first see it, several buttons will be dimmed, indicating that there are things to do before you can merge. In the top of Figure 22.1 a data file is required. You can either use an existing data file or create a new one. Clicking on the Attach Data File... button brings up a file dialog box like the one shown in the bottom of Figure 22.1. Use it to locate an existing data file, or create a new one by clicking the Create Data File... button. This will reveal the Create Data File dialog box shown in Figure 22.2.

This dialog box will actually set up a Word table for you, with field names as columns. Later, you'll enter data into rows in the new table. Give some thought to field names and row content when you create your data files. For instance, if you think you'll want to sort records by ZIP code someday, create a separate field for the ZIP code.

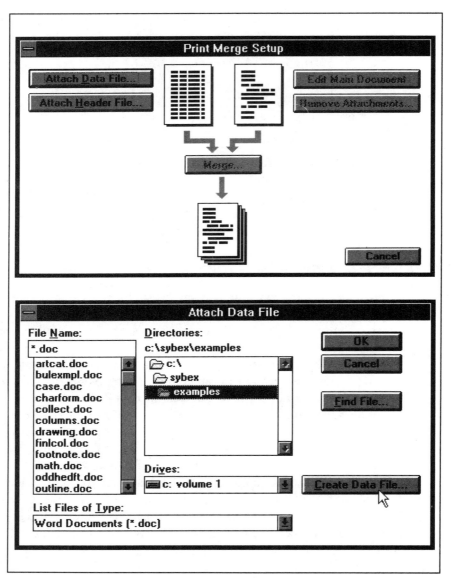

FIGURE 22.1   *The Print Merge Setup dialog box helps chart your progress.*

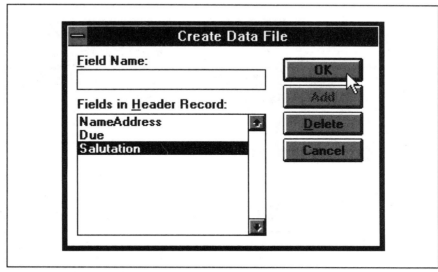

FIGURE 22.2 *Enter field names to create a new data file.*

ENTERING MERGE DATA

When you have named all of the fields for your data file, click OK. Word prompts you to name the document, then opens a new data file document (a Word document with a table), into which you will type data. Figure 22.3 shows a sample data file (Word table) for a collection letter.

Enter and edit data just as you would in any other Word table. Save your work when you are satisfied with it, using Word's regular Save... command.

CREATING A MERGE DOCUMENT

Use Word's Window menu to switch to the main document, where you will type the boilerplate text for your letter. Use the Insert Merge Field... button to place merge codes where you want the data from the data file to print. Examine Figure 22.4 to see how this works.

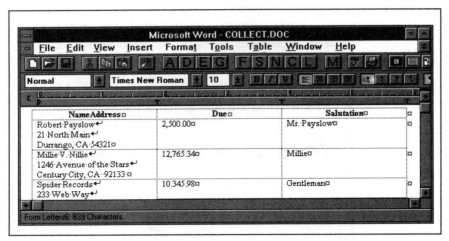

FIGURE 22.3 *Enter data to be merged with the main document.*

The Insert Merge Field dialog box places merge codes at the insertion point. For instance, to create a merged salutation, you might type **Dear** followed by a space, insert the Salutation merge code, then type a colon and press Enter to finish the line.

To alter the style and formatting of merged information, select the Merge codes, then format or apply styles to them. The merged data will take on these characteristics.

MERGING

When you are content with both your data and the main letter, return to the Print Merge Setup dialog box (from the File menu). The Merge button should be undimmed now, as shown in Figure 22.5. Click it.

Word will ask whether you want the merged documents to be sent directly to your printer or to a new document. When setting up a new project it is often a good idea to print to a document file so that you can inspect your results on-screen (and possibly make minor edits). Whenever you attempt to merge, Word will inspect your data and main documents for errors. If you want Word to do this without printing, choose the Only Check for Errors choice.

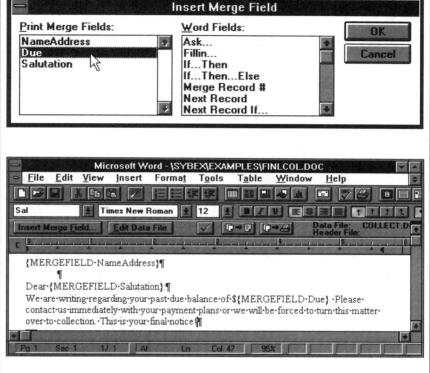

FIGURE 22.4 *Type boilerplate text and enter merge codes to construct your main document.*

You can print selective records by specifying record ranges (records 6 through 12, for instance), or you can print selective records based on criteria entered in a record selection dialog box reached with the button of the same name. For example, you could print letters only for people who owe more than $1,000.

Figure 22.6 shows a typical merged letter created from the first row in the sample data record.

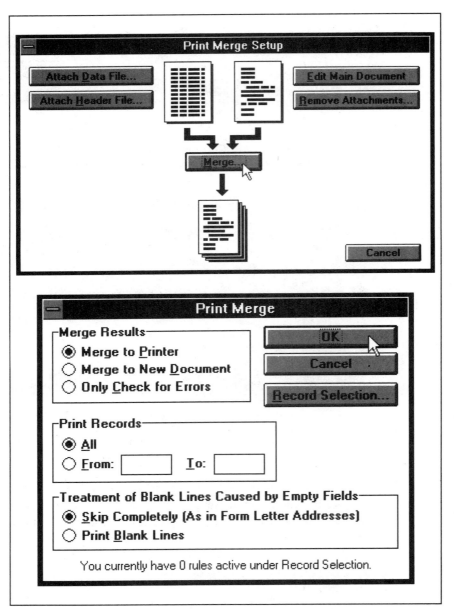

FIGURE 22.5 *Click the Merge button in the top box to merge, then in the bottom box to specify how many records you want to merge. Send them to your printer or a file.*

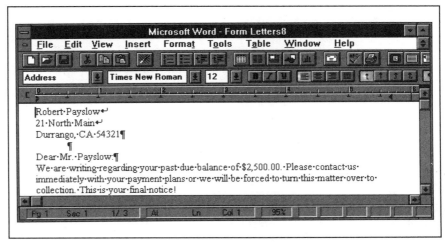

FIGURE 22.6 *Word will merge a new document directly to your printer, or create
a new Word document containing all the merged data and boilerplate text.*

LEARNING MORE ABOUT PRINT MERGE

There's a lot more to know about merging. For instance, you can insert
codes that Word will use to prompt the operator for information when merging. You can use Excel files and other sources of data. If you plan to create
complex merge documents, check out Word's on-line Help and books like
Mastering Microsoft Word for Windows by Michael Young (SYBEX, 1992).

Personalizing Word

The good news is that you have almost total control over the contents of Word's menus, Toolbar, and "personality." That's also the bad news. If you share your computer with another user, or if you work in a large organization, almost any changes to the look and feel of Word can create confusion and training headaches. Some organizations even forbid modifying menus, Toolbars, macros, styles, and other Word elements. If you work in such a place, you might want to contact your menu police before "improving" Word with the techniques outlined in this chapter. There are often good reasons for conformity. That said, let's look at some ways you can make Word better fit your work style.

THE OPTIONS COMMAND

Word's Options… command on the Tools menu is the key to this treasure trove. It displays an Options dialog box similar to the one shown in Figure 23.1.

The actual *options* you see on the *right* of the dialog box depend upon which *category icon* you've selected from the scrollable list at the *left* edge of the dialog box. For instance, clicking on the *General* icon reveals the options you see in Figure 23.1. Clicking on the *View* icon shows entirely different options.

You make changes with the usual bag of Windows tricks—check boxes, drop-down menus, text boxes, and so on. The changes take effect when you close the options box or switch to a different options category.

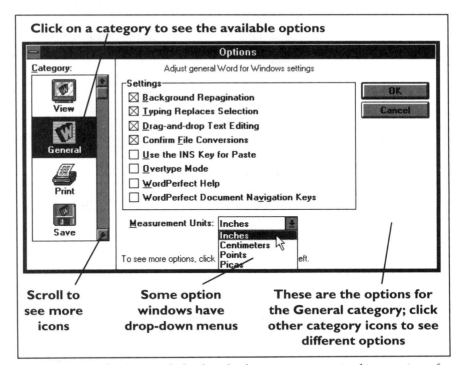

FIGURE 23.1 *The Options dialog box displays options organized in a variety of categories.*

Most option changes are global, stored either in your NORMAL.DOT template or in your WINWORD.INI (intital settings) file.

You can, however, save different templates containing unusual menus, keyboard shortcuts, and defaults. You've seen examples of this in Microsoft's templates. Let's look at the various categories and their options.

GENERAL

The General category (illustrated in Figure 23.1) lets you turn selected editing features on and off. It also lets you specify the units of measure (inches, picas, etc.) that are displayed on rulers and used in document formatting.

The *Background* Repagination option causes Word to update pagination when the program is otherwise idle. On slower computers, this can sometimes make certain operations creep along or cause unsettling delays in your keyboard's response. If you turn off auto repagination, you will be responsible for manual repagination, which is accomplished with the Repaginate Now... command on the Tools menu.

The *Typing Replaces Selection* choice causes any text you type to replace anything you've selected. Normally you'll want to leave this on.

People either love or hate *Drag-and-drop Text Editing*. If, after you've given yourself an honest chance to grow accustomed to it, you want to shut it off, remove the check mark.

The *Confirm File Conversions* switch turns off the dialog box that appears when you try to load non-Word documents. Turning off the box causes Word to use whatever it thinks is the best conversion filter without letting you overrule it.

Here's an interesting option! The *Use the INS Key for Paste* option does just what it says. Although turned off when you originally install Word, the feature when *enabled* lets you paste the contents of your Clipboard at the insertion point by pressing the Insert key. With the feature *disabled*, the Insert key toggles Word between insert and overtype typing modes. (When Word is in overtype mode, **OVR** appears in the status bar, and new characters "wipe out" the ones ahead of the insertion point as you type.)

It follows, then, that the *Overtype Mode* option would permanently place Word in this "destructive" typing mode. And it does. Unless you've also chosen the *Use the INS Key for Paste* setting, you can still use the Insert key to toggle between insert and overtype modes.

The two *WordPerfect* options are used to display, demonstrate, and emulate WordPerfect operations. They can be a boon to users who have migrated from that application.

USER INFORMATION

The *User Info* options shown in Figure 23.2 collect your name, initials, and mailing address.

These entries are used for Summary Info, annotations, and the Toolbar's Envelope button. They are *not* used by LETBLOCK and other Microsoft-provided templates.

VIEW

The View category lets you control the on-screen appearance of documents. The *Window* choices in this category let you turn on and off the scroll bars plus the status bar in new documents.

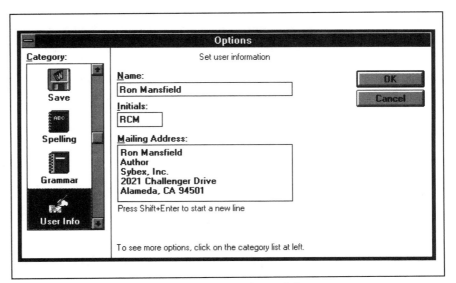

FIGURE 23.2 *Enter your name, address, and initials here.*

Here's a real sleeper: the *Style Area Width* option opens a column along the left of your document that displays the name of the style used by each paragraph! Specify the width of this column in the width box and check this out. About 0.5" should do it. This is a great way to troubleshoot complex documents, or to explain the effects of styles to a novice.

PRINT

Most of the changes made here are valid for all Word printing activities until you revisit the category and make new choices. The *Draft Output* option prints all formatted characters as underlined, but otherwise plain, text. Graphics are represented by empty boxes. This choice can significantly speed up draft printing on some printers.

Use *Reverse Print Order* with printers that pile pages face up. It will cause your work to stack in the correct order.

The *Include with Document* choices let you specify printing of summary information and annotations on separate pages. With the *Field Codes* box checked, Word prints the field codes instead of their contents—{DATE} instead of the actual date, for instance. The *Hidden Text* box forces hidden text printing even if the text is not displayed.

The *Envelope Options* choice lets Word know if you've installed an envelope feeder on the chosen printer.

Widow/Orphan Control prevents the last line of a paragraph from printing on the top of the next page (a widow), and it prevents the first line of a new paragraph from printing by itself at the bottom of a page (an orphan). The *TrueType* option causes Word to use TrueType fonts as the defaults.

SAVE

The *Always Create Backup Copy* option saves a backup copy of your changes with the file extension .BAK. You can't use Fast Saves with this option.

Allow Fast Saves speeds the saving process by saving only changes. Many experienced users prefer to disallow fast saves, which can cause reliability problems. It's often more difficult to recover damaged documents that have been "fast saved."

SPELLING

The Ignore choices let you tell Word to ignore uppercase words, as well as words containing numerals (part numbers, for instance). Particularly on slower computers, if you are a good speller and don't need suggestions, turn off *Always Suggest* to speed up spell checking.

Word will list all dictionary files (with the extension .DIC) it finds in the Word directory (usually called WINWORD) or in the current directory, and any it finds in the spelling path specified in your WIN.INI file (described later).

You can use a maximum of four dictionaries at once. Use the Add… button to create a new dictionary file.

GRAMMAR

The grammar options let you turn on and off rules of grammar. The Customize Settings… button in the Grammar dialog box takes you to lists of rules. To learn more about a rule, highlight it and click the Explain… button.

CHANGING WORD'S TOOLBAR

Suppose you never use the Unindent button on the Toolbar, but you are forever visiting the Picture command on the Insert menu. The Toolbar category lets you delete and add buttons. (You can also use these procedures to add commands or macros to your Toolbar.) Figure 23.3 illustrates the process.

1. From the Toolbar category of the Options dialog box, select a tool to change (from the Tool to Change drop-down menu).

2. Use the Show buttons to list either commands or macros.

3. From the scrollable Commands (or Macros) list, select the item you want to immortalize with a button.

4. Pick a button icon design from the scrollable Button gallery.

5. Click the Change button.

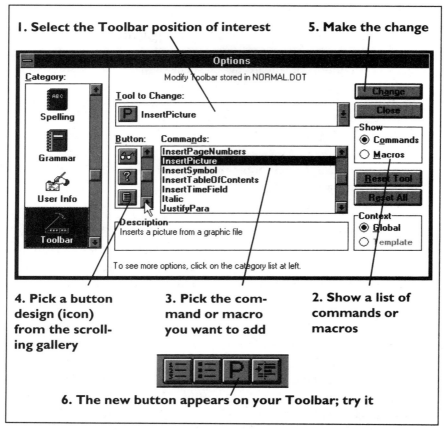

FIGURE 23.3 *Use the Toolbar category to add or delete Toolbar buttons for your favorite commands or macros.*

6. Click the Close button.

7. Admire and test your work.

Incidentally, you can use these techniques to change the button appearance (icons) for *existing* commands too. If you want to make a single button revert to its original design and location, select the corresponding command and click *Reset Tool*. To return the entire Toolbar to Microsoft's defaults, use the *Reset All* button.

CHANGING WORD'S MENUS

Just as you can fiddle with the Toolbar's contents, you can change menus to your heart's content. Suppose, for instance, that you want to add that snappy new PrintOutline macro you've just created to the File menu with the rest of the printing commands. Try this:

1. From the Menus category in the Options menu, show either commands or macros, depending upon what you want to add.

2. Use the drop-down menu list to pick the menu where the command should appear.

3. Pick the command or macro you want to add.

4. Word proposes a command name for your new menu item. Edit it if you wish.

5. Click Add, and the new command is appended to the specified menu.

6. Visit the modified menu and test the command.

Figure 23.4 illustrates the process.

Word *always* places commands at the bottom of the menu list (beneath all standard Word menu choices). There is no good way around this—not even deleting and re-adding standard menu choices.

Notice that all of Word's standard menu choice names in the command list begin with their menu names. For instance, the Exit command can be found in the scrolling Commands list by looking under FileExit.

Notice, also, that the way to underline a character in a command name (and make it the letter to use when picking menu commands with the keyboard) is to *precede* the letter with an ampersand (&). For instance, **Print Out&line** would produce a menu command with an underlined letter l (Print Out<u>l</u>ine). Thus, in our example, pressing an l in the keyboard menu-picking sequence would pick the Print Outline choice. In other words, Alt, F, L would run the Print Outline macro.

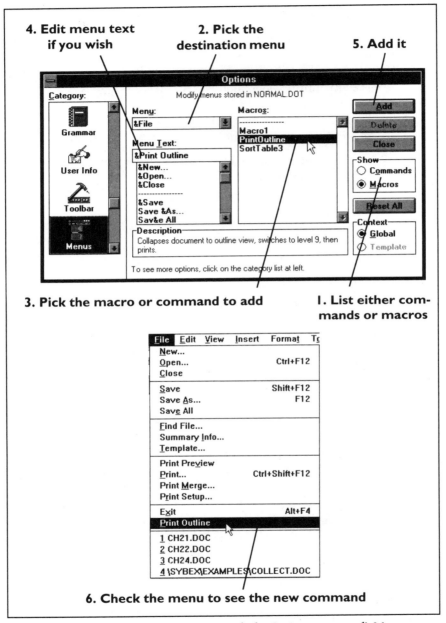

FIGURE 23.4 *Add or delete menu items with the Options command's Menus Category.*

KEYBOARD OPTIONS

The keyboard category lets you assign, view, and reassign keyboard shortcut assignments. Suppose, for instance, that you forgot to assign a keyboard shortcut for your favorite macro. You can simply visit this dialog box, pick the macro from the scrolling list, and assign a shortcut. Figure 23.5 illustrates this.

CHANGING THE WORD WIN.INI INFORMATION

Advanced users sometimes want to change things in the Word section of their WIN.INI file. As an example, they might want to change the default path used for saving with the AUTOSAVE command. The WIN.INI Category in the Options dialog box lets you see and edit this as well as other settings. Refer to advanced Windows and Word books for details, or contact Microsoft technical support for help with INI settings. Figure 23.6 shows the WIN.INI options.

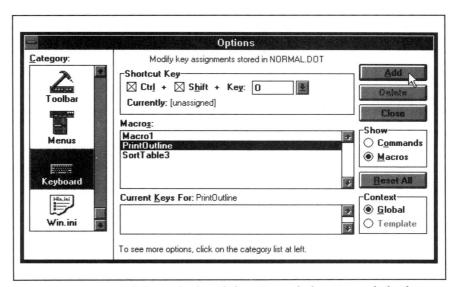

FIGURE 23.5 *See and change keyboard shortcuts with the Options dialog box Keyboard category.*

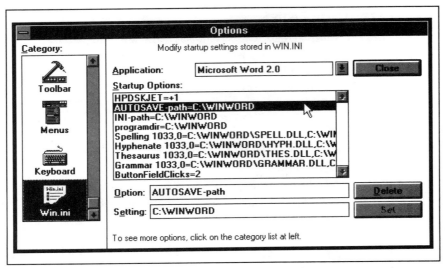

FIGURE 23.6 *Advanced users can change the Word's WIN.INI file with the WIN.INI Category in the Options dialog box.*

PART THREE

EXCEL
Spreadsheets

24

Excel Overview

If you've been using the same old spreadsheet program for years, you are in for a pleasant surprise. If you happen to be a newcomer to spreadsheets, you've made the right choice. Microsoft's Excel version 4.0 is a comfortable blend of old and new. Like Word, it is easy to learn and difficult to outgrow. Users of earlier versions of Excel as well as Lotus 1-2-3 and other spreadsheet programs will quickly feel right at home with Excel's familiar old features—and will grow to appreciate its powerful new ones.

THE USUAL SPREADSHEET FEATURES

Excel lets you create and quickly perform "what-if" analysis of complex, interrelated columnar reports in work spaces called *worksheets* or *spreadsheets*. (The terms "spreadsheets" and "worksheets" are used interchangeably in this book.)

Worksheets are made up of *rows* and *columns*. Rows run across your screen and columns run down. The intersection of rows and columns creates *cells*. You type into cells things like *labels*, *numbers*, and *dates*. Excel *rows* are usually identified with *numbers*, and *columns* with *letters*. The *address* of a cell is a combination of the row and column labels. Thus, cell B5 would be the fifth cell down in the second column from the left of the worksheet.

You also create *formulas* (sometimes called *equations*) in cells. For instance, you might enter five different numbers in cells A1 through A5, then place a formula in cell A6 that adds those five numbers and displays the results in cell A6. Excel helps you quickly build formulas using your keyboard and mouse. Excel also provides *Toolbar tools*, *menu choices*, and *functions* you can employ to create and use complex formulas.

An almost overwhelming array of formatting features lets you "dress up" and print your final work product. A new ChartWizard quickly converts your worksheet numbers and cell labels into all manner of impressive pie charts, line graphs, bar charts, three-dimensional charts, scatter charts, and other visual aids. There's even a way to create automated, on-screen slide shows containing spreadsheet data and charts, complete with audio and special effects!

WINDOWS SAVVY

Because Microsoft designed Excel 4.0 from the ground up as a Windows product, the program offers Windows features you've already learned about in other parts of this book. You edit Excel worksheet text using the same techniques you learned for Word. Many of the commands you'll use are located on the same menus as they are in Word. And Excel offers impressive compatibility with other Windows products. For instance, it's easy to insert graphics from most other Windows programs into Excel worksheets.

Or you can paste Excel worksheet data and charts into Word documents. Data collected in Excel worksheets can be used to create Word Print Merge data files, and so on. But for most people the real Excel advantage is ease of use. Microsoft has created powerful tools to speed spreadsheet construction, formatting, and use. Let's get an overview in this chapter, then create a first worksheet in Chapter 25.

AUTOMATIC NUMBER FORMATTING

Here's an example of an Excel power tool. If you type a dollar sign or percent sign when entering numbers, Excel will format the cells and numbers appropriately as you enter them.

AUTOMATIC SUMMATION

The automation doesn't stop with formatting. Usually Excel can determine where to place subtotals and totals, making it unnecessary for you to type and copy lengthy summary equations! For instance, in the example used earlier, if you enter five numbers in a column, then use Excel's Summation (Σ) button on the Standard Toolbar, Excel will automatically outline all five numbers and offer to create an equation that adds them up, then formats and displays the answer. This can be a real time-saver.

AUTOMATIC WORKSHEET FORMATTING

Then there's the stunning array of 14 automatic worksheet formats. Excel's *AutoFormat* feature presents samples from which you pick the desired spreadsheet appearance. The formats consist of combinations of type styles, 3-D shading, borders around related data, colors, and the like. Once you make your choice, Excel will apply the format to your whole spreadsheet or selected parts. It is usually smart enough to locate and highlight subtotals and totals for you. Adam's Spider survey data in Figure 24.1, for example, have been formatted using Excel's List 1 AutoFormat style.

Since some printers won't reprouce all of Excel's automatic formats acceptably, and since some formats slow the printing process, you'll want to experiment with these features long before starting a project that needs to be completed on a tight deadline.

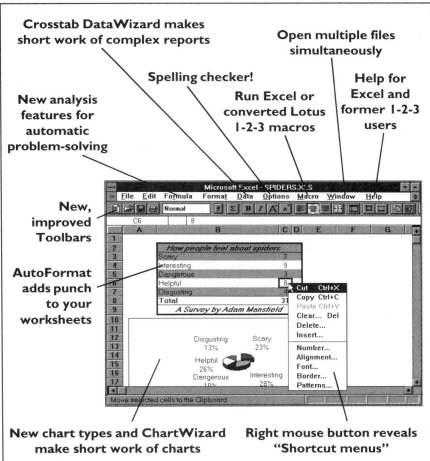

FIGURE 24.1 *Excel 4.0 for Windows offers a number of impressive new and improved features.*

BUILT-IN SPELL CHECKING

How many times have you handed out spreadsheets in an important meeting and noticed a typo or spelling error? Well, apparently this has happened in meetings at Microsoft too. Excel 4.0 comes with a built-in spelling checker. Excel can even share Word's custom dictionaries. This lets you keep unusual words like proper nouns and technical terms all in one place so that the spelling checker in both your word processor and your spreadsheet programs can recognize them.

SHORTCUT MENUS

Microsoft has finally found a powerful use for the right mouse button. Whether you are formatting a document, editing a cell, or working on a chart, commands appropriate to the work you are doing appear whenever you press the right mouse button.

DRAG-AND-DROP
WORKSHEET REARRANGEMENT

Do you want to move a group of cells? Excel's Drag-and-Drop feature lets you reposition selected portions of your spreadsheet by simply dragging them with your mouse, just as you do in Word. Properly written equations automatically adapt themselves to their new locations. It almost makes budgeting fun.

TOOLBARS

Excel offers an improved Toolbar. In fact, as you can see in Figure 24.2, there are many *different* Excel Toolbars. If you don't find one you like, you can create your own, or change Microsoft's.

You are allowed to move many of the Toolbars to different locations on your screen, then point-and-click to accomplish things like formatting numbers or creating charts. It's even possible for advanced users to create their own buttons and spreadsheet functions for the Toolbar.

INTELLIGENT AUTOFILL

Imagine creating an annual budget or other calendar-related project. How many times have you typed **January**, then **February**, and so on, slavishly visiting cell after cell? With the Excel 4.0 AutoFill feature, you need only type **January**, then highlight the next 11 cells by dragging with your mouse.

Choose from a variety of Toolbars —

Some Toolbars can be moved around on your screen —

It's possible to modify Toolbars and button icons —

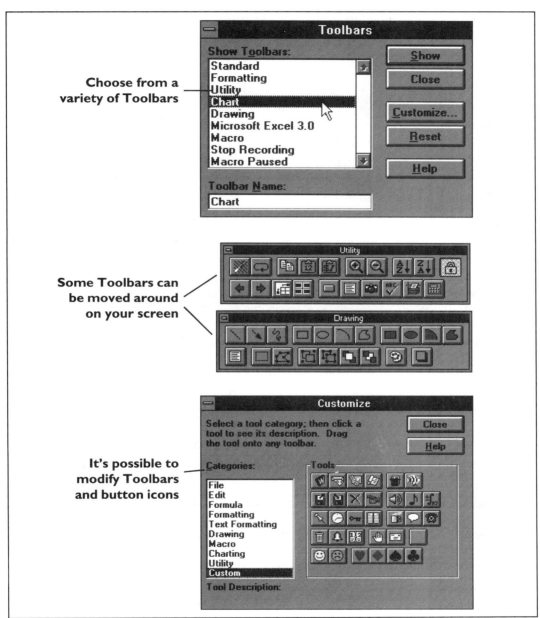

FIGURE 24.2 *Word offers many customizable Toolbars.*

Excel will automatically fill in **February**, **March**, and the rest of the months for you. This works on rows (across) or columns (down). Moreover, AutoFill is intelligent. Type **Jan 1991** and Excel will fill in **Feb 1991**, etc. If the filling reaches the end of 1992, it will change the year to 1993 at the appropriate column or row. AutoFill's not limited to months and years, either. Type **Monday**, AutoFill will provide **Tuesday**, **Wednesday**, and so on. Type **Product 1** and Excel can fill in **Product 2** and on and on. Suppose you want headings with quarterly subtotals. Enter **January 92**, **February 92**, **March 92** and **Quarter 1** as the first four cells, whereupon AutoFill will create the rest of the year or years, complete with properly numbered quarters. Figure 24.3 shows several examples of AutoFill at work.

Besides automatically filling row and column labels, AutoFill can help create forecasts based on sample data you provide. Enter expense dollar amounts for the first quarter and drag the mouse through the cells to fill

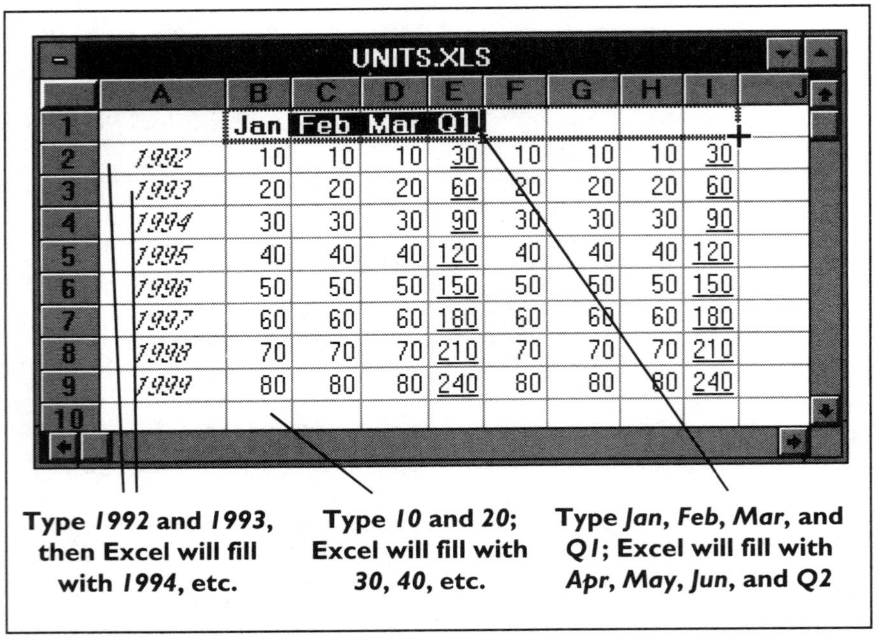
UNITS.XLS
A
B
C
D
E
F
G
H
I
J
Jan Feb Mar Q1
1992
1993
1994
1995
1996
1997
1998
1999
Type *1992* and *1993*, then Excel will fill with *1994*, etc.
Type *10* and *20*; Excel will fill with *30*, *40*, etc.
Type *Jan*, *Feb*, *Mar*, and *Q1*; Excel will fill with *Apr*, *May*, *Jun*, and Q2

FIGURE 24.3 *AutoFill creates new cell entries based on samples you enter.*

them with similar estimates for the remainder of the year. If expenses go up from month to month within your sample quarter (or week or year or whatever), these trends will be reflected in the auto-filled cells. This works great for projections that must account for the fact that some months have four weeks while others have five (sometimes referred to as the 4-4-5 problem). Obviously, you can later fine-tune Excel's automatic projections as needed.

CHARTING

Excel's new ChartWizard steps you through the many possible formatting choices, converting an often confusing process into a few simple steps. There are numerous new chart types including some impressive 3-D charts that can be rotated with your mouse. This makes it easy for you to pick the best "vantage point" for viewing and printing your chart. Figure 24.4 illustrates some of the available chart types.

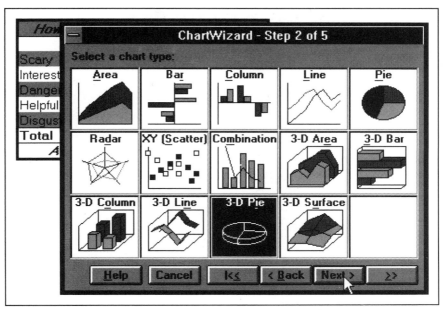

FIGURE 24.4 *Excel's ChartWizard helps create a variety of charts.*

LOTUS 1-2-3
COMPATIBILITY AND TRANSITION AIDS

If you have a ton of Lotus 1-2-3 spreadsheets replete with complex macros, you're not alone. That's why Microsoft has provided a comprehensive Lotus file compatibility. Excel can load from or save to most popular 1-2-3 file formats, including WKS, WK1, WK3, FMT, and FM3. Generally, if your spreadsheet package (including Quattro Pro) can save in one of these formats, Excel can use your old spreadsheets. With very few exceptions, macros you've created in 1-2-3 will also work in Excel. In addition, there is special on-line help for those suffering from Lotus withdrawal.

WORKBOOKS ORGANIZE
AND COMBINE WORKSHEETS

You can combine worksheets, macro sheets, and charts to create *workbooks*. This makes it easier to save, use, and manage related files.

IMPROVED VIEWS

Excel lets you combine multiple worksheets and view them in outline form. For instance, you could have a forecast spreadsheet for each product line or each of your many offices, then combine the data contained in them to produce a "top" summary spreadsheet. Then, by expanding and collapsing the view of these data, you can zero in on specific products and offices— or zoom back to see the whole enchilada.

SCENARIO MANAGER HELPS YOU "WHAT-IF"

Scenario Manager generates tables of values created as Excel tries different combinations of assumptions. Say you wanted to see the tax effects and net profit of selling your home at various prices and sales commission percentages. You could tell Excel's Scenario Manager the selling price and commission ranges to use, then see the results of multiple, automatic computations.

PRESENTATION FEATURES

Excel now offers a "slide show" feature that lets you create on-screen, sequential presentations. Your slide shows can contain spreadsheets, charts, graphics, and even sounds! There are "transitioning effects" that can be placed between slides. Examples include dissolves and wipes and venetian blinds like the ones TV weather forecasters use when switching from map to map. Shows are constructed by copying the various elements (spreadsheets, graphs, sounds, whatever) into a special document, or "script," while specifying the transition effects, length of time each slide will be displayed, and so on. The shows can run over and over again, automatically, or you can advance them manually. This is an excellent, low-cost way to create point-of-sale demonstrations in stores or to make your point at sales meetings or even to create professional-looking displays for trade shows. Figure 24.5 gives you a glimpse of Excel's slide show creation tools.

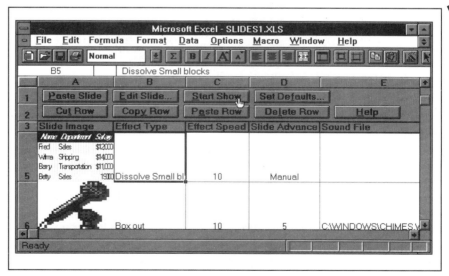

FIGURE 24.5 *Excel lets you create and run slide shows with graphics, sound, and special effects.*

CROSSTABULATION
WITH CROSSTAB WIZARD

As you may know, spreadsheets can also be used as databases. For instance, you could create a spreadsheet containing the names, departments, and salaries of each of your employees. You might have one horizontal row for each worker, and a column titled "Name," another "Department," another "Sex," and another "Salary." Excel's Custom ReportWizard will then lead you through the necessary steps to create reports broken down the way you want them—like a report of salaries by department, or one by sex or by salary within departments, and so on. Here again, Microsoft's "Wizard" feature automates, simplifies, and greatly speeds the crosstabulation process.

MACROS

Excel's macros are collections of automated steps that the computer can perform for you, whenever you ask. For instance, you could teach Excel to sort the information in a section of your spreadsheet, then print an updated report that you need regularly. Excel can learn the macro steps by "watching" you do them and "recording" them in macro files on your disk. If you have old Lotus 1-2-3 spreadsheets containing macros, chances are that Excel can successfully convert and use them.

OLE SUPPORT

Last, but by no means least, Excel supports object linking and embedding, or OLE (pronounced *oh-lay*). OLE makes it possible for you to paste part or all of a spreadsheet or Excel chart into other documents (like a Word document). Then, when something changes in the spreadsheet, the word processing document is automatically updated! This intriguing process is described and demonstrated in Part IV of this book.

Let's get started. The next chapter will show you how to run Excel, get online help, and create a simple spreadsheet.

25

Getting Started
with Excel

The obvious way to start Excel is to double-click on the Excel icon while in Program Manager. Starting it this way opens a new, untitled worksheet. You can also start Excel from File Manager either by double-clicking on the EXCEL.EXE icon in your Excel directory, or by double-clicking on Excel worksheet icons and related files (files with the extensions .XLS, .XLM, .XLC, or .XLW, and possibly others). This starts the program and displays the worksheet whose icon you clicked on.

PARTS OF A WORKSHEET

As you can see in Figure 25.1, Excel follows most of Microsoft Window's conventions. There are scroll bars, control boxes, menu bars, and so forth. There are some new tools in Excel windows as well. See if you can find them in Figure 25.1 as they are described here. (Your screen may look different, especially if someone else has used the program before you. That's because users have considerable control over the appearance of the workspace, as you will learn in Chapter 37, in which you personalize Excel.)

Normally, you will see at least one Toolbar (probably the *standard* Toolbar shown at the top of Figure 25.1). You might also see other Toolbars at the bottom or even in the middle of your worksheet.

By now you should know that worksheets consist of horizontal, numbered *rows* and vertical *columns* identified with letters. The resulting boxes are called *cells*, and the cell where you work is called the *active cell*. It has a dark border around it, or sometimes appears ghostly-white when you select cells around it. In Figure 25.1 cell B4 is the active cell. Notice that the address of the active cell is displayed in a box below the left edge of the standard Toolbar.

When you type *text* or *formulas* (instructions Excel uses to compute results), you'll see your characters scroll across the *Formula bar* and in the active cell. There's normally a status bar at the bottom of your Excel window.

USING THE EXCEL TUTORIALS

Excel contains two tutorials, each containing seven lessons. They are located on the Help menu. Microsoft estimates that it would take you about two-and-one-quarter hours to complete all of the lessons. Since lessons are broken down by topic and skill level, chances are you'll not need to visit all of them. For instance, users of earlier Excel versions will be able to skip the basics and go right to "What's New?" Lotus 1-2-3 converts have their own tutorials in Excel as well.

If you are working on an Excel project when you decide to take the tutorials, Excel sets aside your work, restoring it when you quit the tutorials. The tutorials give you hands-on exercises. Your time will be very well spent to run them.

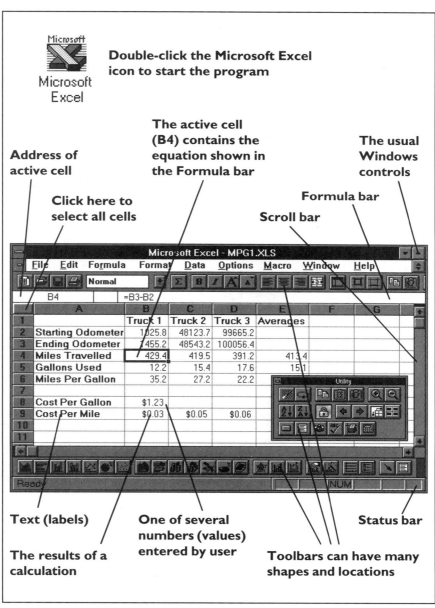

**Double-click the Microsoft Excel
icon to start the program**

**The active cell
(B4) contains the
equation shown in
the Formula bar**

**The usual
Windows
controls**

**Address of
active cell**

**Click here to
select all cells**

Formula bar

Scroll bar

Text (labels)

**One of several
numbers (values)
entered by user**

Status bar

**The results of a
calculation**

**Toolbars can have many
shapes and locations**

FIGURE 25.1 *Double-click on the Excel icon or a related file icon to start Excel.
You'll see either a new untitled worksheet or the worksheet whose icon you
double-clicked on.*

USING EXCEL'S ON-LINE HELP

Like many other Windows programs, Excel offers extensive on-line help. Reach it either with the F1 function key or from the Help menu. Navigate the help files as described in the Windows and Word sections of this book.

GETTING MICROSOFT
EXCEL PRODUCT SUPPORT

Microsoft has set up special telephone support numbers for the Windows version of Excel. You can receive prerecorded voice help and fax support, even speak with humans, at this number. As if that weren't enough, a Microsoft "disk jockey" entertains you when the lines get jammed. In the United States, dial 206–635–7071. A CompuServe Excel forum is also available. Type **GO MICROSOFT** at any ! prompt.

CREATING A NEW WORKSHEET

The best way to learn Excel is to use it. If you haven't already done so, start the program. You should see a new worksheet like the one in Figure 25.1, which calculates mileage costs for several trucks.

PAGE SETUP FIRST

Since Excel can show you page endings, as well as how much information will fit on each page as you work, it's a good idea to make Page Setup decisions right when you start a new project. Use the Page Setup... command located on Excel's File menu. As you will see in Chapter 27, page size, orientation, plus header and footer dimensions are just a few of the things you can control with Page Setup. For your first project you may want to stick with Excel's default settings, but as a rule you will want to get in the habit of changing Page Setup settings when you start new worksheets.

SELECTING CELLS WITH A MOUSE

Before entering or editing cell contents, or before you can format or move cells, they need to be selected. You can select single cells or *ranges* of cells.

To select a single cell, point and click in it. It becomes the active cell. To select an entire column of cells, point to the column's heading as shown in the top of Figure 25.2. Clicking on the raised area above the row numbers and to the left of the column letters (as called out in Figure 25.1) selects the entire worksheet.

Click on a row number to select the whole row. Click-and-drag to select a range of cells. To select noncontiguous (nonadjacent) cells, or groups of cells, hold down the Ctrl key and do any of the aforementioned selection tricks. For example, to select rows 2 and 4 but not row 3, click on the number for row 2, then Ctrl-click on 4.

SELECTING CELLS WITH THE KEYBOARD

While you will probably want to use your mouse for most sections (it's speedier), there are many keyboard selection tricks. Shift-Spacebar selects an entire *row*. Ctrl-Spacebar selects an entire *column*. Ctrl-Shift-Spacebar selects the entire worksheet. To extend selections in any direction, hold down the Shift key and press the appropriate arrow key. The other navigational keys can be used to extend selections also. For instance, Shift-Ctrl-End extends the selection to the end of your worksheet.

THE SELECT SPECIAL COMMAND

The Select Special... command on the Formula menu lets you select cells meeting specific criteria. For instance, you can specify all notes, formulas, blank cells, the last cell, etc. To search the entire worksheet, select a single cell, then use the command. To inspect a range of cells, preselect only the cells of interest.

NAVIGATING WITH
BOTH MOUSE AND KEYBOARD

Use the navigational tools you've read about earlier in this book to move around in large worksheets. Scroll with the scroll bars, use PgUp, Home, and related keys.

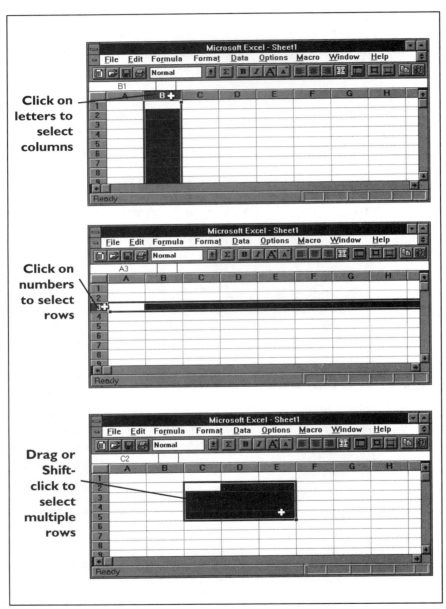

FIGURE 25.2 *A mouse makes it easy to select single cells, all columns, all rows, or ranges of cells.*

The Formula menu offers a number of other navigational aids. For instance, there is a Find… command that will remind you of Word's. It lets you search for text strings, formulas, and other items of interest. The Show Active Cell command takes you back to the active cell.

You can name areas of your spreadsheet and use Excel's *Goto…* command to quickly find them. (Chapter 30 describes this process.)

NAVIGATING WITH THE GOTO COMMAND

The Formula menu's Goto… command can be used to find and activate a cell, or to select a range of cells. Excel remembers and lists your last four locations in the Goto dialog box, making it easy to revisit them. To "collect" and select nonadjacent cells with Goto…, hold down the Ctrl key when you click OK in the Goto dialog box.

ENTERING AND EDITING TEXT

To enter the text used to label things in your worksheets, simply activate the cell where you want the text to appear (point to it), then begin typing. (When you enter text into a cell this way, the text is sometimes referred to as a *constant value*, since it will remain the same until you change it yourself.)

As you start typing, text will appear in the active cell *and* in the Formula bar. Pressing the Enter key or clicking the check mark button in the Formula bar concludes the text entry and places the text in the active cell. If you change your mind before you press Enter, you can press the Esc key or click on the X button in the Formula bar to cancel the entry. Figure 25.3 illustrates this.

If an entry is too long to fit completely in the active cell, only part of the text will show there, but the entire entry will show in the Formula bar, which expands as needed. You can type up to 255 characters per cell. Figure 25.3 illustrates this. (After you've entered text, it is easy to later increase cell sizes or word wrap text to accommodate the entries, as you'll see in Chapter 27.)

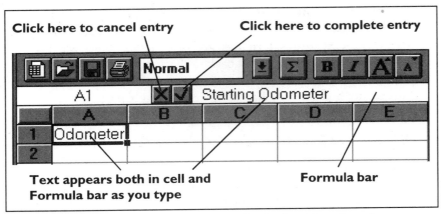

FIGURE 25.3 *Type in the Formula bar. Use the check mark or Enter key to accept the entry. Press Esc or use the X button to cancel.*

EDITING TEXT

If you spot an error while entering text, simply backspace to correct it. If you see an error after finishing the entry, activate the cell and edit the text in the Formula bar. Use your Windows text-editing skills here. Drag or double-click or otherwise select the text you want to delete or correct. Move the insertion point around in the text on the Formula bar if necessary. When the corrections have been made, press Enter or click the check mark button.

REPLACING TEXT

If you activate a cell containing text, then type new text and press Enter or click the check mark button, the new text will replace the old text.

STYLIZING TEXT

You can change the appearance of both text and numbers in cells (make things bold or bigger, change fonts, and so on). The entire cell is affected by the changes. As well as the formatting buttons on the standard Toolbar, there are additional buttons on the Formatting Toolbar, and further choices reached through the Style... command on the Format menu. The process of embellishing cell appearance is described in more detail in Chapter 27.

TEXT BOXES

Besides typing text into cells, you can create *text boxes* and place them anywhere you like on your worksheets. They are a kind of graphic object, described in more detail in Chapters 32 and 33. You have more control over the appearance of text in text boxes than you do in worksheet cells. For instance, you can change formatting of individual characters in text boxes. All characters must have the same formatting in cells. It's even possible to rotate text in text boxes, and draw arrows from text boxes to things the text describes.

TEXT NOTES

Text notes are used to hold notes to yourself that you don't want to display on your worksheets. Notes are attached to cells.

To create a note, start by selecting the appropriate cell. Choose Note… from the Formula bar. Type the note. Don't press Enter to insert line breaks in a note, use Ctrl-Enter instead. Click OK or press Enter to attach the note to the cell.

Double-clicking on a cell containing a note displays the note. The Notes In Sheet dialog box (reached from the Formula menu) lists all notes and lets you select them for viewing. To print notes, visit the Page Setup dialog box and select the desired (self-explanatory) note printing options.

CHECKING SPELLING

Once you've entered the worksheet headings and other text (like chart labels), Excel's Spelling… command on the Options menu will launch the spelling checker shown in Figure 25.4. (There is also a spelling button on the Utilities menu bar.)

If you have a custom Microsoft *Word* dictionary called CUSTOM.DIC in the MSAPPS\PROOF subdirectory of your WINDOWS directory on your hard disk (the default location), Excel will also use this custom dictionary. Otherwise, it will create its own.

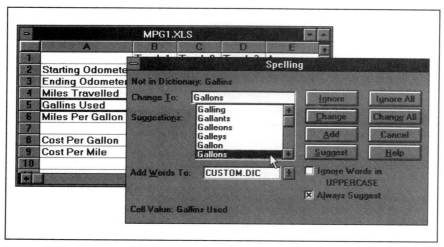

FIGURE 25.4 *Excel's spelling checker can share your Word custom dictionary. You'll need Word version 2.0A or newer to avoid compatibility problems.*

WORD/EXCEL SPELLING COMPATIBILITY CAUTION

Owners of *very early* shipments of Word for Windows 2.0 are cautioned that a serious dictionary compatibility problem exists. The Spelling... command will be visible on your Excel menu Options menu, but nothing useful happens when you pick it. If you plan to use Excel and Word for Windows on the same hard disk, make sure your Word program is at least version 2.0A. You can check this by starting Word and reading the version number displayed on the "splash" screen that shows your name, company, etc. Contact Microsoft technical support for an upgrade and assistance, if necessary.

RUNNING THE SPELLING CHECKER

To check the spelling of your entire worksheet, run the spelling checker *without selecting any cells*. This checks labels, cell notes, embedded charts, text boxes, headers, and footers. It does *not*, however, check text created by formulas.

To check a small portion of the worksheet, select the appropriate range of cells. To check a single word, highlight it in the Formula bar and run the checker.

Accept Excel's spelling suggestions, ignore them, type your own changes, or add words to the custom dictionary as you do in Word. (Refer to Chapter 20 for details.)

UNDOING AND REPEATING ACTIONS

Excel's Edit menu contains Undo and Repeat commands similar to Word's. There is also an Undo button on the Utilities Toolbar. Frequently, if you catch a mistake quickly enough, a trip to the Undo command or use of the Ctrl-Z shortcut will fix it. The Repeat command will often duplicate your last action. The exact names of the Undo and Repeat commands change, based on your prior actions. Sometimes you'll see gray "Can't Undo" or "Can't Repeat" commands indicating Excel's inability to undo or play back whatever you last did.

ENTERING AND FORMATTING NUMBERS

Numbers are the raw materials for spreadsheets. They are often referred to as *constant values*, or simply *values*. You type numbers into the active cell by using either the number keys above the letter keys on your keyboard, or by using the numeric keypad in Num Lock mode. (Most keyboards that have a numeric keypad also have a Num Lock light. When this light is on, you know you can type numbers with the keypad.) Repeatedly pressing the Num Lock key toggles this mode.

In addition to the numerals 1–9, you can enter the following special symbols when typing numbers: +–(),$%E or **e**. Excel ignores the plus sign in numeric entries, and considers a number to be negative if you precede it with a minus sign or hyphen, or enclose it in parentheses. It treats commas and dollar signs correctly, and accepts numbers entered in scientific notation (**2.5E+2**, for instance). When you enter dollar signs, percentages, or commas, Excel changes the number's *format*.

NUMBER FORMATS

Within limits, Excel stores and calculates numbers at the precision you type them, but may display them slightly differently than you typed them.

For instance, if you type **3.141592654** in a cell, that's what will be *stored* in the cell even if you *see* something else. So, if you place that entry in a narrow cell, you might *see* **3.141593**. In this case, Excel *displays* the number at the maximum possible precision under the circumstances and *rounds* it *up* to display it. The actual *appearance* of the number changes with the *number format* defined for the cell. Normally this affects neither the value itself, nor other computations based on the number.

You can control the precision with which numbers are displayed. All new worksheets start out with all of their cells formatted in *General* format, which attempts to show as much precision as possible. You can force cells to use other formats designed by Microsoft, or you can create your own formats. (Chapter 27 discusses this in more detail.) Sometimes, the entry techniques that you use change the cell's number format *automatically*. For example, if you activate a cell in the General format, then type a number with a dollar sign, the cell's format will change from General to a currency format.

Typing a percent sign changes a cell's number format to a percentage with two decimal places (**10.05%**, for instance). There are scientific and fractional number formats as well. You can specify the number format for a cell or group of cells from the *Number Format* dialog box shown in Figure 25.5. Reach it from the Number... command on the Format menu. It is discussed in Chapter 27.

WHEN NUMBERS ARE TOO BIG FOR THEIR CELLS

When a number is too big to be properly displayed in its cell, Excel often displays a series of pound signs (######) instead of the number. Other times, Excel will switch to scientific notation to accommodate a large number. Figure 25.6 shows examples of both techniques.

Making the column wider using techniques described in Chapter 26, or using a shorter number format, will solve the problem. For instance, when dealing with large sums of money, you can often save room in cells by using number formats that don't display pennies and decimal points. They will still calculate correctly. Chapter 27 shows you how.

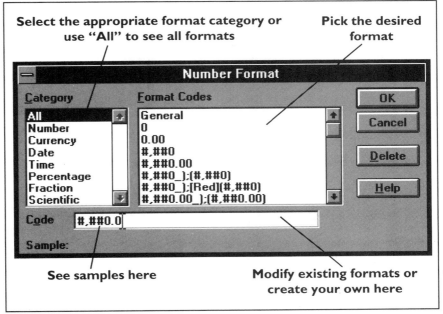

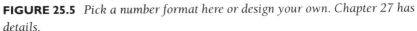

FIGURE 25.5 *Pick a number format here or design your own. Chapter 27 has details.*

Entering and Formatting Dates and Times

Enter dates and times by typing them in most commonly accepted American formats. They include, but are not limited to:

11/7/93

11-Nov-93

Nov 7, 1993

8:10 PM

8:10:12 PM

20:10

20:10:12

11/7/93 20:10

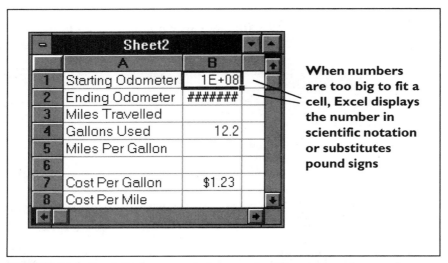

When numbers
are too big to fit a
cell, Excel displays
the number in
scientific notation
or substitutes
pound signs

FIGURE 25.6 *Excel displays pound signs or scientific notation when numbers are too big to fit a cell. Widen the column or change the number format to make things fit.*

You can even create your own date formats. For instance, **mmmm d, yyyy** will display **November 7, 1994**.

Excel will *store* entries like these as dates or times, then *reformat* and *display* them using one of several predefined date formats. Chapter 27 tells you more about date and time formats.

How Excel Stores Dates and Times

Date and time entries are a slightly confusing topic, made tougher by Excel's desire to be all things to all people. If you ever plan to enter dates into cells, you should know the following:

Because Excel is often required to do date-and-time math (determine the number of days between two dates, or the number of hours between two time entries, for instance), it *stores* dates and times as *serial numbers* using January 1, 1900, as the starting date. Here's how it works:

The serial number 1 represents January 1, 1900; the serial number 2 stands for January 2, 1900, and so on.

If you *reformat* a cell containing a *date* and display it as a *number* you will see the serial number instead of the date. Excel will still treat the cell's contents as a date for computations, but the cell will just *look* strange.

Alas, not all computers use 1/1/1900 as the starting point for their date serial numbers. For example, Macintosh computers use 1904. Excel usually converts dates from Macintosh spreadsheets properly when importing and exporting, but check carefully when moving worksheets containing dates from one platform to another. Incidentally, Excel treats 1900 as a leap year even though it is not. This is to maintain compatibility with Multiplan and Lotus 1-2-3.

FORCING NUMBERS TO BE TREATED AS TEXT

If you want Excel to treat numbers or time or date-like entries as text instead of numbers, you need to tell it to do so. Suppose, for instance, you want to enter the part number **12/63**. Excel would try to treat this as a date. Instead of seeing your part number in the cell you'd see **Dec-63** after you finished the entry. To prevent this, precede such entries with a single quotation mark ('), which will not display or print. Alternatively, since Excel treats any cell containing nonnumbers as text, the entries **#12/63**, **12/63B**, and even numbers preceded by a space (**_12/63**) will be treated as text.

ENTERING AND EDITING FORMULAS

Formulas get the work done. When you want to add a column of numbers and see the results, or divide one number by another, or do any other computation, you must create formulas. Formulas are sometimes even used to manipulate text in worksheets.

Usually, you place the formula in the cell where you want to see the results. You type formulas in the Formula bar. Excel formulas always start with the *equal sign* (=), although diehard Lotus users can cheat and use the ampersand (&) instead.

Do you remember the sample miles-per-gallon worksheet at the beginning of this chapter? It contains formulas to compute miles traveled by three trucks, miles per gallon, and cost per mile. Check out Figure 25.7 to see the formulas in more detail.

The mileage formula in cell B3 *subtracts* the ending odometer reading (located in cell B2) from the starting reading (in cell B1) to compute and display the mileage. Notice that the formula does this by *referring to* the two

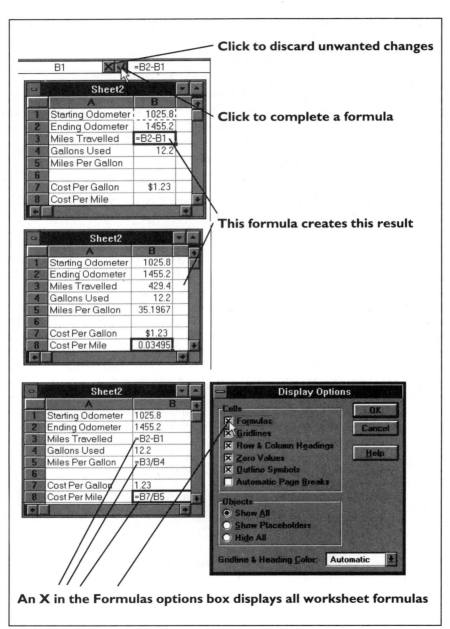

FIGURE 25.7 *See and create individual formulas in the Formula bar. Use the Display Options dialog box to show all of your worksheet's formulas at once.*

cell addresses *B2* and *B1*. Whenever the contents of B1 or B2 change, Excel will automatically compute a new answer and display it in cell B3. That's the essence of worksheet computations! Formulas tell Excel what to do whenever the contents of specified cells change.

The formula in B3 is a very simple one. It would be possible, for instance, to have a more complex formula in B3 that checks to be sure that the ending odometer readings are always larger the starting readings. Take a look at the formulas in cells B5 and B8 at the bottom of Figure 25.7. Do they make sense to you?

CREATING FORMULAS

If you've never used a mouse to create formulas before, you might want to fire up Excel and follow along with this description.

Start by activating the cell where you want to place the formula (point to B3, for instance). Next type either an equal sign or an ampersand to tell Excel you want to create a formula.

You can then either type the formula one character at a time, or *assemble* it using your mouse and keyboard. For instance, you *could* type =B2-B1 and press Enter to create the formula in B3.

But it's often better to reach for the mouse when creating formulas. For example, you could type the equal sign, then point to cell B2 with your mouse. Cell B2 will be surrounded by an dashed outline (sometimes called "marching ants"). The cell's address will appear in the Formula bar. This makes it unnecessary for you to *type* the address with the keyboard. Next, you'd type the minus sign for your equation, then point to cell B1 with the mouse. Pressing Enter finishes the formula. If you have entered values in cells B1 and B2, they will be subtracted from each other and their difference appears in cell B3.

EXCEL'S FORMULA OPERATORS

Operators tell Excel what you want to do (add two numbers, or compare things, for instance). For purposes of explanation, Excel operators can be divided into four general categories—arithmetic, comparison, text, and reference. Most of the time you will use arithmetic operators. The others can be useful for more complex projects.

Arithmetic Operators

You've already seen two arithmetic operators in Figure 25.7—subtraction (−) and division (the slash symbol, /). The others are addition (+), multiplication (*), percentage (%), and exponentiation (^). Simply include them at the appropriate places in your formulas to perform the desired calculation. For instance, the formula =B4*10% would compute 10% of the contents of cell B4. The equation =B4^2 computes the square of cell B4's contents.

Obviously, complex formulas like =E6*B2-(B3*10%) can be created by combining operators and using parentheses.

Comparison Operators

Comparison operators let you inspect two values and come to a conclusion about their relative values. They are usually coupled with Excel's *logical functions* (discussed in Chapter 31).

The operators are Equal (=), Greater than (>), Less than (<), Greater than or equal to (>=), Less than or equal to (<=), and Not equal to (<>).

At the risk of confusing you, here is an example of comparison operators at work with a logical function. Suppose you wanted to display an error message whenever the ending odometer reading in cell B3 was *smaller* than the starting reading in B2. The formula =IF((B3<B2),"**Bad OD!**",B3-B2) would compare the contents of cells B3 and B2. If B3 is less than B2 the text "Bad OD!" is displayed instead of the wrong numeric (negative) mileage value. If the odometer readings pass the comparison test, the math is performed (B3-B2). If you are confused now, this will make more sense after you've read Chapter 31.

Text Operator

Excel's only text operator is the ampersand (&). It is used to combine text. For instance, if you had the word **aero** in cell C7 and the word **plane** in C8, the formula =C7&C8 would create the text string **aeroplane**.

Reference Operators

Finally, Excel offers reference operators. The most common reference is to a range of cells. For instance, the expression B1:C3 refers to cells B1, C3, and all the cells between them. You'll learn more about ranges later in this chapter.

BUILT-IN FUNCTIONS VS. HAND-BUILT FORMULAS

Excel provides a number of built-in functions that automate otherwise time-consuming tasks. For instance, there is a function that computes monthly loan payments given a loan amount, interest rates, and the length of your loan. Another function computes averages for specified groups of numbers. Other functions perform engineering or statistical tasks. You'll learn more about functions in Chapter 31. But there is one worth learning about now. It's called the *SUM* function, and it can be reached with the Summation or SUM (Σ) button on the standard Toolbar.

Suppose you wanted to add the column of numbers in Figure 25.8. You *could* type the equation **=A2+A3+A4+A5**. But the SUM function is a better way to get the sum of those figures.

As you can see at the bottom of Figure 25.8, if cell C6 is the active cell, pressing the SUM button causes Excel to propose a range of cells to include in its range (cell A2 through and including cell A5). Marching ants surround the cells to be included. The SUM equation also appears in the Formula bar, where you can accept or edit it. Pressing Enter or clicking on the Formula bar's check mark button will accept the proposed formula and display the answer in cell A6. The SUM button and related SUM function work on rows, columns, or arrays (described next).

ARRAYS AND FORMULAS

Formulas can include references to *arrays*, or contiguous (adjacent) groups of numbers. For instance, in Figure 25.9 the SUM function will add up all the numbers in the six-cell array B2:C4.

When using the SUM function and similar tools to specify arrays, you can drag the marching ants with your mouse to include or exclude cells.

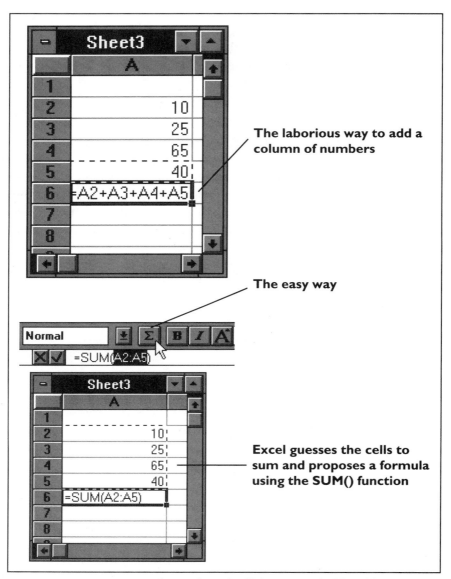

FIGURE 25.8 *Functions make quick work of laborious tasks like adding rows or columns of numbers.*

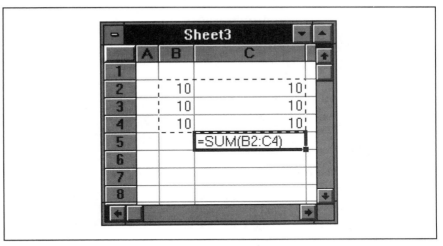

FIGURE 25.9 *Excel can treat groups of cells as arrays.*

CONTROLLING RECALCULATION

Normally, Excel recalculates each time you change any number in the worksheet. And, unless you instruct it otherwise, Excel always recalculates before saving. You can overrule these automatic recalculation options and others from the Calculation Options dialog box, reached with the Calculation... command on the Options menu. Figure 25.10 shows it.

When working on large, complex projects, consider shutting-off automatic recalculation if lengthy recalculation delays bother you. Just remember that once you disable automatic recalculation, you become responsible for telling Excel when to recalculate. If you make changes to your worksheet and forget to manually recalculate, one or more cells containing equations may contain old, incorrect answers. To manually recalculate the worksheet, press the F9 function key. (Put a note on your monitor to remind you to recalculate before you save the worksheet.)

COPYING ENTRIES AND
EQUATIONS TO MINIMIZE TYPING

When creating a large worksheet it is time consuming to type the same values over and over and over again. And, when creating similar formulas

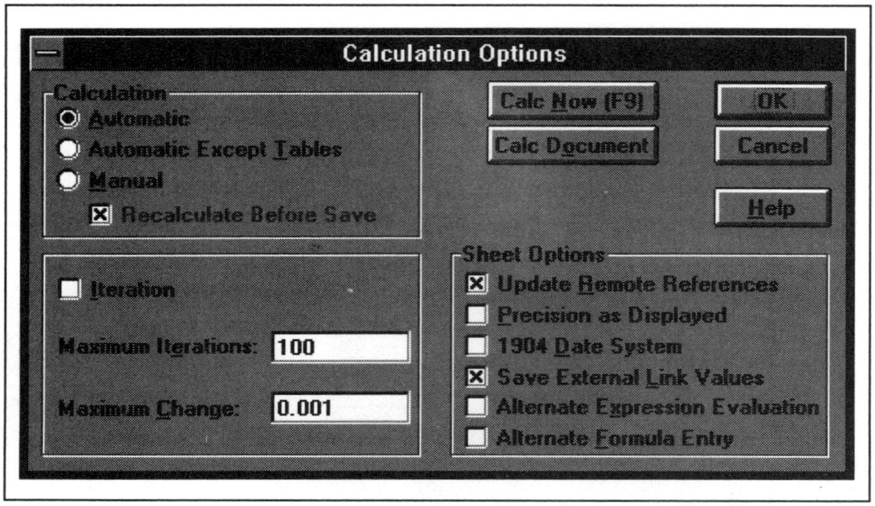

FIGURE 25.10 *Control recalculation from the Calculation Options dialog box.*

in different cells, sometimes the only things that change in the formulas are cell references. For instance, if you create an equation like =A1-A2 in column A, you often want a similar equation like =B1-B2 in column B and =C1-C2 in column C. Excel provides a number of powerful features to minimize mindless typing like this. But you need to use these power tools with care! Take a look.

AUTOFILL

AutoFill is a tool that lets you select cells of interest and make relative copies of them in adjacent cells. Figure 25.11 shows a (partially flawed) example of AutoFill at work.

To use AutoFill, simply highlight the cell(s) of interest, then drag the *fill outline* using the square handle at the bottom corner of the active cell outline. (It's called the *Fill handle*.) Your pointer turns into a large plus sign when it is able to drag the Fill handle.

The *center* part of Figure 25.11 shows the results of auto-filling. There are some surprises, both good and bad. Excel has cleverly guessed that the

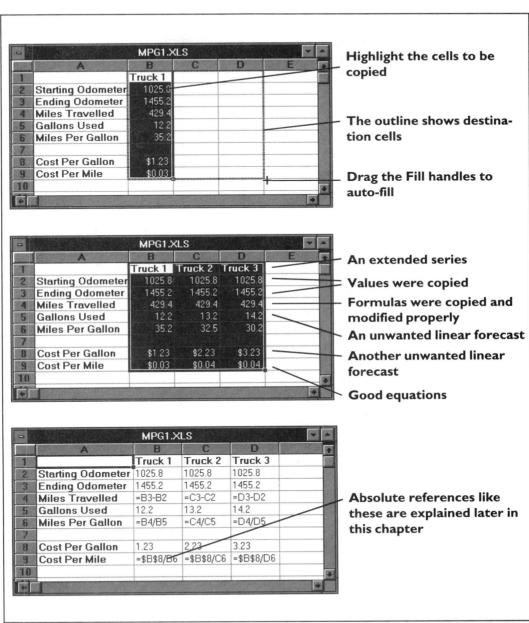

Highlight the cells to be copied

The outline shows destination cells

Drag the Fill handles to auto-fill

An extended series

Values were copied

Formulas were copied and modified properly

An unwanted linear forecast

Another unwanted linear forecast

Good equations

Absolute references like these are explained later in this chapter

FIGURE 25.11 *Features like AutoFill minimize mindless retyping. Use them with care and inspect your work, or you will sometimes create hard-to-find errors.*

second truck should be labeled **Truck 2** and the third **Truck 3**. Not knowing any better, it has *copied* the beginning and ending odometer readings so that all three trucks have the same readings, and thus identical mileages. This is easy to fix by typing corrected odometer readings. (The problem could have been avoided altogether by placing zeros in column A before auto-filling.)

But look at the Gallons Used and Cost Per Gallon cells! AutoFill has *projected* different gas usage and gas prices for each truck, all on its own, by making a *linear forecast* without being asked to do so.

Curiously, this will not happen if you just select cell B5 and auto-fill it to D5, or B8 and auto-fill it to D8. Auto-filling those cells and not the others would prevent Excel from creating the linear projection. Here, too, placing zeros in cells B5 and B8 would prevent this unwanted "assistance."

Obviously, there are times when automatic linear projections are desirable. But this isn't one of them. The message is: if you use AutoFill, check your work carefully.

The bottom screen in Figure 25.11 illustrates automatic equation modifications accomplished by AutoFill and other Excel equation copying tools. Here, we've switched the Display Options to display the formulas created by AutoFill. Notice the formulas in row 4. Excel has altered the cell references in each column so that the formulas subtract the appropriate numbers in each column. This is called *relative addressing*. Sometimes you don't want Excel to do that for you. Use absolute addressing, instead.

ABSOLUTE CELL ADDRESSING

Look at the equations in cells B9, C9, and D9 illustrated in Figure 25.12. They contain examples of absolute addressing.

Here, we want all three trucks to use the same gas price, and want to enter it only once in cell B8. If we just used Excel's Fill features to drag copies of the formula in B9, they would be incorrect. The equation in C9 would look to C8 for a gas price, and the formula in D9 would look to D8. Typing dollar signs in the reference to B8 ($B$8) makes it an absolute reference.

Whenever Excel encounters absolute references while copying, it does not change them, so, in Figure 25.12, each resulting new formula looks to cell B8 for the gas price and the appropriate cell in its own column for miles-per-gallon statistics.

	A	B	C	D	
1		Truck 1	Truck 2	Truck 3	
2	Starting Odometer	1025.8	658	99987	
3	Ending Odometer	1455.2	956.8	100123	
4	Miles Travelled	=B3-B2	=C3-C2	=D3-D2	
5	Gallons Used	12.2	10.7	13	
6	Miles Per Gallon	=B4/B5	=C4/C5	=D4/D5	
7					
8	Cost Per Gallon	1.23			
9	Cost Per Mile	=$B$8/B6	=$B$8/C6	=$B$8/D6	
10					

MPG1.XLS

All three of these formulas refer to cell B8

FIGURE 25.12 *The dollar signs in cell references ($B$8) prevent Excel from changing the references when copying formulas.*

FILLING RIGHT OR DOWN

In addition to AutoFill, Excel offers *Fill Right* and *Fill Down* commands on the Edit menu. You can use these to copy values or formulas in much the same way that you use AutoFill. Select the cell(s) to copy, then drag to highlight destination cells. This time, don't drag the Fill handle. Your screen might look something like Figure 25.13.

PROTECTING AND UNPROTECTING DOCUMENTS AND CELLS

Sometimes you'll want to prevent others from gaining any kind of unauthorized access to a worksheet (say, your employees' salaries). Other times you'll want to let people see, but not change, your work—to prevent you or someone else from accidentally destroying a cell's formula or other contents with an inadvertent entry. Or, you may want to authorize the changing of some cells, but not others.

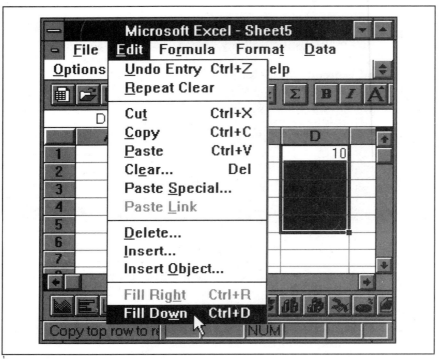

FIGURE 25.13 *Fill Down and Fill Right also copy values and equations.*

PREVENTING OTHERS FROM
OPENING YOUR DOCUMENTS

You can assign a password to prevent unauthorized people from opening your documents. This is done with the Save Options dialog box reached from the Save As... command. Figure 25.14 illustrates the process.

You can completely prevent unauthorized opening of documents from this dialog box, or you can permit people to open and even change things in a worksheet, but not save the changes. It is also possible to let others save changes with a prior warning.

Excel's passwords are case sensitive. That is to say, if you assign **Mickey** as the password, Excel will not accept **MICKEY** or **mickey** or any other variation. You are asked to confirm each password assignment by typing it a second time before it becomes "official."

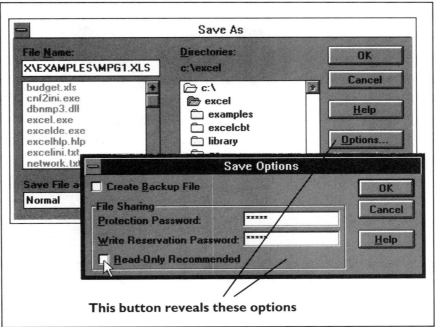

FIGURE 25.14 *Use the Save Options to prevent unauthorized opening or unwanted saving of changes.*

CELL PROTECTION

It is sometimes desirable to protect portions of your worksheets even from your own mistakes. For instance, it is very easy to accidentally enter a value into a cell containing a formula. When you do this, the formula is destroyed and your worksheet will no longer function properly.

For this reason, it's often a good idea to protect cells containing formulas and labels after you are happy with the functioning and appearance of your worksheet. Use the Cell Protection... and Protect Document... commands *in combination* to do this. It's a two-step process. First, you specify which cells you want to protect by selecting them and issuing the Cell Protection... command, then you must turn on protection with the Protect Document... command. Figure 25.15 shows the dialog boxes you'll be using.

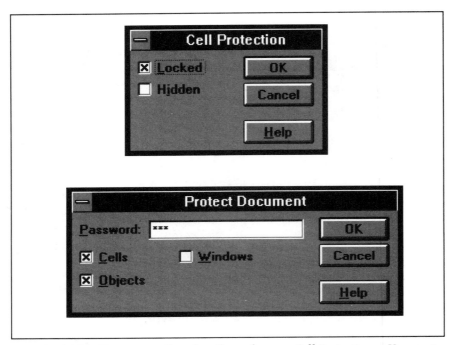

FIGURE 25.15 *To protect cells, select them, then use Cell Protection… You must also use Protect Document… to turn this protection on and off.*

PROTECTING GRAPHICS

Click in the graphic you want to protect, then follow the same procedures used to protect cells, except choose the Objects option in the Protect Document dialog box shown in Figure 25.15.

PROTECTING WINDOW SIZE AND POSITION

To prevent changes to the size and position of a window, arrange it properly, then use the Windows option. Protected windows do not display Control boxes.

26

Rearranging Worksheets

Regardless of how carefully you plan a project, inevitably you'll wish you had put things in a slightly different order. You'll want to insert extra rows or columns, move things around, or just plain delete them. In large measure you'll be able to use Windows and Word skills described earlier in this book. You can cut-and-paste, as well as drag-and-drop, for instance.

MOVING CELLS WITH THEIR CONTENTS, FORMATS, AND NOTES

Normally, when you move cells' contents, you also move their notes and formatting information. If cells contain equations, they move too; and, unless you've used absolute addressing, the references in the moved cells will change.

MOVING CELLS

Sometimes moving the contents of a cell or cells and other objects is as simple as selecting the cell(s), cutting with the Cut command on the Edit menu, and pasting with the Paste command. Since this process uses the Clipboard, any prior Clipboard contents will be replaced. As you might expect, the keyboard shortcuts Ctrl-X for cut and Ctrl-V for paste work too. Excel does not warn you if your pasting will overwrite the contents of a cell when using cut-and-paste. So keep your eye on the screen. Undo works if you do it soon enough.

It is also possible to move cells, rows, and columns by selecting them and using drag-and-drop. Figure 26.1 shows the basic process.

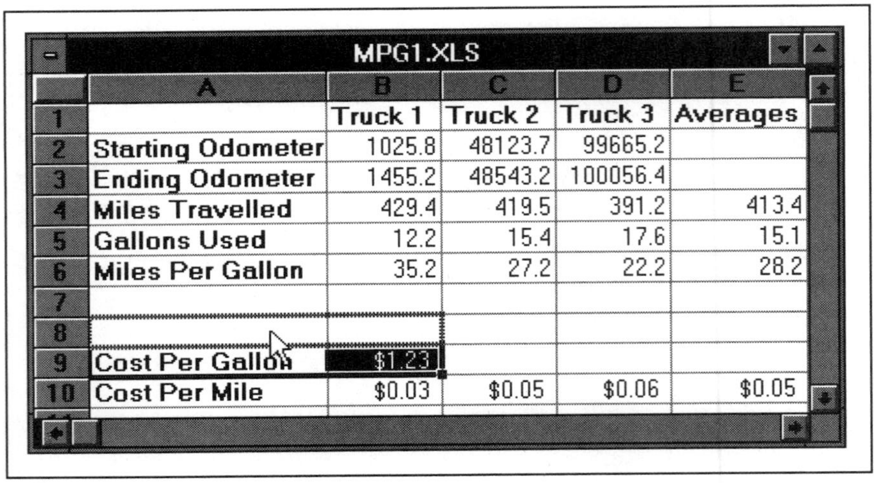

	A	B	C	D	E
		Truck 1	Truck 2	Truck 3	Averages
2	Starting Odometer	1025.8	48123.7	99665.2	
3	Ending Odometer	1455.2	48543.2	100056.4	
4	Miles Travelled	429.4	419.5	391.2	413.4
5	Gallons Used	12.2	15.4	17.6	15.1
6	Miles Per Gallon	35.2	27.2	22.2	28.2
7					
8					
9	Cost Per Gallon	$1.23			
10	Cost Per Mile	$0.03	$0.05	$0.06	$0.05

MPG1.XLS

FIGURE 26.1 *Highlight cells you want to move. Drag at their edges with the arrow-shaped pointer. Releasing the mouse button drops the selected items at the outlined position.*

Unlike cutting and pasting, drag-and-drop *does* warn you if you are going to overwrite nonblank cells. Click OK to replace the previous cell contents with whatever you are dragging, or choose Cancel to abort the dragging and dropping.

COPYING CELLS

To copy cells, select them, then copy with the Edit menu's Copy command and paste with the Paste command. Any prior Clipboard contents will be replaced. The keyboard shortcuts for copying and pasting are Ctrl-C and Ctrl-V respectively (or use the right mouse button to show the Shortcut menu). Excel does not warn you if your pasting will overwrite the contents of a cell when using cut-and-paste. Undo works if you act in time.

It is also possible to copy with drag-and-drop. Figure 26.2 illustrates this.

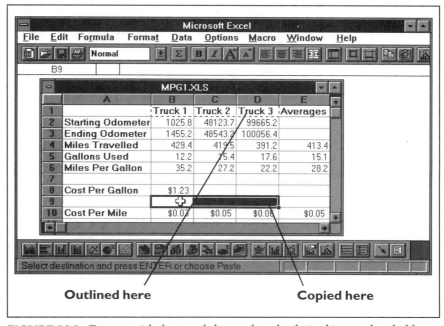

FIGURE 26.2 *To copy with drag-and-drop, select the desired items, then hold down the Ctrl key while dragging.*

Select the cells of interest, then hold down the Ctrl key while dragging. When you release the mouse the selected cells will be pasted in the new location. If this will result in cells' being overwritten, you'll get a chance to cancel the copying.

SORTING CELL DATA

You can sort groups of cells in ascending or descending order, using up to three keys at once. For instance, if you had a spreadsheet containing first names, last names, and test scores, you could simultaneously sort on scores, then last names, then first names so that students with the same scores and last names would appear alphabetically by first name within their score group. Figure 26.3 illustrates this.

Sorting in a spreadsheet is risky business. *You must remember to select everything you want to sort, and nothing else.* For instance, in Figure 26.3 if you select everyone's first and last names, but forget to select their scores, the scores will not move, but the names will, giving some people wrong scores. And, if you select too much (like the headings in Figure 26.3), the sorted data will include unwanted items. An immediate undo can fix this. But it is always best to save before you sort, so that you can close a messed-up worksheet without saving and reload the good, unsorted version. (Or make a copy and try your sort on it.) That said, here are the steps for sorting:

Select just the cells (or rows or columns) you want to sort. Choose Sort... from Excel's Data menu. Specify row or column sorting.

Then, pick the first sorting key. Start by placing the insertion point in the 1st Key entry box. Next, make any cell in the key column (or row) the active cell by clicking. "Ants" will march around the chosen area as if circling the potato salad at a picnic. The key box will contain the active cells' address. In our example, clicking in the Score column specifies Score as the first sort. Next, tell Excel whether you want the sort to produce ascending or descending results. In Figure 26.3 we wanted the high scores first, so a descending sort was specified. If you want to do additional sorts, move to the next key box and repeat the process. Do it again, if necessary, for a three-level sort. When you've set up the sorting specifications, click OK and inspect the results.

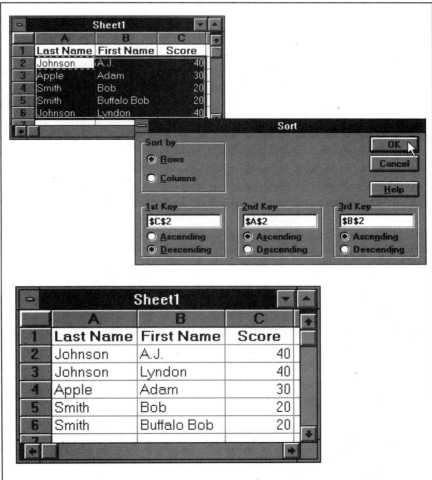

FIGURE 26.3 *Sort on up to three keys at once with the Sort... command on the
Data menu, or use the sort buttons on the Utility Toolbar.*

INSERTING ROWS

It's easy to insert additional rows in a worksheet. One way is to select the
entire row *below* the place where you want a new blank row. Clicking on
the row number at the left edge of row number 4 would select row 4, as an
example. Then use the Insert command on Excel's Edit menu. You will see

a new, blank row 4, and the old contents of row 4 will become row 5. All of the rows that follow will also be pushed down and renumbered. Formulas will usually accommodate insertions like this, but, as always, check your work.

To insert multiple rows, *select* multiple rows before issuing the Insert command. For instance, to insert three rows in our earlier example, you could select rows 4, 5, and 6. This would insert three new rows.

INSERTING COLUMNS

To insert a column, select the column where you want the new column to appear by pointing to the column label. For instance, if you want a blank column at column B, select *it*. Use the Insert command on Excel's Edit menu. You will see a new, blank column B, whereupon the old contents of column B will become column C. All of the columns that follow will also be pushed right and renamed. Formulas will usually allow for insertions like this, but check your work to be sure.

To insert multiple columns, select multiple columns before using the Insert command. That is, to insert three columns in our example, you could select columns B, C, and D. This would insert three new columns.

INSERTING CELLS

You can insert empty cells into an existing worksheet, thereby pushing existing cells either to the right of the insertion point or down from the insertion point. Highlight the area where you want to insert new blank cells, then use the Edit menu's Insert command. The Insert dialog box comes up, asking you if you want to shift cells right or down, or insert an entire row or entire column. This pushes cells as you might expect, although it can ruin the appearance of your worksheet. Undo works here.

INSERTING AS YOU PASTE

Sometimes you'll want to make room for things as you paste them. In these cases, select the items to be pasted, then copy or cut them to the Clipboard. A new Insert Paste... command will appear on the Edit menu. Activate the cell, row, or column where you want to insert the Clipboard contents, and choose the Insert Paste… command. Check the effect upon formulas and the overall worksheet appearance after pasting this way.

DELETING PARTS OF A WORKSHEET

The fact that *three* Excel menus have Delete… commands can be more than a little confusing. The Delete… command on the File menu is used to delete files on your disk, *not* parts of your worksheet. The Delete command on the Data menu is a database command explained in Chapter 35. That leaves the Delete… command on the Edit menu and a companion command called Clear…

Use the Edit menu's Delete command to *remove* unwanted rows, columns, or cells. This places them on the Clipboard and closes up the space made by the deletion. For example, if you select all of column B and use the Edit menu's Delete… command, the contents of column C will shift left and become column C, D will become C, and so on.

The same basic thing happens when you delete rows. Deleting row 4 moves row 5's contents up, making those cells the new row 4, and so on.

If you select an irregular collection of cells (something other than a complete row or column), Excel will ask how you want remaining cells to move when they fill in the newly emptied space.

Deletions of rows, columns, or cells can affect formulas, particularly if you remove cells that are referenced by formulas. Check your work.

CLEARING PARTS OF A WORKSHEET

Clearing removes cell contents but does not move the contents of other cells to fill in the newly emptied space. Highlight the cell(s) you want to clear, then use the Clear… command on the Edit menu, or press the Del key. Excel will ask if you want to clear every aspect of the cell or just selected features like formats, formulas, or notes.

That's the short course on rearranging worksheets. Practice on copies or unimportant projects. Save before making big changes. Next stop: formatting tips and techniques.

27

Excel Formatting Tips and Techniques

Excel provides many formatting features that can enhance the appearance of your worksheets. Some of them will remind you of Microsoft Word's formatting tricks for characters, paragraphs, and tables. Others are unique to Excel. You'll be amazed at how quickly column widths and row heights can be adjusted for "best fit" with a simple mouse click or drag. And Excel's AutoFormat feature can make it look as if you've spent all day on a project, when all you did was make a menu choice. Even if you've used other versions of Excel, be sure you check out this chapter carefully. There is plenty of new material here, including a way to center headings over multiple columns.

EXCEL PAGE SETUP

As with other Windows programs, it's a good idea to make at least preliminary Page Setup decisions when you start a new project. This way you'll be able to see how things will fit when printed. Use the Page Setup... command on Excel's File menu to make a quick trip to the Page Setup dialog box shown in Figure 27.1.

At a minimum, make preliminary page size, orientation, and margin settings. If you have multiple printers, pick the one you'll be using for the project. Later you can revisit Page Setup and fine-tune the settings to improve the final appearance of your document.

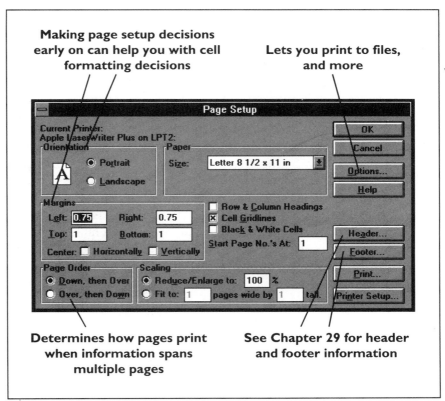

Making page setup decisions early on can help you with cell formatting decisions

Lets you print to files, and more

Determines how pages print when information spans multiple pages

See Chapter 29 for header and footer information

FIGURE 27.1 *Start new projects by choosing paper size, page orientation, margins, and the like.*

CHANGING COLUMN WIDTHS AND ROW HEIGHTS

Sometimes you'll need to change the width of columns or the height of rows. For instance, Excel often displays a series of pound signs (#####) when the results of a calculation won't fit the cell width.

When an entry is too big to fit a cell, you *could* switch to a smaller font or otherwise change the cell's content and format. But frequently you'll want to increase the size of the cell instead. Excel offers a number of ways to adjust column widths and row heights. You can adjust a single row or column, or select multiple rows or columns and change them simultaneously. You can make size changes by double-clicking or dragging, or you can visit dialog boxes. Figure 27.2 illustrates the various approaches, described next.

BEST FIT AUTOMATIC COLUMN WIDTHS AND ROW HEIGHTS

When you place the mouse pointer on or near the right edge of a *column label* (like the one between columns A and B in Figure 27.2), the pointer changes into a thick black bar with arrows pointing left and right. If you double-click, Excel will automatically make the left column (column A in our example) wider or narrower as necessary to accommodate the longest entry in that column. This is referred to as Excel's *Best Fit* feature. When you select multiple columns before double-clicking, *each* selected column will switch to its best fit, potentially making every column a different width.

Row heights automatically increase to accommodate the tallest character in a row. In addition, heights can be changed using techniques similar to the ones used for column widths. Here, too, single rows or many rows can be changed at once. Pointing to a *row* label changes the pointer to a thick *horizontal* bar with *up-* and *down*-pointing arrows. Double-clicking results in a best fit (taller or shorter rows).

While the mouse Best Fit shortcut is the most convenient way to adjust column widths, you can also use the Best Fit button in the Column Width dialog box (reached from the Format menu) to accomplish the same thing.

If you make changes to the contents of cells later, you may need to use Best Fit again, since the feature does not automatically readjust column widths.

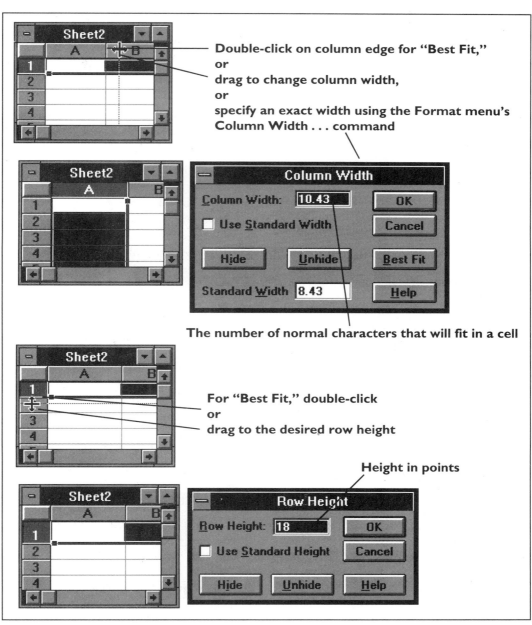

FIGURE 27.2 *Double-click, drag, or use Column and Row dialog boxes to change column widths and row heights.*

Undo (Ctrl-Z) restores column widths and row heights if done immediately after you make changes. Incidentally, best fits are computed using *screen fonts*. As a result, you may occasionally need to readjust columns and rows manually before printing. To see if this will be necessary, use Excel's Print Preview feature.

DRAGGING TO CHANGE ROW AND COLUMN SIZES

If you'd rather make your own manual column width and row height decisions, drag with the pointers rather than double-clicking. As with the Best Fit trick, when you place the mouse pointer on or near the right edge of a row label (like the one between columns A and B in Figure 27.2), the pointer changes into a thick black bar with arrows pointing left and right. Dragging displays a light line showing the column width that will result when you release the mouse button. If you've selected multiple columns, dragging one will make all of them the same width. You can drag to define your own favorite *row height* using similar techniques.

ROW HEIGHT AND COLUMN WIDTH
MENU COMMANDS

The Row Height… and Column Width… commands on the Format menu let you see and specify row heights and column widths. Here you can see row and column measurements, and/or enter your own specifications. Column Width statistics refer to the number of characters that will fit in a cell, assuming that they are formatted in "Normal" style. For instance, in Figure 27.2 the column will hold 10.43 characters. Row heights are displayed and entered in points. In Figure 27.2 the row height is 18 points (a quarter inch).

AUTOFORMAT

Excel's AutoFormat feature uses predefined collections of number formats, fonts, cell alignments, patterns, shading, column widths, and row heights as well as other tricks to embellish ranges of cells you specify. Microsoft calls these *Table Formats*. You can use these formats as-is or overrule some of their characteristics. Because automatic formatting is sometimes difficult to undo, it is a very good idea to save worksheets before experimenting with the automatic formats. Then use the Save As… command to save differently named copies as you experiment. Print before picking your favorite formats.

CHOOSING FORMATS

Start by selecting the range of cells you wish to format. Typically, this is the entire worksheet, but it could be a small range of adjacent cells if you so choose. Then, use the AutoFormat... command on Excel's Format menu to reach the dialog box shown in Figure 27.3.

When you first open the AutoFormat dialog box, you'll see the short version, illustrated in the top of Figure 27.3. Clicking the Options>> button shows the extra check boxes.

Scroll through the list of table formats and click on the names in the list to see them demonstrated in the Sample window. When you find a format of interest, click OK to apply it. (An immediate undo will usually remove the formatting.)

In the process of formatting your document this way, Excel sometimes changes decisions you've made. For instance, if you've made some cells bold, Excel may change them back to plain text or italicize them instead.

To remove some aspect of a Table Format (borders, for example), remove the corresponding X from its name in the Formats to Apply section of the enlarged AutoFormat dialog box. The sample box will show you the effect of these changes as you experiment.

HOW EXCEL MAKES
AUTOMATIC FORMATTING DECISIONS

If you have only one cell selected when you issue the AutoFormat command, Excel looks for what it thinks is a logical range of cells to format. It will highlight the proposed range so that you can see it. If you want to format a different range, cancel AutoFormat and select the desired range before trying again.

Different formats look for—and change—different things when formatting. For instance, the classic formats seek out cells containing totals and subtotals, which receive special formatting. The list-type formats use shading and patterns to make lists more readable. Excel considers outline information while formatting, if you've outlined your worksheet. (See Chapter 30 for more about outlines.)

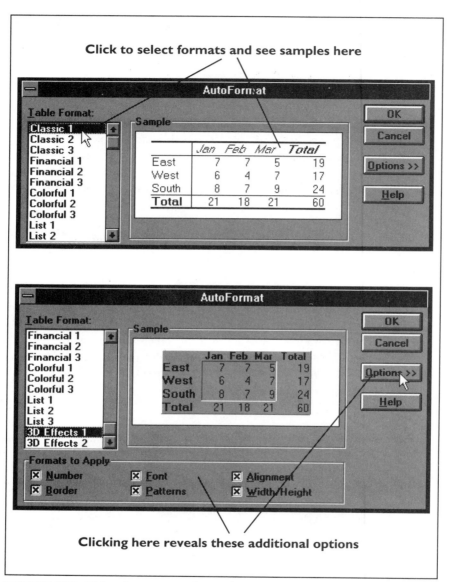

FIGURE 27.3 *Pick a format to apply to selected cells. Save your work before doing this, and experiment on copies of important files, since it is sometimes difficult to undo such widespread format changes.*

MANUAL FORMATTING
WITH THE TOOLBARS AND KEYBOARD

You can make many common formatting changes from the standard Toolbar, from the Formatting Toolbar, and with your keyboard. For instance, to make selected text bold, you can click the Bold button (B) on the standard or Formatting Toolbars, or use the Ctrl-B keyboard shortcut. Figure 27.4 shows the names of the standard and Formatting Toolbars' formatting buttons, plus keyboard equivalents for the buttons that have them.

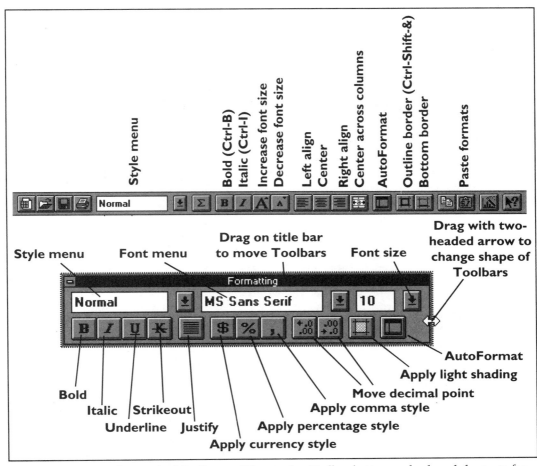

FIGURE 27.4 *Use the standard Toolbar and Formatting Toolbar buttons or keyboard shortcuts for everyday formatting of cells you've selected.*

The Ctrl-7 keyboard shortcut alternately shows and hides the standard Toolbar. Display the Formatting Toolbar with the Toolbars... command on the Options menu. Move this and other Toolbars by dragging on their titles. Reshape by dragging at their edges as illustrated in Figure 27.4.

Remember to select all of the cells you want to affect before using these buttons and keyboard shortcuts. Some style changes will affect the size of cell contents, which may necessitate subsequent changes in column widths, cell heights, and so on. For instance, if you increase a cell's font size and make it bold, text or numbers may be too big to fit within your current column width.

STYLES

Excel provides a number of standard styles, which can be selected from a drop-down menu on the standard Toolbar. Don't confuse *styles* with *number formats*, which are related but not necessarily identical. Styles are collections of formatting decisions that might include a number format, alignment instructions, border specifications, pattern selections, and cell protection decisions. Styles need not specify all of these things. For instance, a style might consist of just a number format and bold character formatting. You can use Excel's predefined styles to create your own. Figure 27.5 shows a typical style list containing both standard and custom styles.

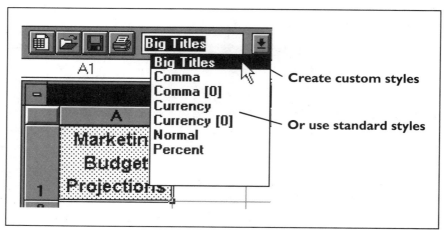

FIGURE 27.5 *Your worksheets can contain standard and custom styles.*

Styles are stored with the worksheets themselves. You can create new styles, edit existing ones, and copy styles from other worksheets.

APPLYING STYLES

To apply an existing style, select the cell or cells you want to format, then pick the desired style from the drop-down style list. You can also apply styles by choosing them from the dialog box reached with the Style... command on the Format menu.

NORMAL STYLE

Excel's Normal style displays and prints numbers using the General format, 10-point sans serif type, no borders, no shading. It is possible to redefine the standard style just as you can redefine any other style using the steps described next.

CREATING AND MODIFYING STYLES

The easiest way to create a *new* style is to format a cell to meet your requirements (number format, font, borders, and the like), then, with that cell still the active cell, type a new style name in the style name portion of the Toolbar. Press Enter to complete the name. The style will be added to the drop-down list and saved with your document.

You can also create, examine, edit, and delete styles by visiting the Style dialog box shown in Figure 27.6.

You'll see the small version of the dialog box when you first open it. From here you can pick and apply an existing style, define a new style based on the contents of the active cell, read a description of styles in the drop-down style list, or enlarge the dialog box with the Define>> button. This lets you modify styles.

Modifying Styles

The easy way to change a *style* is to modify a *cell* containing the style of interest, then choose the style name from the drop-down menu. Excel will ask if you want to redefine the style based on the changes you've just made. Answering Yes will redefine the style. No or Cancel will leave the style unchanged.

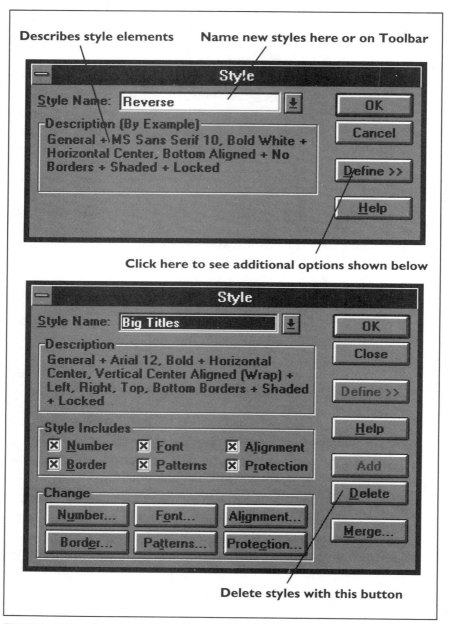

FIGURE 27.6 *Examine, name, edit, and delete styles with the Format menu's Styles... command.*

For instance, if you activated a cell formatted with Percent style, and italicized the contents of the cell, then choose Percent on the Toolbar's drop-down Style list and press Enter, you would be asked if you wanted to modify the Percent style.

When you redefine a style, all of the other cells formatted with the style change too. In our example that would mean that all existing and new cells formatted with the Percent style would be italicized.

The full-size version of the Style dialog box (shown at the bottom of Figure 27.6) lets you see which style elements are used by the style—number formats, borders, patterns, and so on. It also lets you change these style elements by opening the appropriate dialog boxes. For example, to change font characteristics, click on the Font button to open the Font dialog box.

If there is no X next to an item in the *Style Includes* portion of the large Style dialog box, the corresponding button will be dimmed. This indicates that the style currently does not include that characteristic (perhaps no cell protection has been specified, for instance). To include previously un-specified style attributes, click to place an X in the appropriate option box, then use the button to open the desired dialog box.

How Styles Affect Manual Formatting

Styles usually overrule manual formatting, with important exceptions. For example, if you use a style that specifies bold characters, cells that were originally not bold but were italicized will *become* bold and *not* italicized. You can go back to cells thus altered and manually apply (or reapply) things like italics.

Copying Styles to and from Other Worksheets

You can either copy individual styles from one worksheet to another, or you can merge all of the styles from one worksheet with those of another. In either case, start by opening and (optionally) displaying both worksheets. (Use the Arrange… command on the Window menu to tile both worksheets if you like.)

With both worksheets open, to copy a single format from one worksheet to another, copy a cell containing the desired style to the Clipboard, then switch to the destination worksheet and paste the cell into it. The copied style will appear in the Style list, and therefore become available in the destination worksheet. If you don't want to paste a cell's contents—just formats, for instance—you can choose the Paste Special... command from the Edit menu and specify Formats only. (This is frequently more work, however, than simply pasting a cell with the Ctrl-V keyboard shortcut and deleting unwanted contents.)

To copy *all* of the styles from one worksheet to another, do the following (practice on *copies* of important worksheets):

1. Switch to the worksheet that is to receive the new styles (click on it or pick it from the Window menu).

2. Open the large version of the Style dialog box (use the Style... command on the Format menu, then click the Define>> button).

3. Use the Merge... button to open the Merge Styles dialog box.

4. If necessary, select the name of the *worksheet* containing the desired styles from the scrollable list in the Merge Styles dialog box.

5. Click OK to merge the styles of the selected worksheet with the destination worksheet.

Use Care When Merging Styles

Be warned that if the destination worksheet and the source worksheet have styles with identical names, Excel will want to replace the destination styles with the source styles. Excel will caution you about this, and will give you a chance to keep all of the existing styles or to cancel the merge command. You will only be warned *once*—even if you have more than one identical style name!

Deleting Styles

When you delete unwanted styles, all cells formatted with the deleted style revert to the Normal style for the worksheet. Undo does not work here. Use care or, better still, save your Worksheet before deleting styles, so that you can close the clobbered worksheet without saving, then reload the un-modified version. To delete styles, do the following:

1. Open the large version of the Style dialog box (use the Style... command on the Format menu, then click the Define>> button).

2. If necessary, select the name of the *style* you want to delete from the scrollable Style Name list in the Style dialog box.

3. Click the Delete button.

FONT SIZES AND ATTRIBUTES

The Font... command on Excel's Format menu presents you with a dialog box containing lists of available fonts and attributes. This is also where you can specify the color of text. In addition, the Font dialog box lets you pick the font used by the Normal style. (Select the desired font from the Font list and place an X in the Normal Font box.)

ALIGNMENT

A number of alignment buttons are available on the standard and Formatting Toolbars. Use these to shift the *horizontal* position of cell contents flush left, flush right, or to the center of cells. The Formatting Toolbar even has a button for justifying cell contents. In addition, the Alignment... command on Excel's Format menu opens a dialog box like the one shown in Figure 27.7.

From here you can also specify how text and numbers will be positioned *vertically* within selected cells. For instance, you can center short type in tall rows. Text can be flipped with the *Orientation* buttons so that it runs top to bottom or bottom to top within cells. The buttons illustrate their effects. The Wrap option, also found here, is discussed next.

WRAPPING TEXT IN CELLS

Take a look at the text in cell A1 of the worksheet in Figure 27.7. Notice how the words wrap to fit the width of column A. That's because the Wrap Text option choice has been checked in the Alignment dialog box. The text has also been centered vertically and horizontally. It is possible to save combinations like these as styles for easy, repeated use.

CENTERING TEXT ACROSS COLUMNS

Sometimes you'll need to position a cell's contents so that it floats across more than one column. Figure 27.8 illustrates this concept.

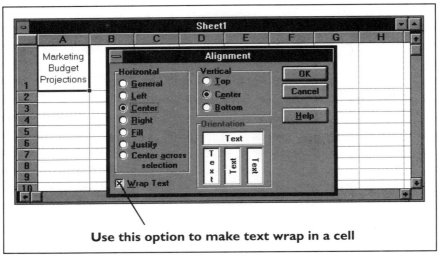

Use this option to make text wrap in a cell

FIGURE 27.7 *Use the Alignment... command to center, justify, and otherwise align cell contents.*

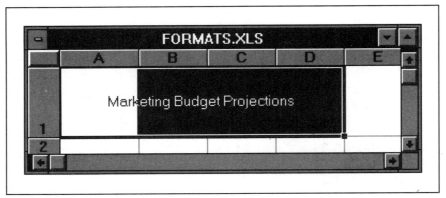

FIGURE 27.8 *To float a cell's contents over multiple columns, use the Center Across Selection button on the standard Toolbar, or pick the option of the same name in the Alignment dialog box.*

Activate the cell you want to "float," then drag to select adjacent cells in the columns of interest. Don't AutoFill by mistake. Click the Center Across Selection button on the standard Toolbar. (The button contains the letter A between two arrowheads.) Alternately, you can use the Center Across Selection option in the Alignment dialog box. If you change column widths, the text recenters properly.

BORDER BUTTONS AND COMMANDS

Borders can be used to set apart related worksheet sections, as well as to emphasize totals and subtotals. Or use them just for decoration, to enhance the worksheet's appearance.

The two most common border types can be created using buttons on the standard Toolbar. To *outline* a cell or range of cells, start by selecting the cells(s) to outline, then use the Outline Border button on the standard Toolbar. Cleverly, the button looks like a cell with a dark border. There's a keyboard shortcut for Border outlining. It's Ctrl-Shift-&.

To place a border line only at the *bottom* of a cell or cells, use the Bottom Border button. It is next to the Outline border button and looks like—well, you know.

You can also construct custom borders using many of the same techniques you learned in Microsoft Word. Select the cells you wish to pretty up, then choose the Border… command from Excel's Format menu. Pick a line type (thick, thin, single, double, or whatever), then click to specify the desired border sides (left, right, top, and so on). The *Shade* check box will fill the selected area with a pattern chosen with the Format menu's Patterns… command.

Consider creating styles for your favorite border and shading concoctions. To *remove* all borders from a selected range or cell, use the Ctrl-Shift-Minus sign (−) keyboard shortcut.

CELL SHADING, PATTERNS, AND BORDERS

The Patterns… command on the Format menu lets you choose from a scrolling list of cell shading patterns as illustrated in Figure 27.9.

The Foreground and Background choices define the colors (or shades of gray) used to construct the patterns. Watch the sample in the dialog box while you fritter away. As you can see from the small sample worksheet at

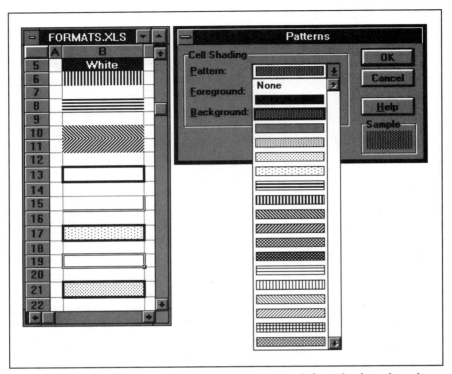

FIGURE 27.9 *Select cells to fill with patterns, then pick from the drop-down list of samples.*

the left of Figure 27.9, you can combine cell patterns, outlines, and colors to create many different attention-getting effects.

INSERTING AND REMOVING PAGE BREAKS

Excel makes page break decisions automatically, but sometimes you'll want to force new pages elsewhere. Do this by activating the cell beneath and to the right of where you want a page break, then choose Set Page Break from the Options menu. Dark dashed lines will mark the new page breaks. Figure 27.10 illustrates this.

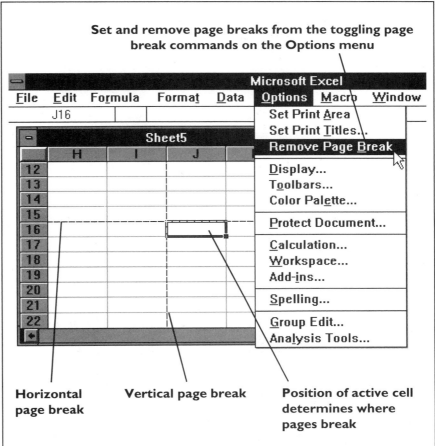

FIGURE 27.10 *Use the Option menu's Set Page Break command to insert page breaks above and to the left of the active cell.*

To remove breaks, activate the cell below and to the right of the break lines (cell J16 in Figure 27.10), and choose Remove Page Break, the command that replaces Set Page Break on the Options menu.

HIDING ROWS AND COLUMNS

You can hide rows or columns without destroying their contents, then reveal them later when you want to see or edit them. Select the row(s) or column(s) you want to hide. Then use the Hide and Unhide buttons in the Format menu's Row Height... and Column Width... dialog boxes.

You can also play hide-and-seek with your mouse, but it takes a steady hand and some practice. If it's morning and you haven't had your second cup of coffee yet, get it.

To hide rows with the mouse, select the row or rows of interest. Place the mouse pointer *beneath* the *heading* of the row or rows you want to hide. For instance, if you want to hide rows 3 and 4, select both rows, then point beneath the number 4 at the left edge of the worksheet. You'll see the pointer shape that indicates your ability to change row height. Drag up until the rows are so thin that they disappear. The line between the visible and invisible row labels will become darker than the rest, and the row numbers will no longer be consecutive (row numbers will jump from 1 to 5, for instance).

Use the same basic approach to hide columns, but drag to the right on column letters.

To *bring back* hidden rows or columns, slowly move the pointer over the dark lines in row or column labels (indicating hidden rows or columns). Watch the pointer carefully. At some position, the dark bar between the two arrowheads will split, indicating that you can drag the rows or columns back to a useful size. Alternately, you can use the Unhide button in the Column Width and Row Height dialog boxes.

TIME TO EXPERIMENT

Go forth and multiply (and divide and format). You now have the basic skills needed to create and format powerful, great-looking spreadsheets. The chapters that follow deal with tools for managing large projects, charting, and other advanced topics. This would be a good point to create some of your own worksheets before continuing.

28

Managing Excel Files

Excel files are saved and opened using techniques similar to those you've used with Microsoft Word. The Excel File menu has familiar New..., Open..., Save, Save As..., and Delete... commands. There is also a Save Workbook... command, used for big projects; it's discussed in Chapter 30. Files can be protected from unauthorized users by defining a password, and can also be write-protected to avoid inadvertent changes. Excel can open documents created by other programs, and furthermore it can save in a number of non-Excel formats. Let's take a look.

SAVE EARLY AND OFTEN

You've read it elsewhere in this book, but it's worth repeating here. Get in the habit of saving early and often. Since Excel does not have an automatic save feature like Word's, it is up to you to remember to save as you work. Every time you answer the phone or step away from your computer, *save.*

SAVING AN EXCEL DOCUMENT FOR THE FIRST TIME

The first time you save an Excel worksheet, you can use either the Save or the Save As... command. The keyboard shortcut for the Save command is Shift-F12. In any case, you'll see a dialog box like the one in Figure 28.1.

Start by choosing a disk drive. When using a floppy, remember to place a disk with ample free space in the floppy drive before attempting to save.

If necessary, specify the path by clicking to open the desired directories. Unless you want to convert your work to a non-Excel file type, make sure the *Save File As Type* option reads "Normal."

Type a legal MS-DOS-style file name of up to eight characters with no spaces or other disallowed characters in the Filename box. Excel will add the proper file extension for you. Click OK or press Enter to save.

If you want to password-protect a file, or specify automatic backups, you can choose those options the first time you save, or later.

Incidentally, while there is a *Cancel* button in the Save As dialog box, Microsoft warns that, under some circumstances, canceling a Save or Save As... command can cause you to "possibly lose data," particularly if the disk you are saving to is "almost full." To be safe, avoid using Excel's Cancel button in the Save As dialog box.

SAVING AS YOU WORK

After the first time you've saved, subsequent use of the Save command or Shift-F12 shortcut will save the file under the same file name, drive, file type, path, and other options you initially specified. To change one or more of these options, use the Save As... command.

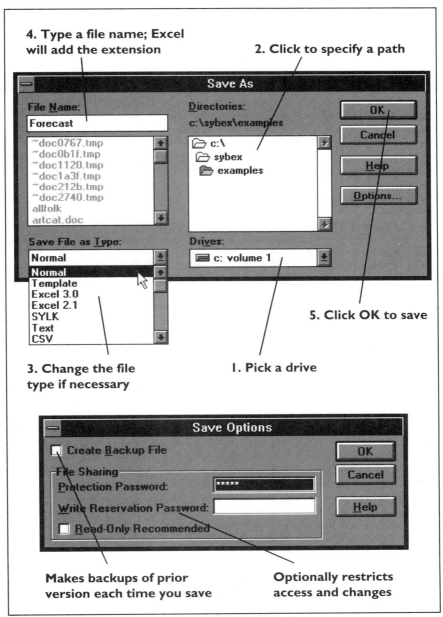

FIGURE 28.1 *Specify the drive, path, file type, and a worksheet name the first time you save. Password and backup options can be reached with the Options button.*

SAVING IN NON-EXCEL FORMATS

Excel can handily "export" files for use with other programs. For example, you can save in earlier Excel formats, a variety of Lotus 1-2-3 formats, various formats that can be read by database programs, and so on. When saving in Lotus WK1 and WK3 formats, Excel automatically creates the necessary FMT or FM3 files containing format information.

Obviously, when saving in different file formats, you may lose styles and other embellishments and features not supported by the other program. Check your EXCEL directory for a README.TXT file containing additional information about compatibility.

To save in a different format, pick it from the *Save File As Type* list. Excel may not be able to save to every format in the list, and will tell you if there is a problem.

SAVING IN EARLIER EXCEL VERSION FORMATS

If you plan to open an Excel version 4 document with an earlier version of Excel, you must first save it using the appropriate version choice on the Save File As Type list. Some new features (chart characteristics and the like) will not be transferred.

MAKING AUTOMATIC BACKUPS

Excel's automatic backup feature is similar to Word's. The second and subsequent times that you save, Excel saves a copy of the *previous* version of your worksheet using the file extension .BAK. This means that unless you make floppy, tape, or network copies of your worksheets at the end of the day, you might *not* have a backup of your most recent work. *Do not rely upon the Excel backup feature as your primary backup procedure for important projects!*

To have Excel create automatic backups, click to place an X in the Create Backup File option in the Save Options dialog box. See Figure 28.1.

PROTECTING EXCEL FILES

Chapter 25 discusses Excel's worksheet protection features, but a review is worthwhile here. You can prevent other users of your system from seeing files, or you can let them see but not modify files.

Password Protecting

You can entirely prevent unauthorized access to a worksheet by defining a password in the Save Options dialog box shown in Figure 28.1 under Save As. You will be asked to type the password a second time after first defining it, to confirm that you've entered and remembered it properly. Excel's password feature cares about capitalization. Be careful that you don't accidentally have the Caps Lock key engaged when you define a password.

Write-Protecting

The Write Reservation Password option is also controlled from the Save Options dialog box. It lets anyone see your worksheets, but only lets password-knowledgeable users make changes to them.

OPENING DOCUMENTS WITH EXCEL

Besides using the obvious Open… command on Excel's File menu, or its keyboard shortcut (Ctrl-F12), you can open Excel documents in many other ways. For instance, you can double-click on their icons in Windows' File Manager. Or you can create files that *automatically* load whenever you start Excel. You can also devise *worksheet templates* to speed the preparation of similar worksheets. And you can often open and convert non-Excel files.

THE OPEN COMMAND

Using the Open… command is probably the way you will most often load Excel documents. It will remind you of similar commands in Word and other Windows programs. Figure 28.2 shows Excel's Open dialog box and summarizes the steps used to open worksheets.

Start by specifying the desired drive (insert an appropriate floppy disk, if necessary), then pick the appropriate file type—Excel files (*.XL*) for Excel 4 files. Click as necessary to open the desired directory, then pick the file of interest from the scrolling list. Double-clicking on a file name loads the file; or you can click once to highlight the file name, then use the OK button.

EXCEL

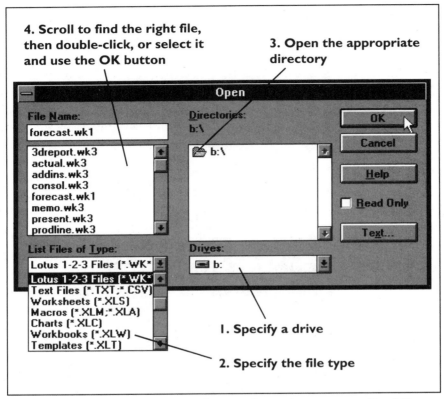

FIGURE 28.2 *The Open… command is one of several ways to open Excel files.*

If you place an X in the Read-Only Recommended box, you will *not* be permitted to save changes under the original file name (you *will* be able to save them with a different name and the Save As… command). Files opened with the Read-Only box checked have the words [**Read-Only**] in their title bars.

OPENING DOCUMENTS AUTOMATICALLY AT STARTUP

Any Excel files you place in the EXCEL\XLSTART subdirectory will load automatically whenever you start Excel. You can also specify another start-up directory even if it's a directory on a network. (Ask your network administrator for assistance, if necessary.) To specify an additional startup directory:

1. Using Excel's Open dialog box, locate and open the ALTSTART.XLA file in the EXCEL LIBRARY subdirectory (double-click on the file name).

2. You will see the Alternate Startup Directory dialog box.

3. Enter a complete path to the alternate directory (**D:\FORMS\XL**, for instance.)

4. Choose OK. Thereafter, Excel will look both in XLSTART and the second directory you've specified.

WORKSHEET TEMPLATES

You can create Excel templates that will remind you of Word's templates. Think of them as patterns for repetitive work. Use them to store formatting, styles, formulas, and anything else you can create with Excel. When you open an Excel template, the program forces you to save your work with a file name other than the template's, protecting the original contents of the template.

To save a worksheet as a template, choose the *Template File* type in the *Save File As Type* list in the Save As dialog box.

Here's a handy template tip: if you store templates in the XLSTART or alternate startup directory, they will be listed in the *New* dialog box you reach with Excel's New... command, making templates easy to find. For instance, in Figure 28.3, a template called *Invoice* has been saved in the XLSTART subdirectory.

OPENING FILES CREATED
WITH EARLIER VERSIONS OF EXCEL

You can open, use, and modify documents created with earlier versions of Excel. If you modify these older files in any way (then save the changes), you must "Save As" using the appropriate version choice on the Save File As Type list in order to use them again with the old Excel version. Some new features (such as chart characteristics) will not be transferred.

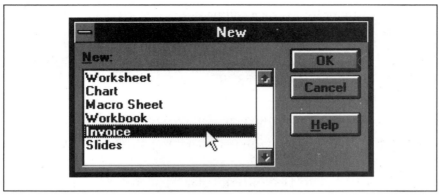

FIGURE 28.3 *Templates stored in the XLSTART subdirectory appear in the New list, making them easy to find and use.*

IMPORTING NON-EXCEL DOCUMENTS

For many reasons you may want to import non-Excel files. If you or associates have non-Excel spreadsheets (from Lotus 1-2-3, for instance), Excel can usually open and use them as-is.

Other times you may want to import tab or comma-separated text for use with Excel's database features (described in Chapter 35).

Use the All Files (*.*) choice on the List Files of Type list in Excel's Open dialog box to see all possible files. The other choices will list only files with certain file extensions. For instance, the *Text Files* (*.TXT, *.CSV) choice will *not* list text files that end with unusual extensions or without extensions. Thus, **README.TXT** would be displayed, but not **READ.ME** or **READ** unless you use the All Files (*.*) option.

DELETING DOCUMENTS WHILE IN EXCEL

Excel's File menu has a Delete… command that is useful for removing unwanted files without quitting Excel. It is particularly handy when you need to make room on floppies. Use care. Undo won't work here.

29

Printing from Excel

When printing from Excel, you can apply many of the Windows skills you learned earlier. This chapter briefly reviews basic printing techniques, but focuses primarily on unique, Excel-specific features. As you will see, Excel's Print Preview and Page Setup features work interactively to help you quickly fit just the right amount of information on each page. Print settings are stored with each document. Be aware that different printers may have additional or varying options that can change the exact appearance of your documents and can even modify some of the dialog boxes used to control printing. For instance, not all printers have the same Print Quality choices.

PREPARING TO PRINT

Always save your work before you print. If you have multiple printers, be sure you've selected the correct one. Check to see that it is on-line, ready to go, and loaded with sufficient supplies. Before printing, it is invariably a good idea to use Print Preview, since display and printer font differences sometimes necessitate minor margin and column adjustments.

PAGE SETUP

If necessary, use the Page Setup dialog box to change page orientation, scaling, and other settings. For instance, you can enter new margins, then ask Excel to center your work horizontally and vertically. You can cause gridlines as well as row and column numbers to print, or you can suppress them. (This does not affect the on-screen appearance of these items when working with cells. It just determines whether they will *print* or not.)

The scaling features can help you cram multiple pages of information onto one sheet of paper, or they can enlarge small images to better fill a page. The Page Setup dialog box also contains buttons that let you define headers and footers. The process is described later in this chapter. You will often find it useful to switch back and forth between Page Setup and Print Preview to fine-tune your work.

The Page Setup dialog box options change slightly when printing from Chart and Show Info windows. This is normal.

PRINT PREVIEW

The Print Preview mode lets you see and adjust margins and column widths. It will also show you how and where pages will end. You can zoom in and out to get either a close-up or a bird's-eye view of each page. Figure 29.1 shows a typical Page View and the Page Setup settings that created the image and margins you see there.

Reach Print Preview... from Excel's File menu. Or, if you place an X in the Preview option in the Print dialog box, Excel will take you to Print Preview whenever you issue a Print... command.

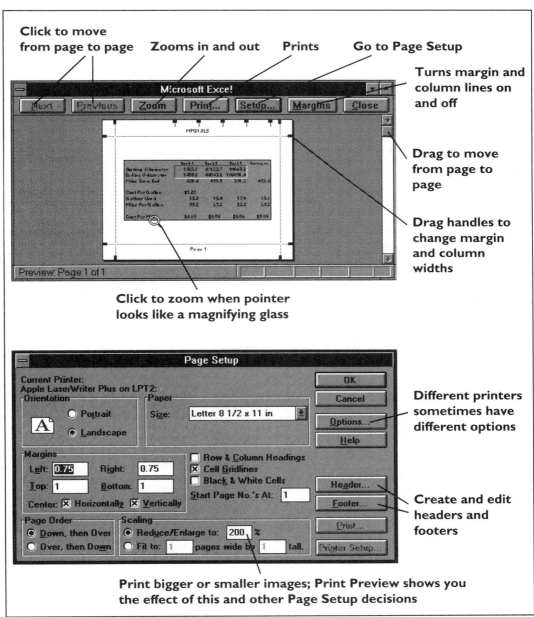

FIGURE 29.1 *Use Print Preview and Page Setup together to fine-tune worksheet page layouts.*

MOVING FROM PAGE TO PAGE WHILE PREVIEWING

When previewing multipage documents, clicking on undimmed Next and Previous buttons will let you move from page to page. A single dimmed button means you've reached one end of the document and can go no further in that direction. Two dimmed buttons mean you are in a single-page document. You can also use the vertical scroll bar to move from page to page.

ADJUSTING MARGINS
AND COLUMN WIDTHS WHILE PREVIEWING

Click the Margins button if necessary to display margin and column lines and handles. Point to the handle of interest. The pointer's shape will change to indicate that you can drag the handle either left and right or up and down. Drag to change margin and column settings. The lower-left portion of the status bar displays the new dimensions as you drag.

ZOOMING IN AND OUT

Zooming makes it easy for you to read small text, to check whether cells are large enough, and so on. There are two ways to zoom. You can click the Zoom button, or, whenever the pointer looks like a magnifying glass (as it does in Figure 29.1), you can click to enlarge the area in the vicinity of the pointer. When the image is enlarged, you can scroll with the horizontal and vertical scroll tools that appear at the window's edge. This is how to see different parts of the enlarged page. Clicking a second time anywhere in the image area, or clicking the Zoom button, returns the image to its normal size.

LEAVING PRINT PREVIEW

If you spot things you want to change while in Print Preview, use the Close button to return to your worksheet. If you are ready to print instead, use Print Preview's Print... button to leave the preview mode and bring up the Print dialog box.

PRINTING AN ENTIRE WORKSHEET

You can begin the printing process in many different ways. As you've just seen, there is a Print button in Print... Preview. And there is the Print... command on the File menu, plus its keyboard shortcut: Ctrl-Shift-F12. There is also a Print button on the standard Toolbar (it looks like a printer).

The Print button in Print... Preview and the File menu's Print... command always take you to the Print dialog box shown in Figure 29.2. The *Toolbar's* Print button bypasses the Print dialog box, but will take you to Print Preview before printing if you've chosen the Preview option in the Print dialog box.

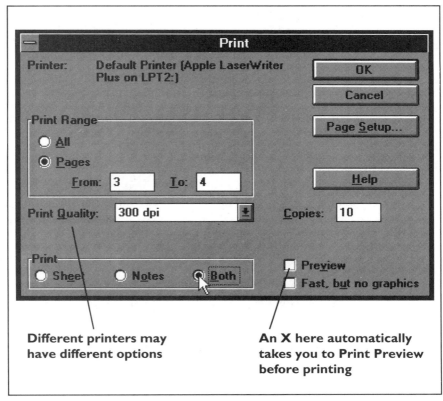

Different printers may have different options

An X here automatically takes you to Print Preview before printing

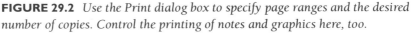

FIGURE 29.2 *Use the Print dialog box to specify page ranges and the desired number of copies. Control the printing of notes and graphics here, too.*

PRINTING PARTS OF A WORKSHEET

Excel's default print settings will print one copy of all pages in your document, but not any associated notes. To print just notes or both worksheet and notes, choose the appropriate options in the Print dialog box.

PRINTING SELECTED PAGES

By default, Excel prints all the pages in your worksheet. You can print ranges of pages by specifying them in the Print dialog box's *From* and *To* boxes. For example, the settings in Figure 29.2 will print just pages 3 and 4.

PRINTING MULTIPLE COPIES

Specify the desired number of copies in the *Copies* box. For instance, the settings in Figure 29.2 will print 10 copies of pages 3 and 4.

PRINTING PARTS OF PAGES

You can print parts of pages by defining *Print Areas*. Begin by selecting only the group of cells and other elements that you want to print. You can select noncontiguous areas (those that are not adjacent) by holding down the Ctrl key while selecting multiple areas.

With the area(s) selected, use the *Set Print Area* command on the Options menu to tell Excel that you want to print only those portions of the worksheet. The words "Print Area" will be displayed to the left of the Formula bar. This is the default name for the print area you've just defined. (You can name and save print areas, as well as other areas of interest. This is discussed in the next chapter.)

In any case, with a print area selected, Excel will print only that area. If you've defined a print area containing noncontiguous cells, Excel will print each noncontiguous area on its own page. The pages will print in the order that the areas were selected. The quickest way to understand this is to experiment, using Print Preview. Remember to use the Next and Previous keys as necessary to visit the separate pages when you define noncontiguous ranges.

PRINTING CHARTS

Either you can print charts along with worksheet cells, or by opening a chart window you can print just the chart. Be patient (or go to lunch) when printing charts. They can sometimes take a long time to play out.

PRINTING REPORTS

Excel lets you create and name reports for large or complex projects. Use the Print Report command on Excel's File menu to show the dialog box illustrated in Figure 29.3.

HOW TO PRINT REPEATING ROW AND COLUMN TITLES

When you have a long or wide report that will span multiple pages, it is sometimes helpful to the reader to repeat column and/or row headings. For instance, you might want to repeat the selected column headings in the amortization schedule shown in Figure 29.4.

Begin by selecting the rows or columns you wish to repeat. Then use the Set Print Titles… command on Excel's Options menu to define the selected area as titles. Marching ants appear around the selected cells. Click OK to

EXCEL

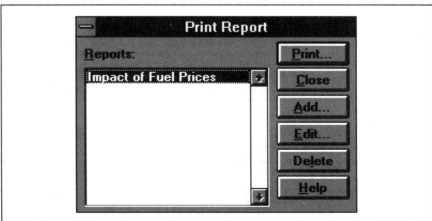

FIGURE 29.3 *Use the Print Report command to view a scrolling list of reports. Use the Print button to print the selected report.*

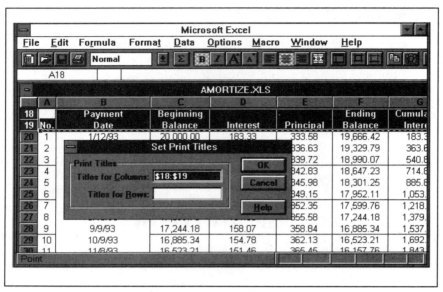

FIGURE 29.4 *Rows 18 and 19 will repeat at the top of each new printed page.*

define the selection as a printing title. The default name "Print Titles" appears next to the Formula bar whenever the area is selected thereafter. The titles will print on each new page of a multipage worksheet.

EDITING AND PRINTING HEADERS AND FOOTERS

You can print information in the headers and footers of an Excel worksheet. These features are not as robust as their Microsoft Word cousins, but they are fine for most applications. By default, Excel prints the worksheet's file name in the center of the header and the text "Page " plus the page number centered in the footer.

You can remove, rearrange, and edit these items or add your own. It's possible to print text, page numbers, a page count, file names, date, and time in headers or footers.

To start, open either the Header or the Footer dialog box by using the appropriate button in the Page Setup dialog box. You'll see something like the top two dialog boxes in Figure 29.5.

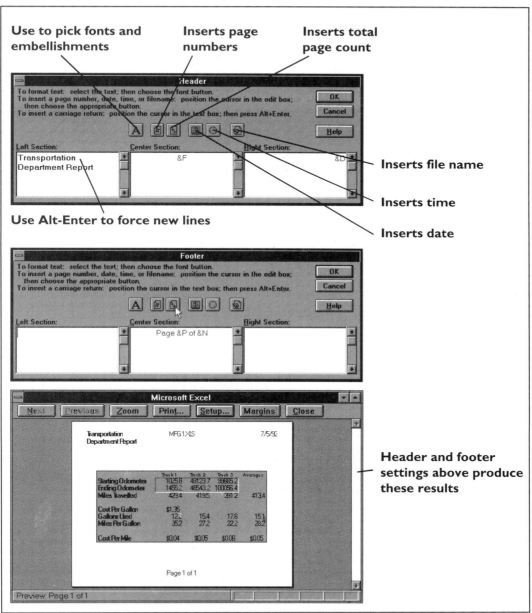

Use to pick fonts and embellishments

Inserts page numbers

Inserts total page count

Inserts file name

Inserts time

Inserts date

Use Alt-Enter to force new lines

Header and footer settings above produce these results

FIGURE 29.5 *Open the Header or Footer dialog boxes from the Page Setup dialog box. The Print Preview screen shows the results of the settings above it.*

Place the insertion point in the section where you want to work (left, center, or right). Either type text or click on the appropriate buttons to insert *commands* for page numbers (&P), the worksheet's file name (&F), and so forth. You can mix text and commands if you wish. For example, in the footer in Figure 29.5, the page number, the page count, plus the text "of " were combined to create the command **Page &P of &N**, which prints page numbers in the format "Page 1 of 2."

Delete commands to remove them. When you want to create multiple lines of text like the "Transportation Department Report" title in Figure 29.5, force new lines with the Alt-Enter key combination rather than just pressing the Enter key.

To change the font and type size, or to make the type bold and/or italic, select the desired text *or command*, then use the Text button (the one with the letter A). It brings up a Font dialog box. Use Print Preview to check your work. You may need to zoom to read the header and footer information.

CANCELING PRINTING

Since Excel uses Print Manager, if you don't hit the Cancel button before the little "Printing" dialog box disappears, you will need to visit Print Manager to cancel the job. This sometimes frustrating process is described in Chapter 12.

30

Organizing
Large Projects

Projects take many shapes and sizes. Sometimes you'll need to deal with a few big worksheets. Other times you'll need to work with lots of little ones. Excel offers a number of features to help you view, edit, navigate, and consolidate big projects. This chapter introduces you to them. You'll read about naming things in such a way that you can quickly locate and refer to them. You'll see how to split windows to make it easier to view widely separated parts of a document. Just as outlines can help you view and rearrange Word documents, they can also change the way you look at big Excel worksheets. And you'll see how workbooks can help you keep related Excel files together, within easy reach.

USING NAMES

You've already seen named print ranges in Chapter 29, but you can also name cells, formulas, and more. Sometimes naming things this way makes it easier to refer to them. Named items are also easy to find with Excel's Goto... command on the Formula menu, or by using the F5 Go To function key.

CREATING, EDITING, AND DELETING NAMES

You can name things yourself, or let Excel name them for you. Take a look at Figure 30.1.

In the top part of Figure 30.1, Excel is being asked to create names for the selected cells. In this instance, it will use the selected row and column labels to name ranges of cells *automatically*. The combination of cells B2 and B3 will be named "Jan." The cell range C2 through C3 will be named "Feb" and so on. Excel will also automatically name cells B2 through D2 "Sold" and cells B3 through D3 "Returned."

You can define names *manually* by selecting things of interest, then using the *Define Name...* command on Excel's Formula menu. You will see a dialog box containing a list of existing names, if there are any. Type the new name and click the Add button. Valid names can be up to 255 characters long. The first character in a name must be a letter or the underline character. Names cannot look like cell references (A$1, for instance).

Editing and deleting names can be a little risky since any formulas that refer to the names will be affected. To make life easier, Microsoft ships a macro that you can use to change or delete names. *Start by saving your work.*

Open the Name Changer add-in macro called CHANGER.XLA. It is located in the EXCEL\LIBRARY subdirectory. (Use Excel's Open command just as you would to open any other Excel file. It will add the command *Change Name...* to your Formula menu.)

Use the Change Name... command to display the *Rename a Name* dialog box, containing a list of names for the current worksheet.

Pick the name you want to change in the From list and type its replacement in the To box. Click the Rename button. Excel will change the name everywhere on the worksheet so that all references will be correct. Use care since Undo won't work here (although you could "re-rename" if you like).

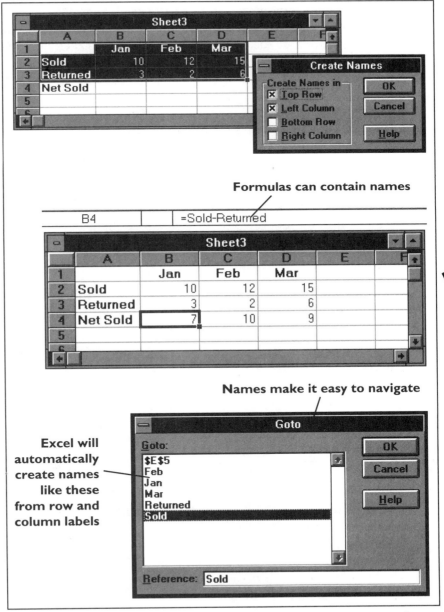

FIGURE 30.1 *Names can help you build equations, locate far-flung parts of worksheets, and more.*

The Rename a Name dialog box also lets you delete names. But be advised that formulas referring to deleted names will no longer work. Undo can't help here, so work on file copies—or save before you experiment and don't save again until you know all is well.

REFERRING TO RANGES BY NAME

Once names like these have been created, they can be used in many ways. For instance, you can create equations like the one shown in the Formula bar in Figure 30.1. As you can see, the Formula =**Sold–Returned** works in place of the traditional =**B2–B3**. The formula =**SUM(Sold Jan:Mar,Returned Jan:Mar)** would compute the total net units sold in Figure 30.1.

While our example is obviously over-kill, you can see how constructing formulas this way in complex worksheets might make them easier to troubleshoot.

The bottom of Figure 30.1 shows how Excel lists named items in Goto and other dialog boxes, making it easier to find or work with them. When constructing formulas containing names, you can either type the names from your keyboard or use the Paste Name… command on Excel's Formula menu. Excel ignores differences in uppercase and lowercase.

VIEWING NAMES IN A WORKSHEET

When you select a named item or range, its name appears next to the Formula bar. For example, if you selected the cell range B3 through D3 in Figure 30.1, you'd see the word "Returned."

SPLITTING WINDOWS AND FIXING TITLES

Excel document windows can be split into two or four separately scrollable panes that make it easy to see different parts of your worksheet. Figure 30.2 illustrates this.

Use the *Split* command on the Window menu to create four panes in the neighborhood of the active cell. Each pane will have its own scroll tools, which can be used to position each pane's contents independently. Use the *Remove Split* command that appears in Excel's Window menu whenever a window is split.

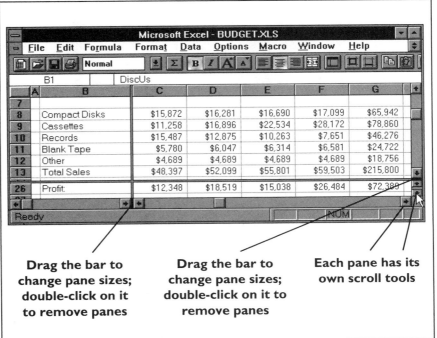

Drag the bar to change pane sizes; double-click on it to remove panes   **Drag the bar to change pane sizes; double-click on it to remove panes**   **Each pane has its own scroll tools**

FIGURE 30.2 *Split an Excel window into panes to see widespread parts of your project simultaneously.*

Alternately, you can drag to create panes exactly where you want them. Here's how: in a single-pane worksheet, there are thick black lines just above the top of the vertical scroll arrow and to the left of the left horizontal scroll arrow. These are called split boxes. Drag on either one or both to create panes. Double-clicking on a split box removes its pane. The Window menu's Remove Split command also removes panes you've created by dragging.

OUTLINING YOUR WORKSHEETS

Excel's *outline* feature lets you expand and collapse large worksheets. For instance, you could create an annual budget containing 12-month totals plus monthly and quarterly subtotals, then collapse it to view and print quarterly subtotals and annual totals. You could collapse it further to show only annual totals. You'll see an example of this in a moment. Moreover, once items have been collapsed, all formatting, cutting, pasting, and similar activities affect all of the subordinate (hidden) detail. To create outlines, all of the references in your formulas must point in the same direction (for instance, every row's sum ranges should be either left to right or right to left).

AUTOMATIC OUTLINES

Excel will automatically outline for you, or allow you to define your own levels of detail. Start by selecting a *single* cell, then use the Outline... command on Excel's Formula menu. Figure 30.3 shows the Outline dialog box reached this way. The default options shown in this figure often produce quite usable results for everyday projects.

VIEWING, PRINTING, PROMOTING, AND DEMOTING

Once you've outlined a document, you'll see outlining tools along the edges of the worksheet as illustrated in Figure 30.4. (These can be hidden with the Display Options *Outline Symbols* choice.)

At the top of Figure 30.4, you see the worksheet shown at its full level of detail. Row and column level symbols in the upper-left corner of the worksheet tell you that there are two levels of detail in this worksheet. It is possible to have up to eight levels.

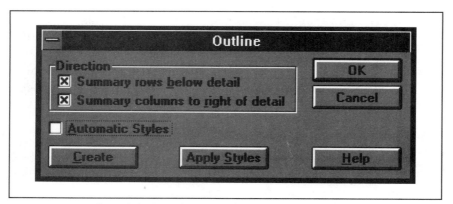

FIGURE 30.3 *These default outline settings were used to outline the budget worksheet shown in Figure 30.4.*

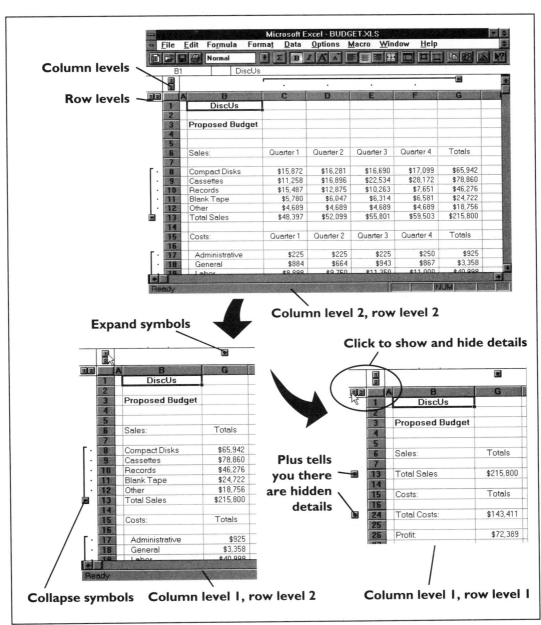

FIGURE 30.4 *Use the outline tools to show or hide various levels of detail.*

Click on the column and row level buttons to show or hide detail. Hidden details don't print.

MANUALLY OUTLINING

While automatic outlines are much easier to create, you can use the Utility Toolbar to outline manually. Use the Toolbars... command to show the Utility Toolbar. The two tools you'll use for outlining are called *Promote* and *Demote tools*. The Promote tool is a thick, left-pointing arrow. The Demote tool is a similar right-pointing arrow. Select *detail* rows or columns and *demote* them, leaving your most major totals at the top level (Annual totals might be the topmost, Quarterly the next lowest, Monthly the third level down, and so on). Outline level markers will appear as you work.

CLEARING OUTLINE STRUCTURES

If you don't mind keeping the outline levels, but don't want to see the space-robbing outline symbols, turn them off using the appropriate check box in the Display Options dialog box reached from Excel's Options menu.

But, to actually clear (remove) outline levels from a worksheet without changing the contents of the worksheet, display the Utility Toolbar as described in "Manually Outlining" above. Show all levels of detail. Select all outlined cells, and promote them over and over until everything is at the top level and the outline level symbols disappear. If you've outlined both rows and columns, you'll need to promote both rows and columns.

WORKING WITH MULTIPLE WORKSHEETS

There are many reasons to work with multiple worksheets. You might have several colleagues sending you their budgets on disk or over a network—budgets you'll need to combine into a company-wide total budget. Or you might have separate and detailed payroll, sales, and other budget worksheets containing totals that need to be included as line items on a summary worksheet. Excel lets you perform tasks like these in a number of ways. Perhaps the most obvious one is to open multiple worksheets and use your Clipboard to cut-and-paste. But there are more sophisticated tools like linking or consolidation that can ensure that, when a number changes in one place, it will be reflected properly in related worksheets.

And, if you've ever worked on projects requiring dozens or even hundreds of related worksheets, you'll enjoy Excel's ability to "corral" related files in workbooks. Ultimately, you may save a great deal of time as well.

LINKING WORKSHEETS

It is possible to *link* the contents of one worksheet with another. For instance, if you have a worksheet containing product prices, then decide to create a second worksheet containing unit sales forecasts and revenue projections based on the number of units sold times the prices on the pricing spreadsheet, you could link the two worksheets. Then, whenever you change prices on the pricing worksheet, the revenue forecasts will change on the forecast worksheet. Figure 30.5 shows a simplified example of this process.

Start by opening *both* worksheets. *Select* and *copy* the cell or cells containing the numbers you want to link (the Prices worksheet cell B5 in our example). Switch to the worksheet where you want to paste the numbers (the Forecast worksheet's cell B2 in our example). Use the *Paste Link* command on Excel's Edit menu. The path to the linked item will appear in the Formula bar.

Henceforth, any change you make to the Prices worksheet will be reflected on the Forecast worksheet. If you open a document that references a link (Forecast in our example), but the referenced document (Prices) is *not* open, Excel will ask whether you want to update from the unopened document(s).

Incidentally, you can link things besides numbers. You can link text, graphics, and so on. Read more about this and related powerful capabilities in Chapter 39.

CONSOLIDATING MULTIPLE WORKSHEETS

Excel's Consolidate... command on the Data menu offers a way to summarize or consolidate information from multiple worksheets. Figure 30.6 illustrates the command at work.

Suppose, for instance, you had three worksheets containing forecasts from three separate stores and you wanted to create a consolidated forecast based on their contents. If all four worksheets have the same basic design, consolidation can be a few mouse clicks away. Start by opening all of the worksheets containing data of interest, and finally opening the sheet where you want the consolidated figures

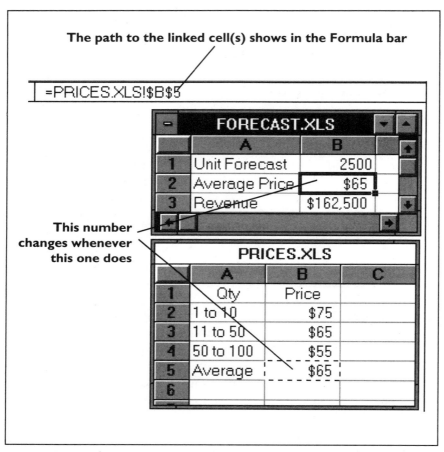

FIGURE 30.5 *When you use Paste Link, changes on one worksheet are updated on other linked worksheets.*

to appear. Select the cell or cells where you want the consolidated figures to appear (in the Allstore worksheet in Figure 30.6). Use the Data menu's Consolidate... command to show the Consolidate dialog box. Point to one of the worksheets to make it the active one. Drag to select the cell range you want to include. Click Add in the Consolidate dialog box and continue adding references until you've specified them all. Clicking OK will update the consolidation sheet (Allstore in our example).

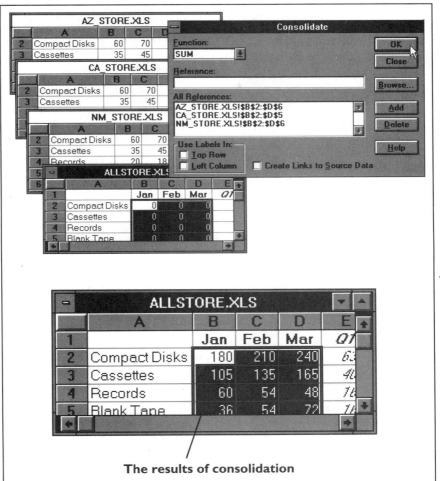

The results of consolidation

FIGURE 30.6 *The Consolidate… command lets you pull together data from multiple worksheets.*

If you want consolidated cells to update automatically, when you change things in the source worksheets be sure you place an X in the Create Links to Source Data option in the Consolidate dialog box. Otherwise, consolidated cells will update only when you issue the Consolidate… command.

USING WORKBOOKS TO COMBINE WORKSHEETS

Excel lets you keep related worksheets and macros together in things called *workbooks*. This way, you can open or close a single workbook rather than many individual files. Workbooks also ensure that any necessary macros are available when and where you need them. Documents stored in a workbook are referred to as *bound* documents. They appear in a special document list, and all become available whenever you open a workbook. Workbook lists can also show files that are not bound but that you need to use with the workbook documents. Figure 30.7 illustrates this.

In Figure 30.7 the Stores workbook contains three bound worksheets (Stores 1 through 3). The list also shows an unbound worksheet (Budget) that is often used with the store documents; it is stored elsewhere, but listed here for quick access.

You open a workbook just as you would any other worksheet, but you'll see the workbook list, rather than a worksheet. You can either choose a worksheet from the list or scroll back and forth through all the worksheets with the icons at the bottom-right corner of the workbook window.

CREATING WORKBOOKS

To create a new workbook, choose *New* from Excel's File Menu, choose *Workbook* from the New dialog box's scrollable list, then click OK. You will see an empty workbook list window.

ADDING AND REMOVING WORKBOOK DOCUMENTS

Use the workbook list window's Add button to bring up the Add To Workbook dialog box, and click on the Open... button therein. Choose files you wish to include in the workbook using the familiar file-opening techniques. Continue finding and adding files this way until you've created the desired workbook.

To remove items from a workbook, select them in the list and use the workbook list window's Remove button. This does not delete documents, it just removes them from the workbook.

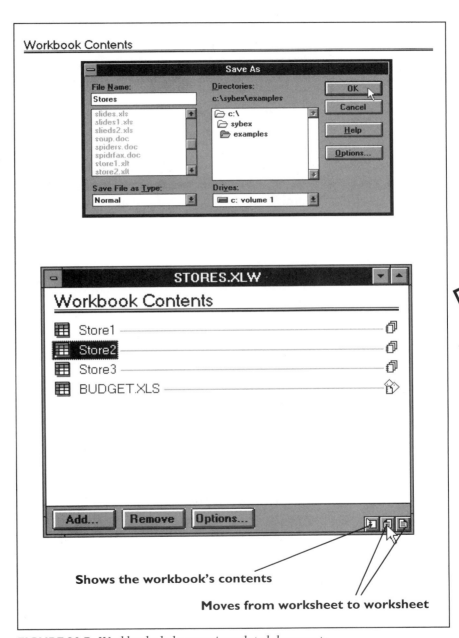

Shows the workbook's contents

Moves from worksheet to worksheet

FIGURE 30.7 *Workbooks help organize related documents.*

NAMING WORKBOOKS

You can give workbooks names that are up to 31 characters long, including spaces. Use the Options... button in the Workbook window to name a workbook.

ANNOTATIONS

You can insert notes to yourself or others using Excel's Text Boxes, Cell Notes, and Sound features. Note Boxes are discussed in Chapter 33.

To add written or spoken cell notes, select the cell of interest and choose Note... from the Formula menu. You'll see a dialog box like the one in Figure 30.8.

Type the note and click OK—or, if your computer is equipped for recording audio, click Record... to bring up the recorder controls. When you've completed your note, click OK to save the note. Cells containing notes have a small block in their upper-right corners. To read or hear notes, activate the cell and use the Note... command on the Formula menu. Yep, the spelling checker will check the spelling of cell notes.

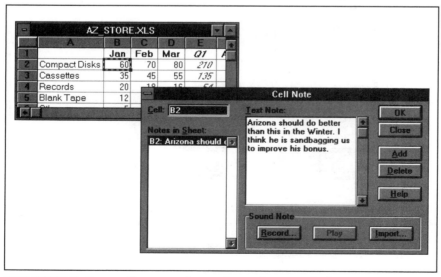

FIGURE 30.8 *Enter cell notes and control sound notes with the Note... command on the Formula menu.*

31

Introduction to Functions

Excel's *worksheet functions* are power tools that help you perform complex computations. Excel has hundreds of functions that facilitate engineering computations, manipulate text, and do much, much more. In addition, Excel offers over four hundred *macro functions*. Macro functions are discussed in Chapter 34. This chapter deals only with worksheet functions.

Worksheet functions can often be used by themselves as stand-alone formulas or they can be built into more complex formulas of your own creation. For instance, the *SQRT()* function finds the square root of a positive number. In the simplest case, you could type the formula =SQRT(9) into a cell and see the results (3). Or, you could include the square root function in a more complex formula like =SQRT(9)*9.

Functions can often refer to other things in your worksheet. For instance, =SQRT(A2) would compute the square root of the contents of cell A2. If you use named items in your worksheets, functions can sometimes refer to them as well. For example, =SQRT(SPEED) might be a legal formula if your worksheet contains a positive number named SPEED.

Some functions *inspect* things and take actions based on what they find. For example, the function *ISEVEN()* can check a cell and tell your formula if the value being tested is even or not. Other functions *convert* things. The text function *LOWER()* converts text to all lowercase, for instance. The engineering function *CONVERT()* transforms values from one unit of measure to another (Fahrenheit to Celsius, feet to meters, and so on).

PARTS OF A FUNCTION

Functions consist of function *names* and (usually) *arguments*. For instance, **SQRT** is the function *name*, while the value (the **positive number**) being evaluated is the *argument*. As you saw earlier in the square root example (SQRT), arguments can be values, references, or names. They can also be text, logical values (TRUE and FALSE), or arrays. You will often see *argument names* included along with function names in documentation, as well as in Excel's Help windows. For example, you might see the functions and their arguments expressed as **SQRT(number)**, or **SUM(number1,number2...)**, or **FV(rate,nper, pmnt,pv,type)**. Arguments are always separated by *commas*.

Notice that in the FV example the arguments *pv* and *type* are not bold. This is sometimes the way *optional* arguments are represented. Often, if you don't provide an argument, Excel uses the default argument for that function. For instance, the *DOLLAR(number,decimals)* function converts numbers into text with dollar signs and, optionally, pennies. The expression =DOLLARS(10) would yield $10.00 (notice the default decimal point and two places for pennies even though *no* second argument was supplied). The expression =DOLLARS(10,1) would create the text string $10.0, while =DOLLARS(10,) would yield $10 (neither decimal point nor pennies). In the first case, leaving out the optional second argument *and the comma* that separates it causes Excel to use the default argument (a decimal point and two places, in this case). In the second example, the comma separates the second argument, which specifies the number of pennies (1). In the third example, where there is a comma and no second argument, the comma suggests to Excel that there *is* a second argument (an argument specifying neither decimal point nor pennies).

The lesson here is that commas are important in functions and that sometimes there is a big difference in the results if you delete a comma instead of leaving it and not entering an argument after it.

You can frequently use *other functions* as arguments. For instance, you could combine the ROUND and SQRT functions to compute the square root of a number, then round the results. The formula **=ROUND(SQRT(A1),2)** would compute the square root of the contents of cell A1, then round the answer to two decimal places.

FUNCTIONS REQUIRING ADD-INS

Some functions require *add-ins*—additional software (such as a utility program) that is provided with Excel, but not automatically loaded when you run Excel. When you attempt to use functions that require add-ins, Excel loads the add-ins automatically for you. For example, the BESSELI statistical function needs the Analysis Tool Pack. If Excel can't load the required add-in, it may be because you chose not to install add-ins when you initially placed Excel on your hard disk. You may need to run the installer program to add these features.

ON-LINE FUNCTION HELP

If we described each Excel function in detail here, the book's size would double, and its title would need to be changed to *The Not-So-Compact Guide to Windows, Word, & Excel*. Fortunately, you won't need to lug around some six hundred extra pages of function trivia.

Excel's extensive on-line *Help* feature will let you find and explore just the functions of interest. To expedite your searching, worksheet functions have been divided into ten categories:

Database

Date and Time

Engineering

Financial

Information

Logical

Lookup and Reference

Mathematical and Trigonometric

Statistical

Text

Use the Help menu's *Search...* or *Contents* commands to get to the Search or Microsoft Excel Help windows shown in Figure 31.1.

For instance, if you want to learn more about the SUM function, you could type SUM in the Search dialog box, then pick the help topic "SUM Math Function" in the scrollable topic list and go to that topic.

If you'd rather browse, start with a general topic like functions, then pick a function category like Financial or Statistical.

Since some of the help provided for functions can often be fairly detailed and complex, you might want to print out the information that you find. Use the Help window's Print Topic feature to do this. Reach it from the File menu in the Help window.

PASTING FUNCTIONS

You can enter functions into your formulas by typing them from the keyboard. But you may prefer to paste them instead, particularly until you memorize their spelling, arguments, and so on. It is possible to paste functions with or without descriptions of their arguments. Use the Paste Function... command on Excel's Formula menu. Figure 31.2 illustrates the process.

Start by activating the cell where you want to paste the function. Begin the formula with an equal sign (=), and place the insertion point where you want to paste the function. Then choose Paste Function from Excel's Formula menu.

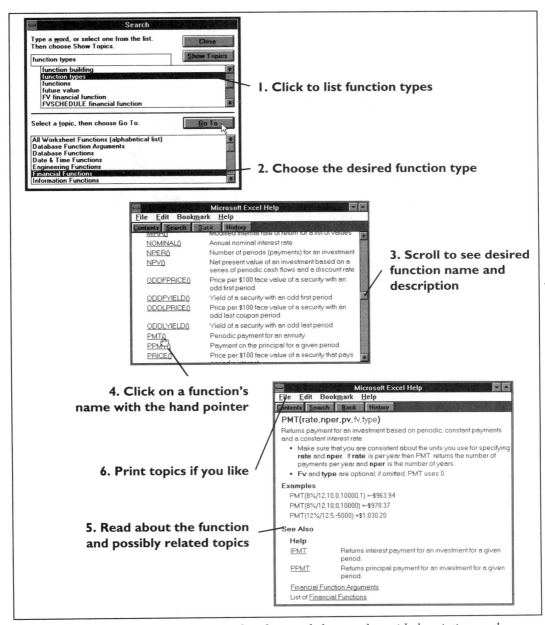

FIGURE 31.1 *Excel provides extensive on-line function help, complete with descriptions and examples of the functions at work.*

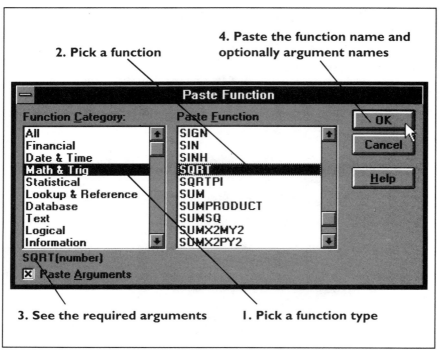

FIGURE 31.2 *Paste functions with or without descriptions of their arguments by using the Paste Function... command on Excel's Formula menu.*

As you can see in Figure 31.2, Excel's Paste Function feature lists the functions alphabetically within the ten categories listed earlier (Database, Date and Time, and so on). Pick a category, then scroll to find the desired function. When you highlight a function's *name* in the scrollable Paste Function list, its name and *arguments* are displayed near the bottom-left corner of the Paste Function dialog box. You can paste *just* the function name and a pair of parentheses, or you can paste the name *and argument names* by placing an X in the Paste Arguments box.

If you paste the names of the arguments, you will obviously need to replace them with the real arguments by editing the contents of the Formula bar. For instance, if you pasted the SUM function with its argument name—**SUM(name)**—you'd need to replace **name** with a number, cell reference, or other legal argument. Excel makes it easy to replace these names by double-clicking on them in the Formula bar.

EXAMPLES OF FUNCTIONS BY CATEGORY

The best way to learn about functions is to experiment with them. Here are a few examples from each category to get you started.

DATABASE FUNCTIONS

As you probably know, Excel worksheets can also be databases, since they often contain organized collections of information. Excel provides a number of database features, designed to help you perform analyses on worksheet data. Consider the information in Figure 31.3, for instance.

Database functions use three arguments: *Database*, *Field*, and *Criteria*. The cells containing people's names, ages, and sex (cells A1 through C7) qualify as a database. The data in Figure 31.3 are organized into fields (columns). The database contains criteria (people's names, ages, and so on).

As illustrated in Figure 31.3, you can find the minimum age of the people in the database with Excel's *DMIM* function. *DMAX* will find the oldest person, using the same function, and so on. Other database functions compute standard deviations, variances, and the like.

Incidentally, while Excel does offer functions that can crosstabulate, use Excel's Crosstab ReportWizard instead. It is demonstrated in Chapter 35, which covers database activities in more detail.

DATE AND TIME FUNCTIONS

Some of the Date and Time functions *return* the current date and/or time. Others do date and time math. Let's first look at a function that finds and reports the current time—the NOW() function. When you use it, NOW() inserts (returns) a new serial number corresponding to the current date and time whenever the worksheet is recalculated.

For example, if you simply paste the formula =NOW() into a cell, it will display the current date followed by the current time, then update the cell's contents every time the worksheet is recalculated (and *only* when it is recalculated).

The actual *appearance* of cells containing the NOW() or other Date and Time functions can be changed by using different date and time *Format styles* found in the *Number Format* dialog box, reached from the Format menu. For instance, Excel's **Date** format will display date and time in the format **m/d/yy h:mm** or in a number of other variations with or without the time. If you want to see only the *time* portion of a date serial number, format

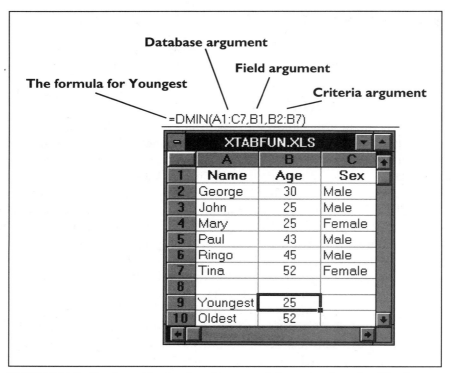

FIGURE 31.3 *Excel provides database features to help you analyze data like these.*

the cell(s) with one of five predefined Time formats, or create your own.

Other Date and Time functions *compute* things using date serial numbers. For instance, the NETWORKDAYS function computes the number of *working* days between two dates. That is to say, it excludes Saturdays, Sundays, and holidays if you specify any. (You can declare a single holiday or a whole list of them.) When you use NETWORKDAYS and some of the other Date and Time functions, Excel will load the appropriate add-in if necessary. Figure 31.4 shows the NETWORKDAYS function in use.

In this example, a calendar has been created by entering the dates (serial numbers) for each day of the month into cells D4 through F8. Those cells were then formatted to show only the *day* portion of their serial numbers.

The NETWORKDAYS function has been pasted into cell K6. This function's syntax is **NETWORKDAYS(start_date,end_date,**holidays).

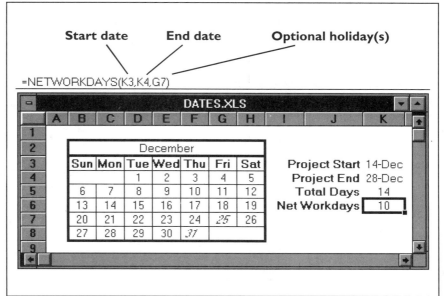

FIGURE 31.4 *Use care when doing date math. The answers are not always what you'd expect.*

The formula in our example looks to cells K3 and K4 to get starting and ending serial numbers (dates), and it has been told that the date serial number in cell G7 is a *holiday*. You can enter date serial numbers *directly* instead of using cell references. For instance, the formula **NETWORKDAYS(33952, 33966,33963)** would produce the same results as you see in cell K6, albeit painfully.

Incidentally, you can create and refer to lists of holidays, if you like.

When you do any kind of date math, check your work very, very carefully. It is quite easy to produce technically correct answers that are not the ones you need. For instance, look what happens when you subtract two date serial numbers. The *Total Days* equation in cell K5 simply subtracts the contents of cell K3 from the contents of cell K4 to get what you might expect to be total days. But that's the wrong technique, as you can see if you count the days in the calendar. Can you explain why Excel says 14? Can you think of a better formula? (Don't you *hate* it when authors and instructors ask questions like these?)

It's largely a matter of *semantics*. There are 15 calendar days *through and including* 14-Dec and 28-Dec. There are 13 days *between* those two dates (15-Dec through 27-Dec). Be sure you know what you are asking for, and label your results correctly. Check your work. If you show up in court a day late because your spreadsheet gave the wrong day count, chances are the judge won't have much sympathy (even if she also has a computer in her lap).

ENGINEERING FUNCTIONS

Many of the Engineering functions require add-ins, which Excel will load, if necessary. At least one of the Engineering functions is of considerable value to non-engineers. It's called Convert, and its syntax is **CONVERT(number,from_unit,to_unit)**. Let's have a look.

Figure 31.5 shows several of the hundreds of possible conversion combinations. Table 31.1 lists the available *conversion units* and their abbreviations (unfortunately, these are *not* all listed in Excel's on-line help).

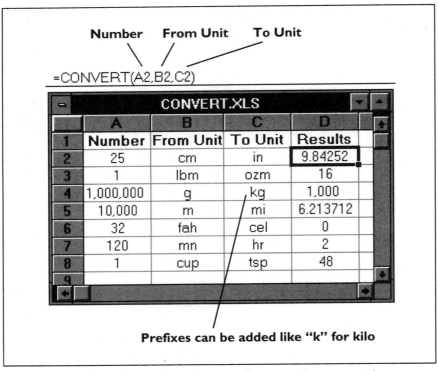

FIGURE 31.5 *Use Convert to transform weights, times, distances, and more.*

TABLE 31.1 *Excel's Conversion Units and Their Abbreviations*

Weight And Mass	
Gram	g
Slug	s
Pounds mass	lbm
U (atomic mass unit)	u
Ounce mass	ozm

Distance	
Meter	m
Statute mile	mi
Nautical mile	Nmi
Inch	in
Foot	ft
Yard	yd
Angstrom	ang

Time	
Year	yr
Day	day
Hour	hr
Minute	mn
Second	sec

Pressure	
Pascal	p
Atmosphere	at

Force	
Newton	N
Dyne	dy
Pound force	lbf

Energy	
Joule	J
Erg	e
Thermodynamic calorie	c
IT calorie	cal
Electron volt	ev
Horsepower-hour	hh
Watt-hour	wh
Foot-pound	flb
BTU	btu

Power	
Horsepower	h
Watt	w

TABLE 31.1 *Excel's Conversion Units and Their Abbreviations (continued)*

Magnetism	
Tesla	T
Gauss	ga

Temperature	
Degrees Celsius	cel
Degrees Fahrenheit	fah
Degrees Kelvin	Kel

Liquid Measure	
Teaspoon	tsp
Tablespoon	tbs
Fluid ounce	oz
Cup	cup
Pint	pt
Quart	qt
Gallon	gal
Liter	lt

As you can see in row 4 of Figure 31.5, it is possible to add prefixes to unit names. For instance, "k" multiplies by 1000. Legal prefixes and the actual abbreviations you add to conversion units follow. Once again, this information is *not* available on-line. Capitalization counts! Work carefully:

atto	a
centi	c
deci	d
deka	e
exa	E
femto	f
giga	G
kilo	k
mega	M
micro	u
milli	m

nano	n
peta	P
pico	p
tera	T

FINANCIAL FUNCTIONS

Excel's many financial functions are pretty well documented with on-line help. Many of them can be used together, or can be included as arguments, one within the other.

Here's an example of one way to use *PMT*, Excel's payment function. Officially, this function "Returns the periodic payment of an annuity based on constant payments and a constant interest rate." In other words, it will tell you what your payments will be, given the loan amount, number of payments, and a fixed rate of interest. The function's syntax is **PMT(rate,nper,pv,**fv,type). Figure 31.6 illustrates PMT at work.

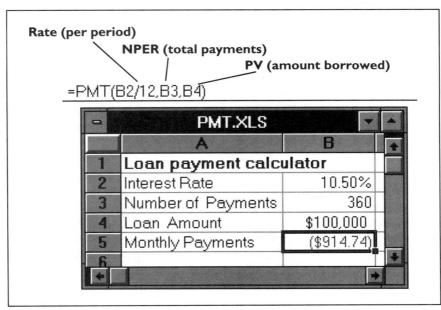

FIGURE 31.6 *PMT is one of many useful financial functions.*

Rate is the interest rate *per period*. For instance, if you borrow at an annual fixed interest rate of 10.5% and then make *monthly* payments, the interest rate is 10.5% *divided by 12*. That explains the division portion of the formula in Figure 31.6.

The argument *NPER* needs the *total* number of payments. Thus, if you are borrowing for 30 years, and make monthly payments, you'll make 30*12 or 360 payments. PV is the present value, or total amount that the series of payments is worth now—the loan amount, in this case. Notice that in this example the optional FV (future value) and TYPE arguments were omitted. Future value is a desired cash balance after the last payment is made. TYPE is either a 0 (zero) or 1. Omitting the TYPE argument or entering zero indicates that you will make payments at the end of each period. Entering a figure 1, on the other hand, tells Excel that the payments will be made at the beginning of the period.

Related financial functions include separate FV, IPMT, NPER, PPMT, PV, and RATE. They are described in on-line help and in many larger Excel reference books.

INFORMATION FUNCTIONS

Some functions inspect things and report back to you. For example, the ISNONTEXT() function will let your formulas know if a cell entry is not text. Other information functions can check things external to Excel, like the amount of RAM in your computer or which DOS version you are using. Figure 31.7 shows INFO() at work. Its syntax is **INFO(type)**.

Cells B1 through B8 each have the same formula that refers to corresponding cells in column A, which contain the arguments that produce the results you see.

LOGICAL FUNCTIONS

You use logic all the time. Chances are, you say things like "If the fruit at the market looks good, please pick up some peaches or grapes, if grapes are less than a dollar a pound…"

You can use logic in Excel, too. Take the IF function demonstrated in Figure 31.8. Its syntax is **IF(logical_test,value_if_true,value_if_false)**.

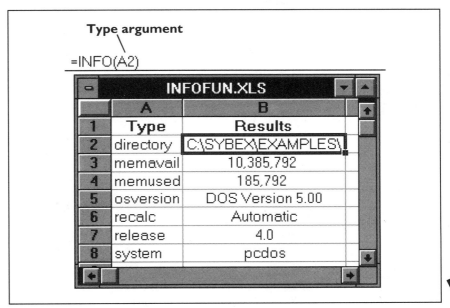

Type argument

=INFO(A2)

	A	B
	Type	**Results**
1		
2	directory	C:\SYBEX\EXAMPLES\
3	memavail	10,385,792
4	memused	185,792
5	osversion	DOS Version 5.00
6	recalc	Automatic
7	release	4.0
8	system	pcdos

INFOFUN.XLS

FIGURE 31.7 *The INFO function can tell you much about your computer, Excel, and files in use.*

In this example, the IF() function checks to see if the ending odometer reading is greater than the starting reading. If it isn't, chances are that the user has made a typographical error when entering readings. Or perhaps the odometer has reached its limit and "rolled over" to zero. If the readings look OK, the IF function causes Excel to subtract the beginning and ending readings (**B3–B2**). If there seems to be an error, the function displays text in the cell (**Check OD**).

LOOKUP AND REFERENCE FUNCTIONS

Like explorers, Lookup and Reference functions go to places that you send them and return with answers. They can be used to create invoices that look up and insert different unit prices based on quantities purchased, for instance. These features can inspect *rows*, *columns*, or *arrays*. Take the simple example in Figure 31.9, for instance.

The INDEX() function has been asked to go to the array bounded by cell addresses A1 through D4, then get the value stored in the cell two rows

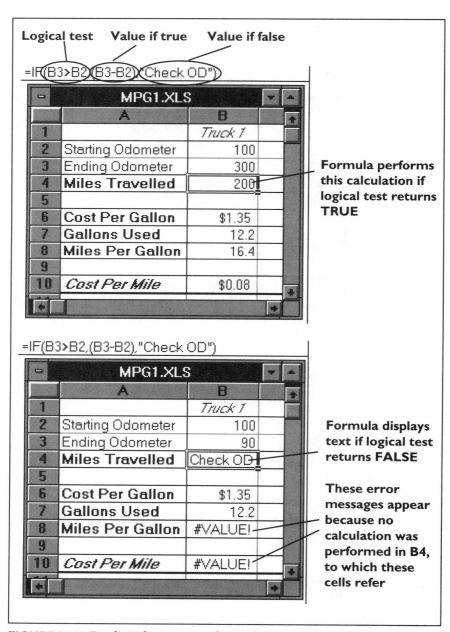

FIGURE 31.8 *Excel's IF function tests for conditions and does different things based on what it finds.*

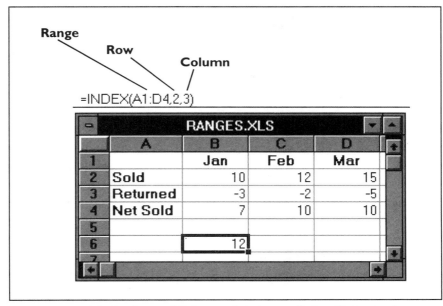

FIGURE 31.9 *Use Lookup and Reference functions to find and bring back information.*

down and three columns across.

Lookup and Reference functions can refer to ranges, names, specific cell addresses, or row and column counts.

MATH AND TRIG FUNCTIONS

You've already seen several of the Mathematical functions in action—SQRT() and SUM(), for example. There are many others, enough to make an eighth-grade math teacher weep with joy. Most are quite straightforward, and well documented with on-line help. Math and trig functions can refer to cell references, names, or plain old numbers.

Two of the Math and Trig functions simply produce *numbers* whenever a worksheet recalculates. RAND() produces evenly distributed random numbers greater than or equal to 0 (zero) and less than 1 each time you recalculate—handy if you play the lottery. The PI() function pastes 3.141592654.

STATISTICAL FUNCTIONS

There are liars, damned liars, statistics, and now Excel. Pollsters and statisticians will want to check out the 71 statistical functions, from AVDEV() to ZTEST(). As is the case with other functions, arguments can be values, addresses, named items, arrays, and so on.

TEXT FUNCTIONS

To manipulate or analyze strings of text in cells, use text functions. For example, CLEAN() will strip away any nonprinting characters stored in a cell. UPPER() converts text to all uppercase. DOLLAR() converts numbers to their spelled-out dollar equivalents and formats them in currency format.

ERROR MESSAGES FROM FUNCTIONS

When you leave out or misuse arguments in functions, you will sometimes see cryptic error messages like **Error in formula**, or a message like **#NAME?** or **#NUM!** will appear in the cell containing the flawed argument.

It is common to get messages like these when you work with names or text strings as arguments. Text strings *must* be enclosed in quotation marks, while names (references to areas, for instance) must *not* be in quotes. For instance, suppose you are using a math function like SQRT. If you enter the formula argument =SQRT(SALES), Excel expects to be able to find a named numeric value or range of cells in your worksheet called SALES. If it can't, you'll get the message #NAME? in the cell containing the formula. If you *do* have a positive numeric value named SALES, the formula will use its contents as the function's argument. If the value of SALES is negative, you'll see the error message #NUM! Suppose you accidentally enclose the name SALES in quotes, then try to use it as an arithmetic argument. The expression =SQRT("SALES") will produce the error message **#VALUE!** since SQRT needs a numeric value to do its thing, and material in quotes is treated as *text*.

Check your work. Use Excel's on-line help feature to see examples of the functions at work.

TO LEARN MORE ABOUT FUNCTIONS

There is clearly much more to know about Excel's functions. While you can learn a lot by experimenting and exploring Excel's on-line help, you may also benefit from the 500+-page *Microsoft Excel Function Reference* shipped with the program. Or for a more tutorial approach, try *Mastering Excel 4 for Windows* by Carl Townsend (SYBEX, 1992).

EXCEL

32

Excel's Chart Features

Excel helps you create charts in two or three dimensions based on data in a worksheet. You can take almost complete control over every aspect of your chart's appearance with Excel's chart Toolbar and charting menus, or you can let Excel's ChartWizard make most of the decisions for you. The 3-D chart in Figure 32.1 was created in less than a minute by answering a few ChartWizard questions. Once you've created a chart, you can print it, hide it, spell check it, modify it, or even include it in your non-Excel projects (such as Word documents). Charts are usually saved as part of a worksheet, but you can also save them as separate documents, in which case their file names normally end with the extension .XLC. Whenever you change data in a worksheet, Excel will update (or at least offer to update) charts that are based on the changed data.

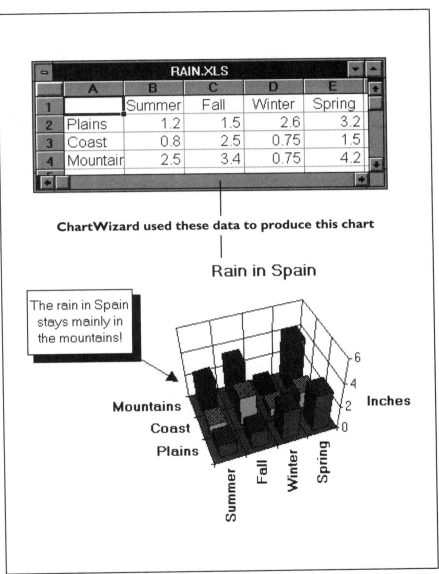

FIGURE 32.1 *ChartWizard can help you make great-looking charts like these in less than a minute.*

CHART PARTS AND TERMINOLOGY

You can fumble along without knowing the names of Excel's chart parts, and there is plenty of on-line help available while you create and edit charts. But you'll be much more productive if you take a moment to understand just a few concepts and terms.

CHART DATA SERIES

A *chart data series* is a collection of *related* values that are plotted on the chart. For instance, in the chart at the *top* of Figure 32.2 there is only one data series—the numbers 133.8, 355.4, and 808.9.

Some chart types can have more than one data series, as you will see in the bottom of Figure 32.2, where a *second* series details government borrowing.

DATA MARKERS

Data markers are the bars, pie wedges, dots, pictures, or other elements used to represent a particular data point (a single value in a series). For instance, the three shaded columns in the top chart of Figure 32.2 are each separate data markers.

When charts have more than one data series, the markers for each series usually look different. This is illustrated in the bottom chart of Figure 32.2. The consumer debt columns are one color (or shade of gray, or pattern), while government debt columns are another.

It is also possible to use different *types* of markers for different series in the same chart. You might, for instance, use *columns* for one series and *lines* for another, as you will see in an upcoming example.

Excel even lets you import graphics for use as markers, a technique also illustrated later in this chapter. For now, just think of data markers as the columns, bars, pie wedges, lines, and other elements used to represent values on a chart.

AXES

An axis is a reference line denoting one of the dimensions of a chart. Excel can plot in up to three axes: X, Y, and Z. Usually the X-axis runs horizontally (left to right) and the Y-axis runs vertically (bottom to top). For instance, in both charts in Figure 32.2 the years run along the X-axis and the billions of

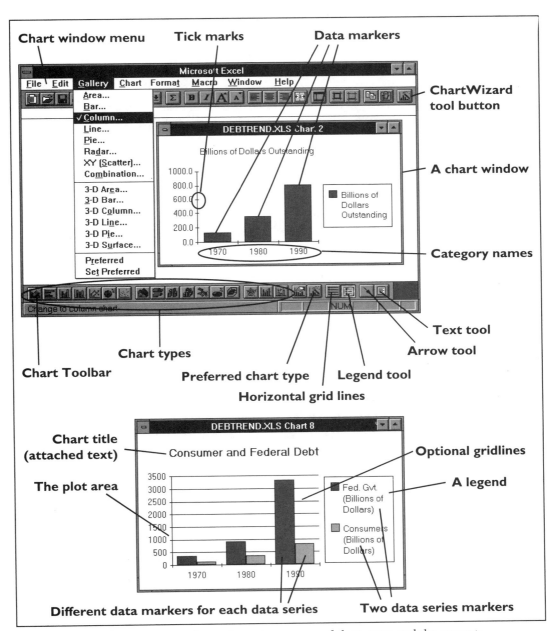

FIGURE 32.2 *Take a moment to learn the various names of chart parts and the concepts behind them.*

dollars run along the Y-axis. In three-dimensional charts, the Z-axis runs vertically.

CATEGORY NAMES

Category names usually correspond to worksheet labels for the data being plotted along the X-axis (horizontally along the chart). For instance, in Figure 32.2 the category names are 1970, 1980, and 1990. ChartWizard identifies and includes category names when it creates a new chart. Some chart types (like bar charts) place category names on the Y-axis.

CHART DATA SERIES NAMES

Chart data series names usually correspond to worksheet labels for the data being plotted on the Y-axis. For instance, in the top part of Figure 32.2 there is only one chart data series name, since there is only one data series (Billions of Dollars Outstanding). The bottom part of the example has two data series names, one for each series. Data series names are usually displayed in a box (called a *legend*) alongside a sample of the color, shade, or pattern used for each data series. ChartWizard automatically identifies category names and creates legends.

TICK MARKS AND GRIDLINES

Tick marks are short lines that intersect an axis to separate parts of a series scale or category. You can also add optional, longer grid lines in any of a chart's dimensions. Using the Gridlines... choice on the Chart window's Chart command. Ticks and horizontal gridlines are illustrated in Figure 32.2.

CHART TEXT

Charts can contain two kinds of text—attached and unattached text. Chart titles and data markers are examples of attached text. They are attached, or connected with, specific parts of a chart and cannot be easily detached.

It is also possible to create unattached text, like text boxes containing notes. Chart text is discussed later in the chapter, because by now you must be itching to create a chart. Let's cut to the chase.

INSTANT CHARTS WITH THE CHARTWIZARD

ChartWizard "looks" at the data you've selected to plot. It also "watches" as you drag to define the size and shape of the desired chart area. Next, it offers you a number of chart styles, and even lets you define chart titles. Faster than you can say, "Next year let's reduce the deficit," you'll have a great-looking chart. Here are the steps for a simple column chart, plus some insights into the other options you'll encounter along the way.

STARTING AND ASSISTING THE WIZARD

Start by creating a worksheet containing the data you wish to chart. In Figure 32.3 the cells A1 through D3 contain the necessary data and labels for a multiseries chart.

Select the data to be included in your chart (probably most easily by dragging). Don't include empty rows or columns. In the sample chart, cells A1 through D3 are surrounded by marching ants, indicating that they have been selected.

Click on the ChartWizard button (it looks like a chart with a magic wand). Marching ants surround selected cells, and your pointer turns into crosshairs. Drag with it, as illustrated in Figure 32.3, to define the size and shape of your new chart. To create a square, hold down the Shift key while you drag. When you release the mouse button, you will see the first of five ChartWizard Step dialog boxes, also illustrated in Figure 32.3.

This box shows you the range of the data to be charted and gives you a chance to alter the selected range. Normally, you'll click the Next> button at this point, taking you to Step 2 of 5.

PICKING THE RIGHT CHART TYPE

ChartWizard can create 14 different *chart types* and many different *formats* for each of those 14 types. The Step 2 window, shown in Figure 32.4, illustrates all the chart types and proposes one (Column, in our example).

It's usually obvious from the chart samples which ones are best for various projects. You can also just experiment, or read on-line help for each chart type. Use Help's Search feature to find information by chart type name (Radar, for instance).

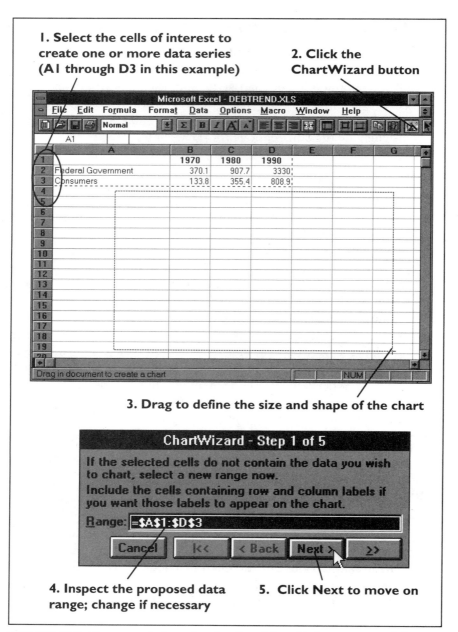

1. Select the cells of interest to create one or more data series (A1 through D3 in this example)

2. Click the ChartWizard button

3. Drag to define the size and shape of the chart

4. Inspect the proposed data range; change if necessary

5. Click Next to move on

FIGURE 32.3 *Start a worksheet, then let ChartWizard help you size and shape it.*

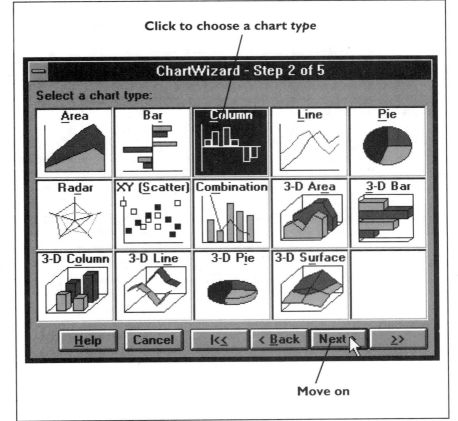

FIGURE 32.4 *ChartWizard presents samples of 14 chart types and suggests one by highlighting it (Column in this example).*

When you've decided on a chart type, click its sample to highlight it, then click the Next> button to continue. Don't worry if you pick the wrong type; you can easily change it later.

Once you've chosen a chart type, ChartWizard presents a Step 3 dialog box showing various *formatting* options, which are different for each chart type. Figure 32.5 shows the formatting options for column charts.

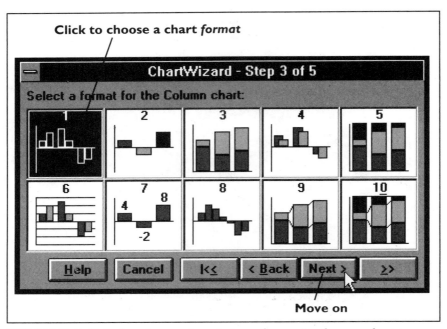

FIGURE 32.5 *Pick chart formats by pointing, after you've chosen a chart type. Format choices are different for each chart type.*

Don't lose any sleep over these choices, either. Formats can be tried on later like hats. Start with the choice the Wizard suggests, and experiment after you've seen those results. Click the Next> button to continue.

In Step 4, you'll see the beginnings of your chart design in a *Sample Chart* box. If you like what you see, forge ahead. Don't worry about the actual shape of the chart at this point, and don't be alarmed if your labels are temporarily truncated (shortened) or replaced with words like "Series 1" and "Series 2." *Do* think about the general presentation of the data at this point. Does the chart help you understand the data? Do you have the appropriate data on the right axis? Do you like the chart type? If not, you can use the <Back button to return to the earlier steps and pick a different chart type or format. Sometimes the option buttons in Step 4 can improve your chart. Experiment. As you'll soon see, the settings proposed by the ChartWizard (and shown in Figure 32.6) are just fine for this sample project.

You're almost done. Step 5 gives you a chance to add chart titles for the chart itself, and for each axis. You will see the titles appear in the Sample

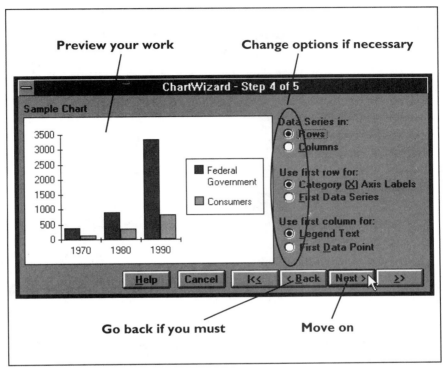

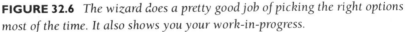

FIGURE 32.6 *The wizard does a pretty good job of picking the right options most of the time. It also shows you your work-in-progress.*

Chart area as you type. The *Add a legend?* option turns legends on and off. Figure 32.7 shows the Step 5 dialog box and the resulting embedded chart. Notice how the year labels in the Step 5 sample appear to be truncated. Don't worry about anomalies like these in the sample. As you can see from the finished chart, the labels look fine in a real chart of the proper size and shape.

If you get cold feet before you click OK, you can still go back to choose other options. When you click OK, Excel will insert an embedded chart in your worksheet quicker than you can say "1040EZ."

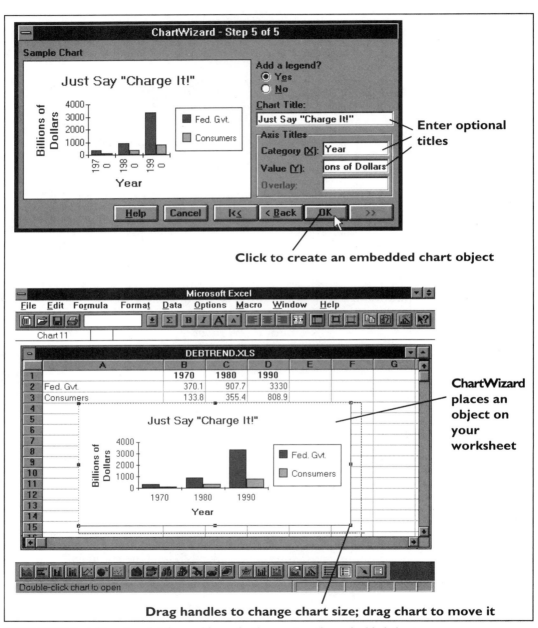

FIGURE 32.7 *Add optional titles and legends, then review the embedded chart.*

CREATING CHARTS WITHOUT CHARTWIZARD

It is possible to bypass ChartWizard entirely. Select the data to chart and press the F11 function key to create a simple chart that can be altered, using the Chart Toolbar and choices on the Chart menu bar.

EMBEDDED CHARTS, CHART DOCUMENTS, AND CHART WINDOWS

I've put off this topic for as long as possible, since it's a little confusing. When you create charts, they can either be *embedded chart objects*—an integral part of your worksheet—or they can be separate *chart documents* that are *linked* to your worksheet. ChartWizard *always* creates embedded chart objects. It's usually the easy way to go. Embedded charts are saved as part of your worksheet file. Even if you create ten different embedded charts for a particular worksheet, they will all be saved as part of one file—along with the worksheet itself. When you make changes to data on the worksheet, affected embedded charts are automatically updated. The whole process is simple, clean, and automatic.

SEPARATE CHART DOCUMENTS

You create a separate chart document several different ways. For instance, if you bypass ChartWizard and create a new chart with the F11 key or New (Chart) command, you will see a new chart window, the Chart menu bar, and a chart Toolbar.

Whenever you attempt to close a chart document created this way, you will be asked if you want to save the chart. If you answer Yes, you will see Excel's Save As... dialog box. Normally, chart documents are saved with the extension .XLC. Excel will add this extension automatically for you if you like. Saved charts are separate documents that are linked (related) to your worksheet.

You can create *multiple* separate chart documents that are all linked to the same Excel worksheet, but, in addition to having a worksheet file, you will have as many separate chart files as you have charts. So if you create 10 charts for a worksheet this way, you'd have 11 files—the worksheet and 10 chart files.

You open these separate chart documents just like you do other Excel documents (other worksheets, for instance). If you open a separate chart document *after* you've opened the worksheet containing the data used to create the chart, the chart will automatically reflect the current data on the worksheet, even if the data have changed since the last time you opened the chart.

If, however, you open the chart and its worksheet is not also open, Excel will ask if you want to "Update references to unopened documents." It is simply wondering whether you want the chart to reflect any possible changes in the data on the linked worksheet. Answering Yes will cause Excel to update the chart, while No will open the chart without referring to the closed worksheet's data.

When you close a chart document, Excel will often ask if you want to save changes. This happens when you've changed either the format of the chart or the data in the open worksheet, as well as when you have answered Yes to the "Update references" question. Before answering No, be sure you understand the consequences of not saving changes caused by new data on the unopened worksheet. In other words, if you open a chart without the worksheet open and answer Yes to the "Update references to unopened documents," you will see current data reflected in your chart. If you then close that chart document and answer No to the Save Changes question, you will not save the updated chart that you see on your screen. Sometimes this is desirable, sometimes not. It's up to you.

If all of this makes sense, move on; otherwise reread the two preceding topics until it all sinks in. There's one more wrinkle ahead and it requires a firm grasp of embedded charts vs. separate chart documents.

CHART WINDOWS

OK, there are *embedded charts* and separate *chart documents*, right? Embedded charts usually look like graphics. They have a thin black outline and eight little size boxes that you can drag to change the shape of the chart area. The *top* part of Figure 32.8 shows a typical embedded chart.

Separate charts (charts stored in their own files) have windows around them including a title bar, control boxes, and so on. They *look* like documents, because they *are* documents. Normally, their names end with the extension .XLC. The *center* chart in Figure 32.8 is a separate chart with the file name TRENDCH.XLC.

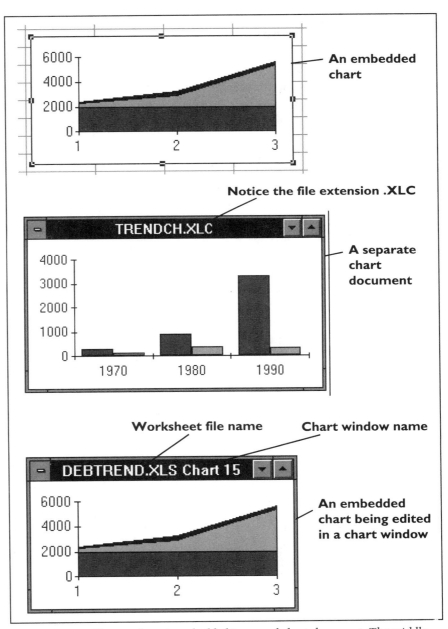

FIGURE 32.8 *The top chart is embedded in a worksheet document. The middle chart is a separate chart document. The bottom chart is an embedded chart being edited in a chart window.*

Whenever you activate a separate chart document, in addition to the Chart Toolbar, you will see the Chart *menu*, giving you access to special tools for editing specific chart elements not found on the Toolbar or worksheet menu (changing chart fonts, data marker shading, and so on).

But what about editing embedded charts? Whenever you select an embedded chart (click in it), the Chart Toolbar appears, letting you change to some but not all chart types, change grid lines, and so on. There are, however, some chart editing tasks that cannot be accomplished with just the Chart Toolbar. The only way to make certain changes is to place an embedded chart into a *chart window*—a third and unique gizmo reminiscent of a separate chart document's window. The *bottom* part of Figure 32.8 is an embedded chart in a chart window. Notice that this kind of chart window shows the *worksheet's* file name in the title bar (DEBTREND.XLS in the example).

To open a chart window of this type, simply double-click on an embedded chart. The window will open with a copy of the embedded chart. (If you move the chart window, you'll be able to see the embedded chart as well.) The changes that you make in the chart window affect the embedded chart immediately. When you are done making changes, you can close the chart window with its Close box or the Ctrl-F4 shortcut.

Incidentally, you can save chart window contents as separate charts (files) by using Excel's Save As... command with an active chart window.

RESIZING AND MOVING CHARTS

You may need to change the size or shape of a finished chart, which is easily done by dragging the little handles that surround a selected (embedded) chart like the one shown at the top of Figure 32.8. When working in chart windows (like the ones shown in this figure), drag on window corners just as you would to change any other Windows window.

Besides making room for previously cramped labels, resizing charts changes their size and shape, and thus the appearance of the chart markers and other chart elements. Resizing is particularly useful if your data labels are invisible or all scrunched up as illustrated in Figure 32.9.

FIGURE 32.9 *Sometimes you'll need to increase a chart's size to see all labels, legends, and data.*

ADDING CHART NOTES AND ARROWS

Often it's nice to be able to draw attention to, or explain, certain items on your chart. The boxed note in Figure 32.10 is an example of this.

To create text like this (often called *unattached text*), work in a chart window or select an embedded chart to reveal the Chart Toolbar. Use the text button on the chart tool. It is the right-most button and it looks like lines of text. Clicking it turns your pointer to crosshairs. Drag to create the outline of a text box in the approximate desired size and shape. Type and edit your note using techniques that should be familiar to you by now.

RESTYLING AND RESIZING TEXT BOXES

To resize the box or move it, point and click on any edge. The outline will thicken and you'll see eight size handles. Drag and resize this outline as you do any similar Windows object. To embellish text, select it and use the standard Toolbar or text-related menu commands.

To change the outline or fill pattern used for the box, or to add a drop-shadow effect like the one shown in Figure 32.10, select the box and use the resulting Patterns... command in the Format menu on either the Excel menu or the Excel Chart menu.

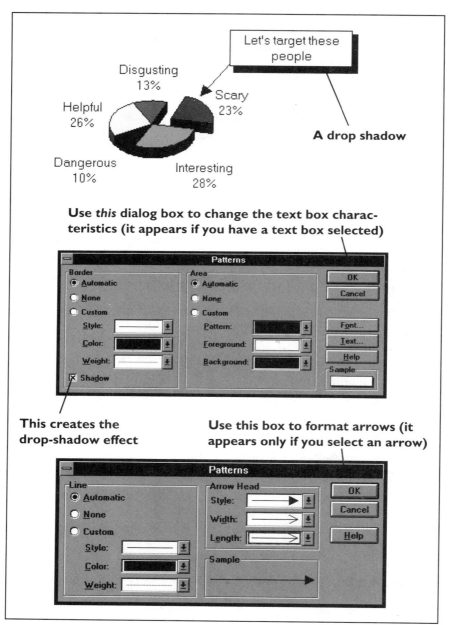

FIGURE 32.10 *Use boxed text and arrows to explain or highlight things.*

DRAWING AND FORMATTING ARROWS

To draw an arrow, use the Chart Toolbar's arrow button (located next to the text button). When your pointer turns into crosshairs, point where you want the arrow to start and drag to the ending point. When you release the mouse button, an arrow will appear. You can drag either end of selected arrows to reposition them and/or change the length of the line. Double-clicking exactly on an arrow brings up the Patterns dialog box shown at the bottom of Figure 32.10, which lets you define arrow styles, line thicknesses, colors, and so on. When done this way, changes affect only the arrow that you've double-clicked on, plus new arrows drawn thereafter. To change arrows drawn earlier, select each arrow you wish to reformat by Shift-clicking, then use the Patterns... command in the Format menu on either the Excel menu or the Excel Chart menu. (The Patterns dialog box provided by the Patterns... command changes, based on what type of chart element is selected when you issue the command.)

EDITING CHARTS

You could spend the rest of your life exploring Excel's chart options. These are nearly endless. It's possible to change chart types and formats, embellish text, choose patterns or colors, add grid lines, insert notes with arrows, and much more. Here's the "compact" tour of Excel chartology:

CHANGING CHART TYPES AND FORMATS

Once you've created a chart, you can quickly change its type by clicking on the chart type buttons on the Chart Toolbar at the bottom of your Excel window, or by picking a chart type with the Gallery... command. Try this with the Debt chart if you've been following along, or use your own creation. Notice how some chart types are good at emphasizing one data series or another, while other chart types are great at comparing data.

Not all of the chart types appear on the Chart Toolbar. Use the Chart window's Gallery menu to pick any chart type and all of the available formats for each one.

CHANGING DATA SERIES RANGES

There are several ways to change the data series ranges. One is to select an embedded chart, then click on the ChartWizard button. You'll see the Step 1 dialog box, which will let you specify a new data range by typing it or dragging with your mouse. To keep all of the other chart design elements intact, use the ChartWizard's >> button in the Step 1 box instead of plodding through all five steps. (Think of this as a fast-forward button.)

You can also edit the series data in chart windows, using Excel's Edit Series... command on the Chart menu bar's Chart menu. (No, that's not a typo.) It's a *menu* called *Chart* on a *menu bar* called the *Chart menu bar*. From here, you can edit the series or rearrange the order in which each series is plotted.

SELECTING AND EDITING CHART COMPONENTS

You can edit specific parts of a chart, like text, grid lines, the shading used for markers, and so on. You must work in chart windows. (Double-click on embedded charts to place them in windows.) Once you have the correct chart window active, point to the item you want to select. For instance, to change a chart title you would click on it once to select it.

Incidentally, when you click to select, some chart items are surrounded by *black* selection squares, while others are surrounded by *white* selection squares. Black squares tell you that you can move or resize the selected item as well as format it in other ways. White selection squares mean you cannot directly move or resize the selected item.

To select a *data series*, click on any marker in the series. For instance, to select the government spending series in your sample chart, you could click on any of the government columns in any year. You will then see a description of the data series in your Formula bar, where you can edit the series definition if you choose.

To select a *single data marker* (like the 1990 Federal borrowing column marker in your sample chart), hold down the Ctrl key while pointing.

To select a *grid line*, click exactly on a grid line. Clicking on any axis selects it. To select just the *plot area* (the columns without their category names, for instance), click in any part of the plot area not occupied by other things like grid lines or markers. There is also a Select Plot Area command on the Chart menu. To select the *entire chart*, click anywhere outside of the plot area, but not on other items like titles or legends. There is also a Select Chart command on the Chart menu.

GENERAL FORMATTING TECHNIQUES

Frequently, you can double-click on chart elements to quickly bring up relevant formatting options. If you double-click on a data marker, for instance, you'll soon see a Patterns dialog box that will let you select a new color or pattern for the marker. Double-clicking on a legend takes you to a dialog box where you can rearrange the appearance of the legends, and so on.

The other general editing technique is to select something, then use the appropriate Worksheet or Chart menu commands and Toolbar buttons.

USING GRAPHICS AS DATA MARKERS

Take a look at Figure 32.11. Instead of containing the normal solid color or shaded pattern for data markers, the chart uses a bit-mapped image of a car. In the top sample, the car's image shrinks or expands as necessary to fill each of the three columns. (It's a little smashed in the Colorado column.) In the bottom sample (using the same data), small cars are piled on top of each other to indicate the relative number of registered autos in each state.

We copied the *cars.bmp* image from the Windows directory for this example. It's reasonably easy to do if you understand graphics and the Windows Clipboard. Here are the general steps:

1. Copy a small bit-mapped image to your Clipboard. (You might use Word's *Insert Picture* command to place a bit-mapped image into a Word document where you can resize and copy it to the Clipboard, for instance.)

2. Switch back to the Excel chart window containing the chart to be modified.

3. Click once to select the *data marker* you wish to change.

4. Paste with Excel's Paste command or the Ctrl-V keyboard shortcut.

5. Resize the chart if necessary to get the desired effect.

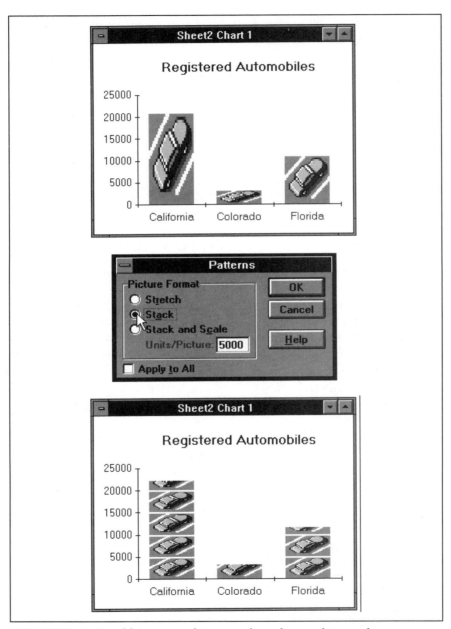

FIGURE 32.11 *Excel lets you use bit-mapped graphics as data markers.*

6. To change to stacked instead of stretched images, double-click on a data marker containing a bit-mapped image to bring up the little Patterns dialog box shown in the center of Figure 32.11. Choose *Stack* or *Stack and Scale*. If you use Stack and Scale, you can specify how many graph units will be represented by each bit-mapped image (the number of registered autos per car image in Figure 32.11).

ROTATING 3-D CHARTS

As you experiment with 3-D graphs, you will find that in some instances tall parts of a chart will obscure inner details. Other times you'll just want to tilt or rotate a 3-D object to get a more dramatic effect. In either case, open a chart window with a 3-D chart, then choose 3-D View from the Chart menu bar's Format menu. You'll see a dialog box like the one in Figure 32.12. Use the Elevation buttons to tilt the chart and the rotation buttons to rotate it. Use the Apply button to preview your changes without closing the dialog box. OK applies the latest changes and closes the box.

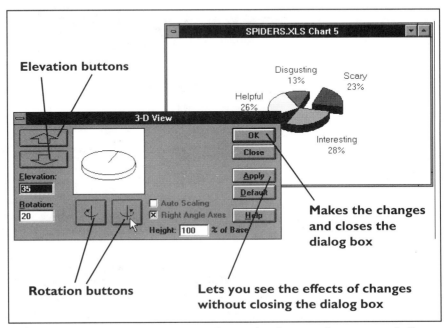

FIGURE 32.12 *Try a 3-D chart to reveal inner details or to achieve a special effect.*

CHANGING WORKSHEET VALUES
BY DRAGGING CHART PARTS

Here's a neat way to "what-if," or to make your data fit a desired scenario. Create a worksheet and a chart—your Debt worksheet, for instance. Then, with the chart in a chart window (and, hopefully, though not necessarily, with your worksheet data in view), try this: Hold down the Ctrl key and point directly to the business end of a data marker (the top of a column, for instance). Figure 32.13 illustrates this.

When you Ctrl-click, just the marker you point to will be selected. And it will have an unusual combination of selection markers—many white ones and one or more black ones. When you *drag* on a black marker, you will be able to move that selected part of the chart *and* automatically change the numbers in the corresponding worksheet cell(s)!

I can hear the voice of corporate America now… "Jones, make the report say we did 26% of our sales in February, truth be damned."

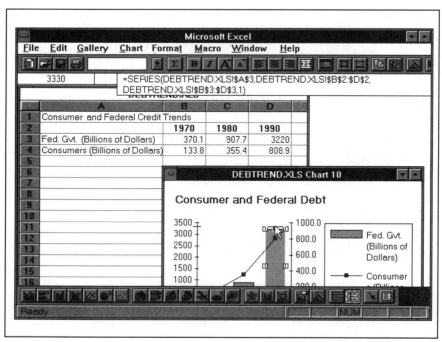

FIGURE 32.13 *You can change worksheet cell values by dragging chart parts!*

PRINTING CHARTS

Unless you tell Excel to do otherwise, it prints all embedded charts. To display but not print an embedded chart, select the chart, then remove the check mark from the Print Object option in the Object Properties dialog box. Reach this box from the Object Properties... command on the Format menu.

If a chart is a separate document, print it like any other Excel document. Remember to update it before printing if that's what you want. Use the Page Setup... and Print Preview features to format these documents, add headers or footers, and so on.

If you experience problems printing Excel's 3-D charts on a *pen plotter*, you are not alone. Contact Microsoft Product Support for assistance or at least condolences.

DELETING CHARTS

To delete *embedded* charts, simply select them and press the Del key or use the Clear command on Excel's Edit menu. Undo works here if you act promptly.

Delete separate *chart documents* as you would any other unwanted Windows file. (Use Excel's Delete command on the File menu, visit File Manager, and so on.)

ABOUT THE PREFERRED CHART

ChartWizard and the New Chart (F11) command normally create new charts using the *Column* chart type and format 1. This is the default *preferred chart style*. You can define a different preferred style by selecting a chart that you like (making its chart window the active window), then using the *Set Preferred* command on Excel's Chart Gallery menu. From then on, Excel will propose using that chart style for new charts. The Preferred Chart choice, also on the Chart Gallery menu, returns a wayward chart to the preferred chart type and format.

EXCEL

TELL ME MORE

These are the basics of Excel charting, and, as you can see, skills you learned in Windows and practiced in Word are often called for and applied in Excel. Many times, just reading the menu, dialog boxes, or the status bar will show you how to do new and useful things.

But there may be other charting details that are not so obvious. For instance, you can link a chart's text with worksheet cells so that chart notes or labels change when worksheet cells change. You can sometimes plot non-adjacent data. There is more to know about forcing axis values than you've read here. And so on... If you don't find the answer to questions like these in Excel's on-line help, check out the 100-plus pages on charts in your Excel manual, or pick up *Mastering Excel 4 for Windows* by Carl Townsend (SYBEX, 1992).

33

Working with Graphics in Excel

You can apply many of your Windows graphics skills to Excel worksheet projects. Worksheets can include imported graphic images, things you draw yourself, arrows, text boxes, and so on. You can use graphics to dress up the appearance of a document or as an integral part of the presentation. For instance, in Figure 33.1, the prices of the individual car options are entered into worksheet cells, and the *Added Cost* figure of $2,095 in the price tag is a worksheet cell containing a formula that adds up all of the items.

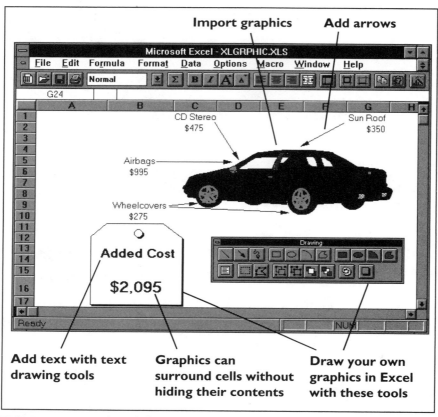

FIGURE 33.1 *Excel worksheets can include imported graphics, or you can use Excel's drawing tools to create your own.*

CREATING AND PLACING GRAPHIC OBJECTS

Excel treats all graphics either as *Microsoft Drawing Objects* (they'll remind you of the text boxes you worked with in the Chart chapter) or as pictures. You can place graphic objects anywhere you desire on a worksheet. By selecting graphics you can move, resize, and restyle them. Copies of graphics can be simply pasted from your Clipboard into a worksheet, or they can be *linked* with the original objects so that changes in the original are reflected on the worksheet.

IMPORTING GRAPHICS

As a general rule, if you can get a graphic onto your Clipboard, you can paste it into an Excel worksheet. Sometimes it pays to visit Excel's Paste Special command rather than using the basic Paste command or the Ctrl-V keyboard shortcut when inserting graphics into Excel worksheets. For instance, if the source program supports object linking and embedding (OLE), you might want to Paste Link, rather than simply Paste. (You'll learn more about this in Chapters 39 and 40.)

EXPORTING EXCEL GRAPHICS

You can also paste parts of your Excel worksheet into other types of documents. For instance, you can copy an Excel drawing or chart to your Clipboard, then switch to another program and paste (or sometimes Paste Link) the Clipboard contents either as a picture or often in other formats. The type of pasting that you do and the program you paste into determines how the pasted items will both appear and behave in the destination document. Again, Chapters 39 and 40 go into more detail about this.

RESIZING GRAPHICS

Chances are, you already know how to resize Excel graphics. Select a graphic by pointing with your mouse. When the handles appear, drag. To change both dimensions at once, drag the corner handles.

POSITIONING GRAPHICS ON WORKSHEETS

To move an object, select it and drag with your mouse. To move more than one object, Shift-click on each of them. Drag them all at once with your mouse and release. To align a graphic object's border with the worksheet cell grid, hold down the Alt key and drag one of the object's corner handles. You can also select graphics, copy or cut them to the Clipboard, and paste them elsewhere.

DRAWING LINES AND SHAPES

Excel provides a number of drawing tools that will remind you of the ones in Microsoft Word's Draw feature as well as the Windows drawing packages described earlier in this book. Excel's tools were used to create the price tag and arrows in Figure 33.1. They work like most similar Windows-savvy drawing tools. Reach them by using the Toolbars... choice on Excel's Options menu. Pick Drawing from the scrolling Toolbars list. You'll see the tools illustrated in Figure 33.2, although they may be in a shorter, two-row box. (As you might remember, you can drag to change Toolbar shapes.)

Since you've probably used similar drawing tools by now, we'll not waste paper here covering what must be familiar ground. If you forget what a tool does, refer to Figure 33.2 or point to the tool in question and read its description in Excel's status bar area. Incidentally, the polygon, oval, text, and drop-shadow tools were used to create the price tag in Figure 33.1.

EXCEL SLIDE SHOWS

Once you've created art and worksheet data charts (and possibly sounds if your computer is properly equipped), you can use Excel's Slide feature to display this information as an animated and entertaining on-screen sequence that will remind you of a 35mm slide show. Unfortunately, you cannot *print* slides from the Slide feature.

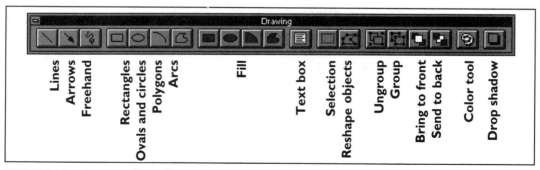

FIGURE 33.2 *Use Excel's Toolbar to create shapes, lines, text boxes, and arrows. Add patterns, group items, and change objects' colors or shades of gray.*

CREATING A NEW SLIDE SHOW

Start by deciding which items you want to include in your show. They need not all be Excel items. In fact, you don't need to include any data from worksheets. You could use Excel's slide show to display just things you've created in Word or an external drawing program or whatever. In any event, make a mental or written list of things you want to show and the order in which you want to present them. Figure out where they are stored if you don't already know. (Sometimes, it is convenient to collect all of the elements into one Word or Excel document via the Clipboard.) When you are sufficiently organized, open a New Slides project by using Excel's New... command and selecting Slides from the scrolling list of New options as shown in Figure 33.3.

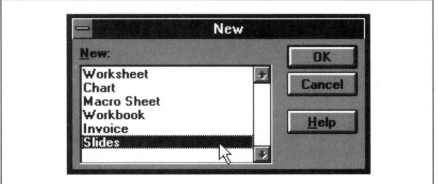

FIGURE 33.3 *After you've planned your presentation and located its elements, use Excel's New Slides choices to start assembling the slide show.*

The new slide worksheet will open with a host of buttons along the top, buttons used to create and run your show, as shown in Figure 33.4. The buttons let you construct, control, and edit the show as well as its individual elements. Starting with row 3, each *row* contains information about a *single slide*.

Figure 33.5 shows a typical slide show.

The first slide in this show is a portion of an Excel worksheet. The next slide happens to be an Excel chart, and the third an organizational chart (a picture drawn in Word). Just about anything you can get onto your Clipboard can be used in a slide show. Columns B through D contain information

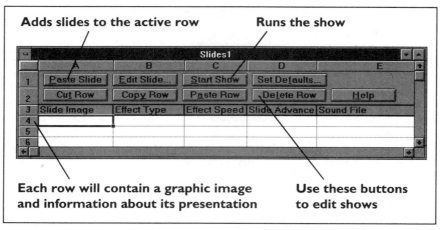

Adds slides to the active row   **Runs the show**

Each row will contain a graphic image   **Use these buttons
and information about its presentation**   **to edit shows**

FIGURE 33.4 *Buttons facilitate and control slide shows.*

about the effects and techniques used to make a transition from one slide to another. Column E indicates the name and location of sound files, if any.

CHOOSING AND INSERTING GRAPHIC ELEMENTS

Start by placing a copy of the desired graphic on your Clipboard. This may require a trip to a different program (like Word or a drawing program), or it may mean switching to a different Excel window.

In any case, with the graphic on your Clipboard, *activate the destination cell* in your slide show document, remembering that the row in which a graphic resides controls its order of appearance in the show. (Cell A4 is the first slide and cell A6 the last in our example.)

Press the *Paste Slide* button. Excel will paste a miniature (often distorted) reproduction of the graphics items you want to display. You will be presented with an Edit Slide dialog box requesting your preferences for transitional effects, plus those for other features. Figure 33.6 shows an example of this.

Transition effects will remind you of those used by television weather forecasters as they switch from map to map. Pick an effect from the scrolling

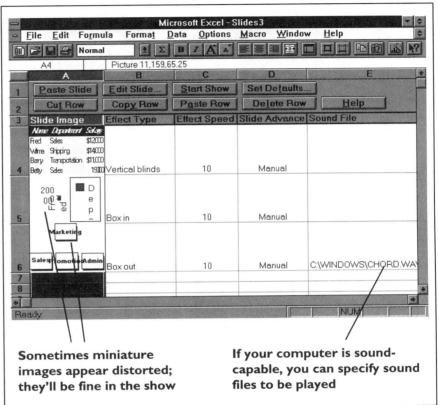

Sometimes miniature images appear distorted; they'll be fine in the show

If your computer is sound-capable, you can specify sound files to be played

FIGURE 33.5 *Excel helps you paste graphics in column A and specify presentation options, which are stored in the rows to the right of each graphic.*

list and see it demonstrated by clicking the Test button. When you find one you like, leave it selected in the list. The Speed slider under the Effect list controls the speed of the transition from one slide to the next. Drag left or right with your mouse to move the slider handle's position. You can test its effect with the Test button.

If you want the slide to advance by itself after it has been on-screen for a specified period of time, enter the length of time you want this slide to be

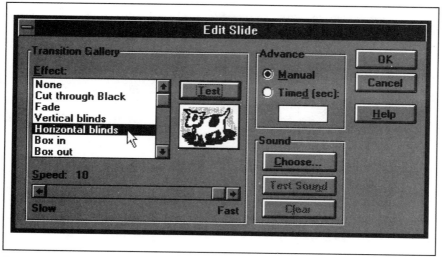

FIGURE 33.6 *Use the Edit Slide dialog box to pick transitional effects, advancement options, and sounds (if your computer can reproduce them).*

on the screen (in seconds). If you leave the Manual option checked instead, the slide will only advance when you press an appropriate keyboard key.

SOUNDS FOR YOUR SHOW

Sound-equipped computers can play sounds if you specify them with the Sound options button in the Edit Slide dialog box. This button brings up a Choose Sound dialog box that will remind you of a typical Windows Open File dialog box. Use it to pick the sound file you want to play at this point in your presentation.

SAVING A SHOW

Save your show periodically as you work, just as you would any other Excel file. Don't use slide show files as the primary repository of your favorite graphics. Save them using the programs that created them, and save *copies* in the show file.

RUNNING AND STOPPING YOUR SHOW

When you are ready to show and tell, click the Start Show button. You'll see a dialog box like the one in Figure 33.7.

You can ask Excel to run the show over and over. Alternately, you can see the show once, then return automatically to the worksheet. Or you can have the show run repeatedly until interrupted with the Esc key. Unless you specify a different starting slide number, shows start with Slide 1. To manually advance slides, press either the spacebar or the right arrow key. Pressing the left arrow key takes you back one slide each time you press it.

When showing slides, Excel expands graphics so that they virtually fill your screen. The worksheet itself will disappear from view until the show is over. If you don't want people to see the worksheet before and after you run your show, place blank, logo, or title slides at the beginning and end of your presentations. Advance to the first slide before the audience arrives, and don't go past the last slide.

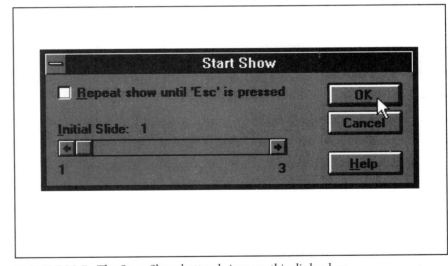

FIGURE 33.7 *The Start Show button brings up this dialog box.*

REARRANGING AND EDITING THE SHOW

Save your work before rearranging a slide show, just in case you want to revert to the old version. To *delete* a slide from your presentation, select its row by clicking in the row number. Then use the Delete Row button in Row 2 of your slide worksheet. Undo works here.

To *move* a slide, select the desired row and use the Cut (*not* the Delete) button. Highlight the row *below* where you want the slide to be placed, and use the *Paste Row* button to insert the cut row.

Use the Copy Row button to copy and paste the same graphic and settings at various places in your presentation.

34

Introduction to Excel's Command Macros

Just as Microsoft Word lets you create macros to automate repetitive tasks, Microsoft Excel will record and play back *command macros*. When you record command macros, Excel watches you work and converts your actions into *macro functions*—a kind of language that describes what you've done. These lists of steps can be saved as named macros and played back at will. For instance, if you always find yourself creating 12 centered and bold monthly column headings (Jan, Feb, and so on), record your typing, auto-filling, and formatting tasks *once*, then use the resulting macro in the future. You can assign keyboard shortcuts to macros. It is even possible to create your own *macro buttons*, or place macros on menus as you will see in this chapter and in Chapter 37.

Advanced users can write and modify macros by working directly with the hundreds of macro functions (called programming commands) described in the *Excel User's Guide 2* and *Excel Function Reference* that come with your Excel program. For now, let's stick with macros that don't require any programming skills, since you can accomplish quite a lot without knowing anything about ABSREFs or ZTETSMs or HENWAYs. (Don't ask.)

RECORDING YOUR OWN MACROS

Start by practicing what you intend to do a few times so that you know what steps to take and are assured that they will work. When you're done rehearsing, choose the Record... command from Excel's Macro menu. You'll see a dialog box like the one in Figure 34.1.

Macro names must start with a letter, cannot contain spaces, and should not look like a reference (no A$1 names, for instance). In place of spaces, use an underline character (**Month_Headings**, for instance).

Decide where you want to save your macro. It is generally best to save macros on the *Global Macro Sheet*. This makes them available in all of your Excel worksheets. You can save different collections of macros on separate *macro sheets*. If this interests you, read about the process later in this chapter.

For a first exercise, click the Global Macro Sheet option to store your macro there, as illustrated in Figure 34.1.

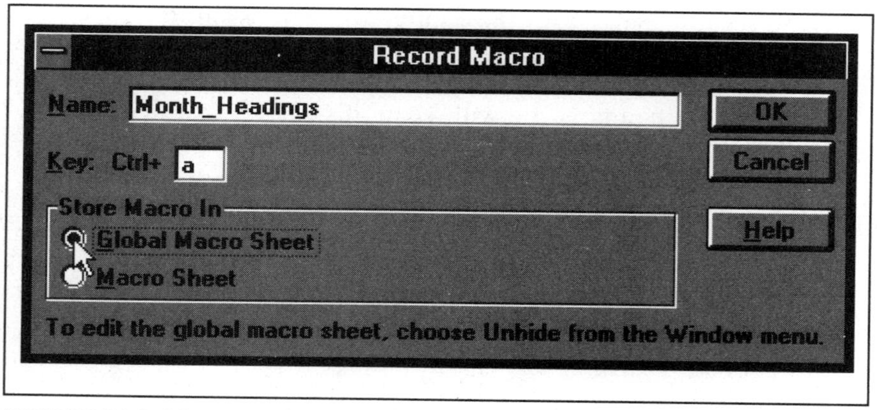

FIGURE 34.1 *Name your macro and decide where you want to save it.*

Excel proposes a keyboard shortcut that you can use in combination with the Ctrl key, and sometimes the Shift key, to execute macros. In Figure 34.1, it is proposing Ctrl-a. Excel cares about upper- and lowercase when creating and using keyboard shortcuts, so you can have both a **Ctrl-a** and a **Ctrl-Shift-a** combination if you like. Excel will not propose key combinations that are already used by Excel itself or by the open macro sheet. If you don't want to assign a keyboard shortcut, delete the proposed letter from the box.

Before we leave Figure 34.1, notice the message at the bottom of the dialog box. It is telling you that the Global Macro Sheet is *hidden* (its normal state) and that you must Unhide it to view or delete macros. Tuck that thought away for now.

Once you have named the macro, chosen a key combination for it, and told Excel where to store the macro, click OK to begin recording.

Live it up! Click, drag, format, enter text or values, construct formulas, use functions, and so on. When you are finished, use the Stop Recorder command on the Macro menu.

RUNNING MACROS

Once you've recorded a macro, use either the keyboard shortcut or visit the Run... command on Excel's Macro menu. If you use the keyboard shortcut, it will run immediately. The Run... command provides a list of macros like the one in Figure 34.2. Pick the one you want either by double-clicking on it, or by clicking once to select and clicking once on OK.

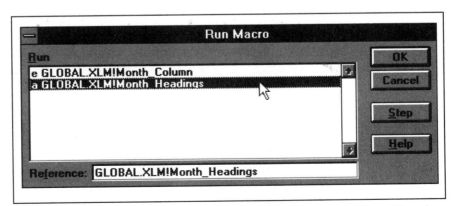

FIGURE 34.2 *Use keyboard shortcuts or this dialog box to run macros. Note that each macro name is preceded by the letter of its Ctrl key shortcut.*

Any way you start it, Excel will repeat your recorded steps, sometimes with surprising results. Remember that you may need to prepare your worksheet before running a macro. If a macro expects cell A1 to be the active cell, you may not like the results if Q7 is the active cell. When you want your macro to sort a table of cells, there had better be the right stuff in them.

There is no short list of macro "gottas," as you will learn the hard way. And, as you will also discover, Undo may not always completely rectify the results of a macro's rampage. It is wise to save your work *before* running powerful macros.

ABOUT MACRO SHEETS

Macro sheets are Excel worksheets containing the lists of macro functions (that is, instructions) used by the macros. Each macro is stored in its own column. The top part of Figure 34.3 shows the macro for filling a row with the months **Jan** through **Dec**, all bold and centered.

The bottom part of Figure 34.3 shows that same macro along with three others in columns B, C, and D. They've been selected prior to deletion.

To see what *your* Global Macro Sheet looks like, you must unhide it with the Unhide... command on the Excel Window menu. Hide it again when you are done snooping.

ASSIGNING MACROS TO BUTTONS

If you have a favorite macro or if you want to make a complex task easy for other users, consider creating *macro buttons*. The process is surprisingly simple. Start by displaying the Utility Toolbar. Use Excel's Toolbars... command on the Options menu. The Toolbar looks like Figure 34.4.

When you click on the button tool, your pointer turns into crosshairs. Use it to drag a button large enough to contain a descriptive label. When you release the mouse button, you'll see a rectangle like the one at the top of Figure 34.5. The box will contain the word Button and a number.

Once you've created the button, Excel will present a list of macros. Pick the one you want to assign to the button (double-click on the macro's name in the scrolling list).

Edit the button name if you like (click on the name and text edit), and you'll see something like the button shown at the bottom of Figure 34.5. Yes, you can use Excel's formatting commands and tools to change the button's font, type size, style, and other text attributes. (See how this all starts to tie together?)

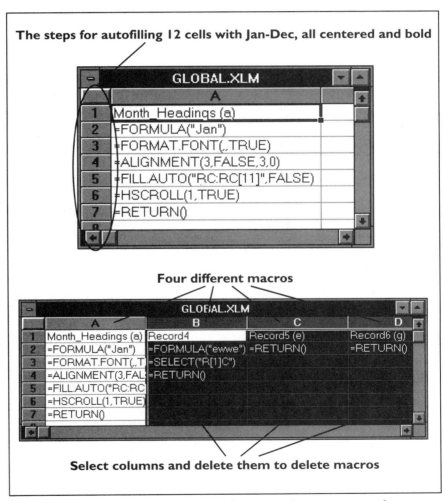

FIGURE 34.3 *Macros are each stored in their own columns on macro sheets. Delete columns to delete macros.*

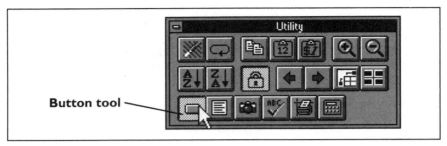

FIGURE 34.4 *Use the Utility Toolbar to create macro buttons.*

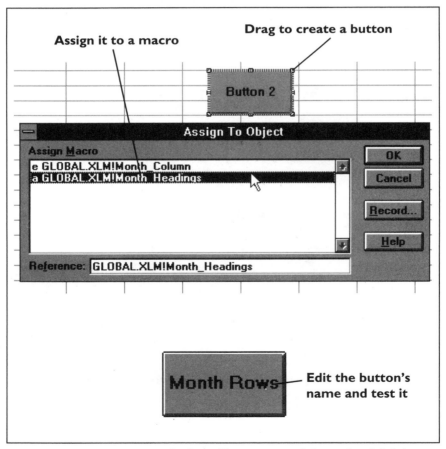

FIGURE 34.5 *Drag to create the desired button size and shape, then label the resulting button and assign it to a macro.*

Clicking on the button should run your macro. To move, resize, or otherwise change a button *without* running the macro, hold down the Ctrl key when you point to the button. The button will take on a by-now-familiar outline that will remind you of a graphic (it will be outlined with size handles). You can reposition a selected button by dragging with the pointer shaped like an arrowhead. To delete a button, select it (Ctrl-click), then use the Del key or Edit menu's Clear command. Deleting a button does not delete the macro that it is assigned to.

TO LEARN MORE ABOUT MACROS

You now know enough about macros to be dangerous. Besides on-line help, plus trial and error, check out the *Excel User's Guide 2* and *Excel Function Reference* that are packaged with your Excel program, or try *Mastering Excel 4 for Windows* by Carl Townsend (SYBEX, 1992).

Using Worksheets as Databases

"When you get a new hammer," the saying goes, "everything looks like a nail." Perhaps that's why many users (to say nothing of spreadsheet manufacturers) turn to spreadsheet packages when they really need a database management program. It is true that Excel has a number of database *features*. It is also true that you can use these features to manage a Print Merge mailing list, to control your inventory, or to do a statistical analysis of complex opinion surveys. But *should* you?

Most worksheet programs, including Excel, have limits that can frustrate database users. For instance, you can only have 16,383 records in an Excel database. If you keep 16,384 people in your mailing list, you'll have a problem (albeit not an insurmountable one).

You can have a *maximum* of 256 *characters* in any one field. So, if you want to collect quotations from famous people in an Excel database, they'd better not be quotes from long-winded speakers. (This paragraph contains *294* characters, for example, so it wouldn't fit in an Excel database field.)

Excel limits you to three sort levels at any one time, so, if you want to sort a list of employees by division, department, last name, and then first name, you will need to take extra (and sometimes confusing) steps.

The biggest concern about using spreadsheets as databases has to do with how easily the *integrity* of your data can be corrupted. For instance, in a worksheet, it is *far too easy* to sort a list of employees and their salaries only to find that you've given each worker someone else's earnings! You'll see an example of this later in the chapter. It's also pretty easy to think you've added records to an Excel database when you haven't.

Nonetheless, there *are* times when Excel's database features can be life savers. You can use them to extract interesting reports from budgets and other "legitimate" spreadsheet data. The moral of this sermon is: before you spend hours entering a mailing list into a worksheet, consider whether you wouldn't be better off with a real database program. But if you have a large budget or other worksheet, Excel's database features can sometimes help you find and manage that information.

DATABASE CONCEPTS AND TERMS

You'll need to know several database terms to make sense of this chapter. Even if you've used "real" database programs before, it's worth browsing the next few topics, since Excel adds a few new wrinkles to "databasics."

DATABASE RANGE

Since your database can be a small *part* of a larger worksheet, Excel assumes nothing about which data in your worksheet are part of the database. You must *define* the *database range*. Figure 35.1 shows a small database range. Notice that it does *not* start in cell A1, and notice that a blank row is included in the database range (row 10).

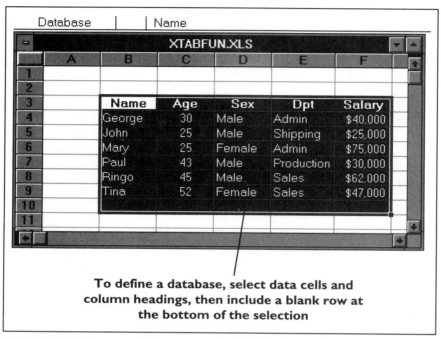

To define a database, select data cells and
column headings, then include a blank row at
the bottom of the selection

FIGURE 35.1 *You must define a range of cells before using their contents with
Excel's database features.*

You define a database by selecting a range of contiguous cells and using
the *Set Database* command found on Excel's Data menu. You can first enter
data, then define the data range—or you can define a range, then enter data.

The selected range is automatically named **Database**. It is possible to create multiple database ranges on the same worksheet, but you must initially
give them *different* names, then may need to *rename* them **Database** each
time you use them. Use the Define Name... command on Excel's Formula
menu to name or rename database ranges.

RECORDS AND FIELDS

Excel treats the contents of each *row* of a database range as a *record*. In Figure 35.1, row 4 is George's record, row 5 is John's record, and so on. The first
row of any database range (row 3 in Figure 35.1) must always contains
column labels, which Excel will use as *database field names*. Field names can

contain spaces. The name **Annual Salary** would be permitted, for instance.

Microsoft calls each column in a database a *field*, and individual cells in a database are also referred to as *fields*. You can enter text, numbers, dates, functions, and formulas in cells. When a field contains a function or formula, it is referred to as a *computed field*. For instance, if you had a **Quantity Ordered** field and a **Unit Price** field, you could create a **Total Cost** field containing a formula that computes total cost based on the other two fields.

CREATING AN EXCEL DATABASE

When creating a database, set up a separate field (column) for any item you'll want to refer to separately. For instance, if you want to sort on *first* and *last* names separately, create a field for each. This is particularly important to remember if you plan to sort on, or search for, things like ZIP codes.

Set column widths right at the start, or go back later after you've entered the data to change widths by dragging or by using Column Width… features (Best Fit, for instance).

ENTERING DATA

You can enter, edit, and format the data in a database just as you would any other Excel cell contents, or you can use Excel's Data Form feature, which is described later. Regardless of which method you use, there are some cautions worth mentioning.

Excel does *not* let you specify "field types," so it's possible to enter either a number or text or a date into *any* field. This can cause problems when entering *numbers* that you plan to display and sort as *text*. For instance, some ZIP codes start with zero. If you want to *see* those "leading" zeros, you'll need to enter ZIP codes as *text*, not numbers, since Excel strips off leading zeros in numeric entries. (You enter numbers as text by first typing an apostrophe.) If you want ZIP codes to sort the way you normally expect to see them, you'll *always* need to enter *each* ZIP code as *text*. Unlike fancier database products, Excel will *not* challenge you if you mix text, numeric, and date entries. Usually, you can see if there is a problem by looking at the appearance of the entries. For instance, unless you format them otherwise, text entries in cells will be left-justified, and general numeric entries will be right-justified within their cells.

ADDING RECORDS TO A DATABASE

Normally, you'll add new records beneath the last record in your database. You can either do this the way you add regular worksheet data (by activating cells in the next empty row and typing), or you can use a database *Form* that "prompts" you for data entries and automatically places new records beneath your last record.

It is also possible to make space for records in the middle of your data range (insert empty rows), then make *mid-database* entries. There are advantages and disadvantages to each of these approaches. To weigh their pros and cons, you must understand what Excel does when new data won't fit in the data range you've defined. Read on.

KEEPING DATA WITHIN THE DATABASE RANGE

Since each added record requires its own row within the defined data range, a worksheet can get quite long. For instance, if you have 1000 records, you'll use 1001 rows (for 1000 records plus their field names). If you know in advance that you'll have a specific or maximum number of records, you can define a data range big enough to accommodate all present and future entries. Do that, whenever possible.

But what if you can't predict the maximum number of records, and eventually you outgrow the defined data range? There are two potential problems. First, if you manually add records beneath the end of the defined data range without redefining the range, Excel's database tools will ignore them. For instance, row 10 in Figure 35.1 is the last row in the defined database range. If you just type new records in rows 11 and 12 without redefining the database range, those new records will be ignored when you sort or do other database functions. Whenever you add records this way, you *must* extend the range.

If you use Excel's Data Form feature to add records, it will automatically *extend* the data range for you, if it can—which brings us to the second problem:

If you plan to have anything in rows directly *beneath* the database range, you will be inconvenienced when you have more data than will fit in the previously defined data range. Suppose, for instance, that in Figure 35.1 you've placed a worksheet equation in cell B10. If you used the Data Form to enter a new record, you'd get the message "Cannot extend database," since the Data Form feature will not write over or push down cell contents. (If the equation was in cell A10, however, you *could* continue appending records, since the equation would not be directly beneath the data range.)

In cases where there is insufficient room to easily extend the database, either you can opt to manually *insert* additional records mid-database, pushing everything else down, or you can insert blank lines at the end of the database range to *extend* it. Don't forget to redefine if you do this! Check your worksheet for formulas that no longer work as a result of your pushing things down this way.

You can also add fields to an existing database. For example, if you wanted to add a Last Name field in column A, you could simply type the field name in cell A3, then enter last names in cells A4 through A9. But you'd also need to—all together now—redefine the data range. If you decided to insert a last name field between Name and Age (by selecting column C and using the Edit menu's Insert command), Excel will extend the database range for you. Placing a field at the right end of the database design (a job description in column G, for instance) requires redefining the range.

WORKING WITH DATA FORMS

Data Forms are handy for data entry, record viewing, and searching. A Data Form is automatically created whenever you define or redefine a database. You can bring the form into view with Excel's Form... command on the Data menu. As you can see from Figure 35.2, Data Forms are dialog boxes containing field names, text entry boxes, and buttons.

Unfortunately, it is possible to design databases with so many fields that they won't all be visible on your form. You *cannot* scroll to overcome this. And, if you place multiple line entries in fields by using the old Ctrl-Enter trick, you'll only see the first line of those entries in your form.

The width of the text areas in a Data Form (and the width of the dialog box itself) is based on the widest field (column) in your database. Thus, if you have an 80-character-wide field in your database, you'll see a pretty big Data Form.

Use the scroll arrows to view different records. Enter and edit text in the Data Form's text boxes as you'd expect. You can use the Tab key to move from text box to box (and to the buttons) in your Data Form. Shift-Tab moves you backwards.

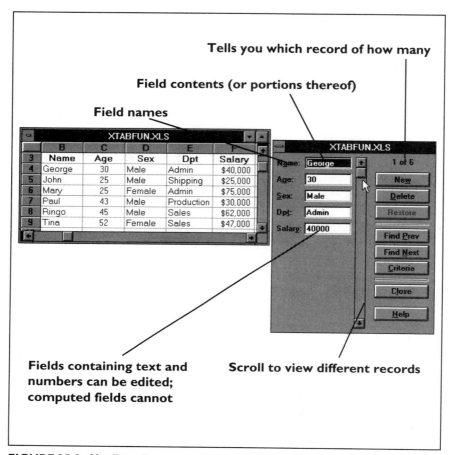

FIGURE 35.2 *Use Data Forms to enter new records, delete unwanted records, or round up records containing data meeting your criteria.*

ADDING AND EDITING RECORDS WITH THE DATA FORM

To add a new record with the Data Form, click the New button, or scroll to the last record, which should be empty. Type as usual, making sure you put the right data in the right fields. Feel free to leave fields empty.

To edit records using the data form, scroll to (or otherwise locate) the record of interest and edit in the text boxes using standard Windows techniques (select and change). Computed fields *can't* be edited. You cannot *format* text in a

Data Form (the Bold and Italic Toolbar buttons won't work here, for instance). Instead, format text in the worksheet itself.

Changes and additions made in the Data Form aren't reflected in the database until you move to a different record or close the Data Form. *Caution*: Even when changes have been made in the database, they reside only in your computer's *RAM* until you *save* the worksheet. Save early and often to avoid datusinterrruptus.

DELETING RECORDS WITH THE DATA FORM

To delete a record with the Data Form, bring the record into view and click the Data Form's Delete key. You will be asked to confirm the deletion. You *cannot* Undo deletions performed from the Data Form. (If, instead, you delete directly in the database using Excel's Edit menu, then act immediately, you can Undo those deletes.)

The major advantage of using the Data Form for deletion is that you can ask to see only records meeting specific criteria. For instance, if you wanted to delete all records for employees earning less than $25,000, you could do that using the techniques described in a moment. Unfortunately, the Data Form doesn't have any way to delete groups of records. After you've rounded them up and inspected them, you'll need to delete them one at a time. To some, this is protection; to others, it's a bore.

SEARCH CRITERIA

You can use the Data Form to create and then scroll through collections of records that meet specific criteria (all females earning more than $50,000, for instance). Start by choosing the Criteria button in the Data Form. You'll see a dialog box like the one in Figure 35.3.

In this example, Excel will gather up just female employees who earn in excess of $50,000. Dollar signs and commas are ignored. If none of your records meet the criteria, frequently some other record in your database that does *not* meet the criteria will be displayed.

This Data Form search feature can locate character strings (text), or records that fall within ranges of numbers or dates.

The comparison operators are = (Equal to), > (Greater than), < (Less than), >= (Greater than or equal to), <= (Less than or equal to), and <> (Not equal to). When you use an equal sign with nothing after it as the single

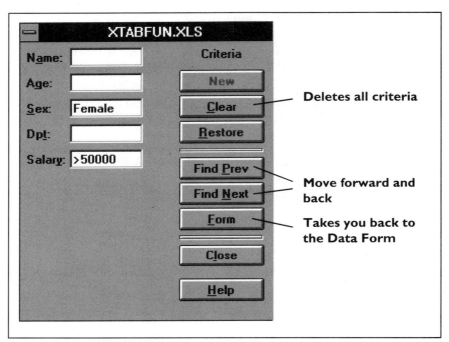

FIGURE 35.3 *Specify search criteria to see a filtered list of records.*

search criterion, only records with blank entries will appear.

These comparisons only work with numbers and dates, not with text. Thus, a search for ZIP codes entered as text like >80000 or >"80000" won't work...

You can use asterisks (*) and question marks (?) as wild cards. For instance, **Sm?th** finds Smith and Smyth (and smithereens). The search criterion **Jo*** will find John and Job and joke, but then so will the string jo, since Excel adds an invisible asterisk to the end of your search criteria. The criterion *****mary** will find Mary and Queen Mary, while the criterion * **mary** (note the space) will only find Queen Mary, and not Mary as the first name in a field. To find an exact text match like **John**, precede the search string with an equal sign. By now you will have deduced that search criteria searches are *not* case sensitive. The search criterion **=John** will also find *john*.

CREATING CUSTOM DATA FORMS

It is possible to create *custom* data forms that display just a few of your fields (this comes in handy when you have too many fields). The process of designing a custom Data Form is rather involved, so we'll leave it to the bigger books, including Chapter 9 of *Excel User's Guide 1*.

SORTING EXCEL DATABASES

Well, gluttons, if you are still reading about Excel databases, it's time to turn to sorting. Figure 35.4 shows a typical before-and-after, along with the instructions for a simple sort.

Start by selecting *each* field for *every* record you want to sort, but do *not* select the field names. Don't select blank rows unless you want to sort them too. If you leave columns out when you select prior to sorting, they will not

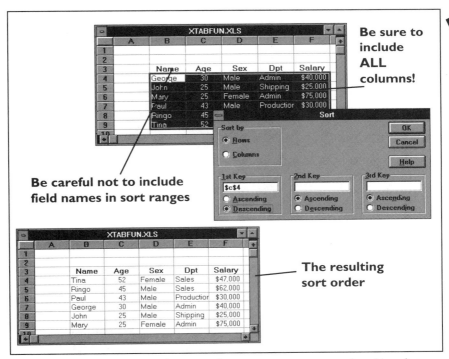

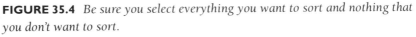

FIGURE 35.4 *Be sure you select everything you want to sort and nothing that you don't want to sort.*

be rearranged. So, if you selected everything except column F in Figure 35.4, most of your employees would end up with someone else's salary after the sort, and you could have a riot on your hands. This kind of error is very easy to make if you have wide worksheets with fields that you can't see. Out of sight, out of mind, as they say…

With your records correctly selected, you can either visit the Sort… command on the Data menu or use the two sorting buttons on the Utility Toolbar. Let's look at the Data menu's Sort… command first.

In the example shown in Figure 35.4, the data will be sorted in descending order, based on employees' ages, resulting in the oldest person being first in the database and the youngest at the end, as shown in the bottom part of the illustration. The data are being sorted by row, and the field names have purposely not been sorted. Keys can be any cell address in the row you wish to use.

You could just as easily sort the list by department, using cell E4 as the first key (in the 1st Key box). But suppose you had a bigger database and wanted to sort it by department to see staffers listed alphabetically *within* their departments. You could do this in one pass by using *two* sort keys. You would make *Dpt* the first sort key and *Name* the second sort key (2nd Key).

In a still more complex database, if you have several people with the *same names* in the *same department*, you could use their age or sex as the tie breaker by specifying one of those criteria as the third sort key (3rd Key).

Incidentally, you can choose to sort by column instead of row, which is one way to rearrange the order in which fields appear in your database. If you rearrange a database this way, you'll want to include the field names in the selection so that the names move with the data.

For simple single-level sorts, you can use the two sort buttons on the Utility Toolbar. They have the letters A and Z in them along with arrows, denoting ascending and descending sorts. The buttons use the field (column) containing the active cell as the sort key.

Excel ignores capitalization when sorting text. Numbers entered as numbers sort before numbers entered as text. International versions of Excel may use slightly different sort orders. Experiment or refer to the big books for details.

To learn more about databases without entering lots of your own data, experiment with the Sales Tracking sample database that Microsoft was kind enough to provide in your Excel EXAMPLES subdirectory. The path is C:\EXCEL\EXAMPLES\SALETRAC.XLW.

CROSSTABULATING DATABASES

"How many women do we have in each department? How do salaries break down by sex around here?" If you ask, or are *asked*, questions like these, you may want to check out Excel's Crosstab features. With a minimum of grunting and groaning, you should be able to create crosstabulated tables like Sheet 3 in Figure 35.5 from a database like the one beneath it. Complex crosstabulation can also be performed on budgets and other large documents.

This may not turn out to be your favorite wizard. It can be slow, confusing, and downright finicky. Save your work before using it. This wiz has been known to lock up a computer or two.

After saving your work, select the data you wish to crosstabulate, including field names, then choose Crosstab... from Excel's Data menu. You'll see the first of many dialog boxes. Use the boxes to define the rows and columns that you want to summarize, plus the type of summaries you wish to see. Figure 35.6 shows several typical dialog boxes.

XTABFUN.XLS

	Name	Age	Sex	Dpt	Salary
3					
4	George	30	Male	Admin	$40,000
5	John	25	Male	Shipping	$25,000
6	Mary	25	Female	Admin	$75,000
7	Paul	43	Male	Production	$30,000
8	Ringo	45	Male	Sales	$62,000
9	Tina	52	Female	Sales	$47,000

Sheet3

	A	B	C	D	E	F
1	Count of Sex	Dpt				
2	Sex	Admin	Production	Sales	Shipping	Grand total
3	Female	1	0	1	0	2
4	Male	1	1	1	1	4
5	Grand total	2	1	2	1	6
6						

FIGURE 35.5 *Use the Crosstab ReportWizard to create tables like Sheet 3 from databases.*

EXCEL

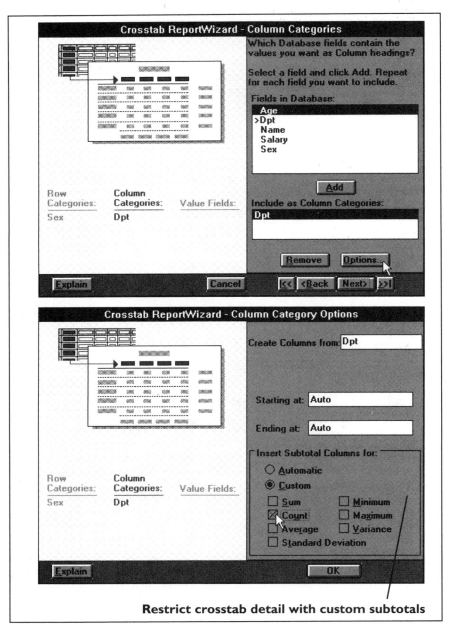

Restrict crosstab detail with custom subtotals

FIGURE 35.6 *The Crosstab ReportWizard asks lots of questions. Use the Explain button to learn more about what it wants to know.*

It is very easy to receive far more detail than you need, so get in the habit of visiting the Options dialog boxes, where you can customize your reports to show just the desired crosstabs. For instance, using the Automatic subtotals in the category Options dialog box in Figure 35.6 will give you more than you'll ever want to know about these people. Specify your own categories.

You will *almost certainly* need to reformat the report generated by the Crosstab ReportWizard. Whenever you change data in your database, you'll need to redo the crosstab report.

The wizard takes its time. Your status bar will give you an idea of what's going on. If nothing changes in the staus area after a prolonged period of time, you may need to restart Excel.

36

Introduction to Automating "What-if" Projects

You know the drill. "What are the effects of changing sales commissions to 3%, 2%, or 4%?" Or "What if mortgage rates fall to 7.25%?" It is questions like these that inspired someone to invent computerized spreadsheets. But the process of preparing them can be pretty tedious, particularly when juggling multiple variables. Excel provides a number of features designed to speed complex "What-ifing." They include the *Scenario Manager*, *What-If add-in macros*, Excel's *Solver*, and related *reporting features*. This chapter introduces you to those tools. Excel's on-line help, sample worksheets shipped with the program, and the bigger books can fill in the details.

GENERAL ORGANIZATIONAL TIPS

When you design worksheets that will be regularly exercised, it is a good idea to organize them logically in a top-down manner. Place introductory text and instructions at the top, followed by the assumptions you'll most likely want to change. Label them clearly. This makes it easy for other people to see and understand your methodology.

If colleagues will be changing or examining your formulas, consider using names (like SALES and COMMISSION) rather than more obscure cell references like B14 or $Q$13.

Protect critical equations so that people don't accidentally overwrite them. Consider breaking complex formulas up into smaller, easier-to-understand parts that display helpful intermediate answers. Test. Test some more. Test again. Dust off that pocket calculator.

SCENARIO MANAGER

Scenarios are named sets of assumptions (inputs) and the resulting computations (results) that you ask a worksheet to compute. For instance, suppose you wanted to explore the impact of interest rates on mortgage payments and total interest paid. You might also want to see the effect of borrowing for 15 rather than 30 years. Scenario Manager can make short work of this, and even create nice summary reports. Figure 36.1 shows you how to start.

DEFINING SCENARIOS

Select or Ctrl-select the cells that you want to be able to change in the scenario. In Figure 36.1 we want to be able to explore changes in interest rates, the number of payments, and the loan amounts, so cells B2 through B4 have been selected. (To select nonadjacent cells, Ctrl-click.)

With the appropriate cells selected, use the Scenario Manager... command on Excel's Formula menu. You'll see a dialog box telling you that no scenarios have been defined yet. Click the Add... button to define some. You'll see an Add Scenario box something like the one in Figure 36.2.

Create as many named scenarios as you want by typing distinct scenario names and different values for one or all of the assumptions in each scenario. Click Add each time you want to save one scenario and start another. When you are done adding scenarios, click OK. You will see a Scenario Manager dialog box like the one in Figure 36.3.

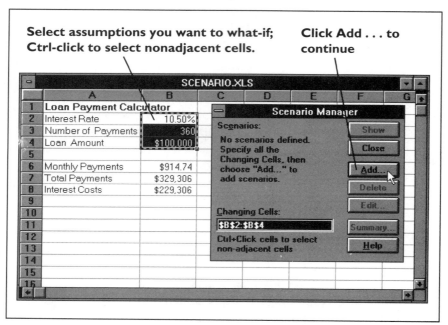

FIGURE 36.1 *Begin a scenario exercise by selecting cells that contain assumptions you want to change.*

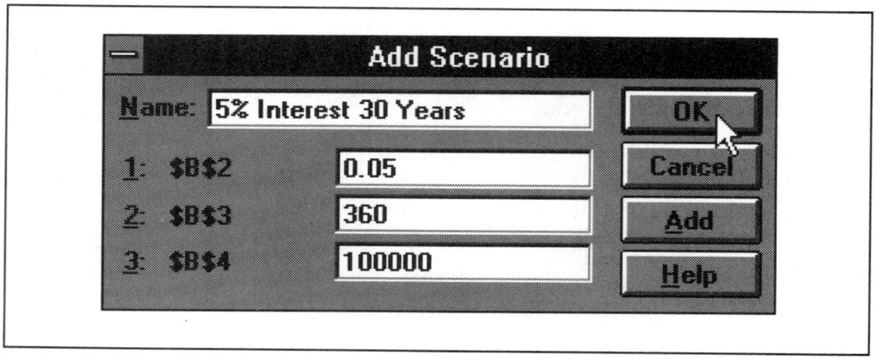

FIGURE 36.2 *Use the Add Scenario dialog box to define multiple scenarios.*

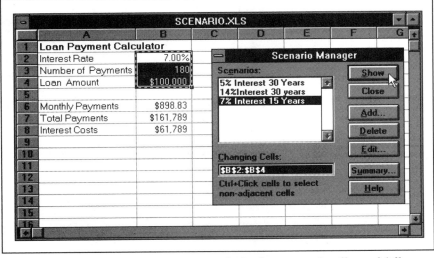

FIGURE 36.3 *Use the Scenario Manager dialog box to see the effects of different scenarios, or to add, edit, and delete scenarios.*

VIEWING SCENARIOS

In Figure 36.3 there are three possible scenarios for cells B2 through B4: 5% Interest 30 Years, 14% Interest 30 Years, and 7% Interest 15 Years. To see the effect of a scenario, select it from the list and click Show. Your worksheet will reflect the chosen assumptions.

OBTAINING SCENARIO SUMMARIES

It is also easy to obtain summary reports that show the assumptions for each scenario and the results of each scenario. Figure 36.4 illustrates two examples of this.

Start by clicking the Summary... button in the Scenario Manager dialog box. Excel asks you to define the changing cells to be displayed. It proposes a range for you. The proposed range usually contains formulas that refer to the changing assumption ($B$8 is proposed in the top of Figure 36.4). You can keep the suggested range or define your own. Click OK when you are satisfied with the results range.

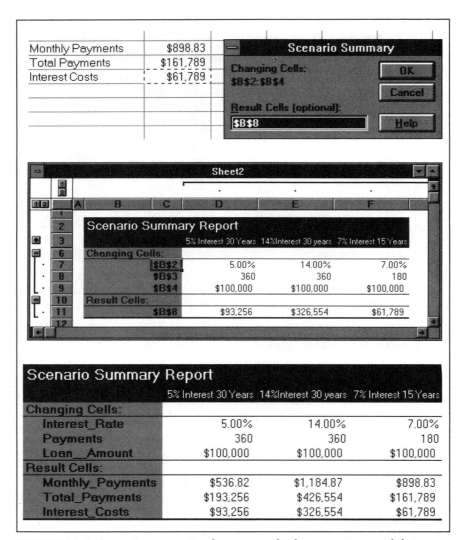

FIGURE 36.4 *Scenario summaries show you multiple assumptions and their results in an easy-to-read report.*

As you can see from the Sheet2 portion of Figure 36.4, Excel then creates and *formats* a report (a separate worksheet, actually), showing the various scenarios and their results. Notice that Scenario Manager labels rows with cell addresses ($B$2, etc.). It makes for pretty obscure reading. You can overcome this by *naming* cells back in your model worksheet. (Use the Define Name... command on Excel's Formula menu to do this.)

Notice, also, that Excel may not propose all of the result cells that you'll want to see. You can overrule the proposed range by entering your own. A revised scenario report at the bottom of Figure 36.4 uses named cells and the Result Cells range of $B$6:$B$8. Pretty slick! It looks like 7% interest over 15 years may be the way to go, if you can afford $898.83 per month.

CHANGING SCENARIOS

Visit the Scenario Manager dialog box to add, delete, or edit scenarios. You cannot undo scenario deletions.

WHAT-IF ADD-IN MACRO

Here's another way to do what-if analysis with many different variables. It employs an add-in macro and requires both a *model worksheet* (like a mortgage calculator, or budget, or whatever) and a *second* worksheet (called a Data Sheet) containing the *values* you want to examine.

The primary benefit to this approach is that you don't need to spell out each possible scenario. If you want to see the effect of 10 different interest rates over both 15 and 30 years, you only need to create a Data Sheet containing 12 values to get 20 results. You can then ask Excel to show you all possible combinations.

First you must load the macro (which adds a What If... command to your Excel Formula menu). The file you need to load is located in the EXCEL\LIBRARY subdirectory and it is called WHATIF.XLA. Load it with Excel's Open... command as illustrated in Figure 36.5. When this add-in macro has been successfully loaded, you'll see a What If... command on Excel's Formula menu.

Open the worksheet containing the formulas you plan to use for the computations (your model). Pick the *What If...* command from Excel's Formula menu to display a dialog box like the one in the top of Figure 36.6.

CREATING A DATA SHEET

To create a new data sheet, click New in the What If dialog box. You will see a *What If Variable* dialog box like the one at the bottom of Figure 36.6.

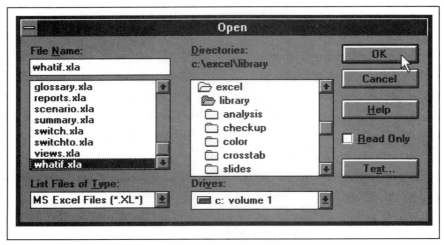

FIGURE 36.5 *Before you can use the What-If add-in macro, you must load it with Excel's Open… command.*

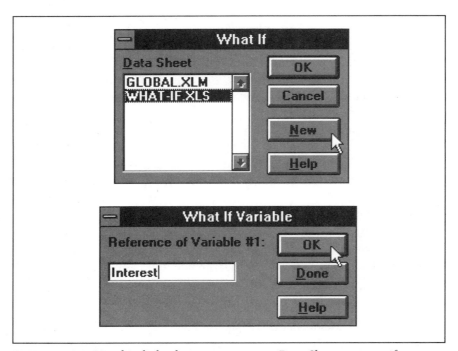

FIGURE 36.6 *Use this dialog box to create a new Data Sheet or to specify an existing one.*

Type a name or cell reference for the first variable. For instance, if your interest variable is in cell B2, you could type **B2** here. If you've named the cell (**Interest**, for example), you could use that name here instead.

When you click OK after typing a Reference name, Excel will ask you for the *values* required to build this part of the Data Sheet. You enter as many values as needed in multiple What If Variable dialog boxes that appear one after the next, until you click Done. For instance, to enter three interest rates, you'd enter the first rate, click OK, see a new dialog box, enter the second rate, click OK, and so on. When you click *Done*, you are asked to enter a different Reference name (number of payments, for instance). When you are "done done," Excel will create a data sheet containing your variables.

You may need to use Excel's Window menu or move things around if you want to view the new Data Sheet. Save it like a regular worksheet if you plan to use the data again. Figure 36.7 shows a very simple example of a Data Sheet and the worksheet it refers to.

SEEING WHAT-IF MACRO RESULTS

To cycle through all of the possible What-If combinations, switch to your model worksheet and use the Ctrl-Shift-T key combination as many times

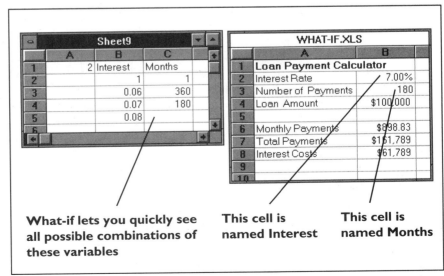

FIGURE 36.7 *The What-If add-in requires a separate data sheet and a worksheet.*

as necessary to see the effects of each combination. To see changes caused by just one variable, activate that cell (the cell containing Rate values, for instance) and cycle with the Ctrl-T key combination.

THE SOLVER

Solver helps you find combinations that reach a goal. For instance, have you ever said, "If interest rates are 7%, and I can afford monthly payments of $1,000 how much can I borrow?" Or you might need to find the most profitable product mix, or examine sales commission scenarios to find the mix that is most profitable. Excel's Solver add-in program can help.

Suppose you know you can spend $1000 per month for 360 months, and you know that interest rates are 7%. Solver will help you determine the maximum loan amount. Figure 36.8 shows an example of this.

Start by constructing and testing your model (a worksheet built around Excel's PMT function in this case). When you know the model works right, save it and choose Solver… from Excel's Formula menu. It's an add-in, so the command may take a moment to load the first time you use it each session.

Soon you'll see a Solver Parameters dialog box like the one in Figure 36.8. Tell Solver which cell you want to solve for (Monthly Payments, or $B$6 in this example). Then define the constraints, or rules to be used. For instance, you know you don't want to spend more than $1000 per month, and you don't want Solver to change the interest rates or number of payments, so you must add constraints for all three of these items. Create each constraint separately by using the Add… button to build constraints like the ones shown in the example. Constraints can refer to cell locations ($B$6, for instance), or to names if you've defined them (like Interest for cell B2).

When you've created all the appropriate constraints, use the Solve button to search for a solution. Eventually the hourglass that pops up will disappear and with luck you will see a Solver dialog box like the one at the bottom of Figure 36.8. If your model worksheet is in view you'll also see a solution.

Solver lets you view your solutions, change the rules, and create reports. You can save solutions for later reuse.

TO LEARN MORE ABOUT SOLVER

This chapter illustrates a very simple Solver example that admittedly could be accomplished other ways. But it illustrates the concepts nicely.

(To see Solver at work on a bigger problem, open the SOLVEREX.XLS worksheet found in your EXCEL\EXAMPLES\SOLVER subdirectory.) Read more about Solver in the *Excel User's Guide 2*.

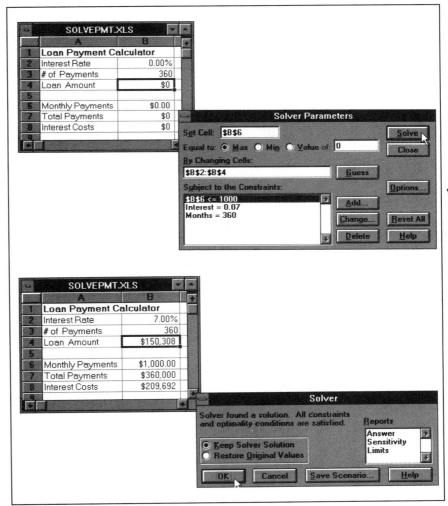

FIGURE 36.8 *An admittedly simple example of Solver at work.*

37

Personalizing Excel

It's easy to adapt Excel to your way of working. For instance, you can place Toolbars all around the outer edges of your screen. You can customize those Toolbars or create new ones of your own. You can even change the way Excel addresses rows and columns. You can turn grid lines on or off, and much more. As with any program that let you change things, keep in mind that this can be disorienting to others who share your computer.

DOCKING TOOLBARS

Perhaps because Microsoft is located so near Seattle's Boeing aircraft facility, you can make your Excel window look like the cockpit of a 767. You do this by placing Toolbars in *docks* around the edges of the window. Figure 37.1 illustrates this trick.

To dock a Toolbar, simply display it, then drag to an outer edge of the Excel window. You'll see the Toolbar's outline shape change when it is ready to be docked. Releasing the mouse button docks the Toolbar. Toolbars with

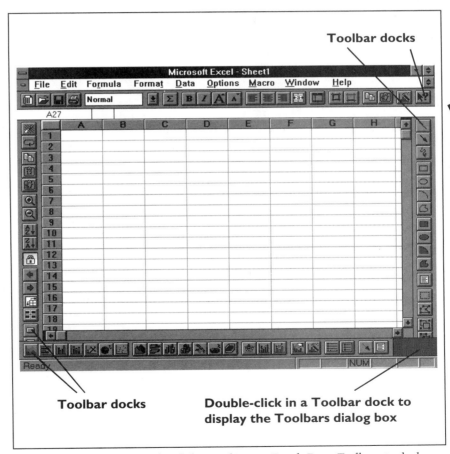

FIGURE 37.1 *The space shuttle has nothing on Excel. Drag Toolbars to docks and they'll be just a click away.*

drop-down lists (like the Format Toolbar) can't be placed on the right or left edges of your screen since the lists won't work there. They can be placed beneath the menu bar or at the bottom of your screen, however.

UNDOCKING TOOLBARS

Double-clicking in a nonbutton area of a docked Toolbar (a space between buttons, for instance) undocks the Toolbar. If necessary, you can then use your worksheet's maximize button to reclaim the now unused real estate.

SAVING TOOLBAR SETTINGS

When you quit (exit) Excel, it saves your most recent Toolbar settings, including the position of any docked Toolbars.

TOOLBAR-DISPLAYING SHORTCUT

There are several quick ways to display the list of available Toolbars without visiting the Toolbars... menu. If you double-click in the background area of a Toolbar dock (like the one in the bottom-right corner of Figure 37.1) you'll see the Toolbars dialog box. Or you can click in the nonbutton portions of any Toolbar with the right (nonprimary) mouse button to accomplish the same thing. Figure 37.2 illustrates this.

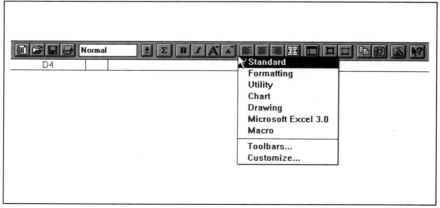

FIGURE 37.2 *Click in the nonbutton areas of any Toolbar with the right (or nonprimary) mouse button to display a Toolbar menu.*

CUSTOMIZING THE TOOLBARS THEMSELVES

It's quite easy to rearrange Toolbars. You can remove buttons you never use, regroup things, and so on. Since there are more than 130 buttons (many of which don't appear on Excel's "official" Toolbars), you may want to create your own custom Toolbars and experiment with them. Here's how.

Begin by displaying the Toolbars dialog box either from the Options menu or from the drop-down menu shown in Figure 37.2. At this point you can change an existing menu or create a new one.

CHANGING A TOOLBAR

To modify a Toolbar, display it first, then click the Customize... button in the Toolbars dialog box to bring up the Customize dialog box shown at the bottom of Figure 37.3.

With this dialog box you can drag tool buttons onto and off of Toolbars. So, if you never use the Save button on the standard Toolbar, but you wish you had a Print Preview button, you can drag the File button off the Toolbar and drag the Print Preview button onto the Toolbar, in the position of your choosing.

To figure out which tool buttons do what, click on them in the Customize window. Read the descriptions that appear in the lower-left corner of the Customize dialog box.

You can drag any tool from any category onto any Toolbar. Deleting a Microsoft-provided tool from a Toolbar doesn't destroy it. You can always revisit the Customize dialog box and drag the tool back.

To reset a Toolbar to its official Microsoft configuration, open the Toolbars dialog box, select the Toolbar name, and click the Reset button.

CREATING A NEW TOOLBAR

To create your own Toolbar, open the Toolbars dialog box (with the Toolbars... command on the Options menu) and type a new Toolbar name in the Toolbar Name text box. Click either Add or Customize... to reach the Customize dialog box. You'll see the beginnings of a tiny new Toolbar on your screen.

Select and drag tools from the Customize dialog box to construct your Toolbar. To space tools tightly, drag buttons partially on top of another. To make wider spaces between tools, don't drag them on top of each other.

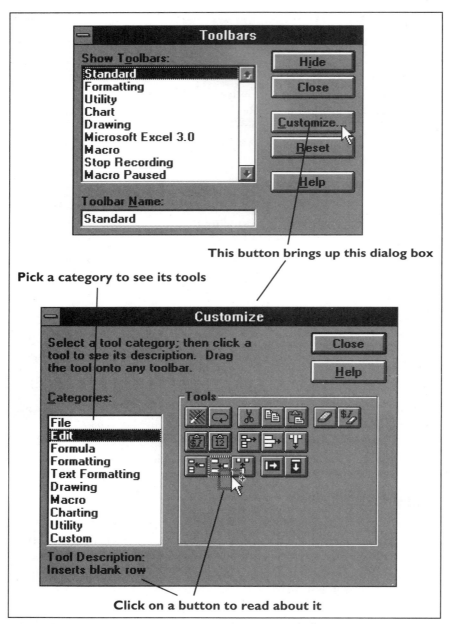

FIGURE 37.3 *Personalize your Toolbars with the Customize dialog box.*

ASSIGNING MACROS TO TOOLBAR BUTTONS

It is possible to create Toolbar buttons that run macros. Start by displaying the Toolbar where you want to add the button. Open the Customize dialog box (with the Customize... button on the Toolbars dialog box). Pick the Custom *category* (shown in the top part of Figure 37.4).

Select a blank button design that will remind you of the function's purpose, and drag that button to the desired Toolbar.

You'll soon see a list of macros in an Assign To Tool dialog box like the one shown in Figure 37.4. Select the desired macro and click OK. Test your new button.

Incidentally, if you don't like any of the button choices provided by Microsoft, you can design your own, or even find them in the public domain. Microsoft's *Excel User's Guide 2* tells you how this is done.

WORKSPACE OPTIONS

Besides changing Toolbars, Excel lets you control many other aspects of your workplace. Many of these changes can be made on the Workspace Options dialog box shown in Figure 37.5.

For instance, have you ever used a calculator that automatically inserts two decimal places—sometimes called an accountant's keypad feature?

FIXED DECIMAL

This is handy for entering dollar amounts or other numbers containing decimals. Placing an X in the Fixed Decimal box and a 2 in the Places area means that when you enter the number **4055** it will be stored as **40.55** (forty dollars and fifty-five cents). The letters FIX appear in the status bar to remind you that you have this feature turned on. You can specify a different number of decimal places with the Places box, if you like. Be sure that this feature is only turned on when you need it. You may find it handy to use in conjunction with your computer's Num Lock feature. If find yourself turning these features on and off a lot, consider creating a macro to do it for you.

ROW AND COLUMN REFERENCES

You can display and work with a different form of row and column numbering (R1C1) if you like. With this option checked, both rows and columns have

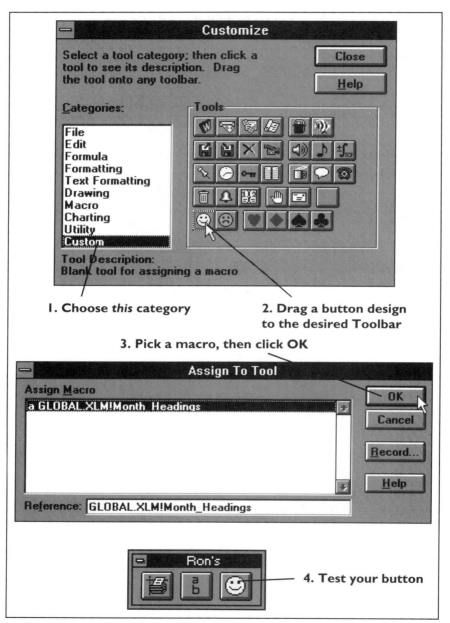

FIGURE 37.4 *It's possible to create Toolbar buttons that run macros.*

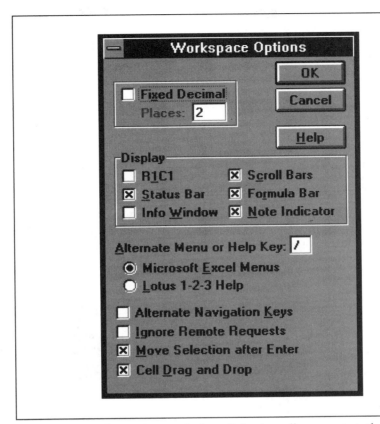

FIGURE 37.5 *The Workspace Options dialog box allows you to tailor certain options to your needs.*

numbers. Cell C2 becomes R2C3. If you've worked with other spreadsheet programs that display references this way, you may prefer it. Excel will renumber worksheets and formulas as necessary whenever you toggle this option.

OTHER DISPLAY OPTIONS

Other display options in the Workspace Options dialog box control the display of the status bar, scroll bars, and other on-screen items. Their names and functions should be self-explanatory.

LOTUS-LIKE OPTIONS

You can switch the key commands used for navigation and on-line help so that they closely mimic those of Lotus 1-2-3. You can also enable help for Lotus users in the Workspace Options dialog box.

DISPLAY OPTIONS

Figure 37.6 shows the dialog box reached with Excel's Display... command on the Options menu. Use it to display or hide grid lines, headings, and other items.

You can also use this dialog box to display all of the formulas in your worksheet to help you troubleshoot. Speaking of which, troubleshooting is the topic of the next chapter.

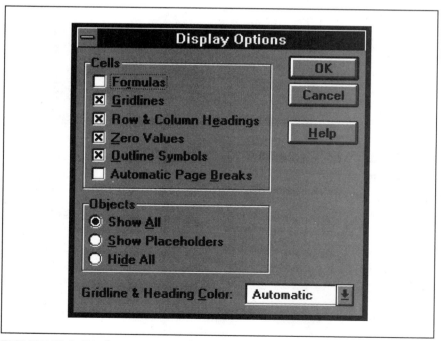

FIGURE 37.6 *Display options can be used to make more room on your screen.*

38

Auditing and Troubleshooting Worksheets

Nothing is more embarrassing than handing someone an important worksheet page containing an error or omission. Blunders can be expensive, both financially and career-wise. Mistakes are inevitable, particularly on large worksheets or in projects where one worksheet refers to another. Excel will help you catch some errors, while others can lurk undetected for years. Make it a habit to test new worksheets using real data. Do the numbers look *reasonable* under a wide range of conditions? If you have time, set the work aside for a day or two and revisit it when you are fresh. Ask a knowledgeable associate to inspect and test your worksheet. Sometimes we get so close to a project that we overlook obvious problems.

Incidentally, just because a worksheet is operating properly on the day you create it does not mean it always will. It's very easy, for instance, to accidentally replace a formula with a value. This is particularly common when you share worksheet files with people who didn't create and don't fully understand them. That's why it is an especially good idea to protect your worksheets—and your formulas in particular—using the techniques described earlier in this book.

Excel provides a number of tools designed to help you locate and stamp out errors whenever they crop up. The tools include *Error values*, the *Info window*, and an add-in called *Worksheet Auditor Macro*.

ERROR VALUES

Occasionally you will see the following error values in cells. They always start with the pound sign (#):

#DIV/0!

#N/A

#NAME?

#NULL!

#NUM!

#REF!

#VALUE!

These values appear both in cells *containing* erroneous formulas, and in cells with formulas that *refer* to the erroneous formulas. Thus, you may need to inspect more than one cell to find the real source of the problem. Sometimes you'll see error values like these when you are creating a worksheet. Although they should never be *completely* ignored, once in a while you will see them simply because you are not finished creating the worksheet. For instance, if you create a formula that performs division using the contents of a cell as the divisor, and if that referenced cell is empty because you haven't entered a value into it yet, you'll see Excel's #DIV/0! value. The error value should disappear when you place an appropriate divisor in the referenced cell.

Let's look at each of the error values and consider what they mean and what to do when you see them.

#DIV/0!

You'll see this error when Excel tries to divide by *zero*, or if a referenced cell is *blank* when it needs to contain a divisor. Some Excel functions return the value of zero under certain circumstances. If your division formula looks to a cell containing a function for a divisor, then the function itself, or one of its arguments, may be causing the problem. Fix the formula if it is referring to the wrong cell, or fix the cell being referenced or the erroneous function or argument.

#N/A

N/A stands for "No Value Is Available." Under certain circumstances, Excel inserts this error value in cells (when you've improperly used certain function arguments, for instance). Other times, *you* may want to type #N/A into cells yourself as a reminder that you need to obtain and enter missing data. Suppose, for instance, that you were creating a worksheet that computes sales commissions for many salespeople and that the commission percentages were still being negotiated for some of them. You could enter #N/A as the commission percentages for the "problem" reps. Then, any formulas that rely upon those missing percentages will display #N/A. The #N/A will "ripple through" the rest of your worksheet and be seen in any cell that can't be computed properly without the missing data (totals and subtotals of sales commissions, for example).

#NAME?

The #NAME? error message usually appears because you've referred to a *named item* improperly. For instance, if you define a cell name **Sales** and create a formula like **=SQRT(Sails)** you'll get the #NAME? error message. (Unless, of course, you also have an item named Sails in your worksheet, in which case Excel will attempt to find the square root of *it*.)

If you name an item, then delete or change its name, you will also get the #NAME? message. Solution: Either rename the item or fix the affected formulas.

You might also see #NAME? if you enter a *function's* name improperly. For instance, the formula =SQR(9) instead of =SQRT(9) will produce a name error.

Forgetting to place a colon between cell addresses in a cell range will make Excel think you are referring to a name rather than a range. For example, =SUM(B1B3) will make Excel think you meant an item named *B1B3* instead of the range *B1:B3*.

#NULL!

The #NULL! message means that you've specified the intersection of two areas that don't intersect, usually in a range specifier. For example, the formula **sum(A1:D1 A3:D3)** produces a null error. Use a comma to separate referenced areas that don't intersect. For instance, **SUM(A1:D1,A3:D3)** is permitted.

#NUM!

You will see the #NUM! error value for several reasons. Unacceptable numeric arguments in functions will produce the error. For instance, trying to find the square root of negative numbers will produce the #NUM! error value.

When worksheet functions that use iterations to solve problems can't reach a workable result, you will also see the #NUM! error value.

#REF!

The #REF! message is commonly seen after you delete something to which other formulas refer. For instance, if you delete rows or columns containing things that remaining formulas need, you'll see the #REF! value in all affected formulas. Either use Undo to restore the deleted items or fix the formulas.

#VALUE!

You'll get a value reminder whenever you use the wrong type of argument, value, or operand. For instance, if you have a cell named **Sales** and you type the formula ="**Sales**"*2, Excel will see the quotation marks and treat sales as text rather than a name.

Sometimes, however, Excel will convert text automatically. For instance, if you make the cell entry '**10.5** (notice the leading apostrophe) in cell A1, the entry will be formatted and entered as text. You can tell this because it will be left-justified. If you then type the formula =**A1/2** in another cell, Excel will continue to display and treat cell A1 as text, but will convert it to a number for purposes of the formula. Thus, the formula will return the answer **5.25**.

CIRCULAR REFERENCES

It is not uncommon to see a dialog box warning that Excel "Cannot resolve *circular references*." That's not completely true. Excel *can* resolve circular references; you just need to use iteration to do it. First, here's a review of what a circular reference is. Take a look at Figure 38.1.

A circular reference is a bit like telling a young actor you'll give her a role in your play if she has experience, but she can't gain experience till she gets her first role.

In worksheet terms, suppose you wanted to pay sales commissions based on company profitability, and wished to include commissions as one of the expenses affecting profit. You might create a profit formula in cell B3 that subtracted the contents of both cells B2 and B4 from the gross sales cell (B1). This would result in a circular reference, since profit will change when sales commissions change. Since commissions change with profit changes, commissions will need to be changed again, and so on. The first time you create a formula like this, and each time you load (open) a worksheet containing such a circular reference, you will see a warning like the one in Figure 38.1.

There are several ways to work around circular reference problems. One way is to redesign the worksheet (and perhaps your commission policy) so

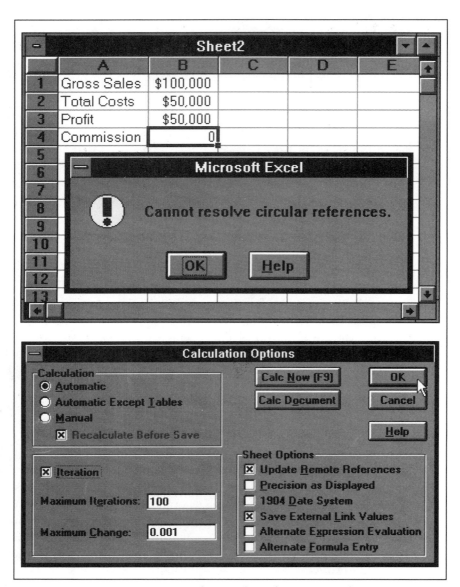

FIGURE 38.1 *Use iteration to resolve circular references, or redesign your worksheet.*

that there is a precommission profit line, then a commission line, then an actual profit line that takes commissions into consideration.

Another approach is to use *iteration* to resolve the circular reference. Start by selecting the cell containing the circular formula (B4 in our example).

Choose Calculation... from the Options menu. You'll see the dialog box illustrated in the bottom of Figure 38.1. Choose the Iteration check box and specify the Maximum Iterations and the Maximum Change options, if you don't like the values shown.

You can see the results without closing the Calculation Options dialog box by using the Calc Now button or the F9 function key. Clicking OK will also run the iteration routine and display an answer in the affected cell(s).

USING THE INFO WINDOW TO FIND ERRORS

The Info window gives you another useful troubleshooting tool. It can tell you a lot about the active cell. Figure 38.2 shows it at work.

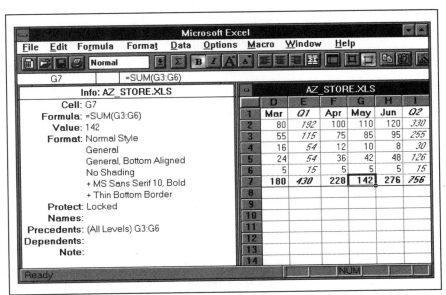

FIGURE 38.2 *Use the Info window to learn about the active cell.*

Activate the cell of interest. Choose Workspace… from the Options menu, and choose the Info Window option. You'll see a window like the one in Figure 38.2, except that it will only display Cell, Formula, and Note information at first. Use the Info choices on the menu bar to add other items of interest (Value, Format, and so forth). Most of the displayed items are self-explanatory. "Cell" is the cell reference of the active cell, for instance. "Formula" is the formula, and so on.

"Precedents" lists all the cells referred to by the formula in the active cell. "Dependents" lists all other cells containing formulas that rely upon the contents of the active cell. This is particularly useful information when working with multiple worksheets that are consolidated.

To print information about a range of cells, select all cells of interest, open the Info window, specify the details needed (with the Info menu), then choose Print from the File menu.

Incidentally, did you notice the error in the formula in Figure 38.2? The SUM range is incorrect.

THE WORKSHEET AUDITOR MACRO

Errors can be particularly elusive in large worksheets. As it happens, there is a huge error in cell F8 of the worksheet in Figure 38.3, but you can't see the error value since it is *hidden* in this outline view and doesn't directly affect any visible cells. Get in the habit of expanding outlined worksheets when examining

	A	B	C	D	E	F	G
1		Jan	Feb	Mar	*Q1*	Apr	May
5	Compact Disks	220	152	240	*612*	100	110
9	Cassettes	105	115	165	*385*	75	85
13	Records	60	54	48	*162*	12	10
17	Blank Tape	36	54	72	*162*	36	42
18	Other	5	5	5	*15*	5	5
19		627	603	815	*1336*	128	252

FIGURE 38.3 *Errors are difficult to spot in big projects, particularly if you've outlined your worksheet and don't display all the details.*

them. You can also use tools like Excel's Auditor Macro to assist you.

The Auditor is an add-in macro named AUDIT.XLA, which can be found in Excel's Library subdirectory. (The path is EXCEL\LIBRARY\AUDIT.XLA.) Use Excel's Open… command to load the macro.

The Auditor macro adds a new choice to Excel's Formula menu—Worksheet Auditor… When you pick this new choice, you'll see a dialog box like the one at the top of Figure 38.4.

To generate an audit report, choose the option of the same name from the Worksheet Auditor dialog box shown in Figure 38.4. Check the boxes in the resulting dialog box to select the desired report elements (Errors, References to blanks, References to text, Circular references, and Names).

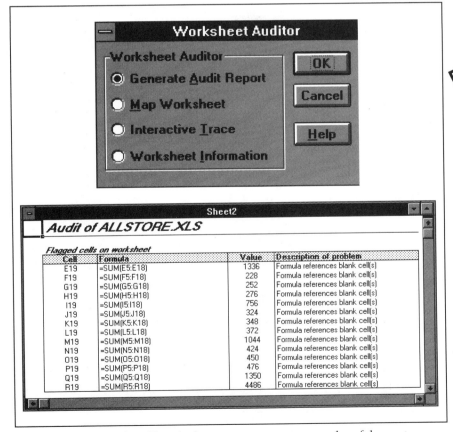

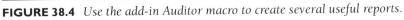

FIGURE 38.4 *Use the add-in Auditor macro to create several useful reports.*

In a moment, you'll see a new window containing information about your worksheet. You can simply review it on-screen, print it, or save it for future reference as you would any other Excel document.

The bottom part of Figure 38.4 shows a list of cells that refer to blanks, in this case indicating that additional values need to be entered.

The Map Worksheet produced by Excel's Auditor macro is a great way to get a bird's-eye view of a troubled worksheet. Remember that problem formula hidden in Figure 38.3? A map makes it easy to spot. Check out cell G8 in the map shown in Figure 38.5.

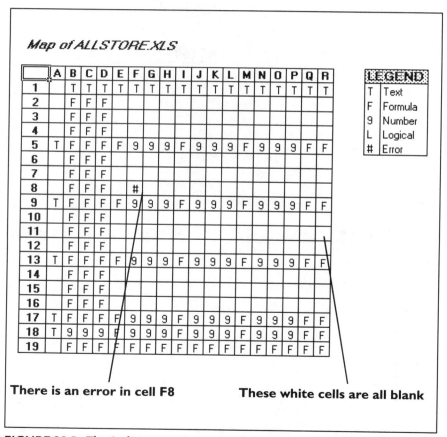

FIGURE 38.5 *The Auditor macro's Map Worksheet feature gives you a bird's-eye view of large worksheets.*

Excel's Interactive Trace option (also provided by the Auditor macro) opens two windows on your screen—the worksheet itself, and a control panel like the one shown in Figure 38.6.

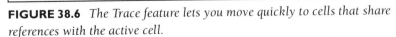

FIGURE 38.6 *The Trace feature lets you move quickly to cells that share references with the active cell.*

Use the Trace controls to visit cells that refer to or are referred to by the active cell. This is a good way to find the real culprit when you get one of those annoying error messages that seem to wind through your entire document. This is also a good way to understand someone else's worksheets. Pick a cell containing results you wish to understand, then retrace the steps to see how the results were created.

Finally, the Worksheet Information choice on the Worksheet Auditor dialog box provides a summary report like the one shown in Figure 38.7. It tells you about the worksheet and points to other worksheets that are related to it.

Worksheet Info

Document Info

Name	ALLSTORE.XLS
	Changes made since last save
Path	C:\SYBEX\EXAMPLES
Protection	None
Version	Microsoft Excel version 4.0
System	Windows 3.10

Worksheet Info

Active Area	19 rows by 18 columns
	342 cells
Blanks	181 (52.9%)
Constants	70 (20.5%)
Numbers	48 (14.0%)
Text	22 (6.4%)
Logicals	0 (0.0%)
Errors	0 (0.0%)
Formulas	91 (26.6%)
Names	0 total
	0 normal
	0 hidden

Precedent Sheets Info

Number	1
Names	C:\SYBEX\EXAMPLES\AZ_STORE.XLS

FIGURE 38.7 *Summary reports can be created via the Worksheet Auditor dialog box.*

PART FOUR

SHARING
Information

39

The Clipboard
and Clipboard Viewer

You've probably used the Clipboard already to move things from place to place *within* a Word or Excel document. You can also use it to move things *between* different programs. This is a particularly convenient way to work if your computer supports 386 Enhanced mode and lets you run and quickly switch between multiple programs without quitting and reloading them. For instance, if you use the Windows Calculator accessory, you can copy the results of your calculations to the Clipboard, switch to Word or Excel, and paste the calculation results into a Word paragraph or an Excel cell. It is also possible to move things to and from *non-Windows* programs via the Clipboard. You can copy an entire screen's contents or just selected portions.

Since many programs use unique control codes, characters, and graphics formats, the results of pasting can be a little unpredictable at times. Windows, and all Windows-savvy applications do a pretty good job of minimizing these often perplexing differences, but the farther you get away from civilization, the more likely you are to have problems. For instance, when pasting from a non-Windows program into Windows, you may need to experiment, and possibly do some manual reformatting to obtain the desired results.

CONSIDER ALTERNATIVES TO THE CLIPBOARD

Before exploring basic Clipboard copying and pasting between programs in this chapter, it's worth reminding you that there are other ways to move data from one application into another. For instance, to turn an entire Word-Perfect or Lotus 1-2-3 document into a Word or Excel document, you are usually better off with Word's and Excel's ability to open and convert these non-Microsoft files *directly* rather than copying and pasting between the two different programs. And some programs offer ways to export and import data without using the Clipboard at all. For instance, many database and word processing programs import and export ASCII files.

Then there is Word's Import Picture... command, which will open, convert, and import graphic files even if you don't have the program that created them. Specialized importing and exporting features like these can sometimes be a quicker, more accurate way to move information from place to place.

Finally, Chapters 40 and 41 describe techniques that are better than a simple Clipboard cut-and-paste when dealing with information that you want to update continually and keep current in multiple files. But for simple, occasional movement of text and graphics, you can't beat the plain old Clipboard.

USING THE CLIPBOARD
WITH TWO WINDOWS APPLICATIONS

As you probably already know, you place things on the Clipboard by first selecting them, then either copying or cutting the selected items to the Clipboard. Remember that the Clipboard is a *temporary* storage area and that its contents are *replaced* each time you copy or cut something new. There is only *one* Clipboard in Windows, even if you are running multiple programs in 386 Enhanced mode. Thus, if you are using Word and copy something (say, a paragraph), then switch to Excel and copy something else (like a formula), when you switch back to Word, your Clipboard will contain the formula and *not* the paragraph. The paragraph will be in paragraph heaven. Even Undo usually won't help.

Clipboard contents also *disappear* whenever you quit Windows or turn off your computer. (Clipboard contents can be *saved to disk*, however. The process is discussed later in this chapter.)

COPYING AND PASTING PORTIONS OF A WINDOW

The act of *copying* is identical in all well-designed Windows applications, including Word and Excel. You can select text, graphics, other objects, or combinations thereof. Start by selecting whatever it is that you want to copy or cut, then choose *Copy* or *Cut* from the application's Edit menu. (The keyboard shortcuts for copying and cutting are Ctrl-C and Crtl-X, respectively.) As you'll recall, the Copy command leaves the original item(s) intact, while Cut removes the selected item(s) from the document. An *immediate* Undo will *usually* restore items you've accidentally cut.

Pasting inserts the contents of the Clipboard at the insertion point. Obviously, if you are cutting or copying from one program (let's call it the *source* program) and pasting into another (the *destination*), you'll need to have both programs running (or at least available) and then switch from the source to the destination program before pasting. In Windows 386 Enhanced mode this can be as easy as repeatedly pressing the Alt-Tab key combination until you see the name of the program you want to use. You can also arrange your screen so that you can see both programs' windows, then point to the one of interest.

When running in Standard mode, however, you'll need to quit the source program and load the destination program. Ah, progress…

What happens when you *paste* depends upon a number of factors. First of all, not every application program can accept everything you can place on your Clipboard. If you tried to paste a graphic in a Windows program that could not accept graphics, for instance, you will fail.

More typically, you'll want to paste things into applications that use different formats and formatting commands. Sometimes Windows and the programs you are using can work around these differences; other times they can't. Occasionally, the results are even better than you'd expect.

For instance, when you copy a range of Excel worksheet cells into a Word document, Word will automatically create a table of the appropriate size to accommodate the contents of the pasted cells. Figure 39.1 illustrates this.

Other times, the results can be downright mysterious. For example, pasted items can look bizarre because they don't fit the destination document's margins or styles. Occasionally, pasted items look fine when you view them on-screen, then have line- and page-ending problems when you print them. This usually happens because of differences in screen and

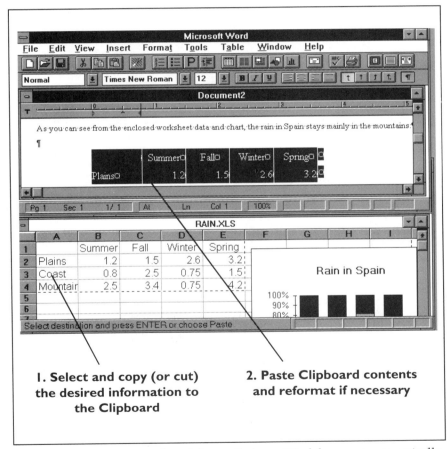

1. Select and copy (or cut) the desired information to the Clipboard

2. Paste Clipboard contents and reformat if necessary

FIGURE 39.1 *Pasting Excel worksheet cells into a Word document automatically creates a Word table.*

SHARING INFORMATION

printer fonts. Check your work after pasting and, as always, save your work before making major alterations with Paste commands.

THE PASTE SPECIAL COMMAND

While the regular Paste command is often all you'll need, sometimes the Paste Special command proves useful. When you copy or cut things to the Clipboard, the *source* program often sends the information to the Clipboard in more than one format. When you use the regular Paste command, the *destination* application pastes the Clipboard contents using *its* default format, which is often, but not always, the best one.

The Paste Special… command will provide you with a dialog box containing an ever-changing list of data types. For instance, when the Clipboard contains a bitmapped graphic, you might see choices like *Picture* and *Microsoft Drawing Object*. If the Clipboard contains text, you're liable to see choices like *Microsoft Word Object, Formatted Text, Unformatted Text*, and so on.

Choosing one of these different formats changes the way the item is pasted, thereby converting the Clipboard contents when you paste. Pick the desired format from the list, then click Paste to place a converted copy of the item at the insertion point. (The *Paste Link* options that sometimes appear are discussed in the next chapter.)

COPYING AND PASTING
AN ENTIRE SCREEN OR WINDOW

When your applications support this feature, you can copy either the entire contents of your screen, or just the contents of the active window, to the Clipboard as a bitmapped graphic. This is a cheap-and-dirty way to create illustrations for programming documentation. While they lack much of the sophistication of true screen-capture programs, you may find these tricks useful.

Start by making sure that the screen contains exactly what you wish to capture. Press the print screen key (PrtSc) on your keyboard (or perhaps Alt-PrtSc or Shift-PrtSc on some keyboards). This should capture the entire screen. Try either Shift-PrtSc or Alt-PrtSc to capture just the active window rather than the entire screen. Some keyboard types require Shift or Alt combinations since they don't recognize plain PrtSc or Alt-PrtSc combinations.

To see what works, use the Clipboard Viewer accessory program, described next.

Once you've placed a bitmapped image on your Clipboard, you can paste it to any application that accepts bitmaps, including Word or Excel. (Using screen dumps like these with Excel's slide show feature can even help you create simple training exercises.)

THE CLIPBOARD VIEWER

The Windows Clipboard Viewer lets you see what's on the Clipboard. It is normally found in the Program Manager's Main Group, and its icon looks like a tiny clipboard.

You may find this accessory program useful enough to place in your Windows Startup folder so that it is loaded each time you start Windows, making it readily available.

Figure 39.2 shows how the Clipboard Viewer displays different types of Clipboard contents.

VIEWING IN DIFFERENT FORMATS

Notice that the Clipboard Viewer can display formatted text, graphics, and most other items in meaningful ways. The Display menu in the Clipboard Viewer window often lets you see items in a variety of formats. The *Owner display* choice shows the item as it would appear in the program that created it. Other viewing options vary with the item being viewed. To return to the first format that was displayed when you opened the viewer, choose Auto from the Display menu.

SAVING CLIPBOARD CONTENTS TO DISK

You can save Clipboard contents as disk files by using the Save As... command on the Clipboard Viewer's File menu. You'll see a familiar-looking Save As dialog box. Get in the habit of noticing where Windows intends to save the file. Change the path if you like. Clipboard files are normally saved with the extension .CLP, which Windows will append for you. It's a good idea to stick with this extension, to facilitate future wild card searches for an elusive file.

SHARING INFORMATION

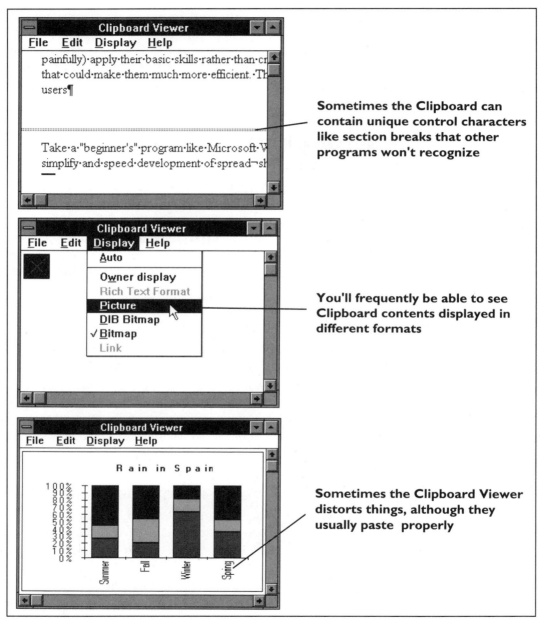

Sometimes the Clipboard can contain unique control characters like section breaks that other programs won't recognize

You'll frequently be able to see Clipboard contents displayed in different formats

Sometimes the Clipboard Viewer distorts things, although they usually paste properly

FIGURE 39.2 *Use the Clipboard Viewer accessory program to see your Clipboard's contents.*

RETRIEVING CLIPBOARD FILES

The Open... command in the Clipboard Viewer will bring up a standard Windows dialog box and let you pick files saved with the Clipboard Viewer's Save As... command. When you open a saved Clipboard file this way, it will replace the current contents of the Clipboard (if any). You will be asked if that's OK.

USING THE CLIPBOARD
WITH NON-WINDOWS APPLICATIONS

It is often possible to paste non-Windows items into Windows documents and vice versa. The steps are only slightly more involved than moving things between two Windows programs. You use additional commands found on the Control menu when running a non-Windows program in a DOS window. For instance, in Figure 39.3, the DOS command **TYPE README.TXT** was used to place some DOS text on the screen in a DOS window. Then a portion of the text was copied to the Clipboard and pasted into Word for Windows.

COPYING AND PASTING
NON-WINDOWS ITEMS TO WINDOWS

Here are the general steps for copying non-Windows items to a Windows application in 386 Enhanced mode.

1. Run the DOS program in a window (press Alt-Enter, if necessary).

2. Choose Edit from the window's Control menu.

3. Choose Mark from the submenu.

4. Select the desired item(s) in the DOS window.

5. Click the right mouse button or press Enter to copy the DOS item(s) to the Clipboard.

6. Switch to your Windows application and paste.

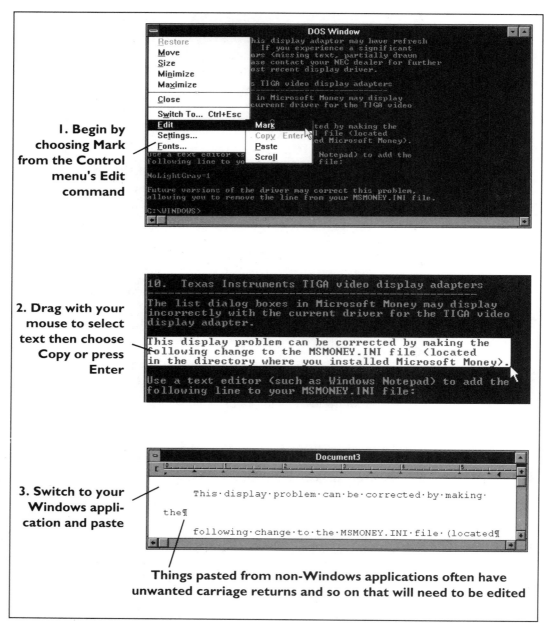

**1. Begin by
choosing Mark
from the Control
menu's Edit
command**

**2. Drag with your
mouse to select
text then choose
Copy or press
Enter**

**3. Switch to your
Windows appli-
cation and paste**

**Things pasted from non-Windows applications often have
unwanted carriage returns and so on that will need to be edited**

FIGURE 39.3 *It is often possible to move things to and from non-Windows programs via the Clipboard.*

Notice that things are not always exactly as you'd like them when you paste. At the bottom of Figure 39.3, the text came in just fine and was reformatted in the Word document's current style (double-spaced Courier). But look at that paragraph mark smack in the middle of the sentence. That happens because there was a carriage return at that point in the DOS text to make it fit the "DOS screen." Things like this may need to be corrected after you paste.

COPYING AND PASTING WINDOWS ITEMS TO NON-WINDOWS APPLICATIONS

Not all non-Windows programs can accept formatted text or graphics. Check with your non-Windows program's documentation, or experiment on noncritical copies of your DOS files. Here are the general steps, assuming that you are using 386 Enhanced mode:

1. Run the DOS program in a window (press Alt-Enter, if necessary).

2. Run the Windows program containing the items to be pasted.

3. Place the items of interest on the Clipboard (copy or cut).

4. Switch to the DOS window and place the insertion point or its equivalent where you want the item(s) to be inserted.

5. Choose Edit from the window's Control menu.

6. Choose Paste from the submenu.

7. See what happens…

COPYING AND PASTING, PLUS RUNNING NON-WINDOWS APPLICATIONS IN STANDARD MODE

Unless your non-Windows application uses the Alt-Spacebar key combination for something else, you can often use it to bring up the non-Windows Control menu. From there you should be able to reach the Edit command.

SHARING INFORMATION

CLEARING THE CLIPBOARD'S CONTENTS

Sometimes you'll want to clear the Clipboard's contents. This is a way to free up RAM when the Clipboard contains a large item in several formats, for instance. To clear the Clipboard, first display its contents with the Clipboard Viewer, then press the Del key, or use the lonely Delete menu choice on the Edit menu. There's no Undo, so think twice or thrice before you delete.

CHAPTER

40

Updating Documents
with Object Linking
and Embedding, plus DDE

If variety is the spice of life, perhaps it is also the cause of heartburn in the computer community. There was a time when people complained about the lack of ways to move information from one program to another. Now it seems as if a new data sharing technology is announced almost daily. Take *object linking and embedding* (OLE), for instance. The two different (but related) technologies of linking and embedding let you create things in one program—say, a chart, a drawing, or several paragraphs—then include those items as *objects* in *other* documents. In many instances, objects created with one program can be used by a different program. For instance, Microsoft Excel worksheet cells and chart objects can be displayed and printed in Microsoft Word.

Sometimes you can set things up so that a change made in one place is reflected in others. For example, if you change numbers in a spreadsheet, and if the cells containing those numbers have been linked with Word documents, the Word documents can automatically reflect the worksheet changes next time you open the Word document. Figure 40.1 illustrates this. The entire miles per gallon worksheet has been paste-linked into a word processing document.

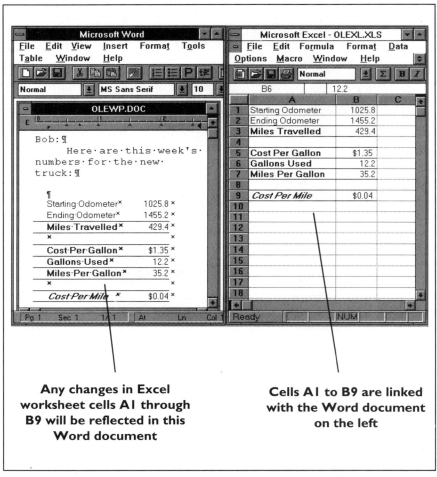

Any changes in Excel worksheet cells A1 through B9 will be reflected in this Word document

Cells A1 to B9 are linked with the Word document on the left

FIGURE 40.1 *Because the Excel worksheet and Word documents are linked, changes in the worksheet appear automatically in the memo.*

In this case, using OLE, Excel and Word were even able to share formatting information. And pasted worksheet cells automatically created a table in the Word memo. The linking tricks that you can play vary with the programs you use, as well as with the linking techniques you employ. Also, realize that even on a fast computer with plenty of RAM, linking can slow things down dramatically. Practice on a few small projects to get a feeling for response times on your system before attempting to link big-time. (Closing or minimizing unused programs can help speed things up.)

Finally, you need to understand that the steps for linking and embedding are slightly different for different programs, even when the programs are from Microsoft. You may need to check individual manuals when linking or embedding.

EXAMPLES OF LINKING

Suppose you create a monthly budget memo in Word, then an Excel worksheet tracking actual performance vs. the plan. If you've linked the two documents, every time you load and edit the monthly budget memo, it will contain the latest budget and performance numbers from the worksheet.

Or you can set up your letterhead stationery and other promotional materials with linked logos, phone numbers, addresses and so on. Then, whenever your logo or letterhead or phone numbers change, new documents will automatically contain the right stuff.

Be forewarned, however, that is possible to set up automatic updating mechanisms that you'll later regret. For instance, if you are in a law firm that has one of those ever-changing lists of partners' names on your letterhead, opening an old letter with a linked letterhead can change the old letter's list of partners so that it incorrectly contains the names of *today's* partners, instead of those in the organization when the document was originally created.

Be sure that you understand the ramifications of establishing links that update automatically. This is particularly important in large organizations. With the cautions out of the way, let's see how these new tools work.

OBJECT LINKING

Object linking is the hot new Windows 3.1 updating tool. It was used to create Figure 40.1. Basically, object linking entails copying selected things to your Clipboard, then *paste-linking* them into other documents. When

SHARING INFORMATION

things are paste-linked this way, they are updated when the original item changes. In Figure 40.1 cells A1 through B9 have been paste-linked into the Word memo on the left. Changes in the worksheet will be automatically reflected in the memo.

THE TERMINOLOGY OF LINKING

To discuss and understand linking, you must know a few new buzzwords. Incidentally, because this is an evolving technology, some manuals and other books and magazines may refer to the same concepts using slightly different terms.

OBJECTS

The word *object* is thrown around a lot in "linkology," sometimes inaccurately. There are *graphic* objects and *sound* objects and *chart* objects and so on. For our purposes, think of objects as things that can be *selected*, then *copied* to the Clipboard and *pasted* into a document.

PUBLISHERS AND SUBSCRIBERS

Publishers are programs capable of *creating* objects that can be copied and pasted into other programs. *Subscribers* are programs that can *receive* pasted objects. Some programs like Word and Excel can both publish *and* subscribe. A few programs like the Windows Draw accessory can only publish. Others like the Windows CardFile accessory can only subscribe. Many older programs can't do either. Check with their makers regarding OLE-capable upgrades.

SERVERS AND CLIENTS

The terms *server* and *client* are OLE synonyms for publishers and subscribers, respectively. Servers can create linkable items, clients can use them. A few programs like the Windows Draw accessory can only act as servers. Others like the Windows CardFile accessory can only act as clients. Some can be both, while many older programs can't be either clients or servers. (Don't confuse the OLE term "server" with network computers called servers. They are not the same thing.)

SOURCE AND DESTINATION DOCUMENTS

A *source* document contains the *original* object. The *destination* document contains a *paste-linked copy* of the object. Destination documents are also referred to as *dependent documents*, since they depend upon other documents for information.

Source and destination documents can usually be created either by the same programs or by different ones. Links are *also* possible within the *same document*. For instance, you can link parts of a Word and Excel document, or parts of two Excel documents, or even two parts of the *same* document.

Why link within a single document? Suppose that you are unsure of what you plan to name a chapter in a long Word document. You can type a working title for the chapter, then paste-link each later occurrence of that chapter name in your text. Later, if you change the first occurrence of the chapter name, all of the linked names in the text will change. What a country!

CREATING A SIMPLE EXCEL/WORD LINK

The easiest way to see how links work is to establish one. Here are the general steps:

1. Create or open a source document (like an Excel Worksheet).

2. Create or open a destination document (such as a Word document).

3. Select and copy the desired "object" to your Clipboard (Excel cells or a chart, for example).

4. Switch to the destination document (a Word document, for instance).

5. Paste-link.

The exact step you'll take to paste-link varies with the subscribing program. For example, to paste-link into a Word document, you use the Paste Link *button* found in Word's Paste Special dialog box.

When pasting into Excel, use the Paste Link *command* on Excel's Edit menu. Other programs use other techniques; check your owner's manuals and on-line help features.

MANAGING AND CHANGING LINKS

Generally, you manage and change links from within the destination program. When a destination document contains a linked item, you'll usually see a command like Links..., often on the File or Edit menus. Figure 40.2 shows the resulting dialog boxes for the Links... commands on Word's Edit menu and Excel's File menu.

While they differ from application to application, Links dialog boxes usually have the same basic capabilities. They will usually do the following:

- Let you open the source document.

- Force an immediate update.

- Cancel a link.

Occasionally, you will need to cancel links elsewhere. For instance, in Excel you'll need to visit the DDE/OLE Options dialog box (use the Links Options... button), then clear the Automatic check box.

PREVENTING AUTOMATIC UPDATES

Normally, if a source document has changed since the last time you've opened a destination document, you will be asked if you want to update whenever you open the *destination* document. Click Yes to update, No to avoid an update. It can take a while to update. If you change your mind, usually pressing the Esc key will abort the update process.

To avoid being asked, and to update only when you demand it, use the manual update options found in most OLE-savvy programs. For instance, when you select a link in Word's Links dialog box, you'll see a manual update option.

In Excel, clear the Update Remote References choice in the Calculation Options dialog box to defeat automatic update prompts.

OBJECT EMBEDDING

Object *embedding* is similar to object *linking*, with several important exceptions. Just as with object linking, you paste (in this case you embed) copies of objects from a source document into a destination document. Embedded objects can be worksheet cells, text, graphics, sounds, and so on.

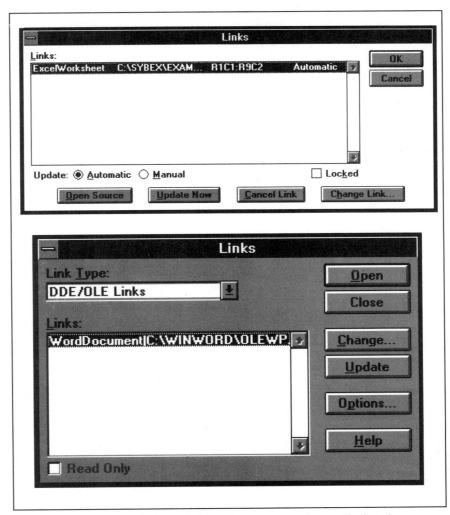

FIGURE 40.2 *Manage links with the Links... commands usually found on a subscribing program's Edit or File menu.*

But here's the difference: changes made in the source are not reflected in the destination documents. You won't even be notified that there are changes in a source document when you open a destination document.

Why *use* embedding, then? The chief reason is that it makes it easy to *edit* embedded things by double-clicking on them in the destination document.

If, for instance, you embed a drawing created with the Windows Draw accessory, double-clicking on the drawn object in the Word document will open the Windows Draw accessory with the embedded drawing as the active window. Similarly, if you embed part of an Excel worksheet in a Word document or part of a Word document into an Excel document, double-clicking on the embedded object in the destination runs the source program and lets you change the object. Obviously, you'll need to have both destination and source programs on your computer. In other words, if you create documents containing embedded objects and give copies of the destination files to other people, they will need both programs on their computers if they will be making changes to embedded objects.

HOW TO EMBED

As you've guessed by now, the act of embedding varies from program to program. You always start by *selecting* and *copying* the item(s) you want to embed while in the source program. Then you switch to the destination program and paste. *How* you paste depends upon the program.

If Word is the destination, for instance, you'll use the Paste Special... command and pick the appropriate data type from a list in the Paste Special dialog box. Usually the data type you'll want will end with the word *object* (Microsoft *Excel Chart Object*, for instance). The data types in the list will change based on what's in the Clipboard when you bring up the Paste Special dialog box. Not all available data types will produce the desired results. For instance, pasting an Excel chart as a drawing instead of an Excel Chart "Object" will not let you quickly switch back to Excel's chart features for later editing. Check your application manuals and experiment to see which data types produce the desired results.

CHANGING EMBEDDED OBJECTS

Assuming that you have the necessary source program on your computer, double-clicking on an embedded object will load the program (if it's not already loaded) and will display the embedded object in the active window of the source program. Make any necessary changes to the source, then close the document window or exit the source program.

You will be asked if you want to save the changes to the *source file* at this point. If you are editing an embedded worksheet, for instance, Excel will ask if you want to save the changes to the worksheet file.

You need *not* save changes to disk at this point to update the destination document. Regardless of how you answer the save-changes question, your changes will be reflected in the destination document. In other words, if you answer No to the save question, the disk file containing the source document will *not* change, but the embedded information *will* change in the destination document. Then, if you save the destination document you'll have two versions of the information—that saved in the source file and that saved in the destination file.

DDE

Dynamic data exchange (DDE) is an early linking technology still supported by many programs that don't yet provide object linking and embedding. Many programs like Word and Excel support DDE so that they can exchange data with older programs. When given a choice, use OLE rather than DDE. For more information about DDE, consult your application software manuals.

SHARING INFORMATION

Packaging Objects

In the previous chapter, you learned how to link and embed things like pictures or the contents of spreadsheet cells. Usually you want to print the resulting documents and hand them to readers. Other times you'll want to share *document files* with people so that they can view and edit them on their *own* computers. Linking and embedding works fine in these instances too, as long as the intended users have the necessary programs on their computers. When you share files with users this way, you can sometimes take advantage of a Windows accessory program called the *Object Packager*. It lets you place *icons* in documents representing things that can be seen and edited on-screen.

You could create a Word memo introducing an Excel slide show and insert the *slide show itself* using the Object Packager. Then, when a co-worker opens the Word memo and reads it on-screen, he or she can double-click on the icon of the slide show to run the actual show. Figure 41.1 illustrates this concept.

ABOUT PACKAGES

Packages created with the Object Packager can contain entire documents or just portions of a document. You can package linked and embedded objects, even entire documents. While you can *package* items that have been created by programs that don't support OLE, you can only *insert packages* into documents created by client (also called subscriber) programs. For instance, because the Windows Paintbrush program is only a server and not a client, you could not insert a package into a drawing created by Paintbrush.

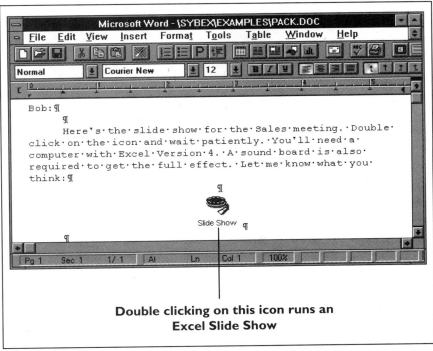

**Double clicking on this icon runs an
Excel Slide Show**

FIGURE 41.1 *Object Packager creates icons that you double-click to edit the actual object or use it.*

SHARING INFORMATION

Since Microsoft Word and Excel are full-functioned client/server programs, you can insert packages into either of them.

While it is possible to package *programs* themselves (like the Windows Calculator accessory) and pass them around with other documents, software copyright laws usually prohibit this practice.

USING THE OBJECT PACKAGER PROGRAM

The Object Packager program is a Windows accessory that can be found in the Accessories window (along with the Clock, Calculator, Notepad, and so on). Its icon looks like an open carton with musical notes, pie charts, and documents spilling out. Figure 41.2 shows the icon and the resulting window that opens when you run the program.

The steps that you take after running Object Packager vary, depending upon what you want to package.

PACKAGING ENTIRE DOCUMENTS

To package an entire document (like an Excel slide show), do the following:

1. Run the Object Packager.

2. Use the Import... command on the Object Packager's File menu. The resulting Import dialog box looks and acts just like a typical Windows Open dialog box.

3. Click and scroll in the Import dialog box to locate the file you want to package.

4. Either double-click on the file of interest, or select it and click OK.

5. You'll see the file named in the --**Content**-- area (right-hand side) of the Object Packager window. The words "Copy of" will precede the file name.

6. Be sure the file name is highlighted in the --**Content**-- area of the Object Packager window. Choose the Copy Package command from the Edit menu as shown in Figure 41.2. The item and its package icon will be copied to the Clipboard.

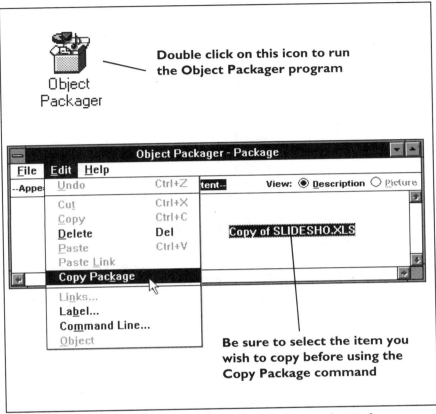

FIGURE 41.2 *Double-click on the Object Packager's icon in the Windows Accessories window to run the Packager.*

7. Switch to the document to receive the package (it must have been created by a client-capable program).

8. Position the insertion point and paste the Package Object.

The exact method of pasting depends upon the *client* program (the program receiving the package). For example, in both Word and Excel, you use the Paste Special... command and choose **Package Object** as the Data Type.

SHARING INFORMATION

A few applications automatically insert packages in the upper-left corner of the document's window.

Once you've pasted a object, you'll see just its icon and file name in the client document. Double-clicking on the icon will let you see, use, edit, or hear the contents of the packaged object. Obviously, the type of object determines what can be done with it.

The appearance of a pasted package icon usually reflects the application program that created the packaged contents. For instance, the icon for a packaged drawing created with the Paintbrush program look like a palette. You can change the icon used for the package, and you can change the text under the icon. You'll learn how momentarily.

PACKAGING PARTS OF A DOCUMENT

The steps for packaging a portion of a document are slightly different from those used to package an entire document. Moreover, the source document must have been created using a program that can act as a server. (Both Excel and Word can be servers.) Do the following:

1. Open the source document.

2. Select the desired information.

3. Copy it to the Clipboard.

4. Open Object Packager.

5. If necessary, click on the word --**Content**-- to select the content part of the window.

6. Choose Paste or Paste Link from the Object Packager's Edit menu (Paste embeds, Paste Link links).

7. Choose Copy Package from the Object Packager's Edit menu.

8. Open the document receiving the package (it must be client-capable).

9. Insert the package by pasting.

The exact method of pasting depends upon the *client* program (the program receiving the package). For example, in both Word and Excel, you use the Paste Special... command and choose Package Object as the Data Type. A few applications automatically insert packages in the upper-left corner of the document's window.

CHANGING ICONS AND THEIR LABELS

The Object Packager lets you change the icons used to represent packages, and it also lets you place different text under the icons. To change the appearance of an icon, click in the left-hand side of the Object Packager window. The word --**Appearance**-- will become highlighted.

By default, the Packager uses the source application's icon. To pick a different icon graphic, click on the Insert Icon... button and assign a different icon graphic. You'll see a dialog box like the one in Figure 41.3.

Either type the file name of a different program to use *its* icon, or use the Browse... button to look for and choose programs whose icon you want to copy.

To change the *text* beneath an icon, pick Label... from the Object Packager's Edit menu. You'll see a dialog box that can be used to enter and edit text. It's OK to enter spaces and other punctuation in this text box.

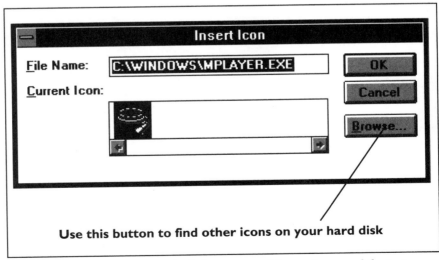

Use this button to find other icons on your hard disk

FIGURE 41.3 *You can change both the icons used for packages and the text beneath them.*

USING YOUR MOUSE TO PACKAGE

When working with programs that support OLE (like Excel and Word), you can embed or link *entire documents*—but not just selected parts—by using your mouse. Do the following:

1. Open the destination document.

2. Switch to File Manager.

3. Arrange your File Manager and destination document windows so that you can see both the *source file* in the File Manager's window and the *destination document's window*.

4. To embed a package, drag the document's icon from the File Manager window to the document window. To link a package, hold down Shift-Ctrl while you drag.

INDEX

greater than operator (>), 400, 537
gridlines
  in Excel, 492, 506
  in Word, 268, 295
groups
  of files, 6
  in Microsoft Draw, 295–296
  startup, 14, 32, 94–95
gutters, 203–204

H

handles
  for graphics, 297
  for margins, 137
hanging indents, 213
hard disks. *See* disks and disk drives
hard hyphens, 216
hardware support for Windows 3.1, 3
Header dialog box, 453
Header/Footer dialog box, 245–248
headers and footers
  in Excel, 452–454
  in Word, 147–150, 244–250,
    252–257
  in Write, 45
headings
  for outlines, 328, 460, 462
  for tables of contents, 338–339
height of rows
  in Excel, 420–422
  in Word tables, 275
help
  in Excel, 350, 386, 471–473
  in Windows 3.1, 17–18
  in Word, 132
hidden files, 64, 123
hidden page breaks, 250
hidden text, 223, 342, 364
Hidden Text option, 364
hidden windows, 33
hiding
  File Manager, 69
  footnote windows, 259
  macro sheets, 525
  rows and columns, 436
  Toolbars, 426

HIMEM Extended memory
    manager, 122
history with Windows help, 17
Home key, 116
Hyphenation dialog box, 216–217
hyphens (-)
  controlling, 216–217
  for negative numbers, 393

I

I-beam pointer, 130, 154
icons
  appearance of, 94
  and keyboard, 113
  minimizing windows to, 22–24
  Object Packager for, 596–602
  in Windows 3.1, 7
IF() function, 482–484
Import dialog box, 598
importing
  files in non-Excel formats, 444
  graphics, 290–297, 515
Include with Document option, 364
indented index style, 343
indents, 134–135, 203–204
  with columns, 281, 283
  with paragraphs, 196
Index dialog box, 343–344
Index Entry dialog box, 342–343
INDEX() function, 483
index lines with Cardfile accessory,
    49, 51
indexes, 223, 245, 342–345
INFO() function, 482–483
Info window, 569–570
information functions, 482
Insert Cells dialog box, 276
Insert Merge Field dialog box,
    356–357
insert mode, 362
Insert Picture command, 290–291
Insert Rows feature, 274–275
Insert Table dialog box, 268–269
insertion point, 114–115, 130, 135
installing
  fonts, 76–78

non-Windows applications, 99
printer drivers, 72–74
Interactive Trace option, 573
international settings, 91–92, 540
international telephone support, 21
IPMT() function, 482
irregular areas, selecting, 157, 160
ISEVEN() function, 470
ISNONTEXT() function, 482
iterations for circular references,
    567–569

K

Keep With Next feature, 283
keyboard, 108
  applying styles from, 228–229
  cursor control with, 115
  delay settings for, 90
  with dialog boxes, 113–115
  formatting with, 425–426
  and icons, 113
  inserting glossary entries from, 239
  menus with, 109–111
  for moving windows, 21–22, 112
  selecting with, 116, 158–160, 387
  shortcuts using, 9, 52, 347, 369, 525
  sizing windows with, 112
  switching applications with, 29, 109
  for Windows tutorial, 17
keys, sort, 414, 540
keystrokes, Recorder for, 51–52.
    See also macros

L

labels
  for icons, 601
  mailing, 315
  on worksheets, 373
landscape orientation, 200, 202
languages with spelling checker, 333
large Excel projects, 455
  annotations for, 468
  multiple worksheets for, 462–465
  names for, 456–458
  outlines for, 459–462

splitting windows for, 458–459
workbooks for, 466–468
layers in Microsoft Draw, 295–296
LCD color setting, 90
left-hand mouse, 88
left tab stops, 263–264
legends for charts, 497–498
less than operator (<), 400, 537
LET templates, 314
Letter Options dialog box, 308, 311
letters, templates for, 307–311, 314
levels in outlines, 460–462
line numbers for paragraphs,
    209–215
linear forecasts, AutoFill for, 406
lines in Excel, drawing, 516
lines in Word
  keeping together, 207
  numbering, 214–215
  without paragraph marks, 204–205,
    211–212
  selecting, 157–159
  spacing between, 206
linking, 587–588
  charts, 499–500
  Excel and Word files, 591–592
  graphics, 514
  objects, 589–590
  worksheets, 463
Links dialog box, 592
lists in dialog boxes, 10, 115
loans, functions for, 481
.LOG files, 43
logical functions, 400, 482–484
lookup functions, 483, 485
lost clusters, 126
Lotus 1-2-3 files, 380
  compatibility with, 380
  exporting in formats for, 440
  importing in formats for, 444
  options for, 562
LOWER() function, 470
LPT ports, 72

M

Macro Name dialog box, 348–349

SYBEX

FREE BROCHURE!

Complete this form today, and we'll send you a full-color brochure of Sybex bestsellers.

Please supply the name of the Sybex book purchased.

_____

How would you rate it?

_____ Excellent   _____ Very Good   _____ Average   _____ Poor

Why did you select this particular book?

_____ Recommended to me by a friend
_____ Recommended to me by store personnel
_____ Saw an advertisement in _____
_____ Author's reputation
_____ Saw in Sybex catalog
_____ Required textbook
_____ Sybex reputation
_____ Read book review in _____
_____ In-store display
_____ Other _____

Where did you buy it?

_____ Bookstore
_____ Computer Store or Software Store
_____ Catalog (name: _____)
_____ Direct from Sybex
_____ Other: _____

Did you buy this book with your personal funds?

_____ Yes   _____ No

About how many computer books do you buy each year?

_____ 1-3   _____ 3-5   _____ 5-7   _____ 7-9   _____ 10+

About how many Sybex books do you own?

_____ 1-3   _____ 3-5   _____ 5-7   _____ 7-9   _____ 10+

Please indicate your level of experience with the software covered in this book:

_____ Beginner   _____ Intermediate   _____ Advanced

Which types of software packages do you use regularly?

_____ Accounting   _____ Databases   _____ Networks

_____ Amiga   _____ Desktop Publishing   _____ Operating Systems

_____ Apple/Mac   _____ File Utilities   _____ Spreadsheets

_____ CAD   _____ Money Management   _____ Word Processing

_____ Communications   _____ Languages   _____ Other _____
(please specify)

Which of the following best describes your job title?

_____ Administrative/Secretarial _____ President/CEO

_____ Director _____ Manager/Supervisor

_____ Engineer/Technician _____ Other _____

(please specify)

Comments on the weaknesses/strengths of this book: _____

_____

_____

_____

_____

_____

Name _____

Street _____

City/State/Zip _____

Phone _____

PLEASE FOLD, SEAL, AND MAIL TO SYBEX

SYBEX, INC.
Department M
2021 CHALLENGER DR.
ALAMEDA, CALIFORNIA USA
94501

SYBEX

SEAL

Cancel an action	Esc	Find a cell with specific contents	Shift-F5	Bold	Ctrl-B
Copy	Ctrl-C			Format as 2 decimals with commas	Ctrl-Shift-!
Cut	Ctrl-X	Formula bar insertion point	↑, ↓, →, ←		
Exit (Quit)	Alt-F4			Format as currency	Ctrl-Shift-$
Help/Help question mark	F1/Shift-F1	Go To…	F5		
		Last cell (lower right)	Ctrl-End	Format as date (12-Jan-93)	Ctrl-Shift-#
Open	Ctrl-F12				
Paste	Ctrl-V	Last cell current row	End, then Enter	Format as percentage	Ctrl-Shift-%
Print	Ctrl-Shift-F12				
Repeat last action	Alt-Enter	Move left, right, up, or down	←, →, ↑, ↓	Format as time (12:00 AM)	Ctrl-Shift-@
Save/Save As…	Shift-F12/F12			General number format	Ctrl-Shift-~ (tilde)
Select entire column	Ctrl-spacebar	Move left/right one window	Ctrl-PgUp/ Ctrl-PgDn		
				Italic	Ctrl-I
Select entire row	Shift-spacebar	Move to next/previous pane	F6/Shift-F6	Normal font	Ctrl-1
Select entire worksheet	Ctrl-Shift-spacebar			Outline border	Ctrl-Shift-&
		Move up/down one window	PgUp/PgDn	Remove all borders	Ctrl-Shift-_ (underline)
Undo	Ctrl-Z				
		Switch to next open window	Ctrl-F6	Select style box	Ctrl-S
				Strikeout	Ctrl-5
		Switch to next workbook document	Alt-PgDn	Underline	Ctrl-U

Navigating

Activate the Formula bar	F2
Beginning of worksheet	Ctrl-Home

Switch to previous open window	Ctrl-Shift-F6

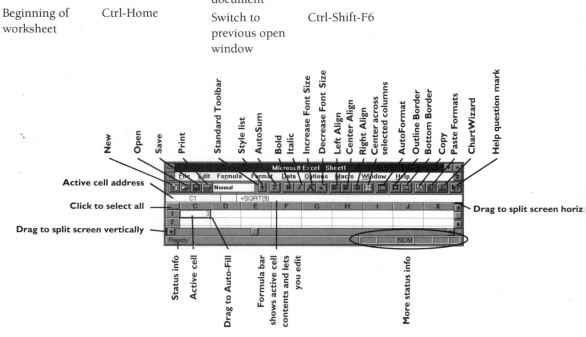

New
Open
Save
Print
Standard Toolbar
Style list
AutoSum
Bold
Italic
Increase Font Size
Decrease Font Size
Left Align
Center Align
Right Align
Center across selected columns
AutoFormat
Outline Border
Bottom Border
Copy
Paste Formats
ChartWizard
Help question mark

Active cell address
Click to select all
Drag to split screen vertically
Drag to split screen horiz

Status info
Active cell
Drag to Auto-Fill
Formula bar shows active cell contents and lets you edit
More status info